Between Two Empires

Between Two Empires

Race, History, and Transnationalism in Japanese America

EIICHIRO AZUMA

OXFORD
UNIVERSITY PRESS

2005

OXFORD
UNIVERSITY PRESS

Oxford University Press, Inc., publishes works that further
Oxford University's objective of excellence
in research, scholarship, and education.

Oxford   New York
Auckland   Cape Town   Dar es Salaam   Hong Kong   Karachi
Kuala Lumpur   Madrid   Melbourne   Mexico City   Nairobi
New Delhi   Shanghai   Taipei   Tokyo

With offices in
Argentina   Austria   Brazil   Chile   Czech Republic   France   Greece
Guatemala   Hungary   Italy   Japan   Poland   Portugal   Singapore
South Korea   Switzerland   Thailand   Turkey   Ukraine   Vietnam

Published by Oxford University Press, Inc.
198 Madison Avenue, New York, New York 10016

www.oup.com

Oxford is a registered trademark of Oxford University Press

Library of Congress Cataloging-in-Publication Data
Azuma, Eiichiro.
Between two empires : race, history, and transnationalism in Japanese America / Eiichiro Azuma.
    p. cm.
Includes bibliographical references and index.
ISBN-13 978-0-19-515940-0; 978-0-19-515941-7 (pbk.)

1.   Japanese Americans—West (U.S.)—History.   2. Japanese Americans—West (U.S.)—Social
conditions.   3. Japanese Americans—Race Identity—West (U.S.)   4. Immigrants—West (U.S.)—Social
conditions.   5. Children of immigrants—West (U.S.)—Social conditions.   6. West (U.S.)—Race
relations.   7. Transnationalism—History.   8. Japan—Relations—United States.   9. United States—
Relations—Japan.   I. Title.

F596 .3.J3A98 2005
973'.04956—dc22   2004050145

Grateful acknowledgement is made for permissions to reprint portions of my articles that appeared in
the following journals.

"Racial Struggle, Immigrant Nationalism, and Ethnic Identity: Japanese and Filipinos in the California
Delta,"*Pacific Historical Review* 67:2. Copyright © 1998 by the Pacific Coast Branch, American Historical
Association. Reprinted by permission of the University of California Press.

" 'The Pacific Era Has Arrived': Transnational Education among Japanese Americans, 1932–1941," *History
of Education Quarterly* 43:1. Copyright © 2003 by History of Education Society. Reprinted by permission.

"The Politics of Transnational History Making: Japanese Immigrants on the Western Frontier, 1927–1941,"
Journal of American History 89:4. Copyright © 2003 by the Organization of American Historians.
Reprinted by permission.

Printed in the United States of America on acid-free paper

To My Teachers and the Memory of Yuji Ichioka

Acknowledgments

This book is the culmination of research and writing that took nearly eight years. At every stage of this project, many people and organizations have supported me in different ways. Without their generous time, understanding, and advice, as well as financial assistance, this project could not have been completed. From the start, my dissertation committee and other UCLA mentors helped me to organize my disparate ideas into a tangible shape, which became the foundation of this book. Fred G. Notehelfer took a genuine interest in my project, even though it did not directly concern his own field. With good will and professionalism, he steered me—morally, scholarly, and logistically. Valerie J. Matsumoto and Don Nakanishi provided me with a strong grounding in Asian American studies, as well as in the history of the American West. Herman Ooms and Miriam Silverberg were instrumental in fostering my interest in social and cultural theories. The late Yuji Ichioka, the foremost specialist in Japanese American history, has been my *sensei* not only in scholarship but in life as well. Ever since I started out as a graduate student in Asian American studies more than a decade ago, Yuji, together with his partner, Emma Gee, has been a guiding force and model for my transformation into a historian. Anyone who is familiar with his scholarship will see the impact he has had on my methodology, framework, and mode of interpretation.

A historian cannot do his work without the help of librarians and archivists. Special acknowledgment is extended to the staff of the UCLA Young Research Library, especially those at the Department of Special Collections and the Microfilm Room. Marjorie Lee of the Asian American Studies Center Reading Room always led me to appropriate source materials when I was at a loss. I also benefited from valuable assistance from the staff at the U.S. National Archives and Records Administration in College Park, Maryland, and in Laguna Niguel, California. The Japanese American National Museum was another stomping ground, where Grace Murakami, June Oyama, Nikki Chang, and Theresa Manalo ably directed me to necessary materials. Other libraries and archives in the United States, including the University of California Bancroft Library, California State Library, Sacramento County Recorder's Office, University of Hawaii's Hawaiian Collections, Oregon Historical Society, and University of Washington's University Archives, proved to be important sources of information for this book.

Because my project is transnational in nature and much of the immigrant-language sources had been lost during the wartime incarceration of Japanese Americans, I conducted lengthy research in Japan to supplement what I could not get here. I thank the following institutions, which allowed me to use their materials: Waseda University History Room and Library, Keisen Women's College Library, National Archives of Japan, Nihon Rikkokai, Shibusawa Memorial Archives, National Diet Library of Japan, Japanese Overseas Migration Museum, and Diplomatic Records Office.

In the course of my research and writing, I have received financial assistance from many institutions. At UCLA, the Institute of American Cultures, Asian American Studies Center, Center for Japanese Studies, and History Department provided me with research grants and fellowships. As a member of the faculty of the University of Pennsylvania, I have been fortunate to enjoy generous support from the University Research Foundation and Center for East Asian Studies. The Civil Liberties Public Education Fund also offered me a substantial grant at a critical time.

The University of Pennsylvania has been a wonderful place, making the laborious task of turning a dissertation into a book manuscript almost enjoyable. The History Department and Asian American Studies Program have given me opportunities for constructive intellectual exchange and learning, as well as much-needed comfort and support. Kathleen Brown, Fred Dickinson, Barbara Savage, Thomas Sugrue, and Beth Wenger shared their valuable time with me, read portions of my manuscript, and gave me critical but helpful comments. Constant encouragement from Lynn Lees, Sheldon Hackney, Thomas Childers, Jonathan Steinberg, Ann Moyer, Ann Farnsworth-Alvear, Lee Cassanelli, Rosane Rocher, Grace Kao, Ajay Nair, Mark Chiang, Karen Su, Josephine Park,

Milan Hejtmanek, Cappy Hurst, and Matthew Sommers has enabled me to carry on when it was especially difficult. Debra Broadnax, Joan Plonski, Paula Roberts, and Kusum Soin have assisted me in navigating through the administrative labyrinths of the big institution.

Many other friends and colleagues rendered valuable support in the research, conceptualization, and writing of this book. They are: Henry Yu, Gail Nomura, Lane Hirabayashi, Gary Okihiro, Franklin Odo, Mae Ngai, David Yoo, Lon Kurashige, Evelyn Hu-DeHart, Sucheng Chan, Gordon Chang, Arif Dirlik, Roger Daniels, Greg Robinson, Takashi Fujitani, Scott Kurashige, John Stephan, Margaret Kuo, Richard Kim, Brian Hayashi, Naomi Ginoza, Yoonmee Chang, Arleen de Vera, Glen Omatsu, Eileen Tamura, Stacey Hirose, Lili Kim, Chris Friday, and Russell Leong. Thanks especially to Brian Niiya who helped to edit various parts of the manuscript, always believing in this project despite its controversial nature. Hiromi Monobe has encouraged me at every step of the way, albeit often having to listen to my half-baked ideas and wild interpretations.

Scholars in Japan have been a source of encouragement, too. To name some, Yui Daizaburo, Sakata Yasuo, Shoji Keiichi, Iino Masako, Kumei Teruko, Hirobe Izumi, Utsumi Takashi, Sakaguchi Mitsuhiro, and M. William Steele. At the Japanese American National Museum, where I worked as a part-time curator/researcher while writing the dissertation, Akemi Kikumura-Yano, Jim Hirabayashi, Lloyd Inui, Art Hansen, Karin Higa, Krissy Kim, Sojin Kim, Jim Gatewood, Masayo Ohara, Glenn Kitayama, and Emily Anderson shared the challenge of doing public history—an experience that has taught me why history writing is as much a pursuit of knowledge as it is a commitment to social justice and public education.

A few chapters of this book are drawn from my previously published articles in the *Pacific Historical Review*, the *History of Education Quarterly*, and the *Journal of American History*. I would like to thank the editors and journal staffs, especially David Johnson, Carl Abbott, Bruce Nelson, Joanna Meyerowitz, and Susan Armeny, for allowing me to reprint portions of the articles, as well as for their editorial advice and assistance, which sharpened my arguments. I am grateful to anonymous readers for these journals and for Oxford University Press, since in tangible and intangible ways the book reflects their contributions as well.

My editor at Oxford, Susan Ferber, has been simply amazing. Not only did her precise advice save me from errors and weak arguments during some critical stages of this project, but her professionalism has kept me on schedule despite the fact that I had to cut my original manuscript by more than a third. She painstakingly went through the entire manuscript and provided helpful comments and suggestions, which guided me through the difficult process of the final revision. Thanks to other Oxford University Press staff for their work in getting this book published. In particular, Tracy Baldwin designed the book and its jacket, making my work visually attractive. Linda Donnelly, the production editor, coordinated the production of the book. And I must acknowledge the important role of Merryl Sloane, who carefully copyedited my manuscript. My book would not have been as readable without their able assistance.

Finally, I would like to thank my parents, Tetsuya and Takako, for their unfailing support. Although they do not have the foggiest idea about my research and writing, they have always been my greatest supporters, keeping faith in me and my project. Even with this book, they will still not understand what I do because of the language difference, but this material object, I hope, is good enough to put an end to their parental worries.

Contents

Note on the Translation and Transliteration of Japanese Names and Words

In this book, the names of Japanese persons are written with the family names first, followed by the given names. For the names of Japanese immigrants and their American-born children, I adopt the customary Western form (the given names first, followed by the family names), because it was the way they transliterated their names in their daily lives. The macrons for long vowel Japanese sounds are not provided in the main text in order to preserve readability. The notes and bibliography offer the complete forms of Japanese names and words with macrons for the benefit of researchers. All translations from Japanese-language sources are mine unless otherwise noted.

Between Two Empires

Introduction

Immigrant Transnationalism between Two Empires

"East is West and West is East," wrote Jizaemon Tateishi, a Japanese immigrant student at the University of Southern California in 1912, criticizing the bipolarities of the Orient and the Occident. "By this I do not mean that the outward manifestations of the two are similar," he continued. "I mean if you go deep into the very heart of the people of Japan, the inner life in which we live, and move, and have our being, is essentially Anglo-Saxon."[1] Riichiro Hoashi, another USC student, challenged the same "too broad generalizations" that failed people like Tateishi and him:

> Born in Japan and educated in America, we are neither Japanese nor Americans but are Cosmopolitans; and as Cosmopolitans we may be allowed to express our opinions, freely and frankly, for nothing but Cosmopolitanism can be our ideal since we have transcended the narrow bound of nationality and race.[2]

Thought-provoking and even postmodern as these statements may sound, neither Tateishi nor Hoashi became a famous intellectual or a leader in the Japanese immigrant community; indeed, their lives in America are scarcely known. But their personal trajectories are not as important as what their utterances signified in the context of their time and place. In the early twentieth century, whether they lived as merchants and store clerks in the urban ghettoes of "Little Tokyos," as farmers and field hands in the remote valleys of California, or as railroad and mine workers in the rugged mountains of the Sierra Nevada, immigrants from Japan formed a group of "aliens ineligible for citizenship," and they were collectively under pressure to justify their presence in the United States. As college students, Tateishi and Hoashi happened to have an ability to present their shared quandary intelligibly in the public discourse and ask for reconsideration of the terms in which their American existence was understood.

Their lives form the story of how Japanese immigrants (Issei) generally made sense of the dilemma of living across the purported East-West divide and related binaries. Not only did the disavowal of bounded national and racial categories by the two students crystallize the heterodox attributes of the Issei under the established orders of the American and Japanese states, but their "cosmopolitanism" is also akin to what scholars have recently celebrated as "transnationalism." Despite the claim to transcend the confines of nation and race, the Issei's transnational thinking was nonetheless constantly counter-checked by orthodoxy that was closely linked to nation-building and the dominant racial politics. The psychic and political engagements that these Japanese had with white America and imperial Japan complicate the meaning of trans-nationalism, which necessitates a new paradigm of analysis and approach to the usual saga of immigrant struggle.

From the viewpoint of America's racial doctrine, the "Orientals" were situated beyond the pale of nationhood, as enshrined in the Chinese Exclusion Act of 1882 and the U.S. Supreme Court ruling against Japanese naturalization four decades later. Accusations of Japanese immigrant communities being "outposts of [the Japanese] empire" were not uncommon in the public discourse. In 1938, a popular travelogue writer contended that even though the Issei had lived in California for years and their sons and daughters (Nisei) were born as U.S. citizens, "there is something that persists in the Japanese heart" that allegedly made them forever loyal to Japan—and, by implication, hostile to America. The blind allegiance that the two generations of Japanese Americans owed to the "Divine Emperor . . . has been there [in their racial heart] for more than two millenniums," the writer asserted, "and it will not be stamped out in a few generations."[3] In much the same way, on the other side of the Pacific, the foreign minister of Japan declared proprietary rights to the Nisei according to that nation's own racial ideology: "I hold their Japanese blood dear and essential. . . . To preserve their racial strength, the Japanese government must exert itself the best it can."[4] The hegemonic constructions of racial and national belonging or nonbelonging, emanating from both states, posed fundamental challenges to the Issei (and Nisei) in terms of how they defined their relationships to, and actually engaged with, both their adopted country and their native land.

This book examines the development of transnational ideas, practices, and politics among Japanese immigrants in the American West prior to the Pacific War. Specialists in European immigration history and African American history have already produced an array of such works that have led to the development of "transatlantic studies" and "African diaspora studies." In the early 1990s, historian Sucheng Chan issued a call to Asian American scholars for a new international paradigm, but it is still uncommon in historical studies of the Asian American experience.[5] To date, most scholars have kept Japanese American history within the confines of the American domestic narrative, treating the subject only as a national(ist) story and disregarding significant parts of the Japanese American experience, which actually extended beyond the boundaries of a single polity.[6] In order to truly appreciate the Issei's insistence on cosmopolitanism, historians need to confront the bounded meanings of nation and race through close analysis of the discursive strategies and everyday practices that the immigrants adopted and deployed relative to the different hegemonic powers.

To present a more complete picture of the Issei's transnational past, I employ what can be termed "an inter-National perspective"—one that stresses the interstitial (not transcendental) nature of their lives between the two nation-states. The findings of this study reveal that Japanese immigrants generally accepted the legitimacy of the meanings and categories upheld by the dominant ideologies of both the United States and Japan. The Issei operated under the tight grips and the clashing influences of these state powers, each of which promoted its respective project of nation-building, racial supremacy, and colonial expansion. Although they constantly traversed, often blurred, and frequently disrupted the varied definitions of race, nation, and culture, Issei were able neither to act as free-floating cosmopolitans nor to enjoy a postmodern condition above and beyond the hegemonic structures of state control. Their strategies of assimilation, adaptation, and ethnic survival took shape through the (re)interpretation, but not repudiation, of the bounded identity constructs that had their origins in the ideological imperatives of each state.[7] My analysis primarily focuses on the basic integrity and potency of the two national hegemonies and modernities, which jointly helped to mold the perceptions of Japanese immigrants, as well as the range of their social practices, in their daily lives.

Though a version of the transnational approach, the inter-National perspective is not limited to viewing the Japanese American experience as one extending across the two nation-states, societies, and cultures. Like other theoretical formulations, transnationalism has acquired different definitions and orientations.[8] *Culturalist-oriented transnationalism* tends to highlight the heterogeneity, hybridity, and creolization of cultural objects and meanings in the context of a diaspora.[9] Its advocates, such as cultural theorists and postcolonial literary critics, stress the constant movements of "transmigrants," the fluidity and multiplicity of their identities, and their simultaneous positioning in a politicocultural sphere inclusive of two or more nation-states. Influenced by Immanuel Wallerstein's world-systems perspective, *structural-based transnationalism* focuses more on the process by which migrants emerge out of contradictions in international capitalism, and how they move, work, and construct new forms of social relationships within the network of a global economic system.[10] These sets of transnational contexts constitute equally important components of this study's conceptual framework, but in light of the interstitial nature of Japanese immigrant experience, the term *transnational*—when casually used— can be quite misleading, for it may connote something "deterritorialized" or someone "denationalized." In order to avoid such inferences, I specifically define my approach as *inter-National*.

Since the consciousness of Japanese immigrants was wedged firmly between the established categories of Japan and the United States, the relationships that they developed and maintained in the interstices were ambivalent, unsettled, and elusive. Because they were always faced with the need to reconcile simultaneous national belongings as citizen-subjects of one state and yet resident-members (denizens) of another, the Issei refused to make a unilateral choice, electing instead to take an eclectic approach to the presumed contradiction between things Japanese and American. Japanese immigrant identities, too, moved across and between the bounded meanings and binaries of race and nation that each regime imposed upon them, rejecting exclusive judgments by either. As such, their ideas and practices were situational, elastic, and even inconsistent at times, but always dualistic at the core. The analysis of Japanese immigrant eclecticism illuminates the intricate agency of these historical actors, who selectively took in and fused elements of nationalist arguments, modernist assumptions, and racist thinking from both imperial Japan and white America.[11] This is the process by which the Issei tried to transform themselves into quasi whites, despite their ancestry, in an effort to present themselves as quintessential Americans.

Notwithstanding its transnational framework, this study highlights the embeddedness of Japanese immigrants within one national order, and hence the limits of their cosmopolitanism. Despite the dynamic interactions that the immigrants and their descendants had with Japan and the United States, their daily physical existence was under the sovereign power of the latter. In other words, while they were caught between the conflicting ideological and often repressive apparatuses of the two nation-states, their bodies were anchored in America, their interests rooted in its socioeconomic structure, and their activities disciplined by its politicolegal system. Giving primacy to the actual physical location of Japanese immigrants, this study pays special attention to the domestic aspect of the otherwise transnational subject.

In considering Japanese immigrant transnationalism, it is essential to ask why and how Japan really mattered. It was in the realms of knowledge production, and of the social practices which the ideas accompanied, that Japan mattered most to the Issei. Their native country—another hegemonic power to which they continued to belong due to the denial of naturalization rights in the United States—strove to control them from afar, but it had fewer apparatuses to achieve that goal. In negotiating their relationships with the homeland, Japanese immigrants were afforded a smaller degree of material nexus than with American society. Ironically, this distance allowed many Issei to use "Japan" as a resource to fight the challenges surrounding their racial standing in the United States and as a point of reference to make sense of their restricted existence there. The command that Japan and the United States exercised over the Issei, albeit unevenly, as well as the mooring of their everyday lives to the American political economy that defined the terms of their engagement with the homeland, form twin themes of the inter-National paradigm.[12]

In dissecting and narrating the transnational history of Japanese immigrants, this book's domestic focus carefully considers the processes of racial formation, by which the combined effects of structural and representational control homogenize the experience of members of a minority group in a given "racial project."[13] The case of Japanese immigrants offers no exception. In terms of class background, the Issei population was diverse, ranging from wealthy entrepreneurs to migrant laborers, educated urbanites to rural farmers, but their racial position and image in American society were so undifferentiated that varied classes of Japanese immigrants came to share a similar, if not identical, collective racial experience. Inasmuch as Issei came to be treated like pariahs in American society, class diversity among them was effectively inconsequential.[14]

While race was central to structuring and representing their overall social world, gender also played a role in the processes of racial formation for the Issei. In Japanese immigrant history, the intersectionality of race and gender was manifested in ways that attached gendered meanings and nuances to the prevailing condition of the Issei's subordination to white America, as well as their reactions to it.[15] In the United States, race inscribed "inferiority" in the identity and positionality of all Japanese, but because it was so cardinal and arbitrary, Issei were quick to learn the politics of manipulating and transforming race for the purpose of their survival in the American West. In this general context of racial formation and transformation, gender ubiquitously prescribed the sexual division of labor and societal roles. In Japanese America, immigrant women concentrated on the construction of ideal domesticity commensurate with the middle-class white model, while their husbands tackled the more public dimension of racial politics, like propaganda, court battles, and economic struggles. By analyzing the interplay of race, class, and gender in Issei lives, this study elucidates the essentially American underpinning of Japanese immigrant transnationalism.

The Issei's embeddedness in the political economy of the United States does not mean that they lived a homogeneous American experience, however. This book often examines the local context—the patterns of social relations and practices within varied regional confines—as opposed to a uniform national context. Recently, the question of the local versus the global has attracted much interest from theorists of transnationalism, who attempt to understand the ambiguous positioning of the Asian American subject in society, economy, nation, culture, and history. This study emphasizes the preponderance of everyday experiences and reality in the immediate surroundings, interpreting identity formation and behavior as "a matter not of ethnic destiny, but of political choice" in the microlevel entanglements of power.[16] As much as Japanese immigrants were situated in the transnational space as a result of their crisscrossing the Pacific Ocean, they also negotiated their in-betweenness through politics that grounded their concerns and agendas in the welfare of each local community dotting the American West. Against the context of international, domestic, and local social locations, Japanese immigrants projected manifold, regionally divergent identities upon their collective self as an American minority that was, at the same time, part of the Japanese nation-state.

This study holds the Issei accountable for their actions and inaction, their choices and judgments, and their complicity and resistance. It scrupulously considers the multiplicity of social positions, which helped to mold habits of mind and behavior among Japanese immigrants.[17] Because intraethnic, interethnic, and international social relations prescribed how they understood and lived their lives, Issei always vied with one another for power within each local Japanese community, clashed with other minority groups for survival under white ascendancy, and tried to rival their homeland compatriots in nationalist contributions. And when reevaluated in this context, Tateishi's reworking of Rudyard Kipling's binarism and Hoashi's rejection of the "narrow bound of nationality and race" reveal more than just academic critiquing. Despite their college educations, the two men probably lived among their countrymen and women of more humble backgrounds in an ethnic ghetto. And like other Issei, Tateishi and Hoashi were accused of posing a threat to the white civilization even though they came to this land to embrace it. Drawing from such real-life experiences, which all "Orientals" shared in early twentieth-century America, their pronouncements of Japanese-white likeness, East-West parallelism, and immigrant cosmopolitanism constituted a radical act of social maneuvering.

Their formulations not only contested the norms of American race relations that kept the Issei socially subordinate but also attempted to debunk the "Yellow Peril" fear, which alienated them from the society in which they wished to claim a place. The idea of cosmopolitanism sought to redefine their relationships with the two nation-states to which they were connected as the consequence of their migration. "East is West, West is East" is an intriguing proposition, indeed, but a full appreciation of its layered meanings requires an analysis of the convoluted immigrant world that developed in the interstices of the divided spheres of civilizations, nation-states, and races. Only by measuring the Issei's agency against the multifaceted relations, interests, and struggles in a transnational space that linked the two sides of the Pacific Ocean can we truly understand the totality of Japanese immigrant experience, which was moved by complex motives and desires, some of which were contradictory and nonsensical at times.[18]

Focusing on the American West, this book chronicles the Japanese immigrant experience from 1885 to 1941. Scholars have divided the prewar history of Japanese Americans into two major phases: the migration of the first generation and the transition to the emergence of all-American Nisei patriots. According to this scheme, Japanese immigration between 1885 and 1908 ushered in the influx of single male laborers—"birds of passage"—who intended to "sojourn" in Hawaii and the continental United States, a practice commonly known as *dekasegi*. Then, around 1908, with the rise of anti-Japanese agitation, the Gentlemen's Agreement between Tokyo and Washington abruptly put a halt to labor migration across the Pacific. Since bona fide residents could still bring their family members from Japan to the United States, immigrants after the bilateral agreement were predominantly women—mostly wives of male Issei residents—whose arrival accelerated the formation of Japanese families and the increase of American-born Nisei in the American West. Meanwhile, the peril of institutionalized racism continued to haunt Japanese immigrants, stripping them of various politicoeconomic rights and relegating them to the status of perpetual foreigners. In 1924, the enactment of the National Origins Act, which prohibited the entry of immigrants from Japan altogether, ended the first migration phase. In the historical literature on this phase, racism and labor have been the two central analytical themes for understanding the Japanese in the United States.[19]

This study incorporates the consequences of nation-building and imperialism into the analysis of the Issei's migration experience and adaptation to American society between the 1880s and the 1910s. Understanding Japanese immigrant history from the inter-National perspective requires close attention to the timing of their departure from Japan and entry into the United States.

Their premigrant experiences were shaped, first, by the emergence of a modern nation-state on the Japanese archipelago that rudely invaded their familiar social world, and, second, by the rise of the two major expansionistic powers in the Pacific.

Though a majority were of working-class origin, Japanese emigrants were still very diverse in their social and intellectual backgrounds.[20] Corresponding to the process of nation/empire-building in Japan, the convoluted nature of Japanese emigration chiefly mirrored how inconsistently various segments of the Issei population were nationalized or "modernized." Because distinct classes of emigrants identified with the Japanese state in different ways, tensions, rather than congruencies, characterized the relationships of Issei with their native country. While the Japanese state attempted to fit the emigrants into the mold of the ideal imperial subject, many Issei interpreted preconceived national categories differently, often blending them with hegemonic "American" meanings posed by white exclusionists and deploying them in defense of their diasporic community.

The American West constituted a borderland where America's westward expansionism met Japanese imperialism around the question of immigration from the late nineteenth to the early twentieth centuries.[21] It was also where different national ideals and ideologies clashed, became intertwined, and fused through the interplay of the nativist push for racial exclusion and the immigrant struggle against it. The turn of the twentieth century marked the consolidation of a Euro-American regime on the "frontier," in which a rigid racial hierarchy was established over the growing "alien" populations of Asian and Mexican origins.[22] Not only did the geopolitical context of the borderland fashion the form of exclusionist and assimilationist politics there, but it also promoted the appropriation of Japanese and American colonial thinking by many Issei, as they fought the Orientalist charges of unassimilability and justified their rightful place in the frontier land. As advocates of the new Western history show, the American West has always been a meeting place of various ideas, interests, and powers; Japanese at this site of cross-cultural mixing must likewise be seen as players in an entanglement and contestation across multiple national spaces.[23] Adopting the concept of the borderland, this book tackles the interconnectedness of the colonialism, migration, and racial struggle that unfolded in the complex social space of the American West.

This book commences by placing Issei migration and their settlement in the contexts of Japan's transpacific expansion and America's continuous conquest of the frontier at the turn of the twentieth century. The massive exodus of labor migrants from Japan, coinciding with the empire's inception, paralleled the development of a major branch of Japanese imperialist thought—"eastward expansionism"—that viewed the Western Hemisphere as its own "frontier."

This impulse was confronted by the westward manifest destiny of white America—one that effected the acquisition of Hawaii, the Philippines, and Guam in 1898. Unearthing this neglected imperialist rivalry, chapter 1 explores Japan's major discourses on emigration, which helped to produce heterogeneous groups of Issei. As various forms of expansionist thought clashed with the pragmatism of *dekasegi* laborers, ethnic solidarity or common identity barely existed among Japanese immigrants at the outset. The first chapter sets the stage for the tumultuous beginning of Issei society and its history in America.

Chapters 2 and 3 trace the contentious processes of community formation. From the turn of the century through the 1910s, a unified leadership of elite immigrants took shape in tandem with the rise of anti-Japanese agitation in California. In partnership with members of the Japanese diplomatic corps, self-proclaimed Issei leaders—mostly urban, entrepreneurial, and educated—institutionalized an immigrant control mechanism in the form of the Japanese association network that crisscrossed the American West. Envisioned as a key solution to racial exclusion, the apparatus of social disciplining sought to transform the masses of laboring men and women into imperial subjects, who could simultaneously partake fully of American life and citizenship. Akin to the mainstream Progressive movement, this project of racial uplift attempted to inscribe onto ordinary Issei a bourgeois middle-class understanding of civility, morality, and womanhood, which underscored the "whiteness" of Japanese immigrants in the language of universal modernity. Central to immigrant moral reform were modernist assumptions of race and nationhood that subsumed classist and gendered expectations. Not only embraced by Japan's elite and immigrant leaders but also vociferously propagated by California exclusionists—albeit against Japanese—in their vision of a Eurocentric America, those assumptions formed a field of accommodation between incoming Japanese and receiving whites in the early twentieth century. Chapter 2 therefore looks at the curious convergence of ideas and practices relative to respective nation-building among the educated elements of Issei men and women, Tokyo's diplomats, and white Californians. The chapter also sheds light on their divergence from ordinary Japanese immigrants, who never seriously heeded the elite vision of ideal citizen-subjects.

Another force, however, simultaneously served to construct the collectivity of a "race" out of Japanese immigrants of all classes and all ideological persuasions on the borderland. Instead of racial uplift, racial subordination was the organizing grammar of this social formation. Chapter 3 deals with the overarching impact on the Issei of American racism, which contributed to the development of a distinct racial identity among them in relation to other borderland residents as well as the people of Japan. This process occurred at the level of their daily struggle as a racial(ized) minority—self-consciously identified as "the Japanese in America [*zaibei doho*]"—on the basis of shared interests in and concerns with power relations in the American West. Examining the critical linkages between white exclusionist politics and immigrant counterstruggles, this chapter explores the grassroots level of community formation, which coincided with the partial consolidation of immigrant leadership during the first two decades of the century.

Situated between the heavily studied subjects of the Japanese exclusion movement and wartime incarceration, the interwar period (1924–1941) is a largely forgotten phase of Japanese American history. The orthodox historical narrative treated the decades of the 1920s and the 1930s as a mere transitional moment in the evolution of two generations of Japanese Americans from "foreign" immigrants to full-fledged Americans. What can be termed the "immigrant paradigm" of Japanese American history has helped to buoy the myth of American exceptionalism, which celebrates the incorporation of foreigners as symbolizing the promise and triumph of American democracy.[24] A part of liberal assimilationist ideology, the paradigm dismisses the Old World traits of immigrants as a major roadblock to national inclusion. As the first generation symbolizes "foreign" in that scheme, the second generation represents the "marginal man," estranged from both the immigrant past and American society. In Japanese American history, the interwar years, especially the 1930s, are generally posited as the time when the Nisei began to grapple, under the obstinate influences of their Issei parents, with the challenges that all marginal men were supposed to encounter along the universal path to becoming Americans.[25] In recent years, revisionist scholarship has complicated that master narrative, instead highlighting the unique "bicultural" or "dual" nature of Japanese American history before the Pacific War.[26] The new studies remind us of the fallacy of seeing Japanese American lives from the standpoint of polarized national/cultural identities and allegiances—the Japan-versus-America binary that has obfuscated the nuanced experiences of Issei and Nisei in a transnational politicocultural space. Japanese Americans' politics of dualism indeed provides a crucial context for a more sensible understanding of the internment years, although this book only suggests certain aspects of the continuities and discontinuities between prewar and wartime Japanese America.[27]

In the five chapters dedicated to the interwar period, this book systematically revisits the historical omissions that have rendered Japanese immigrants as perpetual foreigners in our historical knowledge. Instead of a natural progression or historical inevitability, a politics of social negotiation played a principal role in Japanese Americans' adaptation to the exigencies of the new reality after racial exclusion in the American West. The interwar chapters, like the earlier chapters, draw upon a wide range of primary source documents in both English and Japanese. Because this book probes the interstices of hegemonic meanings and categories wherein the Issei lived and struggled, it is imperative, first and foremost, to apprehend *their* interpretation and appropriation of orthodox ideas, as well as their motives for the actions and inaction that stemmed from them. In an effort to salvage the unarticulated voices and mundane behaviors of Japanese immigrants, this study examines rarely consulted personal and organizational papers, vernacular newspapers, immigrant publications, state records, and government reports scattered in both the United States and Japan.[28]

Chapters 4 through 6 explicate the new thinking and practice that emerged in the community of "the Japanese in America." Bringing together the histories of migration, popular culture, and historiography, the fourth chapter shows how Japanese immigrants placed their collective past within narratives of the American frontier and Japanese expansionism in their relentless pursuit of national inclusion. Between 1924 and 1941, Issei historians writing for a popular audience borrowed from Japanese and American ideologies to draw a parallel between Euro-American frontier settlers and Issei "pioneers," while creating internal aliens among the working-class bachelors unfit for that image. Setting apart *dekasegi* laborers from Japanese American citizen-subjects, this historical vision enabled Issei family men to proclaim themselves archetypal Americans by virtue of their *Japanese* traits despite their unnaturalizable status. During the 1930s, immigrant leaders and parents also engaged in projects of social engineering on the basis of their dual national identity. The making of an ideal racial future for the Nisei involved manipulating their vocational preferences and demographics, advocating the "Japanese spirit" and moral lifestyle, and participating in transnational educational programs that took thousands of the American-born generation to their ancestral land. While expressed in the language of progress, national authenticity, and racial uplift, the visions and practices of Issei transnationalism that those projects embodied reified their overall marginality in American society, as well as added to the pressure experienced by this minority group, which had to constantly defend even the diminutive "ethnic" space it was allowed to hold.

Chapters 7 and 8 examine the intricate meanings of Japanese immigrant nationalism. Uniting ostensibly incommensurate ideas and acts—like their homeland ties and Americanism—is an indispensable step toward gaining a sense of how the world actually looked in the eyes of these immigrant Americans. In the context of racial subordination, the culture of Issei nationalism did not simply assert ethnic pride, cultural superiority, or aspiration toward collective liberation or ascent. Under the spell of nationalist consciousness, Japanese immigrants actually sought peaceful relations with propertied whites for stability and survival. At the same time, without the constraints of hierarchical imperatives in the interethnic relations, Issei nationalism precipitated confrontations with their Asian competitors just as imperial Japan fought and conquered their countries of origin. Finally, this form of nationalism suppressed internal diversity, thrusting heterodox lives, acts, and ideas into the rubric of middle-class citizenry that it strove to construct in the ethnic collectivity. Rather than repelling white supremacy with nationalist indignation, leading immigrants forged an identity of being "honorary whites" around the notion of proper "Japanese" thinking and conduct, and they successfully persuaded the rest of the community to acquiesce to it. Thus, even in the pro-Japan activities of the Issei can be seen a deep-seated desire for inclusion in America. Viewed from this standpoint, the idea of divided loyalties, which the immigrant paradigm presupposes in the problem of immigrant nationalism, simply does not hold up.

This study raises questions and unravels assumptions about race, nation, migration, and history that have misled many scholars into thinking in terms of bounded definitions and essentialized categories. Much of human experience resists being framed into the confines of national histories, and that is most true of immigrants—including Japanese—whose lives unfold somewhere long before they actually immigrate. Although challenging national histories and nationalist historiographies from the Issei's transnational perspective, this study nevertheless does not conclude with an emancipatory vision of escape from, or an inspiring story of opposition to, the tyranny of the national.[29] The most prevalent version of Japanese immigrant transnationalism articulated their profound anxieties about being excluded from white America, being marginalized in the society in which they lived, and being subordinated as the consequence of racist legislation. Unlike black "double consciousness," for example, the Issei's politics of dualism did not stem from ambivalence about the singular nationality of a racist regime and a diasporic self-understanding that aspired to transcend it.[30] Transnationalism instead allowed Japanese immigrants to strategize new terms of national belonging through their claims to their imperial Japanese heritage. Rather than seeking to overcome the constraints of the American state with cosmopolitanism, the Issei spun the meanings of racial authenticity and cultural respectability only to the extent that they did not subvert the integrity of the nation or disrupt the racial order of U.S. society. This paradox—the potency of the national in transnationalism—is the central theme of Japanese immigrant history before the Pacific War.

Part I

Multiple Beginnings

I

Mercantilists, Colonialists, and Laborers

Heterogeneous Origins of Japanese America

> Emigrants (*imin*) and colonialists (*shokumin*), just like the phenomena of
> emigration (*imin*) and colonization (*shokumin*), are often confounded. . . .
> Colonialists embark as imperial subjects with a pioneer spirit under the
> aegis of our national flag for state territorial expansion; emigrants act
> merely on an individual basis, leaving homeland as a matter of personal
> choice without the backing of sovereign power.[1]

In 1910, a Japanese immigrant (Issei) journalist commented on the prevailing
"confusion" over those conceptual categories. Not only were the people of Japan
guilty of this, the writer asserted, but his compatriots in California also erro-
neously identified themselves as "colonialists" not "immigrants."[2] This confusion characterized the historical trajectory of Japanese emigration to the United
States, as well as the heterogeneous nature of the early Issei society. Specifically,
the weaving of colonialism into labor migration, or vice versa, formed a crucial
backdrop against which thorny relations developed among Issei, between them
and white residents, and between the expatriate Japanese community and their
home state. The transnational history of Japanese immigrants in the American
West therefore must begin with an analysis of the ideas and practices that
underlay those confusions and contradictions.

Popularized after the Meiji Restoration of 1868, "emigration" and "colonization" were new concepts borrowed from the West, which the Japanese

political elite and intellectual class came to use interchangeably in their discussion of the most pressing national tasks: national formation and expansion.[3] The dissemination of these ideas to the emergent citizenry through the press, political organizations, and academia was central in the making of a modern empire in Japan. The very notion of emigration or colonization had not even existed under the closed-door policy of the Tokugawa feudal regime. The exodus of various classes of Japanese for Hawaii and the mainland United States after the 1880s prompted the intelligentsia for the first time to seriously contemplate the meaning of popular emigration in tandem with the nascent ideas of national expansion.

In order to explain the nature of early Japanese expansionism with which the practice of emigration was tightly intertwined, it is necessary to delve into three interrelated contexts: geopolitics in the Asia-Pacific region, Japan's incorporation into the international network of capitalist economies, and the formation of the modern nation-state. First, Meiji Japan's entry into modernity coincided with the era in which Western powers had been engaged in fierce colonialist competitions in East Asia and the Pacific Basin. During the 1880s, a new style of imperialism became the vogue as the West sought direct control of overseas territories, replacing the emphasis on hegemonic control in trade to link the metropolis and its colonies. In Southeast Asia, the French took over Indochina, and the British established footholds in Burma, while both powers scrambled for Africa. The Pacific and northeastern Asia subsequently emerged as another sphere of imperialist competition. During and after the Spanish-American War of 1898, the United States acquired Hawaii, the Philippines, and Guam, while the Germans took over the hitherto-neglected Spanish possessions of Pacific island chains in Micronesia and Melanesia. In the meantime, since the mid-1800s, China had become a major battlefield for Christian missionaries and merchants from Europe and the United States.

Meiji Japan, a latecomer, joined this international scramble for new territories and export markets, not only because its leaders felt that the "civilized" had to accept manifest destiny to partake in the practice of colonization, but also because they believed that proactive expansionist endeavors would be imperative in defense of Japan's fragile security.[4] The nation had been on the receiving end of Western imperialism, when it had been forced to open to international commerce in 1854 by U.S. warships under Commodore Matthew Perry, but Japan had diverged from other Asian nations because of its quick "success" in acclimating to the geopolitical environment. No sooner had Emperor Meiji formed a new government in 1868 than imperial expansionism began internally and externally, resulting in the colonization of Hokkaido (1869) and Okinawa (1879); the seizures of Taiwan (1894), south Sakhalin (1905), and Kwantung Province (1905) in northern China; and then the annexation of

Korea (1910). In the meantime, the country fought two successful foreign wars, first with China in 1894–1895 and then with Russia in 1904–1905.[5]

Migration constituted a pivotal part of these state endeavors, both in policy and in practice. Hokkaido, the first colonialist project, was brought under national control by settling with a domestic population. Before the restoration of the emperor's rule, the Tokugawa warrior regime had only loosely incorporated Japan's northern island, but with increasing threats from Russia, the Meiji state embarked on the official colonization of Hokkaido in 1869, modeling it after the conquest of the North American "frontier" by the United States.[6] While building a basic infrastructure and industrial facilities, the government encouraged displaced former *samurai* and peasants in the main islands to immigrate to the new frontier, where the transplanted could farm in peacetime and defend the northern borders in wartime. When the state permitted the departure of common laborers in 1885 for Hawaii and, later, for the U.S. mainland, many officials and educated Japanese viewed their migration in terms similar to the contemporaneous movement of surplus populations to Hokkaido and other new territories.[7]

Japan's late adoption of a capitalist economy further contributed to the blurring of the boundaries between emigration and colonization. Although the nation turned itself from a feudal society into a major military power within the span of a few decades, the development compounded the integration of Japan into the international capitalist network, rendering it perpetually dependent for markets and capital on more advanced industrial economies, particularly the United States. Given its relative underdevelopment, Japan often served as a source of cheap workers for the more advanced economies, transferring manual labor to Hawaii, the American West, and to a lesser degree, various European colonies in Southeast Asia and the plantation economies of Latin America.[8] Insofar as it also enhanced the competitiveness of imperial Japan's economy, the cheapness of domestic labor dovetailed with Japan's own colonialist projects, leading to significant overlap in socioeconomic characteristics between Japanese immigrants in other countries and colonial settlers within the empire.[9] Although the movement of Japanese across the Pacific transpired between the sphere of Japan's sovereign control and that of another nation-state, it was this overlap that caused U.S.–bound emigrants to be often confounded with colonialists who moved and lived "under the aegis of our national flag."

Tokyo's effort to consolidate state control over its populace provided the third context in which expansionism and emigration were interlocked. Aside from setting up formal state apparatuses and a unified capitalist economy, Meiji nation-building sought to make imperial subjects out of village-bound peasants, who would act voluntarily for the benefit of the emperor and the national collectivity.[10] In accordance with this mandate, as the Meiji elite often stressed, emigrants were expected to obey the call of their nation as citizen-subjects. Just as the state dictated that the obligations of every imperial subject included such acts as paying taxes from meager income, working fourteen hours a day under hazardous conditions, and dying while fighting a foreign war, so Meiji leaders defined emigration as a patriotic duty in support of Japan's expansionist cause, whether commercial, political, or territorial. The colonialist discourse therefore usually assigned a nationalist meaning to the act of emigration on the premise that the masses shared the same dedication to the state's collective purpose. Importantly, while it created another point of intersection between colonialism and emigration, the nationalist presumption blinded the elite to the fact that most emigrants of rural origin viewed their endeavors from the standpoint of personal interest without much regard to the purported duties of the imperial subject. Subsuming popular individualism under nascent nationalism, the elite vision of emigration-led expansionism contradicted the logic of most ordinary emigrants and planted the seeds for discord, which would later grow among Japanese residents in the American West.

During the years between 1885 and 1907, when most male emigrants left for Hawaii and the United States, the ideological terrain of Meiji Japan was indeed a diverse one, with competing ideas developing in tandem with the political process of nationalizing the Japanese people. There were three major currents of emigration thought that directly affected the early development of Japanese America. Roughly corresponding with the class origins and mental worlds of the Issei, they were mercantilist expansionism, Japanese-style manifest destiny, and an ideology of striving and success. The heterogeneity of the Japanese emigrant population also provided a background for contentious relations and identities within their communities, based on how individuals, with varied degrees of national consciousness, understood their ties to the homeland, as well as their role and place in their adopted country.

Mercantilist expansionism helped form what was to become the core of urban Issei leadership in the Pacific Coast states. Rather than seizing colonial territories by military force, proponents of this position aspired to establish footholds of international trade at foreign locations, to which Japan could send its export goods while exercising indirect forms of economic domination. The leading advocate was Fukuzawa Yukichi, who took the lead in the learning of things Western and the development of entrepreneurial culture in Meiji Japan. In 1884, dreaming of British-style commercial hegemony in the Pacific, Fukuzawa promoted Japanese export business by the way of entrepreneurial migration to the United States. Through his private Keio academy and commercial newspaper, this foremost scholar of "Western studies" sought to impress his ideas upon the emerging urban bourgeoisie in Tokyo.[11]

Fukuzawa believed that there was an imminent need to shore up the Meiji policy of "enrich the nation, strengthen the military." With a weak industrial base and a small domestic market, Japan in the mid-1880s badly needed to increase its exports to develop foreign exchange holdings. While propagating trade as essential to solidifying the fiscal basis of the state and its military, Fukuzawa defined emigration as a cardinal means of promoting commerce with the United States. Specifically, he anticipated that Japanese immigrants in key American trade ports would serve as a "commercial linkage between their homeland and their new country of residence."[12] In a commentary entitled "Leave Your Homeland at Once," Fukuzawa justified his advocacy of entrepreneurial emigration in terms of the British success:

> In considering the long-term interest of the country, the wealth that [English traders abroad] have garnered individually has become part of England's national assets. The land they reclaimed has turned into regional centers of English trade, if not its formal colonial territories. This is how Great Britain has become what she is today. In a similar vein, [a Japanese emigrant] shall be regarded as a loyal subject. For while sacrificing himself at the time of national crisis is a direct way of showing loyalty, engaging in various enterprises abroad is an indirect way of discharging patriotism. . . . When examining the example of Englishmen, no one would fail to see [that emigration] shall lead to the enrichment of Japan as well.[13]

Not everyone, however, was capable of taking up such an endeavor, in Fukuzawa's opinion. He restricted the practitioners of entrepreneurial migration to the United States to a narrow range of educated, middle-class Japanese, for the national "enrichment of Japan" was contingent upon whether or not emigrants possessed the dispositions with which to remain loyal imperial subjects even on foreign soil. Fukuzawa believed that such individuals should be given an opportunity to leave for "the land of boundless opportunities," because he felt that their intellect, talent, and "superior racial qualities" would ensure their ascendancy in American society. Focusing on people of warrior background, Fukuzawa's emigration discourse offered no room for common people of rural origin, whom he frequently ridiculed as lacking national consciousness and modern sensibilities.[14]

Despite, or perhaps because of, such exclusive elitism, Fukuzawa's mercantilist expansionism had a profound impact on the early Issei community in the American West. Understandably, the business-minded, educated youth were most susceptible to his ideas. Disseminated in Keio classrooms, at public lectures, and through newspaper editorials, Fukuzawa's call for entrepreneurial emigration motivated a number of his early students and others to jump into export-import businesses between Japan and the United States. Some went to New York City to pioneer in the silk trade with Japan as early as 1876, while others rushed to West Coast cities for other opportunities.[15] After the establishment of San Francisco's first Issei import business by one of Fukuzawa's disciples around 1880, a number of individuals followed suit in the ensuing decades and formed a small but pivotal merchant class in early Japanese America.[16] According to one observer, "[T]he many successful Japanese immigrants whom I met during my 1907 trip . . . told me that [Fukuzawa's] extolment of emigration had inspired them to come to the United States."[17] Another source reported that more than 1,000 Keio graduates had emigrated to the United States by 1906, noting the presence of Keio alumni associations in San Francisco and Seattle.[18] As their mentor had taught them, these Issei businesspeople tended to view the significance of their ventures as much in terms of Japan's national interest as in terms of their own personal achievement. Many subsequently returned home to pursue distinguished careers in the Japanese corporate world, but those who remained in the United States formed the core of Japanese immigrant leadership, backed by their wealth and close ties to Japanese diplomats and the social elite in Tokyo.[19]

A more colonialist discourse on emigration overtook mercantilist expansionism from the 1890s on, when the international scramble for colonies reached its nadir in the Asia-Pacific region. The main theme of the new position revolved around the control of a foreign land through mass migration.[20] Historian Akira Iriye aptly summarizes this Japanese-style manifest destiny:

> The line between emigration and colonization was rather tenuous. Most authors, advocating massive overseas emigration, were visualizing the creation of Japanese communities overseas as centers of economic and social activities closely linked to the mother country. . . . Though the outright use of force was not envisaged, such a situation would be much closer to colonization than to mere emigration—like the massive English colonization of the North American continent. Thus, "peaceful expansionism" did not simply mean the passive emigration of individual Japanese, but could imply a government-sponsored, active program of overseas settlement and positive activities to tie distant lands closer to Japan.[21]

Called "a new Japan," "a second Japan," "a new home," or "an imperial beginning," the American West attracted keen attention from a group of Issei intellectuals and students in the late nineteenth century. They took part in the larger current of public discourse that set forth three different directions for expansion. Advocates of northward expansion represented imperialistic ambitions on the Asian continent. Influencing army strategists, it paved the way to the two major wars with China and the Russian Far East and the subsequent influx of Japanese migrants into Manchuria. A harbinger of Japanese naval operations during the First World War, southward expansionism derived from an interest in extending maritime trade into the southwestern Pacific, especially Micronesia. Unlike these two ideas that soon merged into the official state colonialist projects, transpacific eastward expansionism focused on emigration-led colonization without the support of military forces, envisioning the conquest of the overseas hinterland through the transplantation of Japanese masses. The imaginary map of this colonialist vision included Hawaii, the Pacific Coast regions of the United States and Canada, and Central and South America.[22]

Published in 1887, one of the earliest guides to "going to America" contended that North America should be as much a frontier to the Japanese as it had been to the Europeans. "The United States," the Issei authors noted, "is a land for new development, which awaits the coming of ambitious youth. Come, our brethren of 3,700,000! . . . When you come to the United States, you must have the determination to create the second, new Japan there, which also helps enhance the interest and prestige of the imperial government and our nation."[23] Yet, contrary to other Japanese who harbored naked territorial ambitions over other parts of the New World, Issei advocates of Japanese manifest destiny were generally compelled to practice their belief within the confines of existing American power relations. When they rushed across the Pacific in the late nineteenth century, the rigid racialized hierarchy between the white ruling class and cheap labor from Asia had already taken hold on the Western land as the result of Chinese exclusion, and the commanding power of American westward expansionism was about to swallow up Hawaii and other Pacific islands. With no possibility of Japanese ascendancy in the game of mastering the Western frontier, the Issei's Americanized rendition of peaceful expansionism primarily sought to carve out semiautonomous spheres through the building of a collective economic base, the control of farmlands, and the construction of Japanese settlement "colonies," under the established order of the white racial regime.[24]

Toward the late 1890s, a clear pattern of domestic entrepreneurship emerged from the expansionistic Issei intelligentsia. Seeking capital consolidation and ethnic mobilization, many looked to integrate common Japanese laborers, who had hitherto lived in a separate world. In San Francisco, Seattle, and Portland, as well as in smaller regional towns, this ushered in the formation of a class of professional Issei labor contractors. Not only did they promote the influx of additional laborers from Japan, but they also played a major role in increasing landed Japanese communities by facilitating settlement farming in rural districts.[25] In this way, Issei expansionists were being incorporated into the agricultural economy of the American West, conveniently filling the labor vacuum created by Chinese exclusion, as suppliers of farm hands and tillers of undeveloped land.

Based in Portland, Oregon, Shinzaburo Ban was one of the most influential labor contractors. A former diplomat who came to the United States in 1891, Ban explained to his expansionist friends in Japan that he decided to resign his government position and migrate so as "to help [ordinary workers] obtain farmland for the goal of planting the seeds of large-scale settlements." Calling it "suiting the hundred-year scheme of Japan," he elaborated upon his vision of colonization in the Western frontier:

> One has to earn money initially as a common laborer, while learning sentiments, mores, and language [of the host society] to shape the unique character of an immigrant resident. To put it another way, he is going to be hired as a laborer at first given the dearth of capital; as time passes by, he will accrue his earnings to invest in land and build a house, making him an independent landholding farmer. Naturally, he will wish to send for family members from the homeland and settle down [in America] permanently.[26]

Like Ban, a number of expansionistic Issei entrepreneurs took it upon themselves to build "second Japans" as agricultural colonists or as facilitators for others of lesser means, which resulted in the increased landholdings of Japanese in the West. Combined with the business of labor contracting, their "colonialist" practice unfolded without disturbing the existing framework of social relations, and yet many intellectual Issei still interpreted their endeavors in the language of national expansion, or "Japanese development," in America. Such efforts included the formations of the Japanese Village in Dundee (340 acres) and the Nippon Colony in Santa Ana (230 acres) in 1905, as well as of the Yamato Colony (3,200 acres) in Livingston, California, in the following year.[27] Farmers of much smaller scale, too, often understood their meager enterprises in similar terms, characterizing them as part of peaceful expansionism. In 1901, one laboring Issei organized a partnership to pool resources for the acquisition of a five-acre "colony" in southern California—a venture by which to, in his words, "emulate the example of the British [Anglo-Saxons] in marching forward in this world of fierce competition."[28] These landed colonial settlements—large or small—were emblematic of modified peaceful expansionism in early Japanese America, which funneled the resources of colonial-minded Issei into the cause of Japanese development in Western agriculture.

Unlike the ideas of emigration tied to trade and colonization, the third current of emigration thought, an ideology of striving and success, fit into the mental world of many common emigrants. From the mid-1890s through the following decade, what contemporaries observed as a popular "success boom" swept Japanese society, and emigration to the United States was central to this new social phenomenon. As the print media exalted the American Dream, mass-

produced magazines popularized stories of self-made white men, such as Andrew Carnegie, Theodore Roosevelt, Cornelius Vanderbilt, and John D. Rocke-
feller. Because "America" became synonymous with boundless opportunities in
the Japanese vocabulary of the time, many unprivileged but ambitious youth
projected onto these role models their own future trajectories.[29] Portraying emigration to the United States as a crucial step, the success ideology catered to
the aspirations of the indigent students to work their way through school in
the American West and the desire of the rural farming class to make a quick
fortune through manual labor there.

Targeting the first group as their audience, Katayama Sen and Shimanuki
Hyodayu played major roles in disseminating the ideal of work-and-study in
America. Around the turn of the century, these self-proclaimed champions of
the struggling urban students incorporated emigration into their respective social reform programs. Buried in the Kremlin as an Asian revolutionary, Katayama began his colorful political career modestly as a reform-minded Christian
socialist. His interest in emigration was as personal as it was political, for he
had earlier struggled as a student-laborer in the United States. While attending
high school in the San Francisco Bay area, Katayama worked as a houseboy,
cook, and handyman. Eventually he attended Yale Divinity School, where the
ideas of Progressive reformers captivated him.[30] After returning to Japan,
Katayama was recruited to head an American-sponsored settlement house in
Tokyo, from which he promoted emigration as a solution to the lack of educational opportunities for urban adolescents. Also a Christian reformist, Shimanuki during his sojourn on the West Coast was similarly impressed by the
possibility of work-and-study in America as an alternative to aimless struggle
in Tokyo.[31] Instead of clinging to the distant hope of "making it" in dire
poverty, these two social workers encouraged ambitious youth to leave for the
United States for schooling by publishing emigration guidebooks and magazines.[32]

When addressed to student-emigrants, the ideology of striving and success
was not divorced from the prevailing concern with the national whole that
educated Japanese generally shared. Since it was urban literati, like Katayama
and Shimanuki, who articulated the meaning of going to America, the success
ideology was often worded in the familiar language of "extending national
power."[33] Shimanuki resembled a typical expansionist when he argued that it
was the inherent "nature" of the Japanese people to go past their national
boundaries in all directions, in particular, east across the Pacific, to "plant new
homelands."[34] Despite an internationalist outlook, Katayama was likewise "first
and foremost a patriotic Japanese citizen," who compared one's "loyalty to the
emperor and love of country" with "defying the waves of the wide ocean,
entering another country, and establishing one's livelihood."[35] Influenced by

such an ideology, which subsumed self-interest under nationalism, it was not uncommon for many student-emigrants to merge into the earlier group of expansionist entrepreneurs once they arrived in the American West. Indeed, in the first two decades of the twentieth century, many immigrant farmers, business owners, and regional community leaders emerged from this population.[36]

The ideology of success had another keen audience: Japan's rural masses. Unlike students, *dekasegi* emigrants of rural origin were mostly indifferent to the valorization of emigration beyond personal or family concerns. For example, a *dekasegi* returnee ascribed her family's emigration decision solely to the "rumor that [it] would pay off handsomely," while another sought to acquire land in his home village and build a "tile-roofed house"—a symbol of wealth in rural Japan.[37] Upon his return from California, a migrant worker admitted that he had acted on the words of former migrant workers that one could "make a bundle of money in America." Despite his advanced age and family objections, the fifty-three-year-old took the journey to the unknown land, because he knew he could not have enjoyed "his fill of sweet *sake*" had he stayed put as a poor farmer in Japan.[38] These accounts demonstrate no trace of concern for the state, or even for their village communities.

From the standpoint of the government elite and urban intelligentsia, rural Japanese were indeed a great trouble. When a large number of laborers crossed the Pacific for work, the process of molding them into imperial subjects had barely begun at home. Starting in the early 1870s, the Meiji state strove hard to integrate Japan's periphery into its centralized state apparatuses, while inculcating national identity in the population of feudalized peasants. This process entailed the development of suitable ideologies, such as state Shintoism, legally sanctioned patriarchy, and the orthodoxy of emperor worship, as well as the construction of corresponding institutions, including compulsory education and military service. The making of imperial subjects in rural areas was nonetheless uneven and incomplete due partially to the often-strained relationships between the central elite and grassroots leaders. Not until after the Russo-Japanese War of 1904–1905 did the state achieve any notable integration of village Japanese.[39]

Confined to the realm of his immediate surroundings, the consciousness of a typical Japanese migrant was predicated on what was good for him and his immediate family. As historian Carol Gluck observes, this "alternative social ideology to the official one of collective cooperation . . . enjoined not cooperative community spirit but personal striving and brandished the language not of social harmony but of the Darwinian struggle for survival."[40] This heresy, which placed the individual over the nation-state, could easily clash with state orthodoxy. Yet, as long as one acted within the preexisting framework or on behalf of one's family and village community, which provided the backbone of the Meiji body politic, the line between the self-effacing imperial subject and the self-serving individual blurred. Indeed, only after an excess of materialism began to overwhelm the social elite in the early 1900s did Tokyo finally begin to treat the ideology of striving and success as a menace.[41] Labor emigration was part and parcel of this diachronic process, in which the popular logic of success increasingly overrode the national imperative within that ideology.

The departure of *dekasegi* laborers for Hawaii and the United States between 1885 and 1908 signified the zenith of popular pragmatism among ordinary Japanese. In the context of the nation's incorporation into the international network of capitalist economies, the decade of the 1880s ushered in a drastic reconfiguration of its rural economy. What helped to encourage the farming population to emigrate was the overarching effect of commercial agriculture, which alienated so many villagers from their chief means of production, the farmland. These displaced peasants formed a pool of working-class people in need of wage labor. At the same time, the intrusion of market forces into villages opened up the world view of rural residents, allowing some to dream of upward mobility beyond what they could have had under the feudal regime. Depending on varying economic, political, and social circumstances, these developments made some groups of rural Japanese more receptive than others to the idea of going abroad as a way to material fulfillment. The resultant emigrants divide into two major types: distressed contract laborers and entrepreneurial laborers.

Known initially as "government-contract emigrants" (1885–1894) and later as "private-contract emigrants" (1894–1899), *distressed contract laborers* consisted mainly of individuals of "landless or small landowning farming households," who looked to earn American dollars through contract labor in Hawaii.[42] Transportation to Hawaii and other initial expenses were paid for by the employer. In the two phases, there were 29,069 and 40,230 such emigrants, respectively, who were recruited to work on sugar plantations on three-year contracts.[43] When the Japanese government was in charge of recruitment, until 1894, the effort concentrated in a few prefectures in southwestern Japan, such as Hiroshima, Yamaguchi, Fukuoka, and Kumamoto, in accordance with the wishes of government and business leaders.[44] Beneath this political favoritism nonetheless lay a socioeconomic undercurrent that made the ideology of success and striving more influential in some regions than others. The original locations of early contract laborers tended to have undergone a significant transformation from conventional rice farming to the cultivation of commercial crops, like cotton and indigo, as well as the rise of semimechanized cottage industries, since the 1870s.[45]

In order to understand the impact of market forces upon rural emigration, it is crucial to take into account when the fortunes of the landed family farmers declined in such economic circumstances rather than noting merely a state of displacement or want. A typical contract emigrant from Hiroshima was either a household head, his younger brother, or his oldest son, as well as his wife, who sought to work off debts or supplement shrinking family income by three years of hard labor abroad. Such an early emigrant household was among the recent casualties of rapid commercialization in agriculture and Tokyo's deflationary policy. Even though contract laborers tended to be destitute or bankrupt at the time of their embarkation, most had been economically better off prior to the 1880s.[46] In rural Japan, the initial economic change had taken place with the institution of a national tax system in 1873. Levying 3 percent of the assessed land value on all of the landed households, this tax did not reflect fluctuations in the prices of crops nor the value of the currency. When agricultural prices ascended steadily in accordance with the high inflation of the 1870s, it did not affect most farmers, since their growing income could minimize the monetary burden of taxation in relative terms. However, the drastic deflationary measures of the early 1880s not only shrank agricultural prices by half, but they also greatly increased the tax burden in terms of the deflated currency, sending into default many small family farmers who had spearheaded the early growth of commercial agriculture by borrowing and investing. The crisis that these pillars of village communities suddenly faced explains their rising interest in *dekasegi* work for economic rehabilitation, as well as Tokyo's decision to lift its ban on labor migration in 1885 for popular appeasement.[47]

Motivated by the vivid memory of better days in the recent past, rural Japanese formerly of the middle strata were most inclined to jump at what the system of contract-labor emigration promised: a quick recovery from sudden impoverishment without the requirement of personal financial resources or burden. Rural Japanese of other classes were less likely to take the chance even if information on emigration were available. To the most socially deprived, who had been consistently resourceless, the formula looked less realistic. Having lived without hope since the feudal era, they had accepted their socioeconomic standing as a given and had few aspirations beyond daily survival. Further, their chances of being allowed to leave for Hawaii or elsewhere were slim to nil due to the prevailing official bias against them.[48] Meanwhile, very few members of the upper strata would be likely to leave their villages, since they were less willing to risk their familiar lifestyles in Japan by going abroad for temporary work than were those who were financially threatened and desperate. Instead, collaborating with the state, the village upper class often encouraged and facilitated the departure of the fallen middle class in hopes that the scheme of self-help would pacify agitated residents and refocus their energy on local economic development.[49] Official reports indeed attested to the relative success of the contract-labor scheme. According to an 1889 Hiroshima report, "[M]any [returnees] acquired houses and farms, while others used their earnings to start industrial and commercial enterprises" in their communities.[50] Likewise, officials of Okayama and Wakayama prefectures noted that some returnees were even pondering the possibility of growing sugar cane and starting sugar-refining businesses in their home districts.[51]

Critically, these observations also underscore the changing nature of labor emigration, which became increasingly noticeable in the ensuing decades. A growing number of rural Japanese considered it to be a lucrative area of investment. In the regions where many contract laborers originated, their success convinced other villagers of similar or higher strata to follow suit, thus triggering chain migration to Hawaii and the United States. One-time contract laborers, too, often apportioned their earnings for second trips across the Pacific. To his Hiroshima village, for example, a *dekasegi* emigrant brought back more than $350 after three years of toiling on a Hawaiian sugar plantation. Out of that money, his family not only paid off debts and set aside some savings, but also laid out $135 on farmlands and a house, $20 on furniture, and $100 on another *dekasegi* term abroad.[52] When these people paid their own way and embarked on their second transpacific journeys, they were no longer contract laborers bound by specific—and often inferior—terms of employment. Their better economic conditions allowed them to act like the "rational peasant," who was inclined to "make long-term as well as short-term investments" in emigration, rather than the risk-averse "moral peasant" mainly in search of subsistence alternatives.[53] Called *free emigrants*, these rural pragmatists put their own resources into *dekasegi* work abroad for higher returns, often heedless of official mandates or guidelines—a change that increasingly troubled the social elite of Japan.

Between 1895 and 1908, more than 130,000 Japanese—the majority of them *entrepreneurial laborers*—left for the continental United States and Hawaii.[54] The typical emigrant of this group originated from a better-off rural household, and he preferred to go to the continental United States without his wife.[55] An average immigrant in California could earn twice as much as a field hand in Hawaii. Given that even a plantation worker was paid four to six times more than a common laborer in Hiroshima, the benefits of choosing labor on the U.S. mainland far exceeded that of going elsewhere and was well worth the initial expenses, which amounted to at least $100.[56] For the same reason, many Japanese laborers in Hawaii, "liberated" from three-year contracts as a result of U.S. annexation, opted to go to the Pacific Coast states after 1900 instead of continuing to work on sugarcane fields or returning home. From 1902 to 1907, there were reportedly about 38,000 Japanese remigrants from Hawaii to the American West.[57]

Unlike the contract labor scheme, the new pattern of labor emigration soon came into conflict with the diplomatic agenda of the Japanese state. The massive influx of common laborers from Japan incited anti-"Oriental" agitation among white Californians, who had excluded Chinese immigrants on the pretext of their economic, cultural, and racial danger. Quickly gathering political momentum, the anti-Japanese movement in the West became such a liability to Tokyo that the Foreign Ministry was compelled to stop the departure of Japanese for the U.S. mainland altogether in August 1900. A partial relaxation of the ban was effected in June 1902, but it excluded "laborers" categorically from the right of passage.[58] Following this change in emigration policy, when rural Japanese applied for passports, many farmers posed as "businessmen," "merchants," or even "industrialists"—a practice that continued until 1908 with some degree of success.[59] Others went to Mexico and Canada, from which they entered the continental United States.[60] Stringent administrative restrictions only led to widespread popular defiance. Viewed from the perspective of officials, such fraudulent passport applications presented a challenge not only to the diplomatic affairs of the state but also to the very authority of the central government.

Military service formed another notable area of popular defiance by entrepreneurial emigrants. Since the 1870s, rural Japanese had resisted conscription in a variety of ways ranging from mass protests to feigned illness. *Dekasegi* emigration offered many youths a safer means to avoid giving up several years of their lives for something other than their personal benefit and family interests. By virtue of their sojourns abroad, emigrant laborers were able to enjoy annual draft deferments; but in exchange they would be subject to mandatory induction into the army upon their return to Japan without a chance of obtaining reserve status. Yet even this restriction could not match the genius of many emigrants, who simply overstayed in the United States until after their eligibility for active duty expired at the age of thirty-two. The Japanese government was particularly concerned with this problem in the early 1900s, for officials considered it to be not only embarrassing but also inimical to national security. During the crisis of the Russo-Japanese War, Tokyo was compelled to order local offices to scrutinize passport applications from *dekasegi* laborers and crack down on draft evasions, noting that "more and more adolescents due to be draftable in 1905 and 1906 have been attempting to go abroad." Popular individualism seriously challenged the elite/national mandate, producing rebellious rural folks who hardly fit the image of the self-effacing imperial subject.[61]

The Gentlemen's Agreement of 1907–1908 between Washington and Tokyo was a logical culmination of the struggle between the state and rural emigrants. It primarily addressed the problem of anti-Japanese agitation in San Francisco, which demanded immigration exclusion, but also offered the Tokyo elite a solution to the uncontrollable proliferation of the success ideology among labor emigrants. Under the bilateral agreement, the entry routes from Mexico, Canada, and Hawaii into the U.S. mainland were shut down under an executive order of President Theodore Roosevelt, and Tokyo limited the issuance of America-bound passports to specific classes of individuals. Aside from international merchants and students of higher education, the qualified emigrants included only spouses and minor children of bona fide U.S. residents. Until the total exclusion of Japanese in 1924, a smaller scale of labor migration continued in the form of family chain migration, including the so-called picture brides, but after 1908 the control of rural emigrants posed far fewer challenges to the central government.

Thereafter, the main stage of struggle between the commanding state and the defiant emigrant shifted from the domestic sphere of Japan to the society of Japanese immigrants. In the American West, Tokyo's diplomatic agents and the local Issei elite, including expansionistic mercantilists, colonialists, and patriotic students, formed a coalition to keep the immigrant masses in line, while ordinary laboring men and women remained largely oblivious to the imposition of nationalist dictates. And behind this tug-of-war stood white Americans, who, as the chief force of political intervention, inadvertently furnished the framework for the intraethnic contestation and ensuing community-building efforts in early Japanese America.

Part II

Convergences and Divergences

2

Re-Forming the Immigrant Masses

The Transnational Construction of a Moral Citizenry

> Japanese prostitutes in the overseas are a disgrace to our nation. But they
> are unaware of that. . . . It is useless to reprove those who are ignorant,
> for it prompts no response. It is those who understand that must be ad-
> dressed. Who are those people? They are Japan's literati and the govern-
> ment.[1]

In 1894, a Japanese student-immigrant in San Francisco penned these words
for a Tokyo political journal. His message resonated with early Issei leaders,
who disdained the likes of prostitutes and itinerant laborers for tarnishing the
national reputation. Until the 1920s, the question of how to control the behavior of "the poor," both in a moral and material sense, was among the most
important agendas of the Japanese immigrant community. Self-proclaimed Issei
leaders, including mercantilists, colonialists, and nationalist students, attributed
the development of anti-Japanese sentiments in the American West to the contempt felt by the white population for these "ignorant" Japanese. The Issei
literati moreover shared this attitude with members of the Japanese diplomatic
corps and opinion leaders in Tokyo, leading toward their collaborative efforts
to "re-form" the immigrant masses according to common visions of progress
and civilization. Forged in a slow, laborious process from the 1890s to the 1910s,
the transnational elite partnership devoted its energy to producing a self-
governing imperial subject and an acceptable member of the American citizenry

out of an apathetic immigrant through the institutional channels of moral discipline and suasion. This chapter examines how the regulation of popular behavior and the mind was interwoven into the construction of a transnational community of Japanese citizen-subjects from above.

As early as 1889, the Japanese consul in San Francisco expressed his concern about the "deplorable" state of the city's Issei settlement. Many of the 3,000 residents, in his opinion, were destitute laborers who barely eked out a daily living. Even worse were "ex-seamen" who had jumped ship. Having brought women with them illegally, many lived by gambling and by forcing their female companions into prostitution.[2] The situation was similar in the Pacific Northwest. According to an 1891 report, the vast majority of the 300 Japanese in Seattle were prostitutes, pimps, brothel owners, and gamblers, who congregated at Japanese-run gambling dens day and night. Thirty to forty habitual gamblers and pimps reigned over a small minority of "legitimate residents." In 1891, Seattle had twenty-five Japanese brothel owners, who controlled seventy-two prostitutes; Portland had nine and seventeen, respectively.[3] In their reports for Tokyo, diplomats stressed a need for resolute government action against the undesirables, but once immigrants set foot on American soil, the officials had neither legal power nor the bureaucratic means to discipline them. Diplomats instead chose to empower the "legitimate" elements among the resident Japanese in hopes that they would be able to create an overseas community that would properly represent modern Japan. San Francisco offered the best chance, since it had a significant number of well-educated students and politically minded expatriates who shared nationalist concerns, as expressed by the Issei contributor to a Tokyo magazine. Before the 1920s, the city provided a key site for Japanese immigrants of community-building, which was constantly manipulated by certain agents and ideologies.

THE FORMATION OF JAPANESE IMMIGRANT LEADERSHIP AND COMMUNITY

The forging of a cohesive Issei leadership was a gradual and contentious process—one that dovetailed with the development of the anti-Japanese exclusion movement in California.[4] During the last decade of the nineteenth century, the Japanese community of San Francisco experienced a rapid escalation of white antagonism, a problem that targeted not just Japanese prostitutes but common laborers as well. In May 1892, a local immigration officer declared a number of newcomers from Japan to be illegal "contract laborers," thereby refusing them entry. Concurrent with the political effort to extend the Chinese Exclusion Act of 1882 for another ten years, anti-Asia advocates, like union leader Denis Kearney, began to attack the Japanese as another "Oriental menace." With the negative effects of the 1882 law on United States–China relations fresh in mind, Japanese consular officials were afraid that, if Japanese exclusion were legalized similarly, it would become a major setback for Japan's diplomacy in light of its quest for equality with the West. Local Issei leaders would experience additional and more imminent consequences; racial exclusion would threaten their welfare and livelihood. Fears rose as local English-language newspapers published one report after another against the Japanese "invasion," using sensationalized headlines and expressions. The San Francisco *Bulletin* printed "The Japs: Another Rising Tide of Immigration" on May 4, 1892.

> Like the Chinese, they are here for the purpose of acquiring enough money to enable them to end their days in leisure in their native land, and they have no intention of settling down here and making this place their home. In another respect they are like the Chinese, and that is that few of them in this country are married. The [Japanese] women here are of the lowest class, and like the Chinese women, are imported only to lead a life of shame.[5]

Ironically, both diplomats and the immigrant elite agreed with the exclusionists on the key point that the "inferior" quality of Japanese laborers and prostitutes paralleled the excluded Chinese. Fundamentally, this convergence stemmed from the contradiction between their self-image of the Japanese as the civilized and the prevailing notion of the Chinese as the uncivilized.[6] Mired in a hopeless "Asia" that was still stuck in the feudal era, this elite imperial ideology reasoned, Chinese lacked "modern" appearance and "civilized" conduct, offending not only white Americans but also the sensibilities of "educated Japanese." As white citizens of San Francisco had criticized, the city's leading Japanese concurred in the notions that the Chinese living quarters were "filthy," that their persons "stank," that their clothing looked "wretched," and that the men were tong criminals and the women prostitutes.[7] In the midst of the 1892 anti-Japanese agitation, the *Aikoku*, the organ of the Japanese Patriotic League of San Francisco, explained how the types of Japanese with whom the leading Issei associated stood completely apart from the Chinese:

> How do the Japanese in America and the Chinese in America differ? First, the Chinese in America represent the lower class of the Chinese race, and the Japanese in America the upper-class of the Japanese race. Second, the Chinese are so backward and stubborn that they refuse the American way. The Japanese, on the other hand, are so progressive and

competent as to fit right into the American way of life. . . . In no way do we, energetic and brilliant Japanese men, stand below those lowly Chinese.[8]

With Orientalist views of their own, the Japanese elite in San Francisco naturally expected to receive due respect from white Americans—their presumed friends in the modern world—in spite of the unequivocal expression of American racism that lumped the two groups together as the "Yellow Peril."

Distinguishing between the Japanese and the Chinese based on their differing cultural levels, Issei leaders and Japanese diplomats also drew a distinction between themselves and their compatriots from rural Japan, whom the former despised as a "degenerated class," "dirt peasants," and "ignorant fools." To elite eyes, immigrant laborers registered as a group of backward *gumin*, or ignorant masses, who, like Chinese, "prowl about the city with only shabby clothes and straw sandals," oblivious to American customs and etiquette with no command of English.[9] In their opinion, a flock of *gumin* did not constitute what they considered to be representative elements of the Japanese—whether in America or back home.[10] Prostitutes were just as bad, if not worse. Not only did they often embarrass themselves in the public eye by "marching in shoals unashamedly with signature hats on in broad daylight," but they also debauched lowly laborers and, even worse, infected them with venereal diseases.[11] The root of the divergence between immigrant literati and *dekasegi* laborers allegedly rested in their moral qualities, intellectual capacities, and behavioral norms. Although the diplomatic agenda of the Japanese state frequently found itself on a collision course with the practical interests of the expatriate society in America, the Chinese question helped to compound grounds for an enduring partnership between officials and immigrant leaders for the transformation of ordinary Issei from the "Sinified" Japanese to the "truly" Japanese fit for modern life.

Just as the production of Sino-Japanese difference hinged on the transpacific exchange of ideas between the educated Japanese, the "Sinification" of *gumin* was part and parcel of a highly racialized notion of nationhood in prewar Japan. Intellectuals there generally separated the underclass from the rest of the nation, construing their material conditions as manifesting an "alien," not pure Japanese, nature.[12] Likewise, the Sinification of *dekasegi* laborers and prostitutes on American soil derived from their presupposed dearth of bourgeois civilities and moralities that sustained the basic fabric of the modern Japanese (or American) nation-state.[13] Frequently described in racial terms, such difference offered a standard against which to measure one's worth as a member of the national community and of the modern world at large, creating a bifurcation of a people into the upper (civilized, Japanese/white) and the lower (uncivilized, *gumin*/Chinese). This entailed class-based racial formation processes, which fabricated the dual cultural affinities between the elite Japanese and the white American middle-class, and between the lowly *gumin* and the excluded Chinese.[14]

Because Sinification took place in tandem with the rise of California racial politics that homogenized the two Asian groups, the Issei leaders were greatly affected by white Progressive thinking about racial uplift, which sought to tackle the "Oriental problem" indiscriminately. In lieu of immigrant exclusion, some Christian reformers and liberal Americanizers, like Sidney Gulick, considered that the Orientals in their midst could be transformed into being morally capable of governing their lives as citizen-subjects through a rigorous assimilation process.[15] With the rhetoric of unassimilability, however, mainstream California Progressives, like Hiram Johnson, James D. Phelan, and Chester Rowell, led political assaults against the Japanese by drawing the color line between Asians and whites—the two races that "could not mix."[16] It was in this complication of Progressive politics over the question of race that Japanese immigrant leaders confronted the problem of Sinification within their community. As historian George Sánchez contends, the ideological tenets of the "progressive impulse," which celebrated white middle-class cultural norms as the model, often found eager recipients in the upper echelons of many immigrant groups.[17] Issei elite, too, shared the same impulse, and their appropriation of Progressive thinking valorized the meaning of cultural assimilation over that of racial (biological) differences, upon which California exclusionists insisted. The convergence of cultural assumptions between Issei leaders and moderate Progressives induced the former to adopt the project of the latter—moral reform and Americanization—in order to refute the misidentification of the Japanese with the Chinese in American public discourse and politics.

Due to rampant factionalism within the Japanese immigrant population, it took elite Issei nearly a full decade to unite as a reform-oriented leadership. In the spring of 1900, the leading Issei of San Francisco formed the first enduring coalition against Sinification with the blessing of Japanese consular officials. The catalyst was an incident in which Japanese residents, along with their Chinese neighbors, were singled out for compulsory inoculation for bubonic plague by the San Francisco Board of Health.[18] No longer was the problem restricted to the low-class *dekasegi* laborers, for Issei were summarily Sinified in this instance. For the immigrant elite, their worst fear had come true, and this bitter realization accompanied physical pain and humiliation: they "were forcibly detained, violently pushed around and held down tight like an animal to get a needle stuck in the groin." Declaring that "[w]e are not the people of a fallen nation," an angry Issei writer thus posed a rhetorical question in a local Japanese newspaper: "How come we the Japanese have to suffer this when the scourge claimed a few Chinese—the people we have no business with?" The Chinese should be held accountable for the epidemic, he argued, but "the subjects of the Great Japanese Empire" should have been treated with dignity and respect.[19]

What came out of this collective elite rage against ethnic conflation was the Japanese Deliberative Council of America which had the dual goal of "expanding the rights of imperial subjects in America and preserving Japan's national prestige." Despite the involvement of 3,000 Japanese in its inception, the council admitted only the propertied class into its core leadership structure. When it quickly achieved its immediate goal of obtaining a court injunction staying the inoculation order, its leaders shifted their focus to a more fundamental problem: the ever-growing presence and geographic spread of Sinified Issei in the American West.[20]

Whereas sporadic past efforts to "improve social conditions" of Japanese residents concentrated on the urban centers where most undesirables congregated, the council found it necessary to extend its reaches to outlying areas after the turn of the twentieth century. Since the previous decade, Japanese laborers had moved away from the coast for seasonal farm work, railroad maintenance, and mining and lumber work. As early as 1895, the agricultural regions of Vacaville and Fresno already had relatively stable populations of 450 and 220 Japanese field hands, respectively; at the peak of summer harvest, their numbers reportedly approximated 1,000.[21] This transient life and a gender imbalance among the manual laborers were fertile ground for "immoral" activities to prosper in rural districts. The San Francisco consul, for example, observed a 50 percent reduction in Japanese prostitutes in the city between October 1897 and August 1898, which was offset by the comparable increase of such women outside the Bay Area.[22] The vernacular press also frequently reported the eloping of farmers' wives with laborers, as well as cases of "wife stealing" in rural settlements.

Issei leaders believed that the transgression of marital order and patriarchal authority by lawless men was not unrelated to the increase of unchaste women. A story of a prostitute named Tama is a case in point. Though already married to another man, she absconded with a shiftless Japanese gambler whom she had met in Stockton. After finding a hideout in a farm town, Tama plied her trade in a Chinese-owned building, while her companion operated a small pool hall nearby. A few months later, after unsuccessfully trying to make off with her, another vagrant shot Tama's panderer to death in revenge.[23] Typified in this episode, the proliferation of Sinified individuals agonized the elite Issei.

In order to help organize regional chapters for social control at the grassroots level, the founders of the Japanese Deliberative Council dispatched representatives to rural settlements. The first group visited Sacramento, Vacaville, and Winters, where they conferred with the "like-minded" local leaders. The second and third contingents went to San Jose, Fresno, and Stockton. They appealed to the concerns that small numbers of educated rural immigrants shared with respect to the deplorable state of itinerant laborers and immoral women. The ensuing years saw the formation of a regional council of affiliates, marking the first instance in which some of the rural Issei residents came under the direct influence of a unified urban leadership.[24]

The intensified American demand for Japanese exclusion induced the new network of immigrant control to funnel its moral reform directives effectively into rural settlements after initial complications. In 1905, a renewed attempt to Sinify the Japanese occurred in California politics as, buoyed by the Hearst press, labor unions and other agitators called for the termination of immigration from Japan. Comparing the prior Chinese "menace" to the present Japanese "invasion," the rationale for racial exclusion included unfair economic competition, cultural deficiency, and racial incompatibility. This organized political movement culminated in the segregation of Japanese students in San Francisco public schools.[25] At first, except for a few Issei who filed a lawsuit at a federal court on their own volition, immigrant leaders chose to stand aside, because Tokyo insisted that it would settle the matter in direct negotiation with Washington on grounds of treaty violations.[26] Having observed the military victory of Japan over Russia, the Roosevelt administration turned out to be unwilling to offend its new contender in the Pacific. Thus, between 1907 and 1908, the United States and Japan reached a diplomatic compromise known as the Gentlemen's Agreement, whereby the two governments concertedly put a halt to the further influx of *dekasegi* migrants into the continental United States.

This bilateral agreement resulted in discord between many Issei leaders and Japanese officials, setting a stage for the heavy-handed intervention of Japanese diplomats in the construction of a more rationalized immigrant leadership structure. The Issei elite, especially expansionist labor contractors, interpreted the diplomatic solution as a "face-saving" act at the expense of their vested interest in labor migration.[27] As much as educated Issei despised *dekasegi* laborers, their livelihood depended on the steady influx of new immigrants into the American West as workers and clients, and thus they feared the impact of Tokyo's compromise on their economic welfare. In February 1907, when President Roosevelt issued an executive order to prohibit the remigration of Japanese laborers from Hawaii to the mainland, a storm of protest broke out from within Issei society, demanding that the Japanese government fight the American ban and push for more direct migration to the United States. From Seattle and Portland to San Francisco and Sacramento, Issei residents expressed their frustrations and anger at mass meetings.[28] Not only did the question of how to have their voices heard by the government and public at home strain the relations between the immigrant society and the Japanese diplomatic corps, but it also fragmented the nascent Issei leadership built on the loose network of the Japanese Deliberative Council of America.

Some leaders of Seattle and northern California Japanese communities decided to dispatch representatives to appeal to Japan's social and political figures in opposition, who were as eager to gain advantage from governmental "failure" as were the Issei to find support for their agenda at home. Three Issei from Seattle first visited Japan in the summer of 1907, but the Japanese government immediately placed the Issei delegation under close police surveillance as a threat to the volatile balance of power in Japan.[29] In California, the question of whether or not to directly appeal to the home public caused great commotion, which corroded the power of the Japanese Deliberative Council as the central governing body. Fearing the ramifications for United States–Japan relations, the San Francisco consul wasted no time in urging the leaders of the organization "not to take any extreme action."[30] Deliberative Council president Kyutaro Abiko accepted the consul's "advice" as a policy directive, although hot-headed residents in pursuit of direct action had already forced the council to commence a fundraising drive for an official California delegation. For Abiko and moderate leaders, the consul's plea was a welcome pretext to abandon such an extreme measure, but they still encountered intense resistance, particularly from the Sacramento affiliate and segments of the San Francisco community. In order to curb the opposition, Abiko tried to stall the process until cooler heads could prevail. In the spring of 1907, he announced that the delegation would not leave for Tokyo until October, while the *Nichibei Shimbun* newspaper, owned by Abiko, engaged in an extensive publicity campaign to portray the delegation plan as a bad idea.[31]

Sensing the San Francisco leaders' duplicity, many Issei residents continued to press for the delegation to leave in the fall. An association of Japanese laundry owners in the Bay Area—some of whom were council leaders—came forward to publicly castigate Abiko and his inner circle as "irresponsible." Meanwhile, between June and September, the Sacramento affiliate sent its leaders twice to San Francisco in order to obtain a written guarantee for the October dispatch. But as the deadline approached, the Japanese Deliberative Council formally announced the cancellation of the delegation plan—an action that immediately created a schism within the San Francisco leadership and between the council's central body and many of its local affiliates. In the Bay Area, more than fifty Japanese residents united to establish a breakaway organization, the Japanese Association of San Francisco. The Sacramento council branch severed its ties with San Francisco and carried out the delegation plan on its own, sending its president to beseech Tokyo to renegotiate immigration matters with Washington.[32] The Japanese Deliberative Council of America quickly lost its grip on Issei society.

Japanese diplomats decided to restore command over the immigrants by working with a new group of Issei untainted by the recent scandal. Paradoxically, the Gentlemen's Agreement gave Tokyo's agents the upper hand over grassroots Issei leaders. From 1908, Japan's Foreign Ministry issued no passports to new *dekasegi* laborers, but the spouses and children of the immigrants who had hitherto resided in America were still able to travel across the Pacific Ocean. The officials were faced with the practical question of how to determine who was eligible for a passport and who was not. A new administrative mechanism was necessary to certify if an applicant were related to a bona fide resident of the United States. In addition, Japan's new conscription law required that every immigrant without military service records obtain a certificate of overseas residence for annual draft deferment. The handling of various certification applications became such an onerous task for the Japanese consulates that they opted to delegate certain bureaucratic functions to leading immigrant organizations. To set up this new scheme of governance, the Foreign Ministry elevated the San Francisco consulate to a consulate-general and put at the helm an experienced diplomat named Koike Chozo.[33]

Given the disintegration of the Japanese Deliberative Council, Koike had to find an alternative way to meet his new administrative responsibilities while quelling immigrant dissension. Rather than reviving the existing central body, he chose to create a new one with more manageable leadership. To spearhead this endeavor, he named Kinji Ushijima and Taro Hozumi, neither of whom had been involved in the council. Known as "Potato King George Shima," Ushijima was arguably the wealthiest Japanese immigrant in the United States, and he had distanced himself from politics until this time. The San Francisco branch manager of Yokohama Specie Bank, Hozumi was more a temporary business expatriate on assignment than a typical immigrant/resident. While Ushijima could help heal the in-fighting and conflicts within the existing immigrant leadership, Hozumi would lead a new organization in accord with the dictates of Japan's national interests rather than with the "parochial," "selfish" ones of the immigrants. By the end of January 1908, these men successfully brought the fragmented leadership together, inducing both the Japanese Deliberative Council and the Japanese Association of San Francisco to disband voluntarily. Then on February 4, members of the immigrant elite and San Francisco representatives of major Japanese trading firms formed the Japanese Association of America, which served as a virtual arm of the Japanese government.[34]

To establish social control over Japanese residents throughout California, the new central organization administered what were called "endorsement rights," which consisted of verifying certificate applications, processing them, and issuing official certifications as the proxy of the Japanese consulate.[35] Under the umbrella of the Japanese Association of America, the endorsement rights were redistributed to its local affiliates, which played identical roles in their given locales. This scheme allowed Japanese diplomats to keep key immigrant leaders in both urban and rural areas under their command, because they could now arbitrarily decide which local organization would provide these vital services to Japanese residents. Association leaders were reluctant to contradict Tokyo's agents for fear of losing their delegated "rights"—a situation that made less likely the recurrence of open defiance. At the same time, the state-approved authority to issue certificates provided an incentive for rural Issei leaders to set aside internal strife and cooperate with one another in setting up their own associations, since they would otherwise be forced to travel outside their community to obtain this paperwork. The steady income from certificate fees for local leadership created organizational stability, too, which alleviated the financial shortages that plagued rural Japanese associations.

Koike's approach, embodied in the scheme of endorsement rights, was far more effective than sole reliance on a nationalist sense of mission in the mobilization of like-minded immigrant leaders. Indeed, the Japanese Association of America rapidly incorporated remote settlement communities into its institutional fold while grooming a circle of manageable rural elite. Within two years of its founding, the San Francisco headquarters increased local affiliates from twenty-two to thirty-two. In 1916, when the establishment of the Japanese consulate in Los Angeles resulted in the transfer of southern California and Arizona affiliates to the new Central Japanese Association of Southern California, the Japanese Association of America still had thirty-nine locals under its umbrella, which covered the rest of California, Colorado, Utah, and Nevada.[36] The Japanese Association of Oregon in Portland (1911) and the Northwest American Japanese Association in Seattle (1913), other regional headquarters, worked hand in hand with the local Japanese consulates in much the same way.

At the juncture, Koike and other diplomats sought the extragovernmental control mechanisms for another, more imminent political need in addition to the long-standing goal of immigrant reform. Within the power vacuum in Japanese immigrant society following the Gentlemen's Agreement emerged an especially dangerous type of Issei: leftists hostile to Japanese officials and their sympathizers. With the suppression of the nascent socialist movement in Japan, San Francisco had become a refuge for exiled socialists and anarchists, and Tokyo was determined to crack down on these political defiants who increasingly posed threats from overseas. In 1906, a group organized the Socialist

Revolutionary party (SRP) in the Bay Area, and on the imperial birthday the following year, it placed leaflets around the Japanese consulate that blasphemed Emperor Meiji and threatened to assassinate him. Diplomats first attempted to dispose of the culprits with the help of the American authorities, but to no avail. Unable to take legal action against these men outside its sovereign power, the Foreign and Home ministries of Japan agreed to prosecute immigrant socialists when they returned home, ordering the consuls to compile blacklists. Koike purposefully used the Japanese association network, recruiting some local leaders for clandestine information gathering. The president of the Fresno affiliate was specifically ordered to report on the activities of the Fresno Labor League, a leftist organization founded by SRP members.[37]

Whereas the Fresno group quickly fell victim to community-wide disciplining, the remaining Issei radicals in northern California tested the ability of the Japanese associations to serve as unofficial policing agencies—the hurdle to overcome before taking on the project of reform-based community building. Effective in October 1909, Tokyo instituted a new policy of compulsory registration for overseas Japanese. In the United States, all Issei had to register at their nearest consular offices through the agency of the Japanese associations. To ensure their prompt registrations, the San Francisco consul ordered that no certificates be issued unless residents filed the paperwork at the local associations by September 1910. Because the new registration system was mandatory, the Japanese Association of America viewed this additional delegated authority as an opportunity to fatten its coffers. Although Tokyo stipulated no fee for the new bureaucratic function, Issei leaders announced that they would charge an annual fee of $2 to every Japanese resident for the registration service and the maintenance of the registry. While notifying the local affiliates that they would receive a portion of the money, the Japanese Association of America requested that the consul make an exception for charging the registration fees despite the contrary government guideline.[38] No one voiced dissension until Issei socialists in Berkeley criticized this arbitrary bending of the rule.

Immigrant radicals mobilized against the registration plan, first within the Japanese Association of Berkeley. On February 9, 1910, they successfully organized a sizable opposition within its rank and file and managed to pass a formal dissenting resolution. Characterizing the proposed annual fee as a form of "poll tax," the Berkeley resolution maintained that the Japanese Association of America, which it called "a mere private organization," had no right to monopolize such an administrative role. Its attempt would constitute not only the "usurpation of the equal rights that every citizen should enjoy," but also a sinister act of "establishing a separate government within the territory of another sovereign state." Clearly, socialists linked the fee issue to the larger and fundamental question of the Japanese association as Tokyo's proxy. So objectionable was this resolution to immigrant nationalists, however, that most old leaders in Berkeley, including the vice president, the secretary, and twelve board members, resigned their positions while thirty lay members also withdrew. Socialists dominated the vacated offices, and in order to extend the anti–Japanese association movement beyond Berkeley, they distributed copies of the resolution to other regional affiliates, immigrant newspapers, and organizations throughout California. In Los Angeles, their position found considerable support, not so much because Issei residents agreed with the political ideology of the radicals, but because many disliked the idea of giving up two dollars every year to an organization in which they had no part.[39]

Encountering the first real challenge to its authority, the Japanese Association of America attempted to alienate the core group of dissidents from the rest of the Japanese community. On March 9, the San Francisco consul suggested the unacceptability of Berkeley's socialist leadership as the recipient of the endorsement rights. Immigrant elites promptly responded to this veiled directive by severing ties with Berkeley at once. The following day, the central body began to refuse certificate applications from Berkeley on the grounds that the local Japanese association could no longer process the documents. The Japanese of Berkeley had to go to the inconvenient Oakland affiliate to take care of their certificate needs, which quickly turned the area's residents against the radical leaders. Then, following the advice of the consul, San Francisco decided to appease the public by repealing the mandatory registration fee. Instead, residents were "encouraged" to donate fifty cents every time they used the services of the local Japanese association. Moreover, the rule was altered in such a way that registration was necessary only when relocating to the jurisdiction of another Japanese consulate.[40] While this nullified the financial advantage of the registration system, it robbed the Berkeley radicals of an issue around which to rally the public against the transnational elite partnership.

After these counterassaults, the decline of the anti–Japanese association movement was quick and thorough. By the end of March 1910, the socialists were almost completely purged from the Japanese Association of Berkeley. A new conservative leadership was swiftly formed in the organization, which restored formal affiliation with the Japanese Association of America. The dissidents could no longer effectively threaten either the central position of the Japanese associations in the immigrant society or the official-immigrant nexus that they embodied.[41] Now, based on the rationalized network that could channel central directives and programs to the further reaches of Issei society, the Japanese associations were finally ready to undertake their twin goals of popular moral reform and fighting American racism in a concerted manner.

MORAL REFORM UNDER RACIAL EXCLUSION

Supported by Tokyo's policy of extraterritorial nation-building, the apparatuses of immigrant control allowed a relatively cohesive ethnic collectivity to emerge in the American West during the 1910s. To that end, the Japanese Association of America, as well as its counterparts in Los Angeles, Portland, and Seattle, defined basic objectives and goals and coordinated reformist programs, while the Japanese government and opinion leaders furnished funds, personnel, and general guidelines from across the Pacific. The actual work fell largely on the shoulders of each Japanese association affiliate, which adapted the central mandate to local conditions. The transnational collaboration between urban immigrant leaders and a circle of social and political figures in Japan set the basic parameters, focuses, and directions of the effort to re-form the Issei masses and construct a respectable community of Japanese citizen-subjects in the American West.

Moral reform was also a site where Japan's nationalizing impulse, appropriated by Issei literati, came into contact with the domestic project of Americanization. Unlike the white Progressive goal of severing the immigrant from Japanese culture, the Issei reformists aimed to turn ordinary residents into acceptable members of the two nation-states, not just to Americanize them. Having been implored to assimilate by both Japan and the United States, immigrant leaders inevitably understood their position and identity in dualistic, rather than binary, terms. Thus, in January 1911, when inaugurating the first statewide moral reform campaign, Kinji Ushijima, president of the Japanese Association of America, declared before assembled California Issei representatives:

> Like a bridge between the two countries, we, the Japanese in America, occupy the most important place, representative of the Japanese national interests. Not only must we refrain from irresponsible and careless behavior, but we are also obliged to elevate our individual character and moralize our community. We must endeavor to get [whites] to recognize that the civilization of our nation is worthy of utmost respect. . . . Regrettably, in spite of recent improvements within our society, many of the backward customs still stay with us. The most serious ill is the epidemic of Chinese gambling that has poisoned our general populace in America. The solution rests with all of us here—our leadership is essential.[42]

That "Chinese gambling" was singled out as a particular menace was not accidental. Throughout the 1910s, gambling was a chief object of Issei reformist politics, because it was seen as corrupting the basic moral fabric of Japanese immigrant society. Although gambling always held a special place in the male culture of Western frontier society, Issei leaders attributed Chineseness to it.[43]

Most gambling establishments that Japanese frequented were Chinese-owned, and the Chinese lottery called *baahk gap piu* and *fantan* were particularly popular, because these games were simple and language differences were no obstacle to playing.[44] Yet, at the root of the gambling problem was its indiscriminate appeal to the immigrants who wished to achieve their American Dream quickly. Chinese gambling could lure into its trap of Sinification Japanese of any class, not just *dekasegi* laborers but also local residents and even "respectable" entrepreneurs. Its deleterious effects, as the Issei elite worried, ranged from bringing financial ruin to ordinary immigrants to producing new groups of degenerate Japanese. Chinese gambling was blamed especially for the increase of the so-called *shakkotai*, or shiftless vagrants, who habitually gambled and cadged money off law-abiding residents. Although there is no way to know the exact number of *shakkotai*, a Japanese diplomat estimated 8,000 to 15,000 in 1909, or 10 to 20 percent of the working-class Issei in the West, and their number was increasing each year.[45] Consequently, the Japanese associations devoted a large part of their moral reform effort to the gambling problem among rural residents and migratory laborers, who they felt were most helplessly addicted to it.

In 1912, the Japanese Association of America staged its first orchestrated campaign against Chinese gambling. In April, it invited representatives from local affiliates to form a special Committee for the Eradication of Gambling, which resorted to a combination of punishment and education. Each association would compile a blacklist of gamblers, publish in the vernacular press personal information on those who continued gambling despite warnings, notify their families in Japan of their antisocial behavior, and refuse to issue certificates and then inform the Japanese consulate of the fact. The associations also distributed handouts and leaflets and sponsored lectures on the harm of Chinese gambling and the need for a moral lifestyle. Upon request from local affiliates, the San Francisco central committee dispatched a special task force to rural communities for assistance in their popular "enlightenment" program.[46] These efforts were repeated annually throughout the 1910s.

One of the key community projects during that decade, the antigambling crusade provides a glimpse into how the Japanese association system in rural California facilitated leadership formation and community-building concurrently. What transpired in a farm settlement of Walnut Grove, California, exemplified such processes. Situated in the agricultural heartland of the Sacramento River delta, Walnut Grove was known for its slumlike conditions and the prevalence of Chinese gambling.[47] Both the Chinese and the Japanese lived in a crowded "Oriental district" completely separate from the white district across the Sacramento River. Japanese diplomats and urban Issei literati had constantly admonished Walnut Grove residents for their shamefully Sinified state. In 1908, for example, one official depicted what he witnessed there in disgust: "[L]ewd women and lazy men loiter around day and night disgracing the reputation of the Japanese people and the nation." In his opinion, almost all Chinese establishments were gambling dens, where "the Chinese fattened themselves by squeezing dumb Japanese laborers."[48]

Established in August 1910, the Japanese Association of Walnut Grove, which consisted of local merchants and leading farmers, had two specific reform goals: self-segregation from the Chinese community and a direct assault on Chinese gambling. In October 1915, the first goal was furthered by a devastating fire, which reduced much of the Oriental district to ashes. A need for a genuine Japanese town as a deterrent to the Issei's Sinified behavior had been on the community agenda, but financial and other practical hurdles had proved too difficult to overcome. Yet, at this tragedy-turned-opportunity, the fire victims unambiguously declared their intention for self-segregation at a mass rally shortly after the disaster. Characterizing the residents' resolve as a testament to their collective "atonement for their past disgraced life," the Japanese Association of Walnut Grove appealed for support for the reconstruction to the San Francisco headquarters, which subsequently dispatched delegations of legal specialists and financial advisers.[49]

Within two months, a new Japanese residential/commercial district separate from Chinatown arose in Walnut Grove.[50] Residents continued their efforts to keep their town free from "corrupting" Chinese influence by passing resolutions to prohibit gamblers and other undesirables from entering the Japanese section. Whenever there was a renegade, they made an example of him. The first such case involved a Japanese barber, who opened a shop in nearby Locke Chinatown. The Japanese association dropped all relations with his family and resolved to inform his home village in Japan of the "traitorous" deed. Not until the barber made a public apology and suffered intense humiliation did the community lift these sanctions. This effectively inhibited other potential renegades, and in ensuing years, Japanese residents remained in their own quarter.[51]

During the last years of the 1910s, the crusade against Chinese gambling in Walnut Grove, as elsewhere in California, became especially zealous and effective. In the delta region, if self-segregation symbolized a unity of purpose among local settler-residents under the auspices of the Japanese association, the subsequent reformist endeavor was an attempt to stretch the boundaries of the new community by reaching out to laborers on the social margins. The option now was that either they would join the association or they would be outcasts with no place in the local collectivity. The 1918 antigambling campaign unfolded just that way. Meeting with Japanese association secretaries from Fresno, Stockton, and Sacramento, Walnut Grove residents discussed the state of gambling in each community and countermeasures. Resolving to resort to social ostracism, the local leaders formed an antigambling committee, which adopted guidelines similar to the 1912 San Francisco model. Gamblers would be turned over to the local police, their deeds reported to other affiliates, and their names and photographs published in immigrant newspapers. Boardinghouses in the Japanese town were ordered not to accommodate gamblers, and all stores were to prohibit informal gambling on their premises.[52] These strong-arm tactics achieved a considerable, albeit impermanent, success. Many habitual gamblers left Walnut Grove, while others were prevented from wasting their hard-earned wages on the empty dream of quick riches.[53] Until the mid-1920s, when the triumph of the white exclusionist movement made fighting Chinese gambling less important on the general Issei agenda, the Japanese associations exerted themselves to turn the working-class Issei into an integral part of their moral ethnic community.

Tangential to the popular habit of gambling, the Issei elite also felt that the problem of Sinification had to do with the general attitude of ordinary immigrants toward American society. This interpretation led them to look inward even more for a solution as if exclusion was of their own making. Rather than chalking the racist politics up to injustice, the ethnic leadership placed a major blame on the popular Issei disregard for American culture, social customs, and lifestyle.[54] In 1915, the Japanese Association of America officially adopted cultural assimilation as a priority on its general moral reform guidelines. But unlike the white formulation of the linear progression from "Japanese" to "American," Issei leaders embraced a heretical notion of acculturation, envisioning a dual process of nationalization relative to the two worlds to which Japanese immigrants stayed connected. This is because the ideal of East-West parallelism enabled the immigrant elite to imagine the retention of Japanese identity despite, or because of, assimilation.

By distinguishing the external and internal dimensions of assimilation, Japanese association leaders argued that all residents first needed to conform their persons and environment to American middle-class norms, but this external assimilation was not incongruous with the modern ways which Japan's state elite had imposed on the populace in their native land. The Japanese upper class had long favored and promoted the use of Western clothing as a symbol of modernization, for instance, and during the 1910s, the Japanese Association of America similarly encouraged immigrant women to switch from the Japanese *kimono* to Western dress as soon as they landed in San Francisco. Neither did the Issei's internal assimilation deviate from Tokyo's general endeavor to modernize the ordinary Japanese mind, insofar as it aimed to produce a civilized, self-governing individual agreeable to modern societies, including white America.[55] While it was a means of racial uplift in the American domestic context, assimilation also offered Japanese immigrants the way to achieve national authenticity in the transnational context.

For this reason the Issei assimilation project featured intellectuals who could articulate the likenesses of the two cultures in lieu of simply slighting the old. To inaugurate its statewide "campaign of education," the Japanese Association of America invited Ebina Danjo, a well-known scholar and Christian leader who celebrated the ideal of immigrant assimilation as part of Japan's general aspiration for modernization. Touring California from August to September 1915, he gave fifty-five lectures to 7,525 audience members, while his wife spoke exclusively to Issei women on eighteen separate occasions.[56] Other public lecturers were recruited from within the educated circle of Issei, including Stanford University professor Yamato Ichihashi, whose speech at Walnut Grove stressed learning English and the customs of white America, acquiring good homemaking skills, and avoiding gambling.[57] In southern California, informal gatherings for the farming population were held "in every locality about twice a week" with regional leaders as instructors.[58]

During the First World War, the mainstream reformist movement engulfed minority communities, including Japanese, in the coercive "100 Per Cent American" campaign, which added momentum to the ongoing assimilation project within Issei society. This situation differed from the concurrent experience in California of Mexican immigrants, who were reportedly caught between the polarizing forces of Anglo conformity and the "Mexicanization" efforts by their home government.[59] In contrast, Japanese immigrant moral reform was piggybacked on the white Progressive platform, appropriating its Americanizing thrust as its own. In the eyes of Issei leaders, playing along with the white nationalist cause could serve the interests of both Japanese immigrant society and the Japanese state—an idea that Japan's officials and social leaders enthusiastically supported. Americanizing the laboring Issei masses continued to parallel the making of imperial subjects in the United States.

An example in the Pacific Northwest throws light on the harmony between Issei nationalistic reform and the goal of becoming "100 Per Cent American." Joining forces with state and municipal social agencies, local Issei incorporated government-backed educational films into their program. Not only did such films as *Home Improvement* and *Childhood of Abraham Lincoln* "stir the American spirit in children and women," they made perfect companions for didactic lectures foisted upon Japanese residents. The inclusion of white reformists into the ethnic community programs also helped to foster the Issei's sense of connection and agreement with a larger "American" agenda. In addition to lecture meetings held at Japanese halls, churches, and schools, the educational campaign sponsored "community services" at private households, both white and

Japanese, which offered a relaxed atmosphere of interracial friendship and mutual learning. In May 1921, a total of thirteen such meetings were held in Seattle and its vicinity, attended by more than 400 Japanese and white residents, who together sang "The Star-Spangled Banner," watched Americanization films, and listened to reformist preachers while enjoying tea and snacks. White reformists and Issei lecturers also traveled to sawmills and railroad labor camps in remote areas.[60]

A product of transnational collaboration among educated Japanese, moral reform was also deeply integrated into the diplomacy of the Japanese state. With a shared faith in Japanese assimilability, both diplomats and immigrant elites believed that racial oppression would disappear as soon as Americans at large became cognizant of who "real" Japanese were.[61] Hence, moral reform would not suffice without public relations activity. In order to shift the white gaze from the morally deprived working class to the culturally refined bourgeoisie, Tokyo instituted a division of labor, assigning the project of immigrant assimilation to the Issei leadership and a propaganda mission to the consular agents and selected English-speaking immigrant literati. In 1914, Numano Yasutaro, San Francisco consul, devised the plan and recruited as chief publicist Kiyoshi Kawakami, also known as K. K. Kawakami, who held a master's degree from the University of Iowa and had previously served as the general secretary of the Japanese Association of America. With funds from Tokyo, Kawakami established the Pacific Press Bureau, which supplied pro-Japanese English-language materials to the American print media under the guise of an independent news agency.[62] Additional propagandists were recruited subsequently, including Harvey H. Guy, a professor at the Pacific School of Religion and president of the Japan Society; Kiyosue Inui, one-time secretary of the Japanese Association of America; and, occasionally, Yamato Ichihashi. While arguing that this "publicity" program and the existing Issei reform campaigns "would constitute indispensable halves for each other," Numano defined the former as belonging to the domain of governmental affairs and the latter as noblesse oblige for the immigrant elite.[63]

Between 1914 and 1920, Issei leaders accepted this scheme of divided roles, and it afforded the Japanese Association of America a lucrative partnership with Japan's leading entrepreneur, Shibusawa Eiichi. Founder of the Tokyo Chamber of Commerce and head of his own financial-industrial conglomerate, Shibusawa knew that Japan's economy was dependent on exports to the United States, and he feared that California's exclusionist movement would affect bilateral trade relations badly. Allowing San Francisco Issei leaders to use his personal office as their Japan headquarters, Shibusawa lent his full support to the Japanese Association of America.[64] While serving as a powerful advocate for Japanese residents in America and a reliable go-between for Tokyo bureaucrats and corporate heads, the business tycoon held all Issei accountable for their self-improvement and assimilation.

In reaction to the 1913 Alien Land Law of California, which deprived Japanese immigrants of land ownership and restricted their tenancy to three years, Shibusawa sent two of his protégés to the United States with messages of reconciliation to white exclusionists and of self-reflection to Issei residents.[65] While in California, these men admonished the immigrants to "maintain the attitude of a civilized nation and avoid [further] provoking Americans to criticize the Japanese as an inferior race." Yet, what Shibusawa's messengers saw in California did not make them optimistic. They found that "the old undesirable customs of the Japanese peasantry" still prevailed in the Japanese immigrant community. Their dwellings generally fell far short of their white American counterparts and needed better sanitation. The men also emphasized, "The Japanese pattern of living in segregation [from whites] or near the Chinese and frequenting Chinese gambling houses must be stopped."[66] Such a critical observation of Japanese lives in America pushed Shibusawa to get even more involved in the Issei reform program from across the Pacific.

Shibusawa contrived to launch his own campaign for moral education through a brand-new organization in Tokyo, which he envisioned as spearheading the cause of "civilizing imperial subjects abroad" in collaboration with his immigrant allies in San Francisco.[67] With an eye to better preparing new rural emigrants for an "orderly" and "civilized" life in the United States, Shibusawa's Japan Emigration Society set up a center for emigrant training in the port city of Yokohama in February 1914. With an annual subsidy from the Foreign Ministry and an endowment from wealthy businesspeople, the center offered an intensive educational program that supplemented the efforts of the Japanese Association of America. At no cost, individuals bound for the United States and other countries could learn basic Western etiquette and values (six hours); practical English (six hours); living conditions in a foreign land (six hours); vital domestic skills (six hours); household management (six hours); public sanitation and feminine hygiene (three hours); and child rearing (two hours). This thirty-five-hour program was repeated every week.[68]

Many subjects specifically addressed women's needs, since a large number of attendees were "picture brides" summoned by Issei men. Mindful of the critical role that immigrant wives (and mothers) would play in household matters and child care, the Japanese Association of America worked closely with the Japan Emigration Society. Indeed, Yokohama's curriculum mirrored the specific concerns raised by San Francisco Issei leaders. In 1916, they compiled a woman's guide to the United States for use as a textbook at the Yokohama institute and for wider distribution, which laid out gendered expectations along with the familiar nationalistic admonition that they were "obliged to demon-

FIGURE 2.1. A Taste of American Life for "Picture Brides" at the Yokohama Emigrant Training Center, ca. 1916

These women of rural origin received lectures on American life before their disembarkation for America. Notice a contrast between the two male instructors in western attire and the women in traditional Japanese *kimono*. The women were expected to adapt to American material life quickly so that they could properly represent Japanese modernity in the United States. But for most emigrant women, it was the first time to see and touch western utensils, kitchenware, and home furniture. Courtesy of Nihon Rikkōkai.

strate the true virtue of Japanese women and compel [white] Americans to admit them as first-rate women in the world." Their primary goal, the guide stressed, was to "create an ideal household in America" to offer their husbands "comfort" and "a place of relaxation." As mothers, immigrant women were expected to discourage "unsavory conduct and foul speech" and purge "gambling, drinking, and smoking," which second-generation children might mimic. To keep her husband and children from harmful activities, each Issei wife was expected to turn her household into a bastion of moral living.[69]

Other topics of the guide specifically aimed to develop an Issei womanhood suitable for American life. As a majority of female migrants originated from rural Japan and had mostly lived in a traditional way, they were taught the basics of being a modern woman, such as how to wear Western dresses, how to use Western-style toilets and bathtubs, how to walk like a "lady" without

（氏子ぎす生實しりた事幹時當は生先）　ス ラ ク 語 英 の 頃 其

FIGURE 2.2. English Class for Issei Women at the Japanese YWCA in San Francisco, ca. 1916
As a part of the general reform campaign, educated urban Issei women played a central role in instilling middleclass values, teaching white American culture, and promoting modern Japanese womanhood among "picture brides." Unlike emigrant women in Yokohama, the women in this classroom were dressed "appropriately," having traded their Japanese *kimono* for western clothes. Other aspects of "Americanization" than such a superficial change nonetheless proved to be much more daunting for them. Reprinted from the SF Japanese YWCA, *Kaiko nijūnen.*

tottering on Western shoes, and how to prepare meals with Western kitchen utensils. Cooking "fetid" dishes would offend white neighbors, they were told, so it should be avoided. Breast feeding in public would transgress the American sense of decency and be seen as disgraceful. Indeed, "[white] Americans tend to find Japanese life style and customs strange, unpleasant, and even reprehensible," the women were cautioned, "which often leads to the unfortunate misconception that Japanese are unable to Americanize, undesirable, and such." Negative references to Chinese—the example *not* to follow—were always part of reformist pedagogy, thus: "[O]ne of the reasons why the Chinese have been discriminated against more than the Japanese is their stubborn adherence to Chinese life style and Chinese clothing despite their long-term residence in the United States."[70]

The increasing need for the cultural development of immigrant wives during the 1910s prompted the formation of female-centered organizations in the ethnic community, to which Issei male leaders delegated much of the day-today reform operations. One such organization was the Japanese Young Women's Christian Association (YWCA) in San Francisco, which played a significant role in the adjustment of picture brides to American life beginning in 1912. Like their husbands, the city's leading Issei women had long taken exception to being "grouped together with Japanese prostitutes" and unchaste, selfish elopers, protesting the perception that "among Japanese women living on the American West Coast there were none who were of good conduct or who were not shameful."[71] Equating the cultivation of the newcomers' moral regimes for self-governance with the defense of stable marriages and family relations in immigrant society, the female elite felt it indispensable to normalize Issei womanhood to the standards of middle-class white America and modern Japan. Against this backdrop, the transnational venture of female reformers began in June 1915 by following the pattern of the partnership between Shibusawa and the male immigrant elite.

In collaboration with Issei YWCA leaders in San Francisco, Kawai Michi, a Bryn Mawr College graduate and head of Japan's YWCA, took the lead in developing a female-centered program. Though she was well informed of the denigration of picture brides by anti-Japanese advocates, Kawai wanted to see the living conditions of Japanese women in the United States for herself. In March 1915, she traveled to California, where she encountered mostly "uneducated" brides.[72] The pathetic sight of her countrywomen detained for inspection on Angel Island upset this Westernized intellectual profoundly. "The brides were mostly from country communities and looked queer," wrote Kawai in English, "for no one had told them that . . . their efforts to beautify themselves with an excessive use of powder resulted only in giving an impression of uncleanness."[73] The problem ran much deeper than the appearance of these rural women, however. In her subsequent encounters with Issei wives and mothers in California farm communities, Kawai found that they were also utterly ignorant of the basic concepts of sanitation, neglectful of child rearing, and careless about public decency. In her opinion, most Japanese immigrant women "lagged in their intellect and morality" behind their rural Japanese sisters, much less their urban middle-class counterparts. What terrified her most was that they were inculcating these "inferior" behavioral norms in their American-born children.[74] This problem would eventually doom the Japanese community in America unless it were resolutely checked, she decried.

With institutional ties to her like-minded Issei sisters in California, Kawai felt it possible for the Yokohama YWCA to play a significant role in tackling issues facing Japanese emigrant women. Because more brides were leaving for the United States each day, providing them with the proper knowledge and skills prior to their departure would render the women better prepared for their new lives in America. While in San Francisco, Kawai discussed her idea with local Issei YWCA leaders, who were delighted with the support and promised to work together. Soon, the Yokohama YWCA developed its program faithfully around the agendas and pedagogical principles of the Issei women reformers. On the two sides of the Pacific, the coalition of female Japanese literati furnished rural brides with predeparture education and postarrival reinforcement in an integrated manner.[75]

Under the guidance of Kawai, who returned from California, reform workers in Yokohama compiled two instructional handbooks. In terms of its content, the first booklet resembled the guide published by the Japanese Association of America; the second gave immigrant brides information about the moral reform programs in California and where to get additional help within the ethnic community.[76] Armed with these documents, the Yokohama YWCA staff regularly visited the steamships in port, as well as the emigrant inns where picture brides stayed until they passed stringent medical examinations. While distributing handouts, the reform workers explained to each woman why she was supposed to keep her appearance neat and tidy without exposing bare legs, refrain from using a men's toilet on board, and "maintain such a chaste and noble demeanor that would invite no contempt from foreigners even when she has to travel in third-class steerage."[77] After 1917, Kawai successfully convinced steamship companies to place Japanese "matrons" to chaperon the picture brides on the voyage.[78]

Once the newcomers arrived in the United States, the local Christian associations and other immigrant organizations met their needs, offering lessons in American housekeeping methods, child care, and English conversation. In this endeavor, based on the shared Progressive impulse, Issei woman leaders united forces with white churchwomen in San Francisco to organize the Society of American Friends of Japanese Women (Yu Ai Kai). Many of the key white reform workers were former and future missionaries to Asia, who saw their work not so much as the making of Japanese "Americans" in the domestic context of racial uplift, but as part of the larger international project to Christianize "heathen Orientals."[79] Despite the different goals, their Issei partners proved to be indispensable for their missionary work on this side of the Pacific. Sarah Ellis, a former colleague of Kawai and immigration secretary for Yu Ai Kai, was regularly stationed on Angel Island—which was off-limits to non-U.S. citizens—where she assisted incoming picture brides "with advice and introductions to Christian women, Japanese or American, in the places to which they [were] going." Helen Topping of the YWCA Field Committee did "the follow-up work of calling on the newly arrived Japanese brides" up and down California in cooperation with local Japanese pastors and female leaders. As translators and guides, her Issei assistants often accompanied Topping to rural districts for slide shows and lectures.[80]

During the latter half of the 1910s, many local Issei women, especially educated Christians, aided the grassroots reformist crusade within their own communities.[81] In a farming settlement of Hood River, Oregon, the wife of a leading entrepreneur compiled a list of "requests to Japanese ladies." She argued, "We, Japanese wives, are the 'diplomats' who represent all Japanese women, and you have greater influence [on the white perception of Japanese women] than [do] the Japanese government officials."[82] Criticizing their sojourner mentality, this college-educated woman—perhaps the only such female in Hood River—urged the others to commit themselves to permanent settlement in America. She preached the centrality of homemaking in their lives, and warned Issei mothers not to leave their children unattended while working on the farm. This woman also took the initiative in putting together an "informal orientation center," which taught incoming brides "American table manners, how to entertain [white] guests, child care methods, and other American customs." In this way, during a decade of massive female immigration, a viable Issei female leadership was forged in various parts of the West—a leadership that sought to shape a womanhood and motherhood suitable for the emergent community of assimilable Japanese in America.[83]

As the work of the Japan Emigration Society and the YWCAs exemplified, Issei leaders, Japanese officials, and the social elite fashioned out of their transnational partnerships the institutional mechanisms for immigrant moral reform, in the service both of Issei society and of Japan's diplomacy and nation-building. Their reformist endeavors also dovetailed with the white Progressive project of Americanization, creating a movement even larger than an intraethnic one. Despite the powerful system of elite collaboration, however, the divisions between the educated and the laboring masses among the Japanese in America remained significant enough to continue disappointing diplomats. By the late 1910s, many diplomats actually conceded that immigrant moral reform was "a disastrous failure." In 1917, the San Francisco consul criticized the policy of divided responsibilities, disparaging Issei leaders for their "inability" to influence a large portion of ordinary residents. He proposed that the diplomats take back the primary role of re-forming the immigrants in addition to the propaganda work.[84] Two years later, his successor repeated: "No [notable] outcomes have been generated thus far, and many residents remain the same as before in their behavior and character—a situation that feeds the exclusionist politics with tangible and incontestable evidence."[85]

One of the major reasons for such an unimpressive result was that the Japanese association network, despite its ability to mobilize leading rural residents, fell short of infiltrating the furthest reaches of Japanese immigrant society. In May 1909, when the control mechanism was still in an early stage, a Japanese consul calculated that approximately 2,000 Issei men in the Pacific Coast states formed the educated core leadership, encompassing professionals, literati, and other social leaders. An additional 8,000 belonged to the class of "small-scale settler-entrepreneurs and agriculturists," who purportedly had the potential to become the "pillars" of Japanese society in America—the kind of rural leaders that emerged during the 1910s. These 10,000 male residents were expected to participate in the operation of the Japanese associations, with the core elite responsible for the central bodies and the rest responsible for the rural affiliates. Most of the remaining 78,000 Japanese immigrants were laborers of one sort or another, who seldom heeded the Japanese associations, except when they needed specific services or certificates. By 1916, the situation had improved, as the official membership of the associations in central and northern California alone reached about half of the 23,442 adult Japanese males there.[86] Yet, thousands of ordinary Issei, especially single migratory laborers, still lived on the periphery of the ethnic community.

Class differences continued to pose a formidable barrier to the elite attempt to forge national consciousness based on the discourse of civilization. The material conditions of Japanese farm laborers made no significant progress, insofar as they functioned primarily as a source of cheap, expendable labor for the agricultural industry of the American West. In 1919, a vernacular newspaper criticized the unchanging, Sinified state of the working-class Issei in terms of their lack of concern for basic hygiene: "Japanese fieldhands in Walnut Grove nonchalantly stay in dirty labor camps where bedbugs have continuously swarmed since the Chinese lived there fifty years ago." In their 1920 report, California state inspectors concurred that the rural Japanese camps were poorly equipped with only "open toilets, open drains from the kitchen sink, unscreened dining and cooking quarters, and living quarters generally littered with boxes, bags, etc."[87]

Another factor that mitigated the elite project was the increase of *shakkotai* at the grassroots level. Immigrant gangsters expanded their realm of influence during the latter half of the 1910s despite the reformist activities. In 1916, an organized Issei crime ring was born in Los Angeles, where hardcore gamblers in Little Tokyo merged into a Yamato Club. Renamed the Tokyo Club, it controlled numerous gambling dens in California until the late 1930s.[88] In Seattle, there was a similar crime ring known as the Toyo Club, which extended its own network of gambling halls throughout the Pacific Northwest. By depriving the Chinese of the monopoly in the ownership of the business, the Issei gangsters literally turned the racial connotation of gambling from Chinese to Japanese—a situation that ran counter to the elite goal. Furthermore, in the eyes of many residents, the outlaws effectively had established themselves as an alternative to the elitist Japanese associations, providing vital social services,

59

including generous donations and loans, free meals for the poor and elderly, and the enforcement of unwritten law and order within the immigrant society.[89] Often, the crime syndicates placed Japanese association affiliates under their thumb, as they habitually manipulated association leaders with money and the threat of violence.[90]

However, moral reform was ultimately doomed for another reason: the subsiding of the organized anti-Japanese movement. During the early 1920s, the U.S. Supreme Court categorically ruled the Japanese to be an inadmissible race that deserved neither citizenship, land ownership, nor agricultural tenancy.[91] By classifying the Japanese as racial pariahs along with the Chinese and other Asians in no uncertain terms, the court thus nullified the foundations of the Issei's reformist endeavors. So different were the Japanese from the white race that no moral uplift or cultural assimilation could overcome the chasm. Although elite Issei did not discard their sense of superiority to the Chinese and compatibility with the whites, the American judicial system declared the Sinified state of the Japanese to be simply a matter of their "Mongolian" origin—one that could neither be discarded nor covered by cultural changes or assimilation. Symbolizing the decisive triumph of racial exclusion, the National Origins Act of 1924 dealt the coup de grace to transnational collaboration in immigrant control, since its ban on immigration from Japan deprived the Japanese associations of their delegated administrative functions and state-authorized disciplining power. Then, in April 1926, with the formal severance of their relations with Japanese diplomats, the Japanese associations found their control network and their influence collapsing rapidly within the ethnic community.[92]

Yet, convergences and divergences among Japanese in the United States, and between them and people of Japan, were more complicated than the relations revolving merely around the networks of the Japanese associations and the questions of immigrant moral reform and assimilation. Institutionalized racism provided another crucial context, in which a different kind of social formation transpired within the American West and between the two empires during the first two decades of the twentieth century. Unlike the re-form of the immigrant masses, which aimed to construct a community of civilized citizen-subjects according to a modernizationist hierarchy of class and culture, the simultaneous development represented the making of new relations of power in terms of the wholly different logic among three racial(ized) groups— America's Japanese minority, American whites, and imperial Japanese—in a transnational space.

3

Zaibei Doho

Racial Exclusion and the Making of an American Minority

One week before the National Origins Act of 1924 effected the complete ban on Japanese immigration, the *Nichibei Shimbun* of San Francisco elucidated how Japanese residents in the American West had come to form a group distinct from their compatriots in Japan. In response to a call for returning to the bosom of the caring homeland from the anti-Japanese attitude of the United States, an Issei writer hinted at a collective world view that was taking shape in Japanese America: "One sympathetic poet in the motherland ... urges [us] to come back home quietly, as [the people of Japan] are ready to embrace us with open arms and provide for [us] by sharing and sharing alike." While stressing how grateful Issei were for their "sincere sympathy," the editorial added, "But you see, the Japanese in America have reasons not to leave this place, and that is what we want the people of Japan to understand."[1]

As shown by such statements, the first two decades of the twentieth century ushered in the emergence of a community of "the Japanese in America" (*zaibei doho*). That diasporic community evolved around a unique identity, which not only transcended class and intellectual differences among the immigrants but also broke with the Japanese back home. Unlike the collaboration between state officials and Issei elites, this nascent identity did not hinge on the orthodox notion of Japaneseness that was meant to serve the project of modern nation-building on both sides of the Pacific. Instead, what bound diverse groups of Issei was their shared experience of being a racial Other in America, which revealed the futility of the modernist belief that the Japanese should be able to become honorary whites through acculturation. Whereas moral reform could only precipitate a limited degree of community formation among leading Issei, the collective racial experience of Japanese immigrants conjoined them beyond other kinds of differences. By 1924, *zaibei doho* forged a genuine awareness of their restricted lives in the United States, on the one hand, and their emigrant perspective and interests vis-à-vis those in imperial Japan, on the other. Tracing the developments in racial subordination to white America and of the Issei's parting from their homeland, this chapter delineates the making of an American minority, who engaged but never fully belonged to either racial empire.

THE ANTI-JAPANESE MOVEMENT AND RACIAL SUBORDINATION

In the historiography of Japanese immigrant history, the first quarter of the twentieth century is generally narrated according to the "politics of prejudice," in which a call for Japanese exclusion grew from an agenda of organized labor and its allies in California to a major issue of contention on Capitol Hill. Having fought hostilities, discriminatory practices, and racist laws exhaustively but unsuccessfully, Japanese immigrants of the mid-1920s knew all too well that they were subject inextricably to the regime of institutionalized racism regardless of differences in age, social background, gender, occupation, and wealth. While the laws prescribed the universal definitions of the Issei's hegemonized state in America, the varied dynamics of local political economies produced diversified patterns of Japanese-white relations that were nonetheless hierarchically defined. In particular, landless Issei farmers and members of the working class faced intensified dependency, and propertied rural immigrants and urban residents were placed under the forces of racial containment during the decades of Japanese exclusion.

Japanese dependency was the most common pattern of racial subordination, especially in rural districts of the West, where a majority of Issei engaged in agricultural pursuits. Prior to 1941, the nature of relations between Issei and whites was often predicated on a shifting mode of farming and land tenure. In California, as in other Western states, most Japanese agricultural landholdings were leased or contracted farms, but types of tenancy underwent constant change in the white-controlled agricultural economy. Between 1907 and 1923, the percentage of farm tenancy seldom fell below 80 percent. From the first decade of the 1900s, cash tenancy was dominant, and it peaked in 1920 with an aggregate 192,150 acres. Three years later, the combined total of cash and share leases plummeted to 131,991 acres, while the farms under "cropping contracts" jumped to 109,756 acres. Then, in 1929, these three forms of tenancy accounted for only 166,762 acres combined, while the land under the cultivation of salaried "foremen" reached a total of 104,560 acres.[2] These shifts in Japanese tenancy resulted from the enforcement of the alien land laws, whose restrictions on their land leases concomitantly helped to reconfigure the pattern of interactions between Issei farmers and white land owners. From the outset, their relations unfolded vertically rather than horizontally within the preexisting racial order of the West, but Issei could still negotiate or challenge the system until state and federal governments completed legalized Japanese exclusion from Western agriculture. By the mid-1920s, however, interracial relations were uncontestable to the point of nearly total Japanese dependency on propertied whites, who could arbitrarily dictate the use of a few loopholes for their Issei tenants.

The interracial situation in Walnut Grove, California, exemplified what transpired in many other Japanese farm settlements during that period. Solely consisting of tenant farmers, the community had the most common pattern of Japanese immigrant agriculture. Situated in the Sacramento River delta, Walnut Grove includes a vast acreage of reclaimed peat fields where a handful of European Americans monopolized land and power once the United States gained control of the area. Beginning in the early 1890s, Japanese entered the region as farm hands, supplanting the Chinese population after their exclusion. Most

Table 3.1. Japanese Agricultural Landholdings in California, 1905–1929

Year	Owned (acres)	Cash Lease	Combined	Share Lease	Cropping Contract	Foremen	Total
1905	2,442	35,258		19,573	4,775		62,048
1907	13,815	56,889		48,228	13,359		132,291
1909	16,449	80,232		57,001	42,276		195,958
1913	26,707	155,488		50,495	48,997		281,687
1918	30,306		336,721		23,608		390,635
1920	74,769	192,150		121,000	70,137		458,056
1922	51,000		152,000		145,000		349,000
1923	62,773		131,991		109,756		304,520
1929	57,028		166,762			104,560	328,350

Notes. For some years, total figures have been adjusted to correct errors in the original sources. Fractions have been omitted. One special category, "sublease" (4,323 acres), is not included in the 1923 total.

Sources. Nichibei Shimbunsha, *Nichibei nenkan,* vols. 4, 6, 10, 12; *Zaibei Nihonjin jinmei jiten,* 38; Gaimushō Tsūshōkyoku Iminka, *Kashū oyobi Kashū Tochihō shiso keika gaiyō,* 27; Zaibei Nihonjinkai, *Zaibei Nihonjinshi,* 174–175, 187, 192.

rural Japanese farmers came from the ranks of enterprising *dekasegi* migrants, who worked on farms and invested portions of their earnings as a stepping-stone to tenant farming—a main path toward upward mobility in the Western economy. As they accumulated capital and learned farming methods, Japanese tenant farmers appeared increasingly in the delta, as in many parts of the West, by the first decade of the twentieth century.[3] While the numbers of Issei share-croppers and cash tenants there jumped from 254 and 102 to 360 and 198, respectively, the aggregate acreage under Japanese cultivation more than tripled from 2,100 to 7,124 acres between 1904 and 1905, with the especially conspic-uous rise of the cash-tenancy ratio from 12 to 27 percent.[4] The white domi-nation of resources, combined with the exorbitant prices of farmland, none-theless thwarted Issei land ownership in Walnut Grove.

The quick growth of an Issei farming class in the delta coincided with the cultivation of asparagus. Issei discoveries of niche crops that white farmers tended to neglect—such as asparagus, berries, celery, onions, potatoes, and cantaloupes—enabled them to dominate the production of those crops throughout the Western states. In Walnut Grove, the success of Kamajiro Hotta at cultivating this cash crop led to him being dubbed the Japanese "asparagus king" and induced other Issei to follow.[5] When Hotta settled in the delta in 1904, no Japanese was reported to have raised the crop; within five years, Issei asparagus farms increased to 5,549 acres, or half of the aggregate Japanese acreage in Walnut Grove.[6]

Despite these impressive statistics, Japanese tenant farmers worked under the rigid control of white landlords and other business interests, who hand-somely benefited from their relationship to the immigrants. The *Pacific Rural Press* described how the largest land owner in the delta region, Alex Brown, managed his asparagus farms under Japanese cultivation:

> The Brown acreage is leased to tenants who occupy nineteen different camps and each with 100 to 175 acres; though 100 acres is about as much as one camp can handle rightly. Tenants furnish labor only, and get 60 per cent of the crop. They sublet the cutting to [Issei] contractors at about $1.20 per cwt. . . . Cutting requires about 20 men per 100 acres. Hauling, washing, culling, and cutting to proper lengths requires five men more per 100 acres.[7]

After cutting asparagus, the Issei farmers delivered the crop to a packing shed operated by Brown, from which the land owner shipped it to the New York market and to a nearby cannery.[8] This system worked so well for Brown that it brought net profits of $40 to $50 per acre. Since he had nearly 2,700 acres under asparagus cultivation around 1918, his annual net profit could reach as high as $135,000. This land owner–tenant nexus made Brown one of the most successful "farmers" in the region, while his Issei sharecroppers actually cleared, planted, tilled, and harvested the asparagus fields.

Against this backdrop Japanese dependency gradually took hold. Propelled by concerns over the unchecked expansion of the Japanese in agriculture, state governments intervened on behalf of wary white farmers and residents with an eye to circumscribing the modes of Japanese land tenure. In general, land owners preferred share tenancy to cash leasing because of its larger profits, as exemplified in Brown's case. Under sharecropping agreements, the land owners controlled every aspect of farm operations in exchange for supplying land, farming necessities, and financial assistance. Cash leases, many landlords found, gave lessees too much autonomy, allowing workers like Hotta to keep too large a share of the profits.[9]

Enacted in 1913, California's first Alien Land Law produced a socioeconomic condition that unilaterally favored white landlords. In keeping with the euphemism "aliens ineligible for citizenship," the law limited Issei land leases to three years in addition to banning their land ownership, which facilitated rapid conversion of Issei farming to "cropping contracts," a variation of share tenancy. A cropping contract gave no legal rights over the land and was an employment agreement, simply entitling a Japanese cultivator to a designated share of the crops as his "salary." Identical to a sharecropping lease in substance, this mode of farming served propertied whites well, while exempting their Japanese "employees"—not "lessees" in legal terms—from the regulations of the 1913 law.[10] In the ensuing nine years, the Japanese acreage under cropping contracts in the Golden State almost tripled, from about 17 percent to 42 percent.[11] All Issei farmers of Walnut Grove except Hotta were compelled to adopt this method of sharecropping-in-disguise by the early 1920s—a system particularly suited to the cultivation of asparagus and orchard fruit, which require a long-term commitment.[12]

The 1913 Alien Land Law left conflicting legacies. On the whole, the prevalence of share tenancy, including cropping contracts, accelerated the degree to which Japanese farmers were shackled to propertied whites. It also made tenants more vulnerable to their landlords by forcing the Japanese to count on the whites' willingness to assist in their evasion of the law. In this respect, Japanese dependency intensified in both economic and social terms after 1913, but it did not become so manifest until 1920. Combined with a wartime boom in the U.S. farm economy, the legal ambiguity of the cropping contract minimized the immediate effects of Japanese exclusion from agriculture, which the law was designed to achieve. Despite its impact on land tenure, the legislation failed to hamper Issei farm operations in the short term. Like their fellow Issei tenant farmers elsewhere, the Japanese of Walnut Grove continued to expand their acreage during the latter half of the 1910s. As the aggregate figures of Japanese leases in California more than doubled from 179,509 acres in 1909 to 360,329 acres in 1918, so too did the land cultivated by the delta Issei increase from 9,445 acres to 16,541 acres.[13] And during the First World War, as figure 3.1 shows, the Japanese share in the production of the niche crops exceeded the 80 percent mark. Economic empowerment helped to offset racial dependency, which progressed less visibly.

Landed whites and agribusiness interests began to fear a possible change in the status quo in California agriculture and racial order in light of the steady Japanese economic ascent. Through the 1910s, what they characterized as the Japanese "invasion" took various forms in the Western states. In central California, for example, growing land ownership among local Issei accounted for a major part of the racial "problem," while the formation of ethnic wholesale concerns and produce markets contributed to their economic competitiveness, or "menace," in other places.[14] In southern California, a "horizontal and vertical integration" of niche farm industries brought together wholesale, retail, and production into the composite ethnic economy. This enabled local Issei to participate with Italians and Chinese in the operation of the City Market of Los Angeles (Ninth Street Market), which competed with the older, Anglo-dominated Wholesale Terminal Market (Seventh Street Market).[15] Given these developments, as the election of 1920 approached, incumbent U.S. senator James D. Phelan and committed exclusionists like V. S. McClatchy agitated for a more stringent alien land law in order to hold Japanese immigrants in check and to "keep California white," a political platform that met with enthusiastic support from many disgruntled Californians.

What occurred in Walnut Grove was illustrative of the impact of the new Alien Land Law (1920), which was designed to counterbalance Issei economic strength with their intensifying dependency on white patrons. In the delta, the local Caucasian population felt threatened especially by the Issei efforts to build their own asparagus cannery, spurred by the dramatic expansion of Kamajiro Hotta's asparagus farm. In addition to his original 400-acre farm, Hotta had leased in 1917, under a cash rental arrangement, 1,000 acres, which he had sublet to other Issei.[16] In 1920, the asparagus crop on this farm was ready for its first harvest. In tandem with the 5,755 acres of asparagus under cultivation by other Japanese growers in the delta, Hotta's 1,400-acre farm appeared to hold out the promise of controlling supply in the market, since the Japanese acreage in Walnut Grove would amount to nearly 60 percent of the aggregate 12,000 acres in the entire state. Seeing this as their best chance to gain autonomy in farming, local Issei asparagus growers, who had already formed a guild to challenge the white landlords' control, began to draft blueprints for a cannery, and by March 1920, the immigrant press joyously predicted that a Japanese-owned cannery would "come to reality before long."[17]

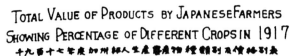

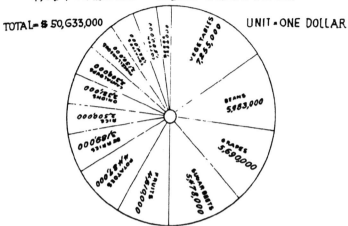

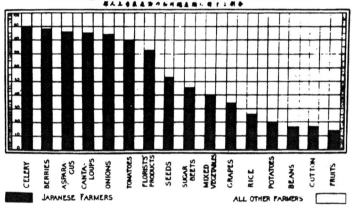

FIGURE 3.1. **Achievements that Illuminate Marginality**

These graphs illustrate the multi-million-dollar Japanese agricultural industry in California in 1917. The comparison of the two graphs shows that Issei dominated in production of labor-intensive field crops such as berries, onions, and asparagus, where much hand labor was essential for crop cultivation and harvest. The cheapness of co-ethnic labor was a major reason for their "success" in such niche farming that was neglected by white farmers. Reprinted from Japanese Agricultural Association, *Japanese Farmers in California* (1918).

This turn of events particularly offended Alex Brown, who had already been forced by collective bargaining to raise the crop share of his tenants in 1918. As the largest landlord in the region, he brooked no further attempts by the Japanese to establish themselves as autonomous farmers. At this juncture, Phelan and exclusionist groups sponsored an initiative to amend the 1913 Alien Land Law. Intended to deny Japanese tenancy altogether, the new land bill offered a practical solution to the local Japanese problem that Brown and other land owners faced. Because even Hotta's farm was under a cash lease, a ban on Japanese immigrant tenancy would nullify the Japanese cannery plan.[18] Indeed, after passage of the law in November 1920, all talks of a cannery ceased among the delta Japanese, exemplifying the poisonous impact that legalized racism had on the lives of Issei farmers in California and, subsequently, in other states.

In the years to follow, Japanese-white relations were transformed in terms both of legal and economic practice and of Issei consciousness. First, institutionalized racism in agriculture circumscribed the Japanese vision of social existence within the narrow bounds characterized by dependency. Not only did legal deprivation strengthen the dominance of propertied whites, but it also cemented their hierarchical relations so firmly that there was no longer much room for Issei to be able to negotiate, much less challenge the regime of consolidated white power in the American West. Without legal entitlement to tenancy, Issei farmers found it virtually impossible to defy their landlords, who could now dictate the terms of their relations in the local political economy at will. White elites still tolerated the presence of the Japanese, continuing to employ Issei farmers rather than lose a good source of profits and able caretakers of their land.[19] As long as such financial incentives remained available, the situation did not cause most Issei significantly greater difficulty than the post-1913 adjustment, and yet, they now were almost totally dependent on the whim and favor of their landlords. In Walnut Grove, a contemporary observer noted that "the close entanglements of interest" between white landlords and Issei farmers made the former still willing to offer a "verbal promise to perpetuate [the Japanese] farming endeavor." In the central California town of Hanford, the situation was similar, but reportedly, local Issei farmers "were put in such a precarious position as to live continuously with a deep sense of insecurity."[20]

Indeed, in light of the contingency of economic ties, white paternalism was never a reliable insurance. With their steadfast grip over rural Japanese engendered by the law, land owners could—and often did—mistreat Issei tenant farmers if and when such actions served their financial interests. A Japanese diplomat chronicled how some Japanese in Placer County found themselves left to the mercies of white exploitation:

Those who have verbal agreements for cash leases with landowners theoretically have maintained close economic ties for a number of years, and
so have sharecroppers built a relationship based on mutual trust. In actu-
ality, these growers never ceased to encounter one trouble after another,
because they are an easy prey to deception. . . . The [Issei] farmers, who
cannot seek help from the authorities [due to their illegal leases], are
placed under the thumb of landowners and fruit-shipping houses that
control the marketing of the crop.[21]

Extreme abuses of course convinced many to give up on farming, as was the
case in the central California community of Armona where the vast majority
of Issei tenants left for urban areas or other states.[22] Yet, for those who managed
to avoid the worst abuses and betrayals, it was still better to count on the
capricious favor of landlords after 1920.

The practice of dependence on white paternalism notwithstanding, there
was a brief moment when Japanese farmers envisioned collective resistance as
a viable option. This popular struggle, spearheaded by ordinary Issei residents,
was short-lived, lasting only from 1921 to 1923. Paradoxically, when the show-
down was all over, the poignant memory of their common experience in defeat
compounded Issei feelings of being a subordinate minority under consolidated
white power. In this sense, the significance of the mass resistance lay not so
much in the act of protest in and of itself but in its impact on the popular
consciousness. While failed resistance further reinforced the general practice of
dependence, it expedited the process in which a racialized identity as *zaibei
doho* took shape among these Japanese in America.

At the heart of this struggle and transformation was the cropping contract.
Initially, during the first half of 1921, a large number of Issei tenant farmers
switched, or planned to switch, to that mode of farming, for it was still a safe
and easy loophole that allowed them to remain virtual sharecroppers.[23] Although most landed whites were no longer dissatisfied with their relationship
to the Japanese, exclusionist zealots continued to press the state government
for vigorous enforcement of the law and prosecution of evasions. The cropping
contract became a prime target of this racist judicial effort, and in the summer
of 1921, California's attorney general, Ulysses S. Webb, himself an ardent advocate for Japanese exclusion, declared in no uncertain terms that the cropping
contract was a form of lease, and therefore illegal.[24]

Webb's attack on the last bastion of Japanese immigrant agriculture provoked grassroots mobilization and resistance of unprecedented form and scale.
Previously, the leading circle of urban merchants and intellectuals set collective
agendas and community policy mandates, like moral reform, which usually
moved downward within the hierarchy of immigrant control mechanisms under

the Japanese Association of America (or its equivalents). By contrast, this popular struggle emerged from rural farm districts where most ordinary Issei resided, thereby thrusting *their* concerns and *their* desires on those in the cities. For the first time, the Issei masses formed a tangible and formidable political force within Japanese immigrant society, marking a significant shift in power relations and community representation.[25] When the core of their self-interest was in peril, the apparatus of immigrant control conveniently functioned as a vehicle for ordinary residents to have their voices heard by the elite and their concerns reflected in its agendas and programs. Not only did residents take advantage of the Japanese associations on their own behalf, but they moreover tried to quell the racist assault by turning the American judicial system against it.

By the fall of 1921, Issei farmers of northern and central California had already reached a consensus about pursuing test cases against the Alien Land Laws in the courts. Given the ambiguous legal status of the cropping contract, the Japanese thought it offered the best chance for defending their interests as de facto sharecroppers. Following Webb's statement, rural representatives met in San Francisco on September 2, 1921, to demand that the Japanese Association of America immediately seek a test case concerning the legality of the cropping contract. The San Francisco elites dragged their feet, first consulting the Japanese consul and requesting his assistance.[26] No sooner had this inaction become public knowledge than rural Japanese association affiliates began to take direct action, lambasting the central body as "useless" and its leaders as "inept"—a rare instance of outright defiance.[27] Backed by popular demands, for example, the Walnut Grove association leaders held a joint conference with their counterparts from nearby Courtland and Isleton, where they agreed to persist in pressing the Japanese Association of America for a test case. On October 2, the region's Issei leaders traveled to San Francisco to meet with other representatives from throughout California, but there was still no response from the central body. Disappointed, the delta's Japanese farmers assembled for a second time and argued that in view of the situation local residents should be prepared to deal with the crisis on their own. To fight for their survival, the immigrants declared that they must disregard the established order of the community hierarchy in their quest of a judicial solution, even if local residents had to bear the financial burden.[28]

The wrath directed against the Japanese Association of America in the fall of 1921 mirrored the urgency of the situation for great numbers of Issei farmers in California. In the north and central valleys, the majority of Japanese tenants expected the renewal of their leases in October or November 1921.[29] Because they had believed in the legality of the cropping contract, they had assumed a simple transition to this arrangement. Nevertheless, as Webb's announcement forecast the real possibility of prosecution, white landlords began to cancel or refused to enter into cropping contracts with the Japanese. According to one source, many Issei in the counties of Placer, Yolo, and Tulare had already been placed in such a predicament by the end of October, and those in Sacramento, Solano, San Joaquin, Stanislus, and Kings counties were on the verge of losing their contracts. The acreage under the threat of state prosecution amounted to more than 90,000 acres, or about 30 percent of the total Japanese leases in California.[30]

On October 13, 1921, overwhelmed by popular pressure, the Japanese Association of America finally filed a bill of complaint for a cropping-contract test case, followed by another lawsuit that challenged the ban on Issei holding stocks in landholding companies—an issue that imperiled many farmers in Fresno and Yolo counties.[31] Similar grassroots efforts compelled the Central Japanese Association of Southern California, based in Los Angeles, to contest the constitutionality of the ban on leasing, which was most crucial to this area's residents. After the Washington state legislature passed its own Alien Land Law in the spring of 1921, the Japanese association headquarters in Seattle sponsored its own test case.[32]

Two years later, the Issei's legal battle ended in great disappointment. The prospect for the cropping-contract case looked deceptively bright at first, whereas most other test cases in California and Washington were quickly rejected. On December 20, 1921, a lower court in California upheld the Japanese argument that the cropping contract was not in violation of the 1920 statute, which the state of California swiftly appealed to the U.S. Supreme Court. In the meantime, while other Western states, including Arizona in 1921 and Oregon, Idaho, and Montana in 1923, enacted almost identical laws against Japanese immigrant agriculture, the Supreme Court also heard and rejected a Japanese plea for citizenship in the historic *Ozawa v. U.S.* decision of 1922, a decision that made the application of the alien land laws to unnaturalizable Issei a permanent fact of life. Consequently, Japanese farmers of the American West braced anxiously for the definitive judgment on the last bastion of Japanese immigrant farming, but in November 1923, the Supreme Court failed the Issei, declaring the cropping contract to be illegal.

"Dumb-founded," the immigrant press uniformly expressed disbelief and anger after the ruling, which nonetheless soon gave way to a call for acquiescence.[33] Having exhausted every means of fighting legalized racism, "most growers cannot but engage in farm labor from now on," wrote the *Rafu Shimpo* of Los Angeles resignedly. "It will surely be painful to bear the downfall from an independent farmer to a mere laborer, but nothing can be done about it."[34] A Sacramento Japanese daily urged readers to accept the grim reality with good grace and endeavor to procure the "sympathy" and "trust" of white landlords through hard work.[35] Speaking of the social status that would necessitate such attitudes, one editorial compared Issei to *burakumin*, Japan's outcast group that was often thought to be of alien origin, and another paper paralleled their lot to those they viewed as marginalized and powerless races, like "Mexicans, Armenians, Poles, and Negroes."[36] These comparisons poignantly show that Issei collective consciousness began to incorporate the notion of Japanese in America being socially and racially subordinate at the core, as depicted in a cartoon in a San Francisco Japanese daily (fig. 3.2). Interviewing Issei in the northern California town of Suisun, a Japanese diplomat reported the psychological state of rural residents: "[Japanese farmers] are in such low spirits. . . . One would

FIGURE 3.2. Issei under Racial Subordination, 1921
Printed at the height of exclusionist agitation, this 1921 cartoon exemplifies an emerging sense of the collective self among many Japanese immigrants. Here a struggling Issei man personifies the "Japanese in America." Despite his heavy bundle, labeled "exclusion," he still envisages a better future. In English and to the right in Japanese, the weeping sun promised him: "Be patient and do your best, someday you will win." Reprinted from *Shin Sekai* (New World, San Francisco), Jan. 21, 1921.

feel as if the [Alien] Land Law of 1920 and 1923 had robbed them of their arms and legs, leaving no autonomy to them. When land ownership and leases were legal, they had so much hope and vigor; today, all you see are dejected old men."[37]

Adding nuances to this process of racial formation, however, the Issei's chorus of acquiescence also manifested a future-looking rhetoric that attempted to mitigate their degraded position in American society. When addressing the issue at hand after the Supreme Court ruling, immigrant writers chanted a specific Japanese phrase, *innin jicho* (prudence and perseverance) as if it were a new motto for all Japanese in the United States. Reified in the cartoon, the concept corresponded to what the empathic Sun advised the struggling Issei omnisciently: "Be patient and do your best; some day you will win." Not only did it offer confused immigrants direction, the promise of *innin jicho* also helped them to historicize their bitter experience as simply an unexpected set-back. Because the land laws applied only to the immigrants, their negative effects would pass with the growth of Japanese American citizens, the Nisei. Believing that their subordination was tied to their legal status, not to racial heritage, many Issei felt that this was a temporary situation. Rather than wasting their time lamenting what they had lost, the immigrants agreed that they might as well consolidate forces and rebuild the ethnic agricultural economy.[38] The situation, in their opinion, would only improve if they persevered, hence they accommodated racial subordination as a matter of expediency.

Whereas the legal defeat placed rural Japanese immigrants in utter dependency, the Issei's consent to their powerlessness ironically spared them from total exclusion from Western agriculture. Among available loopholes, the "foreman" system emerged as the most prevalent replacement for the cropping contract. This method allowed Japanese to maintain a standard of living equivalent to tenant farmers, while playing the role of salaried workers. It of course required the blessing of landlords even more than a cropping contract, and depending on the degree of interracial bonds, there appear to have been many variations of farm foremanship. In Holister, California, for example, many Issei foremen received a flat salary of $300 every month, three times greater than the income of a mere laborer ($80–$100), while their Vacaville counterparts tended to use the foreman arrangement simply as a front for sharecropping. Walnut Grove Japanese, meanwhile, preferred to combine a monthly payment of $100 to $175 with an annual cash bonus of $2,000 to $3,000.[39] Foremanship, albeit a symbol of racial subordination and economic retreat, still enabled many Issei to remain forward-looking, since they thought the arrangement continued to help them lay sound foundations for the next generations. In this reconfiguration of race relations in Western agriculture, however, Japanese tenant farmers coalesced an awareness of being a minority with their understanding of their collective self on the basis of their frustrated past struggles, restricted present circumstances, and shared optimisms for the future.

While dependency accounted for the situation of most rural Japanese, land-holding Issei experienced a different kind of racial subordination. In California, the farms under Japanese land ownership constituted between 10 and 20 percent of the aggregate acreage from 1907 to 1923. The ratio of Issei land ownership in Washington, on the other hand, neared 30 percent around 1923, due likely to the absence of an alien land law in that state until 1921.[40] Despite this relatively low percentage, propertied Issei tended to concentrate in certain rural areas, engendering distinct race relations there. According to the 1914 California data, landholding Issei farmers of Fresno and Los Angeles counties controlled about 24 percent and 12 percent, respectively, of the total 29,735 Japanese-owned acres in the state. In smaller communities, like Florin, Vacaville, Loomis, and especially Livingston, Japanese farmers held markedly higher shares. In other states, similar patterns of concentrations were evident, as in Hood River in Oregon.[41] These communities and regions witnessed different patterns of Japanese-white entanglements than the tenancy-dominated areas.

Around 1920, many Issei land owners encountered the forces of racial con-tainment, whereby they were forced into living in accord with the will of their white neighbors despite their ostensible autonomy. The passage of the alien land laws effectively arrested the expansion of independent Japanese farming, squeezing the settlements of Issei land owners into tighter areas. California landholding statistics reveal a steady decrease in property from 74,769 acres in 1920 to 62,773 acres in 1923 and to 57,028 acres in 1929.[42] As landed Issei saw their settlements diminished under the pressures of legalized racism, they sought a greater degree of integration into the local white societies and political econ-omies. While Japanese tenants seldom collided squarely with their landlords over economic issues, independent Issei farmers tended to compete directly with their white neighbors, which reinforced strained relations and the latter's fever-ish support for discriminatory legislation. Out of concern for their own survival and for interracial peace at the local level, these Issei often became obsessed with their image as loyal community members, and therefore they allowed the dictates of local whites to take precedence over general ethnic concerns when necessary.[43]

The central California town of Livingston offers a good example of Issei containment. Known as the Yamato Colony, the ethnic community there started with the expansionistic vision of Kyutaro Abiko, publisher of the *Ni-chibei Shimbun*, who imagined an agricultural settlement comparable to New England's original Puritan colonies. In 1906, Abiko formed a landholding com-pany and purchased 3,200 acres of undeveloped land in Merced County. The tract was subdivided into 40-acre parcels, which were then sold to Issei families who wished to settle permanently as pioneer farmers and live frontier Christian lives. Thus, the Yamato Colony consisted solely of land-owning farmers, who later organized their own agricultural cooperative equipped with a packing shed and private railroad platform.[44] After enlarging the Yamato Colony by adding more tracts, Abiko proceeded to establish a similar agricultural colony in neighboring Cortez in 1919—when exclusionist groups were engaged in a fierce propaganda campaign focused on the Japanese "takeover" of California before the upcoming election.

Led by the coalition of the Livingston Board of Trade and the Farm Center, anti-Japanese advocates organized a local political movement specifically targeting the influx of new Issei settlers into the region. Many white townspeople believed that Abiko was financed by Tokyo to advance "a great Japanese invasion" in the area. In January 1920, they hastily resolved to erect signs announcing "No More Japanese Wanted Here" alongside the highway entrance at both ends of the town.[45] Although local agitators stressed that they opposed the arrival of "low class Japanese," not the current Issei residents, whom they described as "high class men," this distinction came with a veiled threat. These agitators effectively demanded that Japanese land owners align with them, not with their compatriots who wished to move to the Livingston-Cortez area. At an informal conference with Issei residents, the director of the white Farm Center argued: "[W]e don't want them [new Japanese settlers] and I am sure you don't want them either. . . . You must join us in this movement to protect you[r] interests as well as ours. We must work together." To local Japanese, the consequences of declining this "proposal" were frighteningly clear; a mob of exclusionists had already threatened in a mass meeting "to treat roughly any who might sympathize with the [low-class] Japanese."[46]

The responses of Livingston Issei illuminated their "fragile position" in the local political economy despite their landed status.[47] Because the Japanese residents were fully aware that their own safety and livelihoods were under threat, they were left with no alternative than to join forces with local whites in their fight against "Japanese invasion." As soon as the uproar began, the Japanese Yamato Colony Association (YCA) convened an emergency meeting, where the overwhelming majority voted to stage an exclusionist campaign of their own. First, they decided to circulate a petition to all Japanese households in Livingston, urging them to pledge steadfast opposition to the entry of any more Japanese into Merced County. The YCA formed a three-person disciplinary committee to severely punish anyone who refused to sign the petition. As an example to the community, they then singled out a renegade who had prepared to enlarge his farm operation by bringing in new Issei tenants and workers. The YCA set up a sort of kangaroo court to coerce him into abandoning the plan, which this man did at the loss of several thousand dollars already invested in the project.[48] Pitting the "interests" of Livingston Issei against those of their co-ethnics, white racism induced local Issei farmers to act as accomplices in blocking further Japanese settlement and land acquisition in the area.

The local exclusionist pressure was so strong that Yamato Colony Japanese continued to pursue interracial "cooperation" despite criticisms from their fellow Issei, who reprimanded them for their "shameless treachery" and "disloyalty."[49] Faced with ostracism from their compatriots, Livingston's Japanese residents were compelled to defend their position by issuing a statement in the Japanese immigrant press. It argued that local Issei had never approved the injustice of racism per se, but they had to "respect" the prevailing "public opinion" there. In the document, the YCA president emphasized that the specific social dynamics of Livingston required this response. The solution to race problems must first take into account the "locally particular circumstances," he reasoned, dismissing any criticisms without such consideration as "worthless." And their informed compromise, according to the YCA statement, had helped to rehabilitate the Japanese race in the local perceptions.[50]

Ever faithful to the cause of their neighbors, a Livingston Japanese representative also appeared with white exclusionists before a congressional hearing on the "Japanese problem," testifying against further immigration from Japan. Asked if he thought there were "enough" Japanese in the United States, the Issei told the chairman: "I think it is quite hard to Americanize [them]. I think we have plenty of foreigners in this country; that we should first Americanize those foreigners who are here, and after that I think it is better to prohibit the newcomers." Following this statement, a local white leader unabashedly praised this Japanese speaker—and other Livingston Issei in effect—for their cooperation and loyalty to Livingston, while hinting at a contrarily sinister image of the rest of the Japanese in California:

> [I]n about February or March Mr. [X] lived here actually in danger for the attitude he took in attempting to solve the problem locally in Livingston; and also in Oakland and San Francisco, Mr. [X] was in danger when he was there [to explain his position to other Issei]. His thought is in harmony with ours, and we have these people [Japanese residents in Livingston] with us.[51]

By adhering to this accommodationist thinking to the temporary detriment of ethnic unity, Livingston Issei sought further integration into the local society. They collaborated with whites in forming the Livingston Anti-Japanese Committee, which served as "an American-Japanese clearing house for all matters affecting the two people[s] in the district."[52] By stipulating a local ban on the sale or lease of land properties to Japanese, the institutionalized interracial partnership decidedly slowed down the influx of Japanese settlers into the area to the extent that local whites no longer made it an issue by the fall of 1920. And in exchange for their compliance, Livingston Issei succeeded in securing from the white residents an affirmation of their presence there. Several months after the campaign, the town's white leader praised the area's Japanese for proving themselves to be "the only [Japanese] group in the state who have maintained independence from their strenuously objecting and fighting countrymen."[53]

Tranquillity came to Livingston, but at no minor cost. The pacification of local interracial relations precipitated the self-induced containment of Issei under the dictates of white townspeople. Local ethnic agriculture stagnated, and the colony struggled to grow thereafter.[54] Critically, moreover, the 1920 episode revealed the pliability of landed Issei to immediate political pressures, as well as the contingency of their racial identity. The "racial" consciousness of Livingston Japanese was so responsive to the will of their white neighbors—or what they termed the "locally particular circumstances"—that it was easily manipulated to function as a wholly localized identity, if necessary, even in disagreement with the larger concerns of their fellow Issei. A shared notion of being *zaibei doho* did not emanate out of a single, monolithic racial experience; it stemmed from an amalgam of experiences and understandings that varied in separate locations and for different classes of people, albeit under the overarching effects of legal discrimination that categorically defined them as a racialized Other. Without external interventions to distinguish the local Japanese from the rest, the Yamato Colony did not witness any more instances of intraethnic divergences after 1920, but the potential for such conflict was always present there, as elsewhere, despite the general condition and consciousness of racial subordination.

In the early 1920s, many urban Issei also encountered forces of racial containment, which manifested in a different manner. In addition to occasional instances of commercial competition, the chief issue was whether or not interracial interactions should be permitted beyond the realm of economics. With the rapid increase of the Japanese population during the war years, the lines of racial demarcation had become blurred in some urban residential areas. Because the remarkable expansion of agriculture and farm-related ethnic industry in southern California induced many Japanese to relocate from the north, notable exclusionist drives against the cohabitation of whites and Japanese took place in Los Angeles and its vicinity. Some of these campaigns prescribed restrictive covenants or deed restrictions regionwide, while others lobbied the City Realty Board to "recommend that Realtors . . . not sell property to other than Caucasians in territories occupied by them."[55] Despite tenacious demands for residential segregation, a considerable number of Japanese immigrants still managed to move into new areas—a situation that provoked violent white reactions and localized efforts to contain Issei in Little Tokyo and other "colored" sections.

Influenced by the statewide exclusionist movement, anti-Japanese agitation surged in Los Angeles around 1922. In the district of Rose Hill, the acquisition of a residential tract by an Issei-owned firm stirred a commotion. While housing was being built, nearby whites threatened to destroy the construction company unless it scrapped the project. The same year, a proposed plan for a new Japanese Methodist church building met staunch opposition from the neighborhood association of Pico Heights. In 1923, an Issei found that the house he had just acquired in the Belvedere section of Los Angeles was burned in an arson attack, and afterward white residents erected a "Japs Keep Out" billboard. In Sherman, an immigrant family encountered anti-Japanese signs, placards, and banners when they moved into a new house there. Hollywood emerged as another hot spot for segregationist activities. Local whites sought advice from veteran agitators in Pico Heights and Belvedere, and, in a combination of political lobbying and intimidation, they used the newly established Hollywood Protective Association to fight "the invasion and colonization of the Japanese in that section."[56] Such racist harassment successfully deterred Issei residential development in Rose Hill, frustrated the establishment of Japanese Christian churches in Pico Heights and Hollywood, forced the Japanese family to abandon their property in Belvedere, and likely discouraged other Issei from moving to new neighborhoods.[57] This experience taught the area's Japanese immigrants that white America would not tolerate them unless they remained segregated in Little Tokyo.

Whether through dependency or containment, by the mid-1920s, racial subordination had become the inescapable reality that pragmatically oriented much of Japanese immigrant life. When the National Origins Act added further insult by terminating Japanese immigration, no visible uproar or anger emanated from Issei, who rather calmly interpreted it as a natural culmination of the white supremacy that they had fought in vain. On July 1, 1924, the day that the law became effective, an Issei woman resignedly wrote in her diary, "We, the [Japanese] residents in America, are so accustomed to the unfair treatment that this immoral nation has waged upon us, that we no longer find it unfair. We are made to take it as business as usual." A Los Angeles man likewise recorded the community consensus, noting that "the Japanese in America . . . do not seem to think much of it any longer."[58]

Vernacular newspapers all expressed similar sentiments, but they valorized the idea of *innin jicho* (prudence and perseverance) as usual. While lamenting the "failures of the past twenty-some years of struggles against white exclusionists," the *Shin Sekai* of San Francisco expressed an ironic sense of closure and determinedly swore to still "work out our destiny by ourselves." Right after the passage of the law by the U.S. Congress, the immigrant newspaper wrote: "Now it is all over. . . . We are clearly branded as pariahs in America. . . . Yet, even if [America] dealt with us as pigs, or perceived us as dogs or cats, we must focus on our work obstinately." Admonishing against "rashness," Seattle's *Taihoku Nippo* echoed the importance of *innin jicho* by urging readers to "be only concerned with defending [their] interest." A few months later when the law was enforced, the *Nichibei Shimbun* repeated the prevailing view in its editorial statement: "[W]e can easily lose our livelihood in America unless we acclimate . . . to our [new] circumstances."[59]

Candidly admitting that there existed very few options or leeway, the *Rafu Shimpo* of Los Angeles summed up the situation for all Japanese residents in the American West at this juncture. If an immigrant wished to stay in the United States, he could not but "resign to the reality of being excluded." Anyone who found it too hard to swallow would either have to "return to Japan" or "leave for other countries."[60] Accepting their shared status as pariahs was hence a prerequisite for remaining "the Japanese in America." As much as the long social process of marginalization contributed to the Issei's feelings of oneness, they also crafted their racial consciousness calculatedly in order to "acclimate . . . to [their new] circumstances," "defend [their] interest," and above all, "work out [their] destiny" in the United States. Such mental (re)orientation provided for what an Issei leader aptly characterized as their emergent "spiritual alliance," or a teleological collective identity, as racially subordinate.[61]

ISSEI "DIASPORA": AN ESCAPE FROM RACIAL SUBORDINATION

While most Issei chose to stay, many immigrants rejected lives under the command of another race. In order to break away from such social conditioning, they left the United States for their homeland, or for third countries, where they believed they could remain "the people of a first-class nation." The departure of these people further accelerated the formation of a relatively cohesive, self-contained group by moderating the multiplicity of racial identities within the population. According to U.S. government statistics, annual Japanese disembarkation peaked in 1923 and 1924. An analysis of the occupational breakdown reveals that the figures of these two years included more than twice as many farmers as in other periods—a direct consequence of the alien land laws and defeated test cases.[62] Local Issei statistics corresponded to this trend. Between 1920 and 1925, Walnut Grove's Japanese farming population was cut in half from 158 to 80, and the community of Turlock shrank by 80 percent. The grim reality likewise caused an exodus of Issei from Oregon; in the four years following 1924 the Japanese population of the state dropped from 2,374 to 1,568, a decrease of more than 30 percent.[63] Observing each transpacific steamer departing with several hundred Issei, a Los Angeles writer reported in 1922:

> Having handed over their farms and businesses to others, they take [their] entire families along with all the wealth they have amassed here. It is doubtful that most have a plan to return to the United States. Should they find some means of making a living in Japan, they are going to stay there. If any of them happen to return here again, it is not because they truly wish to do so, but because they are forced to, being unable to get viable work [in Japan].[64]

In the meantime, a number of Issei made their way south of the border. In April 1924, the Pacific Coast Japanese Association Deliberative Council—an assembly of all associations in the American West—passed a resolution to investigate the prospects for mass remigration to other U.S. states or other countries. While the Japanese Association of America conducted a series of agricultural surveys in the American South and in a few central states, the Central Japanese Association of Southern California took charge of studying Mexico.[65] Many Issei there argued that the country was pro-Japan, free from an ideology of white supremacy, and possessed an undeveloped frontier where the Japanese could legally own land. The *Rafu Shimpo* was a leading advocate of these ideas, but as its editor, Shiro Fujioka, warned, the remigration to Mexico was not recommended for ordinary laborers, and anyone who decided to stake the rest of his life in Mexico had to carry enough capital to start out as a land owner.[66] Although Fujioka did not relocate to Mexico, some Issei took his advice and crossed the border to become self-sufficient colonists.

Many remigrants appear to have been relatively well-educated immigrants, who either shared or appreciated the views of early expansionists. Some resembled romantic colonialists in a return to the 1890s. Too humiliated to resign themselves to racial subordination, this group of Issei, albeit small in number, entertained the idea that the Japanese could conquer the wilderness of Mexico "by providing guidance for Mexicans, assimilating them, and cooperating benevolently with them."[67] Others fell into the category of expansionist entrepreneurs, who invested in farming or fishing ventures in Baja California and Sonora. By 1927, for example, two dozen Japanese from southern California had acquired barren land near Ensenada for the development of vegetable farms for a growing Los Angeles consumer market.[68]

Hachiro Soejima was a quintessential expansionist entrepreneur, who rejected the ideology of white supremacy. Founder of the *Shin Sekai* newspaper, he was part of the core leadership in the nascent community of San Francisco Japanese around the turn of the twentieth century. Born a samurai in 1861, he attended the Japanese Army Academy after the Meiji Restoration and came to California in 1890 with a dream of building a "new Japan" on the Western frontier. His parting with the *Shin Sekai* and subsequent business failures led to his relative obscurity during the 1910s, but at the peak of anti-Japanese exclusion, Soejima published a weekly newspaper in which he advocated the colonization of Mexico's northern frontier. Then in 1926, with the purchase of 500 acres near Hermosillo, Sonora, this sixty-five-year-old man, along with two other Issei from California, took it upon himself to do just that.[69] Planning to build several dozen residences for additional Japanese colonialists, both from California and Japan, he had delivered boxcars of furniture, construction materials, farm tools, machinery, and even a large motorboat for coastal fishing. Soejima's ambitious venture was nonetheless short-lived; in 1928, a Mexican employee murdered him and another Issei in the course of a robbery, resulting in the dispersal of other Japanese and the abrupt demise of his colony.[70]

With better luck, some Japanese founded similar colonial enterprises in Brazil, a popular destination of emigrants from Japan after the Gentlemen's Agreement. Nagata Shigeshi, a one-time Issei who had taken over Shimanuki Hyodayu's emigration society called Rikkokai, was most responsible for the remigration of these Issei to South America. In late 1923, Nagata visited California and personally witnessed the defeat of the cropping-contract test case. Incensed, he had local Rikkokai disciples form a Brazil Study Group in Los Angeles. Following the passage of the 1924 Immigration Act, Nagata had a tight network of Issei Rikkokai alumni spread propaganda to encourage Japanese to leave racist America for friendly Brazil, where experienced Issei farmers could take the lead in creating a colonial utopia with their compatriots from Japan.[71] Nagata's disciples in California eventually obtained 2,600 acres in the forest of Paulista near São Paulo, Brazil. One group established a Christian settlement named Cultural Colony, and another established Tokyo Colony.[72]

Another group of Issei traded lives as a racial minority in the United States for those of colonialists in Manchuria. Toyoji Chiba, president of the Japanese Agricultural Association in San Francisco, played a pivotal role in this movement. Educated at Waseda University in Tokyo, Chiba was a typical Issei intellectual who interpreted Japanese immigration to North America as part and parcel of Japan's overseas expansion.[73] In light of exclusionist agitation, he became progressively pessimistic about the future of Japanese immigrant agriculture in the United States. He predicted how badly the new Alien Land Law would affect Issei farmers, noting in one of his commentaries in 1921: "[T]he Japanese in America will not be able to withstand the troubles caused by the strict enforcement of the law, which should eventually impel them to quit farm operation, abandon permanent residency [in America], and relinquish their vested interests there."[74] A few months later, Chiba himself abandoned permanent residency and headed for Manchuria, because he expressly wished to "live in the sphere where Japan's sovereign power extends, and work under the Japanese flag in such a way that the fruits of our labor can directly benefit our homeland."[75] Hired as an agricultural specialist and colonial planner by Japan's South Manchurian Railway, Chiba found the Issei's farming expertise beneficial for agricultural development in Manchuria and called for remigration to Manchuria. The successful case of a former Fresno resident, Man'ei Awaya, who developed a large apple orchard near Dalian, Manchuria, convinced Chiba of the promise which that part of Japan's "frontier" held for experienced Issei farmers.[76]

The departure of these expansionists and colonialists narrowed differences among Japanese immigrants in the United States. Inasmuch as their frames of reference and the material bases of their livelihood were both embedded in American social relations, the remaining Issei became a unique group of Japanese, who not only shared a lived racial experience but also endeavored to forge a common destiny under racial subordination. In terms of their perspectives and identities, white racism had brought different cohorts of the immigrants much closer, and an awareness of mutually comparable social positioning and collective interests had taken shape among them. The exodus of those, like Soejima and Chiba, who would rather have lived as colonial masters than as the racially subjugated helped further to facilitate the racialization of Japanese immigrants as an American minority. This does not mean that "the Japanese in America" came to form a homogeneous community; it continued to be full of internal friction and divisions. Yet, initial diversities within the populace, including nationalist mercantilists, colonial expansionists, and *dekasegi* individualists, became less pronounced, because all Japanese immigrants had to grapple with the totalizing forces of American racism. The Othering and domination of Japanese immigrants not only produced the appearance of an undifferentiated race in the eyes of whites but in fact propelled Japanese immigrants to categorize themselves consciously into a corporeal group, which they began to call *zaibei doho*.

Whereas the much-desired label of honorary white slipped through the Issei's fingers in the context of America's hierarchalized race relations, the formation of the new community set them apart decisively from their home compatriots in a transnational context. Borrowing from Rogers Brubaker's formulation of "triadic relational interplay," we can envision that the society of Japanese immigrants (a racialized national minority) came to stand tangentially between white America (a disciplining racial regime) and imperial Japan (the external national homeland) by the mid-1920s.[77] The cases of Japanese-white entanglement and estrangement underscored the trajectory in which the Issei were transformed into minority "Americans," marked by their racial Otherness, in the constellation of power on the borderland of the American West.[78] Questions of race and power were also at the center of the growing cleavages between the Issei society and their external national homeland, Japan. Whereas the manner in which the Japanese in America understood their relationship to whites was contingent on their everyday experiences of rejection, subjugation, and cooptation, the imperial Japanese perception of race relations drew on how their empire interacted with Western powers. In contrast to the Issei's localized perspective, most people in Japan interpreted their racial identity and position in terms of geopolitics and international power relations.

RACIAL DIVERGENCE: AN AMERICAN MINORITY AND THE "LEADER OF THE ASIATIC"

Unlike the Issei's strategic compliance with white America, the people of Japan countered Japanese exclusion from the United States with their own racism. After the passage of the U.S. Immigration Act on April 12, 1924, a whirlwind of anti-Americanism swept the Japanese islands. Domestic newspapers carried sensational stories of racial oppression across the Pacific, and opinion makers registered fury against the treatment of the Japanese as inferior. Shibusawa Eiichi dispatched a telegram to white friends and associates in the United States: "We earnestly pray that [the] proposed exclusion provision will not become law for in that event we fear all past efforts for [the] promotion of good will between the two nations will be nullified."[79] After the president signed the bill into law in May, optimism vanished, and intense protests emanated even from America's most ardent supporters in Japan. Kaneko Kentaro, a Harvard-educated statesman, abruptly resigned his post as the president of the America-Japan Society, professing that he "felt as if the hopes of [his] life were destroyed" and that "the wounds will not be healed so long as the racial discrimination clause remains in the law." Nitobe Inazo, an alumnus of Johns Hopkins and undersecretary general of the League of Nations, echoed Kaneko's ire, declaring that he would never set foot on American soil again unless the United States repealed the racist immigration law.[80] Meanwhile, anti-American meetings were convened throughout Japan. Between April and early July, Tokyo alone witnessed more than a hundred anti-American gatherings, some of which attracted several thousand participants. The day that Japanese exclusion officially went into effect, July 1, was solemnly observed as a day of national humiliation.

America's rejection of racial equality made a significant dent in the collective Japanese mind. Major themes of discussion in the enraged nation included the hypocrisy of American democracy, the domination of the world by Americans and Europeans, and even the notion of immigration exclusion as a declaration of war against Japan, but the crux of the debate converged upon the matter of race.[81] In light of white American definitions that insisted on scientifically rationalized boundaries, many Japanese intellectuals also started to accept the biological basis of differences among racial/national groups. Highlighting the physiognomic proximity of the Japanese to the peoples of the neighboring region, a new appreciation of scientific racism by many Japanese ironically propelled them to embrace an idea of racial responsibility for their "Asian brothers." In the scheme of global power politics, this perspective saw California's exclusionist movement as yet another manifestation of ongoing confrontations between whites and other races throughout the world. As Japanese understandings of American race relations were projected onto the worldwide hierarchy and struggle of races, protesters of the U.S. Immigration Act in Japan came to consider it their own destiny as the "leader of the Asiatic" to assemble a unified racial front against white Americans. While immigration exclusion helped to steer Japan's diplomacy away from international conciliation, the Japanese idea of race relations underwent a notable shift, one which, some historians have argued, paved the way for the wartime ideology of the Greater East Asian Co-Prosperity Sphere.[82]

Generally, Issei showed little sympathy for anti-Americanism and overly confrontational racial attitudes in their native land. From their standpoint, the Japanese were getting caught up in the same kind of irrational rhetoric that they had long fought in the United States. Los Angeles leader Shiro Fujioka warned the Japanese people "not to give measure for measure." Even if the United States humiliated Japan by classifying its people as unworthy of admission, he stressed that the nation must avoid lowering its standard to the level of the "moral losers," that is, the white exclusionists.[83] A San Francisco vernacular paper criticized the Japanese for retaliating against American racism with unreasonable boycotts and unjustified attacks on white Christian missionaries in Japan. Comparing the plight of American residents in hostile Japan with the sufferings of their own under white supremacy, Issei writers took exception to the Japanese confusion of local social relations with international politics—the very rhetorical manipulation that had allowed California exclusionists to construct a notion of "Japanese invasion." In their criticisms, immigrants focused squarely on the ramifications that anti-Americanism would have on their livelihoods in the United States. A *Shin Sekai* editor characterized the homeland reactions as "a nefarious nuisance" to "the Japanese in America," arguing that antagonism toward Americans in Japan would likely come back to haunt them. "You may all feel good afterwards, but what will become of us?" asked the writer of his home compatriots.[84] Yet, Japan's new politics of racial confrontation demonstrated no real concern for overseas residents, whose welfare was only of secondary significance to the empire's overall quest for power and its ascent in the global order.[85]

White American racism, while binding Issei closer together, cleaved their identity and community from their native land during the first half of the 1920s. Divergent paths—one characterized by Issei struggle for survival under racial subordination and another that led to the racial supremacy of the imperial Japanese—complicated the relationships between *zaibei doho* and their homeland in the ensuing years. Until the attack on Pearl Harbor, however, these paths did not directly collide with, or completely repel, one another, as much as Japanese America never simply confronted or completely cast away from white America. In the changing historical contexts of domestic race relations and international relations, the Japanese immigrant community and its native state continued to find each other useful for their respective goals. While grappling with the dilemmas of life as a racial minority in America, Issei maintained intricate ties with Japan and yet strenuously guarded their new identity and ethnic interests from cooptation by imperial racism. The triangular relationship among *zaibei doho* and the two empires turned even more convoluted during the turbulent decade of the 1930s.

Part III

Pioneers and Successors

4

"Pioneers of Japanese Development"

History Making and Racial Identity

In 1922, during the peak of anti-Japanese agitation, an Issei writer called atten-tion to the need to preserve the record of their American experience.[1] Despite his concerns about a steady "disappearance" of history, Japanese immigrants had actually been quite interested in leaving chronicles of their doings since the first decade of the twentieth century. From 1908 to the early 1920s, more than a dozen such books came out in the Japanese community in America. These books, however, differed considerably in their shared themes, narrative schema, and thematic organization from a new kind of history writing that would com-mence after racial exclusion.[2] In 1927, Yoichi Toga, an immigrant in Oakland, California, published a chronological history of what he characterized as "Jap-anese development in America," which marked the beginning of the new his-torical constructions and interpretations. He explained the meaning of that history:

> A great nation/race [*minzoku*] has a [proper] historical background; a na-tion/race disrespectful of history is doomed to self-destruction. It has been already 70 years since we, the Japanese, marked the first step on American soil. . . . Now Issei are advancing in years, and the Nisei era is coming. . . . I believe that it is worthy of having [the second generation] inherit the record of our [immigrant] struggle against oppression and hard-ships, despite which we have raised our children well and reached the

point at which we are now. . . . But, alas, we have very few treatises of our history [to leave behind].[3]

In December 1940, just one year before Japan's attack on Pearl Harbor, a 1,300-page masterpiece entitled *Zaibei Nihonjinshi* (The History of Japanese in America) completed that concerted project of history writing.[4] Not the work of trained academicians, this synthesis—edited by a team of educated Issei, including Toga—represented the collaboration of many Japanese immigrants, including the self-proclaimed historians who authored it, community leaders who contributed funds toward its publication, and ordinary people who offered information and bought the book. In this instance, history writing was synonymous with history making, as it entailed not only the privileging of specific self-images over others but even the fabrication of historical "facts." The result was a systematic discourse that asserted Issei compatibility with, and placement within, Anglo-American society while affirming the ties they maintained to their homeland despite, or maybe because of, the legacies of racial exclusion and national divergence. This chapter unveils how history making helped to forge an undifferentiated memory that would guide the population of *zaibei doho* through the turbulent years preceding their wartime internment.

Issei history writing was an important signifier of larger change in the immigrants' perspective on their life in the United States. The success of the Japanese exclusion movement led many Issei to grope for something in which to take pride and for which to hope, albeit under the general principle of acquiescence. As immigrant writers often opined in the vernacular press, the mid-1920s marked the end of an era, an end that fostered a sense of collective destiny among the residents. Writing a common history was the Issei historians' attempt to replace the group's crisis of racial subordination with a shared memory of their "glorious" past in the post-1924 years. The notion of a racism-induced break in history prompted many writers to make sense of their victimization by crafting a narrative of their past accomplishments—or "development" (*hatten*), as Toga and other historians usually put it—in light of the new journey that Issei en masse appeared to be undertaking in the American West. Cast in a transnational framework, this endeavor revealed an important aspect of the Issei's intellectual adaptation and a new strategy for dual national belonging, resulting in the racialized reinvention of a collective self—concomitantly as American frontiersmen and as Japanese colonists/colonialists—acceptable to both their adopted country and homeland.

THE ISSEI PIONEER THESIS AND THE CONCEPT
OF JAPANESE DEVELOPMENT

The year 1927 was a watershed in the emergence of a new historical perspective among Japanese immigrant intellectuals in addition to marking the debut of Yoichi Toga as a semiprofessional historian. Shiro Fujioka, a community leader and journalist in Los Angeles, published a treatise whose title translates to "Pioneers of Japanese Development," which helped to set the basic tone and direction of the subsequent historical construction of the Japanese community from the exclusion movement to 1924. The author characterized the Issei as "the pioneers of racial development [*minzoku hatten no senkusha*], [who] have endured poor living conditions, patiently fought exclusion and persecution day and night, and still established the basis for social progress."[5] He also contemplated what measures Japanese residents should take for their future in the United States.

Taken together, the publications of these immigrant authors established the Issei pioneer thesis. The term that Fujioka casually used throughout his work, *the pioneers of Japanese development*, led to a variety of interpretations for years to come by immigrant historians, who were usually well versed in the intellectual trends of both the United States and Japan because of their academic backgrounds.[6] Like its formulators, the pioneer thesis was duly transnational and drew on both national political ideologies. The popular American frontier discourse dictated how Japanese American historians conceptualized their collective past as a glorious story of pioneer colonists who conquered the untamed land. By emphasizing Japanese development, the Issei challenged the Anglo-American monopoly on frontier expansionism, arguing for their own relevance to the settling of the West. The narrowly defined nexus between mastery of the frontier and racial agency in it was reworked to include Issei pioneers as legitimate participants "in the annals of American literature and history," to borrow the expression of one Issei writer.[7] "Along with the story of the white man's advance to this frontier land," the Japanese were rendered an indispensable partner in a story of conquest seen as continuing beyond the purported "closing of the frontier" in 1890.[8]

To supplement the self-serving revision of the frontier discourse, Issei historians turned to the Japanese *kaigai hattenron* (discourse on overseas development) that fueled Japan's colonialism and emigration. Often accompanied by pseudoscientific theories that stressed the overseas origins of the ancient Japanese, this popular discourse, much like Frederick Jackson Turner's thesis, posited the "expansionist traits" of the Japanese, which presumably still remained in their "racial blood." It extolled the maritime destiny of the island empire and its people not only as a colonial power but also as a nation "racially-endowed" for expansion to "new Japans" overseas.[9] Many leading Issei historians, including Toga and Fujioka, who had initially come to the American frontier in the hope of establishing a basis for Japanese national expansion, subscribed to this idea. Influenced by their writings, other immigrant historians appropriated the notions that the American West was as much a frontier to the Japanese as it was to the whites and that they too, as a civilized people, had the right to partake in socioeconomic development, if not outright territorial colonization.

Under the spell of bilateral intellectual traditions justifying colonialism, Issei historians discursively hijacked the American frontier as their own without disturbing its rhetorical foundations of conquest. Elements of the racial ideologies from Anglo-American manifest destiny and imperial Japanese expansionism were joined to form the Issei's vision of the past, which placed them on a par with white frontier settlers and above the rest in their expropriation of the wilderness. Thus, as a 1932 newspaper editorial exemplified, immigrants tended to postulate a historical mandate for "the downfall of certain races," such as "American Indians, Eskimos, and Mexicans," in the West while normalizing the Japanese ascendancy.[10] Such reworking of the dominant Japanese and U.S. discourses gave shape to the pioneer thesis after 1927.

In celebrating Japanese "tribulations and triumphs" on the frontier, Issei historians took particular pride in their contribution to agriculture not only by the taming of forsaken land but also by effecting a revolution in productivity. The *Zaibei Nihonjinshi* aptly summarized this aspect of the pioneer thesis:

> Back in 1849, California was an importer of food stuff, which totaled over-$10 million. . . . By 1919, it was an exporter with the income of $750 million. In the same year, Japanese farmers grew approximately one-tenth of the net export. Our total population was smaller than one-twentieth of the three million Californians, but we were responsible for that much produce. It is a product of Japanese diligence and superiority in [farming] skills. Despite the alien land laws, Japanese have always kept their farms green and supplied the produce of higher quality. That even anti-Japanese legislation has failed to divorce us from California farms crystallizes our exceptional ability and talent.[11]

Just like Europeans in other parts of the New World, the Japanese writers also often portrayed themselves as responsible for the arrival of modern civilization on the frontier.[12]

Comparing the experience of Japanese with that of European settlers was a pivotal rhetorical strategy in the pioneer thesis. Masasuke Kobayashi, leader of the Japanese Salvation Army in San Francisco and one of the most prolific contributors to the pioneer thesis, even declared that Japanese were "chosen by

God" to cross the Pacific a few hundred years after the Puritans crossed the Atlantic. According to him, their quick ascendancy in the American West before exclusion should have come as no surprise, since they were "selected from all the [racial] stocks of the Orient" to live among "a chosen people (Anglo-Saxons) from the Occident."[13] Another Issei leader called the Japanese "the Puritan brothers of the Orient, who [had] landed on the West Coast of the United States."[14] This line of argument often underlay Issei history writing. A typical example argued:

> We, the Japanese in America, all crossed the Pacific [and] entered North America with such a heroic determination. Unfamiliar with the language and customs, we still managed to build today's foundations with many tears and much sweat. . . . We all have done our best for our own lives and this society [America]. . . . No one can deny that we have performed distinguished service for the [industrial and cultural] advancement of North America.[15]

By adapting the dominant society's categories, such as tribulations and triumphs accentuated by their illustrious contributions, Issei historians discursively empowered themselves, spinning their racial/national identity from "unassimilable Orientals" into mainstream Americans. This social negotiation was not dissimilar to the frustrated endeavor to re-form the masses into citizen-subjects, for members of the Issei literati articulated and propagated the notion of reverse racialization.

The skewed vision of *zaibei doho* unarguably favored certain segments of Japanese immigrant society. As indicated by the celebration of their agricultural achievements, the history of Issei pioneers was first and foremost a story of "successful" entrepreneurs, who deserved respect not only for their individual merits but also for the group traits they epitomized. Many histories featured biographical sketches of the well-off farmers and, to a lesser degree, business people and other community leaders who financed or sponsored their publication.[16] Issei history making inflated the roles of these patrons by centering the narratives around their personal anecdotes of triumph and tribulation. The books therefore bestowed historical agency solely on the entrepreneurial class of Japanese immigrants and on the intelligentsia, including the writers themselves. The production of such narratives reflected the fundamental problem of funding, authorship, and audience. While the community-wide endeavor of *Zaibei Nihonjinshi* and a few other major publications involved teams of renowned writers with substantial expense accounts for international distribution, most history projects, which aimed to produce books for limited circulation, employed single local intellectuals who received only modest financial support from individuals or small organizations. This general pattern determined who undertook the writing, as well as the market for the books. It also underscored the considerable power and privilege that the proponents of the pioneer thesis enjoyed in the intellectual topography of interwar Japanese America by their access to the community leadership and the immigrant press.

A good example of such biases in history making is manifest in a chronicle of the Japanese in the Santa Maria Valley, California. This treatise gave Yaemon Minami and Setsuo Aratani, the two most affluent Issei farmer-shippers in the area, the privilege of writing prefaces, in which both men espoused their personal experiences as the model for their fellow residents and posterity. The commissioned author, Hisagoro Saka, one of the best-educated local Issei and the Japanese association secretary, constructed the community's history around the past activities of organizations in which Minami and Aratani had held leadership. Combined with biographies of other lesser Issei who, like the big two, had lived pioneer lives, albeit not as impressively, the narrative offered a varied but unified story of Japanese development in rural California.[17] Likewise, a volume edited by a *Rafu Shimpo* reporter appropriately entitled "Records of Japanese Fighters in America" contained a large assortment of life stories and featured dozens of leading local Issei who were frequent advertisers in that Los Angeles newspaper. The editor pointed out that despite individual differences, each of the life stories represented "a microcosm of . . . [the Issei's] pursuit of the ideal of Japanese development [in America]."[18] Narrated by the elite cohorts of Issei men who financed history writing, the integrated life stories also demonstrated the American dream fulfilled—a Japanese version of the Horatio Alger story that reinforced the pioneer thesis in the domestic context.

Such a narrative strategy led to an elaborate scheme of progressive history, tracing the trajectory of Japanese Americans from migrant laborers to sharecroppers and from tenant farmers to idealized land-owning farmers.[19] In that scheme, which *Zaibei Nihonjinshi* most articulately presents, the Issei's control of the farm labor market in California characterized "the first era of Japanese immigrant agriculture." After the passage of the Chinese Exclusion Act of 1882, Japanese arrived in California in large numbers. Because they were "far more effective and quick workers" than the Chinese, the Issei soon "chased out the Chinese from fruit orchards and later from vegetable and grain fields."[20] The second phase involved their advance into sharecropping. Accumulating capital and farming experience, Japanese displaced Chinese and others as sharecroppers. With their "superior" skills in farming—due to their "expansionist traits"— they further raised themselves to cash tenancy after the turn of the twentieth century. During the ensuing decades, many became independent farmers, moving on to individual land ownership before the racist laws stripped the Japanese of that crucial right.

This four-stage narrative was not completely fictitious, since many men became land-owning farmers in that manner. However, the story focused only on a specific class, and the narrative excluded the vast majority who had not followed this path, as well as those who regressed to farm foremen and other lesser statuses. Not only did the class biases obscure some essential aspects of minority experiences in a racist society, such as exploitation, poverty, and the dearth of opportunities, but the class specificity of Issei history also presupposed a causal nexus between particular group traits and the "exceptional success" of *zaibei doho*. In addition, this historical construction privileged the role of men, excluding women's historical experience in building family, community, and economy.[21] With such multifarious biases, the homogenized memory fabricated certain forms of intraethnic unity among the Japanese in America, as well as a false image of their racial superiority to other non-Anglo peoples.

Although few dissenting voices found their way into the mainstream ethnic press due to the monopoly of the print media by Issei historians and their sympathizers, a handful of leftist immigrants publicly attacked the biases in history making. In a sarcastic commentary entitled "Pioneers of Japanese Development," one writer in a communist journal argued that "capitalists" and their allies, including historians, had obfuscated the oppressions that migratory Issei laborers and prostitutes had to endure in the past. Comparing those "real pioneers" with African slaves and Chinese coolie laborers, the writer asked readers whether or not they should see those immigrants as "victims of the capitalist system" instead of simply celebrating their "tribulations."[22] In his letter to the *Nichibei Shimbun*, another leftist lashed out at history making itself, which he interpreted as a bourgeois pastime that bore no relation to the daily survival of ordinary Issei during the Great Depression. Living from hand to mouth, he stressed, his fellow farmers could not allow themselves the luxury of "wasting their time on searching for the graves" of pioneers. In response, letters to the editor all rationalized history writing as contributing to the welfare of the ethnic collectivity and deemed the leftist to be an "outcast."[23] Considering the peripheral positions these dissidents occupied in public discourse and their failure to present or publish a coherent counternarrative, their criticisms of the pioneer thesis could not pose a substantial challenge to the emerging orthodoxy.

White racism figured centrally as the force that sidetracked this class-specific progressive history. All publications by Issei historians included at least a chapter that detailed the political and legal processes that led to the enactment of the alien land laws and the passage of the Immigration Act of 1924. Such a narrative premised a set of unique social conditions with which Japanese pioneers had to grapple on the Western frontier. Not only did racial exclusion eventually terminate "the numerical increase of Japanese immigrants, a requirement of their development," but it also "made it impossible [for Issei] to become either landowners or tenant farmers." By the 1920s, according to a typical explanation, Issei were "put in circumstances under which their struggle could no longer produce any result other than defending [what they had]."[24] At the end of the narrative, Issei writers presented a picture of stagnation, with anti-Japanese legislation temporarily impeding what they viewed as the normative process of Japanese development in the West.

While usually ending with discouraging depictions of the present, Issei history making was intended to restore hope for the future and to imbue the immigrant community with a sense of historically mandated unity in purpose and identity. Yoichi Toga's opening statement in his 1927 treatise—"Now Issei are advancing in years, and the Nisei era is coming"—is indicative of that double message.[25] Projecting the idea of temporarily thwarted development onto this generational change, immigrant leaders foresaw the continuation of their progressive history with the growth of a new generation. Outlines of this vision were already manifest in the immediate aftermath of the defeat in the Alien Land Law test cases, but they subsequently became a theoretical underpinning of the pioneer thesis. According to it, Nisei citizens would not face the legal obstacles that had tormented their parents. And because they were endowed with the same superb racial attributes, Issei expected that their children would be able to take over what they had built, set Japanese development back on track, and take it to a higher level.[26] Just as the immigrant generation was the pioneer, the second generation would become the successor of racial development.

Critically, in the context of history making, the boundaries between the Issei and Nisei were forged as a matter not of simple age differences or cultural divides but of political exigencies. Contrary to the culture-based formulation of white assimilation theorists, Japanese immigrant historians found "generation" to be a political construct under the condition of racial subordination, where the arbitrary division of citizenship status created specific historical roles for the American-born. Indeed, as immigrant sources noted, it was not until around the 1922 *Ozawa v. U.S.* ruling against Japanese naturalization rights that the concept of "Nisei"—and the term itself—was purposefully introduced into Issei public discourse as a new category by which to distinguish the Japanese youth with U.S. citizenship from those without.[27]

All Issei history books subsequently narrated the story of the pioneers for the sake of the successors. In the narratives, there was deliberately little reference to the first generation post-1924; they usually included just a short postscript commenting on how anti-Japanese laws adversely affected the Japanese community and agriculture. Instead, coverage of the post-1924 years was primarily concerned with the Nisei and prospects for their future. Some authors even inserted short English sections, speaking of the significance of race history directly to a second-generation audience. One example read:

To you the second generation whose whole future lies before you, and to all our descendants in America, we wish this saga of the Japanese pioneers to be a cherished legacy to inspire you and to instill you with pride and confidence in whatever task or venture you may undertake. Then in generations to come when our great-great-grandchildren or perhaps their great-great-great-grandchildren wish to seek new worlds to conquer . . . may the incentive provided by the stirring epic composed by their forefathers produce an atavistic recurrence of the spirit of the Japanese pioneers to guide them.[28]

Issei historians' teleological optimism, however, did not simply emanate from their abstract faith in racial heritage or reliance on the "evidence" of their past development. They prophesied advances for their community with a conviction buoyed by the current ascent of Japan in a world dominated by the West and the white race.

An inflated expectation for the future made another dimension of the Issei pioneer thesis increasingly important during the 1930s. Extending the notion of *pioneer* beyond the discourse of American national formation on the frontier, Issei historians began to lay claim to their rightful position in the history of modern Japan. Borrowing the language of Japanese imperialism, they contended that their emigration to the United States and the subsequent "conquest" of the Western frontier constituted the first instance of Japan's rise as a colonial power in modern history. According to this transnational narrative, the Issei, the pioneers of Japanese development, took it upon themselves to spearhead an expansionist venture for the homeland, preceding their compatriots in South America, on the Asian continent, and in Micronesia.[29] One writer boasted: "We have been here for over sixty years. Ever since the beginning of [modern] Japan, no other group of Japanese spent as long as sixty years abroad. We are indeed the first ones. Our [emigrant] history is not quite the same as our homeland's, but it is still part of it. Our history is the first page of the history of Japanese expansion."[30] Thus the notion of *development* came to have a double meaning.

In this rhetoric, the racial difference that had marked Japanese for victimization by white America, as well as the stigma attached to their racialized identity as unassimilable aliens, came to look less daunting, for Issei historians could now juxtapose their racial development in America with the ongoing expansion of their homeland in the world. In their eyes, Japan's competition with Euro-American powers overlapped their own struggle against racial persecution in the United States. And they often defined their native country and the immigrant community as "partners" in the fight against racism, local and global.[31] Masasuke Kobayashi most eloquently expounded the international meaning of the Issei pioneer thesis, contending that wherever they resided, the

Japanese were saddled with the mission of extending their influence and bringing peace and harmony among all the peoples in the East and West. According to Kobayashi, the Issei and Japan had been striving together to rectify not only racial injustice within the United States and other nations, but also the monopoly of the New World by whites. Their fights in tandem would end, he predicted, in "the fair rearrangement of Oriental and Occidental populations" and "harmonious relations between Oriental and Occidental races" around the globe, including in the American West.[32] Paradoxically, the emphasis that he and other immigrant historians placed on the Japanese as the leader of the Oriental races made them look even more American than whites, for their endeavor corresponded squarely to the national ideals of justice and equality *for all*, as the historians often argued.

Without contradicting the domestic dimension of their historical thesis, this emerging (sub)concept of the Issei as the pioneers of Japan's *overseas* development (*minzoku no kaigai hatten*) came to have greater significance particularly after the mid-1930s. Concurrent with state-sponsored mass migration from Japan to Manchuria, Issei historians began to express their hopes that the record of their American experience would offer valuable lessons to other overseas Japanese and the homeland itself. In the preface of *Zaibei Nihonjinshi*, for example, Yoichi Toga declared: "When it is read by the residents of other overseas settlements, this [book] shall serve as a good reference for them." Depicting the Issei as "the advance group of Japanese national expansion abroad," he explained that they published the volume in part to educate fellow Japanese about the immigrants' tribulations and triumphs, especially their firsthand experience of racial competition with Westerners. Entering the established order of white society, they had withstood the unprecedented "racial/national challenge" that their compatriots were currently facing throughout a world dominated by the West.[33] Suggestive in this comparison was the Issei's presentation of their ascent to parity with Anglo Americans, which seemed to predict the eventual fulfillment of Japan's "cause" in geopolitics as well. While portraying the Issei as quintessential American frontiersmen, *Zaibei Nihonjinshi* forcefully and decisively defined them as ideal Japanese colonialists as well.

THE ARTIFICE OF HISTORY AND THE CONSTRUCTION OF PUBLIC MEMORY

To rationalize the Issei's possession of dual national attributes—a theme that had obsessed the immigrant intelligentsia since the early 1900s—the making of a monolithic race history entailed "genesis amnesia" and the homogenization of their historical origins.[34] Replacing moral reform after the mid-1920s, that project sought to counter the unequivocal rejection of Japanese immigrants by both the United States and Japan through the forgetting and remembering of selected "facts." And with the aim of creating a new mythology of a pioneering past, Issei historians focused specifically on the juxtaposition of "settler-colonists" and "sojourners," which the American frontier discourse and Japanese expansionism posited as central to each conceptualization. The immigrant artifice of history therefore had to take into account the two national spheres and discourses simultaneously.

The endeavor began with the problematization of rampant biases in Japan against emigrants (*imin*). For ordinary Japanese, the term evoked images that defied what imperial subjects were supposed to be. Encompassing the elite disdain for common migrant laborers, *imin* connoted to the public someone without education, manners, and good grooming and with hardly any trace of national consciousness. In short, as the Japanese often contemptuously stated, *imin* deserved to be treated as no more than *kimin* (people abandoned by their own nation), and Issei intellectuals hoped that the pioneer thesis would refute such a view. A number of their publications indeed commenced with strong words of protest against anti-*imin* stereotypes, after which the authors sought to disprove them with a celebratory explication of their tribulations and triumphs. Before extolling the pioneers of Japanese development in his 1927 treatise, Shiro Fujioka lamented: "[O]ur homeland compatriots have wrongly perceived us as inferior beings, treated us as an abandoned people, and thought of us as if we were a bunch of the useless scum."[35] To transform the Issei's marginality in the Japanese national discourse, the dominant meanings of *immigrants* first had to be reversed.

Such discursive practices drew on the preexisting theories of cultural compatibility between Japanese immigrants and white Americans. Part of the larger national discourse that was popular in Japan before the militarist era of the 1930s, this peculiar racial thinking primarily countered American racism, which had offered the basic vocabulary and framework for the negative stereotypes of *imin* in Japan. Originally, much of the affront that the Issei suffered at the hands of Japan's populace had derived from the accusations put forth by California exclusionists, who viewed Issei, like the Chinese before them, as uncivilized, unassimilable, and un-American. Rather than protesting such characterizations, the upper echelons of Japanese society embraced the white rhetoric, because the elite did not construe it as harmful to their own identity as modern. Because culture, rather than biology, dictated the scripting of race in their minds until the 1920s, it was not aberrant that the people of Japan blamed Issei, the lowly *imin*, for their racial victimization on grounds of their alleged cultural inferiority.[36]

Nevertheless, given the contingencies of racial differences and the magnified shades of meaning in the transnational discursive space, there was room for Issei writers to contrive binational authenticity through the selective representations of their cultural state and intrinsic traits as a uniform group. Moreover, the culturalist approach allowed the Issei historians to circumvent the question of citizenship when asserting the American dimension of their dual identity. Having been disenfranchised by judicial action, they could never argue for their authenticity in the American national community on politicolegal grounds. In light of the dominance of assimilationist theories at that juncture, indeed, acculturation offered Issei the only rhetorical possibility, for which Japan's ideology of national/racial compatibility served most conveniently.[37]

Based on the categories and language presented by champions of Japanese exclusion in California and critics of *imin* in Japan, immigrant authors asserted their "whiteness" (and hence "Japaneseness") by calculatedly invoking favorable group images through historical artifices. Like Irish immigrants, who "whitened" themselves through mainstream political participation and the scapegoating of non-Europeans as America's racial/national Others, many Issei fashioned their historical identity around the prototype of Anglo-American conquerors and distanced themselves from other minority groups in the American West.[38] Drawing a parallel between Japanese pioneers and white frontiersmen comported with this very American mode of social legitimization.

In the orthodoxy of each country, what most saliently rendered Japanese immigrants un-American and hence less Japanese, or vice versa, was their *dekasegi* (sojourning) mentality. Both anti-Japanese agitation and anti-*imin* sentiment often centered on this issue, thereby making it the focal point of efforts to establish Japanese immigrant whiteness after 1924. The disparagement of sojourners was predicated on a distinction between them and "permanent settlers," which ineluctably privileged earlier immigrants of Western European origin over newcomers from other areas of the world.[39] With no commitment to their "host" society, the notion implied, *dekasegi* Japanese, much like excluded Chinese, refused to assimilate into the American fabric of life and therefore formed an undesirable element that disrupted the national integrity of the United States. Whereas white accusations focused on the cultural, political, and economic menace of the "alien" race in the domestic context, Japanese criticisms of the Issei's sojourning also referred to its ramifications for the goal of overseas development. From the standpoint of Japanese colonialism, sojourning symbolized the Issei's dearth of self-awareness as members of the expansive nation and of commitment to its larger colonialist cause.[40]

Expropriating the culturalist concept of race, immigrant historians put the Issei pioneer thesis to full use in the disavowal of their sojourning mentality. A variation of the Issei's ongoing identity politics, this practice nonetheless diverged from the earlier reformist crusade against Sinification on one account.

Whereas the project of moral community-building presupposed internal class divisions to be overcome before Issei could truly claim the privilege of American whiteness, history making propagated a contrary notion that the population of Japanese immigrants differed entirely from the stereotypical sojourners in their dispositions, values, and consciousness. The resulting manufactured images all sought to convey a theory of distinction for the purpose of rehabilitating the Japanese in America.[41]

In order to fabricate a separate origin from the unruly *dekasegi* migrants despised by the two national publics, the Issei pioneer thesis worked in multiple ways. The standard pattern of historical artifice first and foremost entailed the misrepresentation of all current Issei residents as authentic Japanese citizen-subjects: moral, civilized, progressive, and modern. Designed to draw readers into a state of genesis amnesia, this narrative strategy was employed most effectively in two canonical works of Issei history. Published in 1931, *Nichibei taikan* (Compendium of the Japanese in America) devised what became the orthodox historical construction of the *dekasegi* question. According to this book, the definition of the original "pioneers" should be limited to "a group of young students and ambitious entrepreneurs" who had come to the Western United States between 1885 and 1895, the decade prior to the massive influx of common *dekasegi* laborers from Japan. Called the "brain of Japanese immigrant society," this early wave of immigrants was described as the antithesis of *imin* as perceived by the people of Japan (and by white Americans), and hence as full-fledged settler-colonists. Unlike stereotypical *imin*, they came from a decent social class and had considerable education. They all came to the American West with a larger ambition than simply earning money, this book stressed, since they were determined to work out their own destiny on the frontier from the outset. Later, when the number of the Japanese in the United States increased, they led the construction of an ideal settlement community.[42] Perhaps, from the vantage point of Issei elder leaders, this was not tantamount to a fabrication, since many of them had actually seen the American West as their own frontier, a "new Japan." But *Nichibei taikan* also implied that these trail-blazers had transformed the ordinary laborers who had followed them.

Nine years later, *Zaibei Nihonjinshi* advanced the theory by claiming that no Issei were ever *dekasegi* laborers. Whereas *Nichibei taikan* was suggestive, this 1940 synthesis elaborated on the sort of Japanese who came to the mainland United States after 1895. Their exodus from Japan paralleled their sudden transformation from apathetic peasants into nationalists during the homeland's first foreign war in 1894–1895. According to the book, these emigrants, that is, "most of the [present] residents in America, rushed to the United States following the Sino-Japanese War in order to amass wealth for Japan by developing natural resources in a foreign land." Not only had "such an ideal" enabled them to "build today's community and attain the present level of development," but it had, by extension, helped to shape the basic disposition of Issei pioneers. Thus, *Zaibei Nihonjinshi* asserted that the Japanese in America were from the beginning upright citizens and colonists with a sense of commitment to the Japanese nation and a mission larger than mere self-interest.[43] Given that modern Japanese and white Americans were congruent in their cultural level and consciousness, it was not altogether surprising that the Issei authors made a case for their Americanness, too, after having dedicated their lives to the "conquest" of the West, like other white frontiersmen of foreign extraction. A typical explanation unfolded in an expectedly transnational manner: "We are not legally [able to become] American citizens, but in spirit we have become American citizens. We are loyal to our native land, but in that loyalty we find nothing incompatible with loyalty to our land of adoption."[44]

Since male Issei were not posited as the inferior stock of *dekasegi* laborers, immigrant women had to match their husbands' qualities as pioneer settlers. To counter the negative perception of early immigrant women, many of whom came to the West Coast as prostitutes, Issei historians introduced the famous legend of Okei—claimed to be the first Japanese female in America. The romanticism of Okei's story, as well as her virginal state and short life, enhanced her heroism and cleanliness in stark contrast to the "disgraceful" lives of prostitutes. Okei was supposedly among a small group of Japanese, led by a German named John Schnell, who came to settle in El Dorado County, California, in 1869. Brought as a nanny for Schnell's two children, she was only seventeen years old, according to the legend. Within a year, financial problems ruined this first Japanese settlement. The German leader, his Japanese wife and children, and a few immigrants were said to have returned to Japan, while the rest, including the young Okei, were stranded in California. A sympathetic white neighbor took her in, but Okei died of malaria at age nineteen. A few decades later, a former member of Schnell's expedition visited the area to erect a modest gravestone in her memory.[45]

Not until the 1920s did Okei's story appear widely in historical publications. Her tombstone had been known to nearby Japanese residents for some time, but they assumed it belonged to one of the early prostitutes. Earlier in the decade, a curious Issei newspaperman had come to the site of Schnell's former settlement, where he interviewed local white residents, who told him Okei's story. He later detailed his findings in a San Francisco Japanese newspaper, stressing that Okei was not a prostitute, but a pioneer who had dared to immigrate to this alien land and tragically died young. Inspired by the report, Masahei Kawamura, a Japanese-language teacher in a nearby town who became known for his expertise in Okei's story, popularized her account in Japanese immigrant society. While exalting her as the ideal pioneer woman in magazine

FIGURE 4.1. Gravestone of Okei, Gold Hill, California, 1871
The headstone reads, "Okei, nineteen years old, died in 1871." The Japanese caption on
the right identifies her as "the first female Japanese immigrant." Thanks to the lobbying
of local Nisei leaders, her grave was designated part of a state historic landmark in 1969.
Reprinted from Zaibei Nihonjinkai, *Zaibei Nihonjinshi*, 1940.

articles and books, Kawamura wrote that the significance of Okei's grave lay in
its "spiritual effect that runs like an electric current through the hearts of those
who stand before it." It could not help but revive a sense of history in visitors
and invite them to look back at their own experiences as pioneers on the
Western frontier, according to him. Kawamura also contended that the community ought to commemorate the inspiring story of this courageous woman
as "a first instance of overseas Japanese development."[46]

Zaibei Nihonjinshi duly incorporated the story of Okei in its master narrative of Issei pioneers, embellishing it with a poignant image of her historic
tombstone. Although an early section briefly mentioned "women of disgraceful
profession," the book did not connect them with Issei women, who came to
join their husbands mainly after the Gentlemen's Agreement of 1907–1908 and
who were credited with "the healthy development of Japanese society in America." Because Okei was celebrated as "the first Issei woman" at the beginning
of the narrative, readers were led to see the similarities between her and post-
1908 female immigrants.[47] And so the legend was made. Overshadowing the

presence of any female immigrants diverging from the pioneer thesis, Okei cleansed the Issei woman and glamorized her as the admirable companion of the male pioneer.

Such homogenization of their origins not only helped to purge undesirable aspects of the immigrants' past, but it also dovetailed with the production of material symbols, like monuments and memorials, that cemented suitable memories in the public realm. Like any other ideological project, the politics of history making worked in a two-way process. Many ordinary immigrants— most likely consumers of invented history—undertook the task of public commemorations in tandem with the Issei historians and community leaders, who organized knowledge through research and writing. The monuments that ordinary people built or enshrined served as powerful mnemonic aids that permanently inscribed historical memory on the Western landscape where the people ordered their everyday lives.[48]

In the early 1930s, Okei's grave turned into one such public marker of history, as Japanese residents in the local area began to monumentalize her tombstone as a tangible testimonial to the pioneer thesis. They cleared the grass and brush around it and made the fading inscription legible by adding black ink. Incense and flowers decorated the grave at all times. At the biannual convention of the Japanese American Citizens League (JACL) in 1934, the second-generation leaders unanimously resolved to "beautify the grave of Miss Okei, the first Japanese woman pioneer." Setting up a special Okei Memorial Fund, the JACL proclaimed: "Miss Okei has carved a niche in the memory of her contemporaries and her posterity. Her name is now tradition, an inspiration that has guided others to pioneer along the same lines."[49]

Similarly, other graves of unknown Issei, hitherto forsaken in the bushes, were suddenly cared for by nearby residents, who constructed their localized ethnic identity around these nameless pioneers. In 1935, two generations of Japanese Americans in the Salt River valley of Arizona celebrated their monumental achievement—a defeat of racist bills in the state legislature—with a mass pilgrimage to an area cemetery, where "the spirits of the 73 pioneer Japanese farmers . . . were informed of the victory . . . in silent prayer." These modest graves symbolically reminded later generations of their own need to defend their place in that part of the frontier. As a *Rafu Shimpo* English-language reporter wrote, "Standing before each of the 73 tombstones marking the remains of the first Japanese who perished . . . in their effort to convert the cactus and sagebrush land into the fertile farm land that it is today, the living successors recalled the struggle endured by these Japanese who did the impossible where any white man had not even made an attempt."[50]

Ordinary immigrants elsewhere erected new monuments to commemorate their pioneer struggles, often in a transnational manner. While secular organizations usually took the initiative in such efforts, many individual residents contributed enthusiastically. In June 1937, for example, the Federation of the Southern California Japanese Women's Associations launched a community-wide fundraiser to build a twenty-foot-high tower in memory of "the nameless who had fought a peaceful war [for Japanese development] in this land till they perished." Donations poured into the federation's coffers, and in less than six months the memorial was dedicated before a crowd of more than 3,000, and the president of the federation compared the Issei's contributions to the con-quest of the American frontier with the "brave Japanese soldiers who died glorious deaths for our homeland" on its Manchurian frontier.[51] Commonly built in the midst of Japanese cemeteries, such monuments set up permanent sites where Issei and their descendants could readily claim both their unbreak-able ties to the Western land and their dual heritage. This memorialization went hand in hand with the building throughout rural Japan of material sym-bols that celebrated the pioneering role of the Issei in overseas development. Public memorials, built by Issei in their Japanese hometowns as well as their American destinations, gave many lay people a way to collaborate with the historians in etching their place in the national histories and on the topogra-phies of Japan and the United States.

THE TRANSNATIONAL AND THE LOCAL IN THE ISSEI PIONEER THESIS

The image of the Issei as dedicated Japanese colonists proved to be open to distortions and a variety of interpretations. The transnational exchange of ideas in history making did not simply place Japanese immigrants at its receiving end; the process was reciprocal. During the late 1930s, imperial Japan found the Issei pioneer thesis a convenient justification for a policy of expansionism in Asia. Tokyo's cooptation of Issei history also took place in its anti-West racial ideology and its own history making. Many Issei publications, such as *Zaibei Nihonjinshi*, found a keen audience across the Pacific, because they served the political agendas of the empire, which self-righteously proclaimed to seek global racial justice in confronting Euro-American powers. Often, Japanese intellec-tuals manipulated the pioneer thesis to bolster their assertion of supremacy to Westerners—an idea that ran counter to the Issei's eclectic belief in racial com-patibility. According to imperial orthodoxy, Japanese exclusion in the American West was explained by "the whites' fear of Japanese superiority," and legal discrimination had crystallized the Anglo Americans' "confessions of defeat as a race."[52]

安らかに眠れ——海外開拓の人柱

南加婦人會聯盟主催の下に千九百卅七年十一月十二日

エバグリン墓地にて除幕式を行ひたる

在留同胞先亡者慰靈塔

IREI-TO......A Lasting Memory To the Pioneers
Evergreen Cemetery, Los Angeles Unveiled November 12, 1937

FIGURE 4.2. Issei Pioneer Memorial in Evergreen Cemetery, Los Angeles, 1937
The Federation of the Southern California Japanese Women's Associations collected donations to build this monument, dedicated in November 1937. Its Japanese caption reads,
"Rest in peace: martyrs of overseas development." Reprinted from Rafu Shimpōsha, *Rafu
nenkan, 1938–1939*. Courtesy of the *Rafu Shimpo* and the Japanese American National Museum, Los Angeles (96.5.65).

Printed in Japan's bestselling magazine in 1933, the image of an Issei farmer with his two "American" workers on their hands and knees, tethered to a plow like farm animals, exemplified a decisive rupture in racial consciousness between imperial Japanese and Japanese immigrants.[53] This misinterpretation effected two forms of denial. Divorcing the immigrant discourse from its constitutive context, Japan's rendition replaced the Issei's survivalist tenet with a racist vision of Japanese hegemony. Concurrently, immigrant dualism fell victim to Japanese domestication of a transnational history.

Given the utility of Issei history, Tokyo took a formal step to make the immigrant discourse serviceable for its imperialist orthodoxy through a nation-wide commemoration of the pioneers of overseas development in November 1940. Convened under the aegis of the Japanese Ministry of Foreign Affairs and the Colonial Ministry, the Tokyo Convention of Overseas Japanese gave the first official sanction to the international aspect of the Issei pioneer thesis. To participate in the national celebration of the 2,600th anniversary of the enthronement of the first Japanese emperor, Tokyo invited nearly 1,500 representatives from Japanese settlements in North America, Hawaii, Latin America, Southeast Asia, Micronesia, and the Asian continent. The United States accounted for the biggest delegation with 794 representatives, including Toga and many other historians. A distant second was the Southeast Asia–Micronesia group (314), followed by East Asia (198), and Latin America (193).[54] To arouse the interest of the Japanese people in state-sponsored colonial endeavors, the government hailed the Issei and, to a lesser degree, other overseas Japanese as national heroes. In the process, Japan claimed ownership of the Issei pioneer thesis as a national past and convinced the Japanese masses of this through spectacular ceremony.

On November 4, 1940, the Grand Celebration March kicked off a five-day program. The 1,500 "overseas compatriots" marched through central Tokyo, accompanied by musical bands and thousands of domestic participants. Following the rising sun flag were the leaders of the procession, two elderly Issei from northern California. Japanese officials handpicked them to head the march because they were the actual "forerunners" of Japan's "70-year history of overseas development." Indeed, the pageant was the visual manifestation of that history, which was still unfolding and progressing. After the Issei elders came the Hawaii delegation, followed by contingents from the mainland United States, Canada, Southeast Asia–Micronesia, Latin America, and finally those from China and Manchuria—the rough chronological order of Japan's emigration history. The remainder of the march consisted of 3,000 domestic high school and college students aspiring to join the ranks of the "overseas compatriots" in the near future.[55] This pageantry brought together different trajectories of past overseas development and fused the disparate, often contradictory ex-

FIGURE 4.3. **Issei Pioneer Thesis, appropriated by Japan's imperial racism, 1933**
In 1933, a popular Japanese magazine printed this cartoon, showing a successful Issei
farmer with his two "American" workers on their hands and knees like farm animals. It
mirrored mainstream racial thinking in Japan, which asserted superiority over westerners.
In its stark contrast to the self-image of "the Japanese in America" under the heavy burden of "exclusion," this Japanese appropriation reveals the gap between the perceptions of
Issei and those of people in Japan. It also testifies to the political utility of the Issei pioneer thesis for Japan's imperialist agenda. Reprinted from *Kingu* 9 (Oct. 1933), 171, Tokyo.

periences of Japanese abroad into a monolithic, grand narrative of imperial
expansion. The rest of the convention featured the presentation of historical
data through exhibitions and public lectures, including Toga's well-attended
colloquium on Issei history.[56] Demonstrating a national expansionist history
personified and related by actual Issei pioneers, the five-day ceremony received
extensive coverage in the rigidly censored print media in Japan, and it impressed
on the domestic populace the patriotic services their compatriots in America

had purportedly rendered to the homeland at the early stage of its expansion. Up until 1945, imperialist orthodoxy continued to enshrine the Issei as pioneers.

Not only did most Issei not protest Japan's appropriation of the pioneer thesis, many were ecstatic about the historical mythologizing because they felt that their role in overseas development was finally receiving due recognition from their homeland.[57] The decoration of meritorious Issei by the state further reinforced the conviction that their national contribution was second to none; many saw the honors as conferred not on selected individuals but on all Japanese in America.[58] Along with the usual list of honorees, like politicians, military men, and scholars, the Issei—formerly the mass of national disgrace—entered the ranks of national heroes. A wave of joy and pride led to a local reenactment of this pageant in virtually every Japanese immigrant community on the West Coast. In Los Angeles, November 10 was designated as the day of celebration. The main gathering of community leaders included speeches, Shinto rituals, and three cheers of *banzai*, after which they proceeded to the local Issei memorial to pay tribute to the fallen pioneers. Coupled with these formal proceedings was a variety of cultural and athletic programs. Most notable were tournaments of various martial arts and sports, where Nisei were the contenders.[59] The public display of their youthful vigor, competitive spirit, and physical might formed a striking contrast to the commemorations of the past that preceded it.

Although these developments in late 1940 may appear to have signaled the end of Issei dualism, Japanese immigrants still maintained a degree of autonomy in defining the meaning of their history on their own terms. In other words, the transformation in Japan of immigrant history into imperialist orthodoxy did not supersede the meaning of this race history in Issei society, since Japanese immigrants continued to insist on a corporate identity as an American minority. From the American West to Japan, and back, the Issei pioneer thesis underwent yet another process of reappropriation to mitigate the effect of its arbitrary domestication by Japan, although the immigrants still embraced what seemed to be beneficial to them, such as state recognition. The manner in which the Issei reenacted Japan's national pageantry was a case in point. In Los Angeles, it took the form of commemorating the deceased Issei of yesteryear and celebrating the growing Nisei of tomorrow. Japan, as enacted in the martial arts and cultural demonstrations, served as a reference point to the fundamental local change, that is, the transition from the first-generation to the second-generation era, which Issei history predicted would lead to the resurrection of Japanese America. It still rested with their rendition of the national pageantry to principally articulate the teleology of the generational shift within their own community.

The Issei's insistence on the local therefore deserves further analysis beyond what was written in the pages of their chronicles. Japanese immigrant history making had its ideological roots in the Issei quest to overcome racial subordination in the American West. The dualism of the pioneer thesis constituted a pivotal rhetorical strategy that countered such inequality by appealing to the theory of Japanese-white compatibility and the example of Japan's ascent in international relations. Transnational as the Issei consciousness appeared prima facie, this narrative construction did not transcend the concrete realities of existence. Far from suffering from false consciousness, Issei historians and their audiences were perfectly cognizant of their constrained and restricted lives as a racial minority in the United States. Candidly, in their publications, immigrant authors always intimated the enduring presence of an overbearing power: white hegemony.[60] The paradox of celebrating development in spite of subordination was a notable feature of the Issei pioneer thesis that can be fully understood only in the local context of race relations.

As important as it was, history making formed but one of the diverse currents in the social and intellectual efforts of Japanese immigrants after racial exclusion. Instead of looking back at their pasts, other endeavors directly addressed the dilemmas and challenges with which the ethnic community was grappling in order to prepare for the coming Nisei era. In complex ways, history making was intertwined with these community projects in the service of the racial successors in America.

5

The Problem of Generation

Preparing the Nisei for the Future

The related themes of the Issei as pioneers and the Nisei as carrying on Japanese development in the United States were central discourses in the upbringing of many American-born youths. During the 1930s, the average age of male Issei approached sixty, and although most of the Nisei were still in their teens, the second-generation era appeared to be looming closer. As a way to call the Nisei's attention to this point, Japanese immigrant dailies often featured English-language essays and editorials that highlighted key aspects of the pioneer thesis; immigrant educators taught racial history to their Nisei pupils at Japanese-language schools.[1] Oratorical contests, usually sponsored by regional Japanese American Citizens League (JACL) chapters or other youth organizations, provided the Nisei with a venue for demonstrating their understanding of Issei tribulations, as well as the mission of their generation. Many juvenile orators— usually local honors students—recited passages that seem to have come directly from Japanese immigrant chronicles. At the San Francisco Bay Region JACL Oratorical Contest in 1936, a young woman addressed her fellow Nisei in English:

> Our parents have provided us with a good, strong foundation, which
> they have created through many untold hardships and sacrifices. They
> came to this strange land, unable to speak the language of the people
> who dwell here. They have gone through thick and thin to make a good

name for the Japanese people . . . We must, and should, show our appreciation for their work, and carry on the work which our parents have so well planned for us . . . It is our duty to lay an even stronger foundation for the coming generation—the third.[2]

As Issei leaders and writers had desired, their history had apparently inspired many Nisei to base their personal aspirations in creating a positive future for the Japanese in America.

Yet, neither the Issei pioneer thesis nor its interpretation by Nisei orators revealed a concrete picture of what the future might really hold for the new generation of Japanese Americans. How did Issei leaders expect the American-born to carry on Japanese development in the face of racial subordination? In what ways did immigrant parents attempt to enable their children to do this? What did Nisei "duty" really mean in the sociohistorical context in which these concepts were enunciated? The answers to these questions are to be found not so much in the intellectual productions of immigrant historians as in their social practices. This chapter explores some of the key community-wide efforts made by immigrant leaders and parents to promote a positive prospect for the Japanese minority in America in the postexclusion era.

TACKLING THE "NISEI PROBLEM"

The hopes of Japanese immigrants for the coming era manifested in a number of social programs to grapple with the so-called Nisei problem (*Dai-Nisei mondai*)—a concept that resonated with the contemporary mainstream discourse on the "marginal man."[3] Formulated by University of Chicago sociologist Robert Park, the marginal man theory placed a transitional category between the two ends of an assimilation process. This scheme sees children of immigrants as being caught between the obstinate influences of the Old World, embodied by the first generation, and the forces of Americanization emanating from the larger society. Neither completely alien nor fully (Anglo) American, the second generation stands somewhere between the divided worlds. From the late 1920s, Chicago sociologists theorized on the types of problems that marginal people, like the Nisei, would face in American society, and the theory quickly caught on with the general public.[4]

Weaving this dominant formulation into their peculiar sense of history and the idea of Japanese-American compatibilities (not divides), Issei leaders and parents categorized the post-1924 challenges to racial development as specifically the "Nisei problem," which ranged from questions of marriage to employment, and from education to the racial inferiority complex.[5] It is important to note that the Issei's conception of generational dilemmas did not presume naturalness as did white assimilation theorists, since the immigrants treated the Nisei problem as a racially prescribed one, a product of exclusion, rather than that of ubiquitous cultural conflict. In other words, the marginality of the second-generation Japanese Americans was construed as a unique racial condition in the postexclusion era, not simply as a legacy of alienation from the mainstream cultures of Japan and the United States. Historicizing the difficulties of the Nisei marginal man in terms of the Issei pioneer past was hence a standard practice among Japanese immigrants. Following the narrative of the glorious yesteryear wronged by white racism, indeed, concluding chapters of Japanese immigrant chronicles usually concentrated on discussions of second-generation issues. Revealing the particular visions of a racial future that many Issei shared, such a scheme appeared to diverge from the ordinary project of history, that is, a rendition of the past. Yet, the very purpose of Issei history making validated this divergence insofar as the pioneer thesis was meant to augur a resurrection of Japanese Americans as a race. The immigrant generation believed the Nisei problem could be solved only by drawing on the spirit of race history instead of by merely losing the influences of the old culture and traditions and merging into white America.

Based on this principle, Japanese immigrants took a two-pronged approach to tackle the Nisei problem. Some programs were designed to construct socioeconomic conditions suitable for the activities of the younger generation as an integral but distinct racial element of American society. The manipulation of Nisei occupational patterns and demographic composition formed the centerpiece of this endeavor. Other Issei programs sought to mold the Nisei mind, using education to preserve a "proper" racial lineage and "uniquely Japanese" qualities. Japanese immigrant social engineering encompassed the production of external and internal conditions that would help steer the Nisei in prescribed directions for the ultimate purpose of racial development.

Just as Issei writers posited the Nisei problem as unique to American-born Japanese, not ubiquitous to all second-generation Japanese abroad, the meaning and scope of Japanese development hinged entirely on the political economy of the American West. In the 1930s, one of the few conceivable spheres of development was farming. The Japanese preeminence in some areas of Western agriculture, notwithstanding legal discrimination, reinforced Issei historians' claims that Japanese had "racially endowed" farming skills, and also strengthened the general conviction that agriculture was—and would remain—the principal industry for Nisei citizens, who would face fewer artificial obstacles.[6] Indeed, as late as 1939, statistics showed that Japanese farmers were responsible for producing approximately 97 percent of the berries, 82 percent of the onions, 59 percent of the celery, 45 percent of the asparagus, and 36 percent of the potatoes in northern California. In southern California, they grew over 97 percent of market greens, 96 percent of cauliflower, 93 percent of berries, 92 percent of celery, 83 percent of tomatoes, and 51 percent of cantaloupes and other kinds of melons.[7] What Issei writers often described as "solid foundations" pointed to this occupational concentration.

The semicolonial conditions of Japanese farmers in the West belied these impressive statistics and the Issei's flowery characterizations of the Japanese as agriculturalists, however. The Japanese farmers occupied a subordinate position within an industrial pyramid headed by a white agribusiness elite. Due to the alien land laws, the vast majority of Issei farmers barely eked out a living working as illegal tenants or hired foremen during the Depression. The kinds of crops in which they specialized demanded intensive labor in lieu of capital outlay. More prosperous white farmers usually avoided raising these crops. When speaking of development, Issei writers and parents anticipated that their children would maintain the economic niche that they had carved out in Western agriculture, thereby preserving the occupational structure and the distorted socioeconomic orientation reserved for this racial minority.[8] It is ironic that the overall exclusion of the Japanese from most other economic sectors, which caused their lopsided involvement in agriculture in the first place, gave them this hope, when in reality Issei farming underscored the severe limitations to Japanese livelihoods in the United States. In defense of their agricultural niche, the source of their optimism, the Japanese community launched two programs: the Back-to-the-Farm movement (*Kino undo*) and the Return-to-America campaign (*Kibei undo*).

Officially inaugurated in 1935, the Back-to-the-Farm movement aimed to persuade young Nisei men—and Nisei women as their wives—to return to the countryside to take over their parents' farms. Throughout the 1930s, many Issei were troubled by their children's apparent indifference to farming. The vernacular press frequently lamented the Nisei's inclination to "swing away from land into white-collar pursuit[s]" and their tendency to move into cities after completing their secondary education.[9] An editorial in the *Kashu Mainichi* of Los Angeles warned that because the Japanese community's livelihood revolved around agriculture and allied pursuits, such as wholesale distribution, transportation, and retailing, the move to urban living could "presage a serious crisis in the occupational status of the Japanese in America."[10] Similarly, comparing the significance of Manchuria to imperial Japan with that of agriculture to themselves, Shiro Fujioka called the industry their "life-line" and insisted that the Nisei must defend the vested interests of the ethnic community. The Issei historian and community leader urged his fellow immigrants to "guide and nurture the majority of the nisei toward the farming industry as our successors."[11]

Fueling Issei wariness was the prevailing Social Darwinist notion of "racial struggle." This theme frequently appears within contemporary chronicles of immigrant history. For example, one historian argued that Issei laborers had been forced to compete with Chinese, Italians, and Greeks before they climbed to a "dominant" position in the farming class of California. "Just as we, the Issei, did," he continued, "our Nisei are also destined to compete with all enemies in our race war."[12] In the 1930s, the Japanese community foresaw confronting diverse "enemies," including Filipino and Mexican immigrants. In that the Nisei would inherit this racial competition, they were urged to follow in their parents' footsteps and preserve Japanese agriculture at all costs.

As a product of such anxieties, the Back-to-the-Farm movement involved a variety of measures. In many parts of California, Japanese associations provided intensive agricultural lessons to the sons of immigrant farmers. In Walnut Grove, for example, an agricultural specialist from San Francisco taught such topics as the cultivation of tomato and seed crops, spraying, and soil analysis for two days, after which some twenty Nisei participants received certificates of completion. Between 1935 and 1938, a total of 182 Nisei—sixty-three in the San Joaquin Valley, forty-five in the Sacramento area, thirty-eight in Watsonville, and thirty-six in San Jose—completed a similar lecture series and received certification. To further facilitate their learning of different farming methods and to foster intraethnic ties among the successors, Issei leaders advised Nisei youngsters to form agricultural study groups whose members would visit settlements throughout rural California.[13]

Farm organizations often sponsored oratorical contests in which selected youngsters addressed audiences on the importance of agriculture. In Los Angeles, with the backing of the immigrant press, the Southern California Japanese Farm Federation and the Cooperative Farm Industry (the latter consisting mainly of wholesalers) coordinated a massive regional effort to promote Nisei interest in agriculture. One of the organizers told Issei parents that he wished Nisei orators to help "arrest their tendency to leave farms for city life and give a hopeful vision to their fellow Nisei in farming."[14] With the "future of Japanese agriculture in California and their [generational] mission" as its organizing theme, the All–Southern California Oratorical Contest drew an audience of 800 Issei and Nisei to Los Angeles's Little Tokyo in December 1935. As Issei leaders anticipated, the key thesis put forth by all three top speakers centered on the Nisei as the successors to Japanese agriculture.

For example, Isamu Masuda of Orange County, the first-prize winner, emphasized that the immigrant generation "ha[s] built a foundation for us" despite anti-Japanese laws, language barriers, and cultural differences. He believed that the second generation shared a special talent for farming with their parents that no other group possessed and also mentioned that the Nisei held a privileged position as native-born Americans exempt from the restrictions of the alien land laws. Agriculture, according to Masuda, would enable the Nisei "to raise [their] standard of living, and to leave conditions in a much better state for the Sansei [the third generation] than the Issei [were] leaving for [them]."[15] The Nisei's return to the soil was more than a matter of personal preference, the speaker stressed. Not only was it supposed to preordain the restoration of their collective economic strength but it would also salvage a progressive race history that malicious whites had temporarily subverted.

To shore up the propagandizing effect of these endeavors, Los Angeles leaders commissioned local Japanese movie makers to produce a film on behalf of the Back-to-the-Farm movement in late 1936. Titled *The Growing Nisei* (Nobiyuku Nisei), this full-length silent film featured a mostly Nisei cast with a few Issei and one white American. Scripted by an immigrant writer, it dramatized major aspects of the Nisei problem from the Issei standpoint, including the generational conflict, the tragedy of interracial love affairs, lack of opportunity in urban America, juvenile delinquency and moral decay, and, finally, the need to return to the soil for regeneration. The plot focused on a young Nisei man in a rural community who falls in love with a white girl, leading to a serious conflict with his immigrant father, a farmer. Rebelling against his father's order to break up with his girlfriend, the Nisei asks her to elope, but she refuses. Dejected, he runs away to Los Angeles, where he finds employment in a Japanese vegetable market. Later, he gets into a fistfight in a gambling joint. Believing that he has hurt the other party, he returns to his family farm, only to clash again with his father. At the height of their argument, his Issei father is fatally stricken with a heart attack. The death of the old man signifies the ultimate sacrifice of the older generation for the younger generation, leading to the son's rebirth as a person and as a Japanese American. Realizing the madness of the urban jungle, he decides to stay on the farm where there is familial love and a viable future. With the help of his dedicated Nisei fiancée, he ends up organizing a cooperative movement among the young Japanese American farmers in his community.[16]

Mediated by the theme of the unbreakable bond between the Western land and Japanese America, this film was full of Issei teleology. The transformation of the protagonist from a selfish delinquent/rebel into a community-minded farm leader exemplified what many immigrant parents wished to see happen with their seemingly shiftless sons. Likewise, the supporting role of the Nisei girlfriend and future wife provided a prototype of the idealized Japanese American woman, which parents projected onto their Nisei daughters. The birth on the land of the racially conscious second generation was seen as naturally leading to the formation of a monoracial Nisei family and a consolidation of community resources for the further development of all Japanese Americans. The vernacular press frequently reported that *The Growing Nisei* enjoyed enthusiastic receptions throughout California and beyond, although perhaps more from Issei audiences than from Nisei.[17]

As the film's ending suggests, the Back-to-the Farm movement culminated in the birth of a central Nisei farm organization. In June 1939, under the joint sponsorship of the Japanese Association of America, the Central Japanese Association of Southern California, and the Federation of Japanese Farmers, the two-day All-California Japanese Farmers Conference paved the way to what appeared to be a historic shift in Japanese ethnic agriculture. Dedicating the first day to an intergenerational meeting, the conference commenced with a moment of silence in memory of deceased Japanese pioneers in the United States. The next day, Issei leaders officially passed the torch to the second-generation delegates, who resolved to form their own association. To entice more American-born youths into farming, Nisei farmers also proposed to cooperate with the JACL, which agreed to establish agricultural bureaus within its organization. They further requested that the vernacular press promote "the solidarity of Nisei farmers and the importance of their future" in their English-language sections.[18] Two ongoing programs—lectures on farming and study tours—would also receive renewed attention and better coordination from the first- and second-generation farmers organizations in each community.

In April 1940, the first Nisei farmers convention met in Los Angeles. Drawing fifty-two delegates from all over California, it passed a unanimous resolution to establish the Nisei Farmers' Federation of California. An Issei farm leader confessed before hundreds of Issei and Nisei in the audience, "Until five or six years ago, I worried so much about the Nisei's ability to inherit our agricultural base. Today, about 90 percent of the attendants at agricultural lectures are Nisei, and they do not have a 'get-rich-quickly' [sojourner] mentality; they are committed to farming, which looks really promising."[19] Several months later, *Zaibei Nihonjinshi* commented that, based on the April meeting, "[W]e can deduce how seriously the Nisei are trying to take the legacy of their ancestors to a higher stage of development."[20] Meanwhile, influenced by the success of the California endeavors, the North American Japanese Association of Seattle began to sponsor an annual Second Generation Conference on Agricultural Problems. Convened first in November 1939 and again in December 1940, this one-day conference brought from each Japanese farm settlement in Washington two to four Nisei, who sat through lectures and discussions offered by experts from state and county agricultural experimental stations.[21] The organization of these institutional structures marked the dawning of the Nisei era in Japanese agriculture in the American West.

The actual impact of the Back-to-the-Farm movement is hard to gauge because there are no statistics on how many Nisei returned to, or stayed in,

第二回全加州邦人農家大會

增の中央は議長 茅野恒司氏立てはる加州二世農家聯盟會長 恵古勝氏

FIGURE 5.1. Inauguration of the Nisei Farmers' Federation of California, April 1940
Under the watchful eyes of Issei farm leaders, Nisei farmers formed their own organization for the cause of "racial development." Standing in the center is Thomas Yego of New
Castle, declaring the formation of the federation. Some 160 Nisei and 125 Issei from all
over California attended this conference, marking the climax of the Back-to-the-Farm
movement. Reprinted from *Beikoku Chūō Nihonjinkaishi* (1940).

agriculture as a result. Whether it was a direct effect or simply a consequence
of an aging immigrant generation, there was considerable turnover of farm titles
and actual operation of farms from the first to the second generation by the
early 1940s. In Los Angeles County, for example, the number of Japanese farms
under Nisei operation had increased to 757 by February 1942, compared to only
634 still under Issei operation. Nisei farmers were already responsible for 58
percent of the 26,045 acres being cultivated by Japanese in the county. Even
among the 634 farms run by Issei, 247 had one or more Nisei at least twenty-
one years old working on the premises.[22] Most of these Nisei were the sons of
Issei farmers; they would probably have taken over the farms after a few years
of practical training had it not been for the Pacific War.

Another notable program that supported the idea of the Nisei as racial
successors was the so-called Return-to-America campaign. Typical of minority
middlemen in a racially stratified industrial structure, Japanese immigrant farmers originally forged their strength around uninhibited access to the cheap but

able labor of their compatriots, who in turn required the intermediary roles of Issei farmers as employers and translators.[23] The abundance, as well as the vitality, of the Japanese workforce therefore preconditioned the integrity and competitiveness of ethnic agriculture. The Return-to-America campaign was integral to the Issei effort to safeguard their agricultural interests and was based on the unbreakable link between group labor and farming success. Designed to bring back the American-born who had been reared in Japan (known as *Kibei Nisei*; hereafter Kibei), the campaign was principally intended to maintain an influx of fresh Japanese workers, despite the 1924 Immigration Act, in order to fortify the agricultural basis of racial development. If American-educated Nisei took over their fathers' farms, Japanese-educated Kibei were meant to collaborate with them as loyal employees once back in their native land. In this manner, the Back-to-the-Farm movement and the Return-to-America campaign were interwoven in the immigrants' general quest for Japanese development.[24]

Although some local communities had already carried out an informal Kibei campaign starting in the early 1930s, the passage of the Filipino Repatriation Act of 1935 accelerated an official statewide effort. To remove Filipino immigrants (colonized U.S. nationals exempt from the 1924 law) from the continental United States, the legislation provided them with transportation to the Philippines at the expense of the U.S. federal government on the condition that they forfeit the right to reenter the country. Because Filipinos had become an indispensable part of the labor force on Japanese farms since the mid-1920s, the government's initial prediction that the law would reduce the Filipino population by half alarmed many Issei farmers about the prospect of an acute labor shortage. At the same time, many saw the situation as a great opportunity to take back the labor market from a racial "enemy."[25]

In September 1935, the Japanese Association of America and the Japanese Association of Los Angeles launched a joint Return-to-America campaign, dispatching two envoys to Japan to persuade second-generation youths there to join their Nisei brothers and sisters across the Pacific. While asking for financial support from the Japanese government, the Issei representatives crisscrossed southwestern Japan, giving lectures on the conditions of the Japanese in America and publicizing the goal and scope of the campaign in local newspapers. These direct appeals were repeated the following year, even though Tokyo opposed the campaign from a diplomatic standpoint. Meanwhile, Issei leaders back home hastily compiled a pamphlet, *Kibei no shiori* (Guide to Returning to America), which detailed legal procedures, offered practical advice, and delineated the rationale behind the campaign.[26]

Estimated at 40,000 to 60,000, the American-born living in Japan formed a crucial age group needed by the ethnic community because of immigration exclusion. The guide predicted that under the poisonous effects of the 1924

Immigration Act, the number of Issei males would drop quickly from 34,000 to 12,000 between 1935 and 1940. At the same time, there would be fewer than 8,000 Nisei men over twenty years old residing in the United States. With the most productive group in the immigrant generation rapidly decreasing, the consequences to Japanese agriculture in the West would be severe. The pamphlet for the Kibei thus noted:

> Such a situation will resemble the perilous state of Chinese agriculture in California around 1892. By that time, the impact of the 1882 Chinese Exclusion Act was felt everywhere, and within the next ten years, the Japanese easily took over Chinese farms, which lacked their own heirs. With the shortage of Nisei successors, our agriculture has already lost the labor market to Filipinos and Mexicans because older Japanese laborers cannot compete . . . Our farms, which we, the pioneers of this new land, established in the last four decades, despite anti-Japanese exclusion, are panting under the shortage of racial successors; now we face the same fate our Chinese counterparts succumbed to forty years ago.[27]

Given the significant pool of young Nisei in Japan, many Issei believed that their return migration to America would allow the ethnic community to circumvent such a fate.

Their sense of fear and urgency was so deep that, in addition to an orchestrated effort by the central community organizations, a number of individual immigrants and local associations strove to arrest the depletion of the Japanese population in the United States. In 1936, eighty-year-old Matsunosuke Tsukamoto of San Francisco volunteered to go to Japan. He spent two months in Tokyo and another two months traveling throughout major "emigrant prefectures," where he met with local politicians, journalists, and high-ranking bureaucrats and attempted to sell them on the idea of systematically returning the Kibei to America.[28] His argument faithfully followed the logic of the pioneer thesis. Speaking before a group of elite Tokyoites, he said:

> It is my advice that second generation Japanese who possess full rights in the United States return there in this emergency. It is for them to take up the work started by the first generation in America. The "isseis" have worked their entire lives to create a place in America for their children . . . The first generation has developed the possibilities for the Nisei in America—in basic industries, farming, marketing and merchandising. I wish these Nisei [in Japan] would cherish this heritage from their parent generation.[29]

The appeal of this elderly immigrant pioneer understandably attracted much media attention in Japan.[30]

Others spent their own funds and time bringing Kibei back to Pacific Coast states. A leading farmer in the Sacramento delta financed a newspaper advertisement in Kumamoto, his home prefecture, announcing that he would pay the steerage fare for those youths who wished to come back to the United States. Thirty Nisei applied. After examining their school records and family backgrounds, the Issei employer selected four men to work on his asparagus farm. Another immigrant farmer visited his hometown in Japan, then brought five Kibei back to California, where he helped them find work and housing.[31] The Wakayama Prefectural Association raised a special fund of $3,000 so that it could offer $200 loans to Kibei men who had no family members living in the United States, then helped them to secure employment upon their arrival in Los Angeles.[32] Likewise, Walnut Grove added a dozen Kibei to the local agricultural labor force through the office of its Japanese association secretary during the last five months of 1935. The success of this local campaign continued with the return from Japan of thirty-nine American-born youths in 1936 and twenty-three in 1937. According to a boardinghouse owner in Walnut Grove, these Kibei were "the finest and most efficient workers," and they, along with some Hawaiian-born Nisei and students, already constituted half of the entire Japanese labor force in the delta community by 1938.[33] Many Issei there viewed the increase in the local Kibei population and their competitiveness as signaling a promising future.

The Kibei campaign had an additional purpose: to solve the second-generation marriage "problem" that Issei leaders defined as a priority in 1938. With the most recent statistics, the Japanese Association of America announced that an estimated 3,500 Nisei women in their mid- to late twenties were yet to be married. Until the middle of the 1910s, immigrant couples had produced more female babies than male, whereas the gender balance more or less normalized thereafter.[34] To this was added the time-honored immigrant practice of sending older sons to Japan for education while grooming daughters for womanhood under their parents' watchful eyes in America. The 1930s witnessed the increase in the Nisei population of the "old misses," who were prevented from fulfilling their supposed roles as wives and mothers of their co-ethnics. Unless the ethnic community enabled those Nisei women to marry within, Issei leaders feared the problem might eventually endanger the racial integrity of the Japanese in America. Some regional Japanese associations set up marriage introduction bureaus and hosted dance parties and other events for Nisei, but hundreds of marriageable women still failed to unite with Japanese mates of their age cohorts.[35] Issei reasoned that the "immigration" of adult Kibei men would be the best, and perhaps only, solution, thus tying the objectives of the ongoing campaign to the overriding concern over racial preservation. Not only would the Japan-educated Nisei men revitalize the ethnic economy, but they would also facilitate intraethnic family formation.

Like the Back-to-the-Farm movement, the Return-to-America campaign seemed to have achieved a degree of success after 1935, despite Tokyo's refusal to lend support and the sporadic agitation of white exclusionists.[36] The *Shin Sekai* reported that a total of 850 Kibei returned to the United States during the first nine months of 1936. Since the previous yearly average ranged around 500, it was indeed a big increase. The number of Kibei returnees rose higher after the beginning of the Sino-Japanese War in 1937, when young American-born men with dual citizenship left Japan to avoid conscription into the Japanese army.[37]

MOLDING THE NISEI MIND

The manipulation of the Nisei occupational structure and demography constituted only part of Japanese immigrant social engineering during the 1930s. The Issei recognized that the transformation of their community depended upon Nisei choices made within the political economy of the American West. Many immigrants therefore felt it necessary to mold the Nisei mind toward an understanding of the collective racial ideal so that they would effectively undertake their generational mission. Immigrant leaders, educators, and parents attempted to nurture what they termed *Nippon seishin*, or Japanese spirit, in each and every Nisei. They interpreted the Japanese spirit as the wellspring of inner strength that would regulate the Nisei world view and practices. When Issei talked about this highly elusive concept, they generally referred to two core elements. The first was a set of moral values that they regarded as authentically "Japanese"; second was a strong sense of racial pride or racial consciousness. Together these would instill the second generation with uniquely Japanese self-discipline and a sense of obligation, and motivate them to cooperate in pursuit of a meaningful future for the racial collectivity.

In order to teach the Japanese spirit to Nisei children, the Japanese immigrant community set up various educational programs in the late 1920s following an intense debate on appropriate curricula and pedagogies from the standpoint of racial development. Like other aspects of the discourse on the second-generation problem, the immigrant discussion of Nisei education unfolded under the general influence of anti-Japanese racism. Advocates of Japanese exclusion first raised the issue of what they perceived as an apparent contradiction between American citizenship and the education that Nisei were receiving at community-based Japanese-language schools. This agitation culminated in the enactment in 1921 of a California law, which censored the content of textbooks used at those schools and required Issei teachers to be certified by the California superintendent of public instruction. Thereafter, until the court ruling against the constitutionality of Hawaii's equivalent law in 1927, legally mandated Americanization was forced on the Nisei even at Japanese-language schools. Their educational program during this period included replacing stories about a heroic Japanese warrior and his self-effacing and chaste wife with stories about George Washington and Betsy Ross. Though no legal restriction was instituted in other Western states, most Issei educators there followed the example of their California colleagues, compiling sanitized textbooks or providing pupils with "American" instruction in Japanese.[38]

Even before the court decision invalidated state intervention, a fierce debate started in May 1925 with regard to the new directions of Nisei education. Ohashi Chuichi, the Japanese consul in Seattle, provoked public discourse by printing a series of newspaper commentaries which ascribed a cause of racial discrimination to the presence of Japanese-language schools. Published in Issei papers in Seattle and San Francisco, the diplomat's articles strongly opposed Japanese-language education and reproved community schools for producing "half-baked Americans who are neither American nor Japanese." Ohashi was also concerned that Japanese education would result in a racist backlash, which might seek to strip the Nisei of American citizenship. For the Japanese community to avoid "a suicidal death" because of the language schools, he recommended that the Nisei be raised as "[one] hundred-percent American," with absolutely no instruction in Japanese language or history.[39]

Ohashi's articles invited a storm of criticism, as well as sporadic but enthusiastic support. The Seattle-based *Taihoku Nippo* printed both pro and con articles from many immigrants throughout the month of June 1925. In the *Shin Sekai* of San Francisco, two leading Issei educators contributed counterarguments. One of them interwove his article with positive personal experiences of teaching Japanese to the Nisei.[40] While the *Taihoku Nippo* seems to have devoted almost the same amount of space to both sides, the San Francisco newspaper, with one exception, only carried articles critical of Ohashi. Newspapers that had not printed Ohashi's original series contested his viewpoint in editorials as well.[41] The list of reasons given to support Japanese-language education were both practical and philosophical. It was seen as necessary to promote better communication between parents and children and to enable the second generation to understand their parents' homeland, appreciate their cultural background, and take pride in their racial heritage. The command of Japanese language would also expand the range of employment options for the Nisei, given their general exclusion from the mainstream job market. While the opinions voiced by the Issei in the newspapers were not unanimous, the anti-Ohashi argument appears to have been more prevalent.

The 1925 dispute between pro-Americanization advocates and Japanese-school supporters reflected two contesting views regarding the future of the Japanese community at an early stage in a wholesale epistemological shift following exclusion. Insisting that the Nisei be fully assimilated into Anglo America, Ohashi and a minority of the Issei optimistically envisioned merit-based upward social mobility for the second generation.[42] The majority of the immigrants, however, predicted that the endurance of white racism would circumscribe the Nisei activities and continue to relegate them to an inferior sociopolitical status, the same social conditions that had necessitated the Back-to-the-Farm movement and the Return-to-America campaign in the first place.[43] In their eyes, Anglo conformity and assimilation would not suffice.

In accordance with the emergence of Japan as a conceptual frame of reference in the Issei pioneer thesis, Ohashi's idea quickly became obsolete. By the late 1920s, whether or not Japanese education was necessary for the Nisei was no longer a matter of dispute. A case involving one immigrant leader was indicative of this dramatic shift. At the end of July 1928, Naoki Oka, a Japanese association secretary and language teacher in Isleton, California, attempted to revive the old controversy by reiterating Ohashi's argument in the *Shin Sekai*. Praising the consul for his "farsighted" ideas, Oka condemned Japanese-language schools for "producing [culturally] deformed Nisei" through "an education based on the Japanese spirit," and instead called for Japanese development through total assimilation into Anglo America. Despite his work as a Japanese-language schoolteacher, he claimed that it was the height of folly for the Issei to impose on the Nisei a Japanese code of ethics which was "anathema to the American public."[44] His appeal rang hollow and drew no response from other Issei, except for severe censure by his community. Less than a week after the series of seventeen articles appeared, Oka faced a unanimous no-confidence resolution from both Issei parents and the local Japanese association. By the end of August, he was forced to resign and abruptly left Isleton.[45] This incident illustrates that by 1928 most Japanese immigrants had come to share a consensus on pedagogical principles.

Within this common vision, however, Issei leaders and educators agreed that the conventional Nisei education was inadequate and in need of revision. It is crucial to contextualize this development within the pandemonium following an infamous crime involving a Hawaiian Nisei. In September 1928, a nineteen-year-old Honolulu Nisei, Myles Yutaka Fukunaga, murdered the son of a white business executive, whose financial company had threatened his Issei parents with eviction for overdue house rent. The oldest of seven siblings, Fukunaga was incensed at the callousness of the firm. Seeking revenge and a ransom to save his family from economic ruin, the Nisei kidnapped the boy and killed him.[46] Reports of this crime became a sensation not only in Hawaii but also among mainland Japanese immigrants. More than anything, the incident showed the real possibility of a Nisei becoming a public menace and disgracing the entire community. As a prominent writer noted in the *Nichibei Shimbun*, most Issei feared for the welfare of their own communities and did not regard the Fukunaga case as merely incidental or irrelevant. "Having struggled in the United States for the past fifty years," wrote one journalist, "we have produced a 'clean record' as those least likely to commit crimes. Now I feel that the good name of the 280,000 Japanese in the [continental] United States has been also tarnished by this one misguided delinquent [in Hawaii]."[47] Calling the incident a "disgrace to our race," other Issei writers warned that similar incidents might occur if immigrant leaders and parents did not take effective measures immediately.[48] The Fukunaga incident was not just a Hawaiian problem; it was a harbinger of Nisei delinquency in the West, which threatened to nullify the Issei dream of racial development.

From the late 1920s on, the vernacular press frequently printed reports of Nisei transgressions, often with such menacing headlines as "Steadily Worsening: The Nisei's Criminal Tendency" and "Nisei Crime Wave." According to Los Angeles County data, Japanese juveniles committed eighteen crimes in 1931; however, many of these were traffic offenses. In the first ten months of 1932, there were fourteen cases involving Nisei, some of them crimes of a more aggressive nature, like possession of a deadly weapon, a felony hit and run, and two cases of manslaughter.[49] Three years later, a San Francisco newspaper highlighted the fact that the trend was worsening. According to a Nisei writer, "[T]he frequent participation of young Japanese-American[s] in crimes has become a serious problem and it [needs] immediate solution in order to stop further outbreaks of offenses against the law. The [Japanese] used to be proudly called 'law abiding people.' Now it is no longer so."[50] There were also sporadic stories of Nisei street gangs in Los Angeles and San Francisco.

After the Fukunaga incident, Issei leaders and parents made every effort to arrest the Nisei delinquency problem. In order to deal with actual and potential transgressors, the entire community exerted "almost a direct control upon the moral life of the individual." An agent of the Federal Bureau of Investigation (FBI) observed that the community began to play multiple roles as police, court, and correction agency, "to eliminate the possibility of the Japanese criminal rate acting as a point of ridicule against the Japanese . . . as a whole." He continued:

> Whenever a young Japanese boy became involved with the law or was considered morally unstable, . . . he would be brought before a meeting of leaders in the Japanese Association, and of the Ken [prefectural] or-

ganizations, and other organizations which might have an interest in the boy, and they would discuss with the boy the course of his future life. If the parent of the boy at that meeting stated that he or she could do nothing more with the lad, the committee with the boy's automatic consent might decide any of several things. It might place the boy under the direct supervision of a person other than the parent, who would gainfully employ the boy, or if he were a bad case, he might be sent to a Japanese farm to work for his livelihood.[51]

Close analysis of the Fukunaga case allowed Issei to recognize the underlying problems, which demanded preventive measures more than simply discipline or punishment. Fukunaga was often characterized as a "genius" and was reportedly one of the best students in his high school graduating class in Honolulu. The Issei agreed that his crime had nothing to do with intellectual capacity. They pointed instead to his lack of appropriate "values" and "spiritual cultivation" as the most likely cause. In their opinion, Fukunaga's action signified a failure of moral development—a deficiency that they feared many second-generation children on the mainland might share. A number of immigrants blamed excessive Americanization among the Nisei, a blind imitation of American "hedonism" and superficial "mammonism" that had allegedly effaced basic discipline. To prevent another Fukunaga from appearing in the Japanese community, some immigrant leaders emphasized family education, while others talked about the positive influence of religion. A majority, however, proposed an intensified effort to teach Japanese social ethics and norms, called "the Japanese spirit," which they believed American public schools did not, and could not, teach effectively.[52]

The solution lay in the education provided by Japanese-language schools. Kyutaro Abiko, a respected leader, expressed the view shared by many Issei parents, which explains the sudden shift from language instruction to moral education in schools after the late 1920s. Criticizing the alleged lack of character building in American public education, Abiko argued that Japanese-language schools had the important mission of "molding the mind." This, he said, means "to foster a strong will and an indomitable spirit in a Nisei boy, thereby enabling him to grow up as an upright man; it means to develop in a Nisei girl gentleness, tranquillity, and chastity—the virtues of an ideal [Japanese] woman . . . Their mission is not just to provide language instruction."[53] While the moral characteristics that Abiko advocated reflected conventional gender roles, others added more politically oriented virtues such as loyalty and patriotism.[54] Taken together, these moral qualities comprised the Issei's definition of the "Japanese spirit" that they considered indispensable for the second generation.

Japanese immigrant educators responded to the demand for the new pedagogy swiftly. During October 1928, less than a month after the Fukunaga incident, extraordinary community forums were convened in many settlements, including Stockton, San Francisco, and Los Angeles, to formulate new strategies for second-generation education.[55] At the same time, the Northern California Japanese Language School Association resolved to "make greater effort to foster [the Nisei's] inner development" and discussed the need to "study appropriate methods of moral cultivation." Educators in southern California called for a new textbook series that would incorporate the Japanese code of ethics.[56] In 1931, Kohei Shimano, the chairman of the Revisory Editorial Committee, proposed a blueprint for a new Japanese reader that would replace the one that had been edited under the now-defunct California foreign-language school law. Intended "to bring up patriotic, loyal American citizens of Japanese ancestry," the sixteen-volume series would cover literature, geography, science, industry, experiences of the Japanese in America, "social and public etiquette, morals, and ethics," as well as what Shimano termed the "racial ideals" found in the national history of Japan. In concrete terms, he explained that of "the outstanding culture and virtues of Japan, only those worth dedicating to America, should be introduced and encouraged, e.g.[,] patriotism, loyalty to nation, respect for elders, filial piety, to name just a few."[57] For the time being, however, economic difficulties kept educators from making significant progress in this ambitious project during the 1930s.

With the dearth of ready-made instructional materials for the moral development of Nisei, more schools opted to adopt the textbook series authorized by the Japanese Ministry of Education for domestic use than preexisting state-approved texts. In 1935, out of ninety-eight elementary-level schools in southern California, seventy-nine adopted textbooks from Japan, three used state-approved textbooks, eleven schools employed both, and five had "special" textbooks.[58] Advanced grades read more imported textbooks than did lower grades. All of the twenty-eight Japanese middle schools in southern California taught Nisei students using Japanese Ministry of Education textbooks. In northern California and the Pacific Northwest, the trend was the same. In 1935, the San Francisco consulate reported that approximately 65 percent of 149 schools employed Japanese national textbooks, and over 23 percent combined them with California textbooks in language instruction. Only seventeen schools based their education wholly on state-approved textbooks. In Oregon, Ministry of Education textbooks were the choice of all but one of fourteen schools; the same held true for most of the Japanese-language schools in the Seattle and Tacoma areas.[59] While practical need compelled them to use these imported texts, immigrant teachers generally thought that the "textbook printed in Japan but not prepared for use in this country was . . . [often] inadequate in its theme and materials" for American citizens.[60] They used discretion and care with regard to what elements of Japanese ethics to teach.

The instruction of selected national virtues proceeded in tandem with the promotion of racial pride, without which the Issei felt it impossible for second-generation children to appreciate the Japanese spirit. Many immigrants condescendingly argued that the Nisei could avoid the "pitiful" circumstances of other racial minorities, such as Native Americans, blacks, or Mexicans in the United States, as long as they preserved a "superior national spirit" and "racial consciousness."[61] The converse was also implied: but for their unique traits, the American-born Japanese could lose their distinction from other minorities, who had surrendered to a tragic fate as a result of their defeat in the racial competition. Issei educators may well have interwoven such rhetoric into everyday instruction in their classrooms. One senior teacher in Seattle, for example, listed two "don'ts" at the core of his teaching to the Nisei: "Do not kowtow to other races; do not think that the Japanese can ever be outstripped by other races."[62]

Immigrants often justified such racialist/nationalist pedagogy in terms of the dominant American ideology, arguing that "Japaneseness" could be an asset to white America as well. One section of the Issei's official curriculum, submitted to the California Department of Education, read:

> Japanese-Americans should be given what may be termed a special education which should be at once recognized as a privilege and an advantage. We firmly believe that possessing and maintaining racial pride is not altogether incompatible with America's "melting pot" theory. We believe that racial pride and self-confidence go hand in hand; that their loss is not conducive to the dissemination of worthwhile foreign cultures and virtues . . . One of the highest justifications, we believe, for the existence of the Japanese-American is the opportunity that is their heritage, to contribute the highest essence of Oriental culture to America for its future benefit.[63]

This theme of eclecticism, which attempted to (con)fuse distinct national attributes, formed a guiding principle for Nisei education throughout the 1930s.

At first glance, the focus on the Japanese spirit and racial consciousness seemed to signal a growth of immigrant nationalism during the 1930s. It was certainly a product of that trend in Japanese America, but the racialist mode of thinking that the Issei came to embrace, as well as the unusual pedagogical theory stemming from that, had more to do with their belief in what they posited as the value of a uniquely Japanese morality. From the perspective of this racial minority, Japaneseness was the most basic reality that influenced their individual and collective lives in the United States. In terms of skin color, it was the cause of racial exclusion, oppression, and subordination. When defined as moral attributes and cultural traits, however, Japaneseness became their treasured monopoly, enabling them to dream of transcending their current predicaments and excelling in American society. In that it mirrored the Japanese immigrant experience in the United States, the Issei's extolling of the Japanese spirit was an American social phenomenon.

By the same token, their idea of *Nippon seishin* tended to differ from that of the militarists and right-wing intellectuals in their homeland—another point of contestation. In Japan, pundits construed and propagated it as a national principle that "propels a person to dedicate himself to the Emperor and promote the imperial interest."[64] Forming an ideological underpinning of fanatic patriotism, the extolling of the national spirit fed the ascendancy of the militarist regime in the 1930s that mobilized the masses around the imperial symbol. The Japanese spirit, according to the orthodox definition, had enabled the nation to prevent the invasion of Mongols in the fourteenth century, to defeat the Qing Dynasty in 1894–1895, and to overwhelm czarist Russia in 1904–1905. The Japanese spirit continued to be drawn upon in Japan's ongoing struggle against Chinese "bandits" and for the "liberation" of East Asia from white hegemony.[65] This statist version of *Nippon seishin* offered a powerful political ideology that justified all kinds of individual or collective actions so long as they appeared to serve the national cause.

Although Issei similarly highlighted the necessity of loyalty and patriotism in the inner development of the Nisei, most professed no intention of producing Japanese subjects out of their American-born children. Whereas their compatriots in Japan embraced the imperialist ideology of the Japanese spirit, immigrant educators and parents generally posited that spirit as the reification of old-time Japanese ethics, concentrating on its universal moral implications for American citizens of Japanese ancestry.[66] An FBI agent reported that white American teachers in Seattle "have never found any indication that the Japanese language schools . . . intend to influence the children away from loyalty and patriotic ideals respecting the United States." A leading Issei educator in the Pacific Northwest even told the agent that he would "dismiss" Nisei pupils from his school should they "begin to exhibit a lack of loyalty or patriotism toward the United States."[67] Of course, not all immigrant teachers went to this extreme, but when it came to the question of Nisei education, they usually reduced the essence of the Japanese spirit to a set of moral precepts and behavioral norms that they felt would help their children grow, first and foremost, into good citizen-subjects of the American state.

A logical explanation for this gap lies in the Issei's faith in the compatibility of the Japanese spirit with Americanism. In the characteristics of respectful white Americans, Japanese immigrant leaders and educators found many virtues that supposedly epitomized *Nippon seishin*. Sei Fujii, publisher of the *Kashu Mainichi*, observed that those of outstanding character, whether Japanese or American, always possessed identical moral qualities. In the United States, these qualities happened to be called "Americanism," whereas they were known as *Nippon seishin* in Japan. He thus saw no distinction between instilling the Japanese spirit in the Nisei and Americanizing them.[68] Likewise, Issei educators declared in unison that the racial heritage of the Nisei would "contribute the highest essence of Oriental culture to America for its future benefit."[69] Along similar lines, Takeshi Ban, a renowned Christian minister-educator, adopted the following message as the guiding principle of his pedagogy. In clumsy but heartfelt English, he wrote:

> We glory in the privilege of our being Japanese, and are grateful. You, Nisei, the Americans of Japanese parentage, should comprehend the true Japanese spirit that has effected the formation of the spiritual culture of Japanese [*sic*], your parent's home, and should, with this same spirit, serve America your mother country. The present brilliant culture of America has been built up in less than five centuries since it was opened, by the various peoples each bringing a different culture from Western Europe. We Japanese, too, by bringing ours generated by the history and tradition of three thousand years, should enrich the contents of the spiritual culture of America, contributing toward the realization of the ideal of its foundation.[70]

The rhetorical origin of this perspective can be traced to the ideas put forth by the Japanese scholar Nitobe Inazo in his famous *Bushido* (The Way of the Warrior). First published in 1905 when many Westerners were awed by the defeat of Russia by the small Asian nation, Nitobe's popular treatise aimed to convince the West to admit Japan as its equal despite its "Oriental" origin. Nitobe, a Johns Hopkins graduate and dedicated Quaker married to a white American, as well as a son of a *samurai*, was arguably the best candidate to delve into the cultural traditions of both worlds and to explicate a theory of commonalty between the Judeo-Christian tradition and *bushido*, the warrior heritage of Japan. Not only did the book contain an extensive survey of Japanese "virtues instilled by Bushido," such as justice, courage, sincerity, honor, and loyalty, it also offered a well-reasoned comparison of these qualities with matching examples drawn from the Bible and historical anecdotes of the West. According to him, "no one quality of character was its [*bushido's*] exclusive patrimony." Instead, it held much in common with the Christian code of ethics.[71]

On loyalty, for instance, Nitobe drew an analogy between the stories of Genzo and Abraham—historical figures of the East and West who each opted to sacrifice their own sons for the sake of greater good and higher duty. "In both cases," wrote the Japanese Christian scholar, there "was obedience to the call of duty, utter submission to the command of a higher voice, whether given by a visible or an invisible angel, or heard by an outward or an inward ear."[72] Nitobe made a compelling case for the compatibility of *bushido* and Christianity, the Orient and Occident, and Japan and the United States. This theory of bilateral compatibility laid a philosophical foundation for the Issei's unique pedagogy during the 1930s, as shown by frequent references to the Japanese scholar or his publications.

Cultural affinities did not mean a complete parallel between the conceptualizations of Japanese and American moral characters, however. The Issei instead anticipated that the Japanese spirit would enhance some "American" qualities in the Nisei, reinforcing what Americanization offered to them. At that time, it was a common understanding that the Japanese lacked some virtues, while excelling in others. The Japanese assumed that they were weak in such traits as individuality, frankness, and creativity, while surpassing other nationalities in honor, obligation, respect for elders and parents, and loyalty. Loyalty in particular was an emblem of Japaneseness; Nitobe argued that the Japanese carried it "to a degree not reached in any other country."[73] This point—an excess of loyalty—was at the core of the Issei rationalization that a Japanese moral education would make good American citizens of their children.

Japanese immigrants took for granted that holding American citizenship meant that Nisei owed their loyalty to the United States. They stressed this point repeatedly at educational meetings, in newspaper editorials, and at public lectures. Because the spirit of the *samurai* absolutely disallowed Nisei from serving more than one country (or master), they would become better Americans if they were properly educated in this national/racial virtue. In other words, unflinching loyalty to one's country, a special characteristic of the Japanese people, would ameliorate the Nisei relationship to America, their native land.[74] Reiterating that the essence of *bushido* "has no national boundary," a Seattle immigrant leader explained in English its relevance to the Nisei:

> The United States citizens of Japanese ancestry should feel proud for having the spirit and virtue of Bushido in their blood, that spirit which has made the country of their ancestors one of the greatest among the Nations of the World. They are the descendants of loyal Japanese, so are imbued with their ancestral ethical and loyal spirit. They are expected to be loyal and true to their country, the United States of America, the country which gave them birth, education and protection. Bushido do despises [*sic*] one who is coward[ly] and untruthful to the country of his birth.[75]

In addition to the belief in Japanese American cultural compatibility, there was another reason that many Issei saw no contradiction in instilling the Japanese spirit in Nisei citizens. While being caught between the generally polarized notions of what was Japan and what was America, they managed to make sense of the Nisei's ambiguous position by distinguishing race/nation (*minzoku*) from state (*kokka*). Never was this distinction crucial to the Issei themselves, since they were denied rights of naturalization and thus remained Japanese subjects. The notion of the Nisei's future development, however, revolved around this very distinction. Without dispute, according to Issei thought, the Nisei were Japanese in terms of race and nationality, yet they were also full-fledged Americans in terms of citizenship. The Japaneseness of the Nisei derived from their "natural" attributes, devoid of "political" ties to the Japanese state.[76] This is not to say that the Issei did not wish their children to have sympathy or an affinity with imperial Japan, but their American citizenship took precedence. In the opinion of many immigrants, the teaching of the Japanese spirit was necessary for the enhancement of the Nisei's racial/national strengths, the positive effects of which would manifest in making members of the second generation better U.S. citizens than members of most other races. Therefore, as Issei leaders often contended, the Nisei had to remain upright Japanese to become loyal Americans.[77]

The Issei's eclectic interpretation of the Japanese spirit helped many Nisei leaders to form nuanced identities as ethnic Americans. James Y. Sakamoto, publisher of the *Japanese American Courier* in Seattle and prominent leader of the JACL, frequently borrowed the *bushido* rhetoric to illuminate the importance of what he called "undivided allegiance" and "full-blooded Americanism." In response to a question about the general policy of his newspaper, Sakamoto insisted that he wished to make "true American citizens" out of the Nisei. To explain how this was possible, he noted:

> In bushido there is the saying, "Chu-shin wa ni-kun ni tsukaezu," which means the same as, no loyal person or patriot shall serve two masters. The second generation in following the bushido of their ancestors cannot fail to grasp the meaning of these words and by following them I do not think that they will be treading on the wrong path . . . In other words our policy is in pursuance of a character program, to build the character of the young people along right lines so that they will understand and sense what is important and what requires their support in pushing their individual welfare as well as that of their country and community.[78]

Sakamoto's view was perfectly consistent with the immigrants'; no other statement could have made his parents' generation happier.

A small minority of Issei nonetheless reproved educators and community leaders for promoting the Japanese spirit among Nisei youths. They seemed to have managed to maintain what Consul Ohashi once termed the "hundred-percent American" principle. These individuals refused to recognize any compatibility between the Japanese spirit and Americanism. In 1935, a small group of San Jose Issei, who called themselves the Permanent Settlers Association, studied the various educational issues and pedagogical principles that Japanese educators and parents had been discussing at community meetings. Reaching the conclusion that "part of the current educational policy" could fuel agitation for Japanese exclusion, they took a stand against instilling the Japanese spirit in the Nisei.[79]

The most notable and sustained opposition came from a few dozen leftists associated with the *Doho*—a Japanese communist organ published in Los Angeles. The newspaper often identified Japanese moral education with the wholesale indoctrination of Japanese militarism in Nisei children. Showing no interest in prevailing cultural and spiritual arguments, the *Doho*'s writers perceived the Japanese spirit as an ideological weapon of the Japanese state controlled by the military clique. From this materialist perspective, Japanese virtues were never universal nor inherent, but always political and class specific.[80] While a vast majority of Issei highlighted the universality of Japanese national morality, the leftists saw in it an unbreakable political relationship with Japanese imperialism.

These minority criticisms struck at a fundamental conceptual flaw in Issei eclecticism. For the vast majority of Japanese immigrants, the issue of militarism had little to do with the Japanese spirit. Concerned with group survival in America, most Issei expected the moral effect of the Japanese spirit to foster racial subjectivity in the Nisei and allow them to hold a competitive edge over other minorities under white hegemony. Yet, the Issei use of the concept of the Japanese spirit was premised on the Nisei being an extension of the Japanese race/nation, albeit not the Japanese state. The core of their spirit still lay inside Japan. The doctrine of Japanese development demanded that members of the second generation maintain a strong connection with, if not an allegiance to, the homeland and its sovereign emperor, regardless of their citizenship. When national political membership was defined in racial terms, whether in Japan or in America, Issei eclecticism, based on an artificial dichotomy of the natural and the political, likely failed to resist state orthodoxy. Just as Tokyo freely exploited the Issei historical discourse on the grounds of this ambiguity for its expansionist politics, Nisei education frequently approximated emperor worship and Japanese patriotism while affirming the obligations of American citizenship. It is for this reason that some Japanese-language schoolteachers taught Nisei pupils to have an affinity with the emperor as the father of the nation/race.

At times, this flaw even served to invalidate the delicate separation of race/nation and state, upon which Japanese immigrants insisted so steadfastly for their children. The Issei's unabashed praise of the Japanese empire and culture sent some second-generation youths a mixed message that mitigated against their Americanism. No matter how strongly Issei leaders and parents preached the importance of unflinching American loyalty, some Nisei became befuddled over their political identity as they struggled to balance their primary allegiance to the United States with their natural racial ties to Japan. Characterizing "the [Nisei's] racial angle" as "the controlling factor" in determining their attitude toward Japan, an American intelligence agent observed that "in any matter in which the lines are drawn along racial lines, the Nisei will predominantly favor Japan," even though they remained loyal to the United States when the question of race did not enter the picture.[81] Some of the Nisei's Japanese writings suggest that Issei eclecticism might well have generated a degree of confusion in their children's minds. At the community movie showings, too, youths often praised Japanese soldiers as models of "heroism" and applauded passionately when the rising-sun flag or a hint of the emperor's presence appeared on screen.[82]

Immigrant eclecticism would become increasingly vulnerable to the ever-intensifying nationalizing pressure when within reach of Japan's state control. In this sense, Nisei education posed a risk outside the multiracial American West, where transnational practices had a better chance of keeping their nuances and ambiguities alive. As the following chapter shows, the schooling of Nisei expatriates in Japan put the immigrant vision and Japan's political agenda directly on a collision course. The disciplining of the Issei's heterodox imagination, reified in the American-born students, by Japan's regime only foreshadowed what would happen to their eclecticism in the United States when it also began exerting nationalizing power over Japanese immigrants and Japanese American citizens in the early 1940s. An important backdrop to the mass incarceration, the contradiction that immigrant eclecticism embodied would prove deadly in the face of intolerant wartime nationalism.

6

Wages of Immigrant Internationalism

Nisei in the Ancestral Land

> Scattered throughout the far-flung island empire of Japan are the nisei—
> Americans of Japanese ancestry . . . [T]heir migration to Japan did not
> become conspicuous until shortly after the Manchurian Incident of 1931
> when the rise of Japan first impressed the nisei in America. Since then
> there had [*sic*] been a continuous stream of these youngsters, both men
> and women, coming to Japan to study.[1]

So wrote Goro Murata, news editor of the *Japan Times* in Tokyo and former
English editor of the Los Angeles *Kashu Mainichi* newspaper, in 1940. Throughout the decade of the 1930s, there was a flock of second-generation youth, like
Murata himself, aboard every transpacific steamship that sailed into the harbors
of Yokohama and Kobe. Race relations in America and imperial Japan's growing
presence in geopolitics ushered in the Issei's redefinition of their relations with
their homeland, and this change led many immigrants to long for its value
system, language, and national essence. Just as Issei parents and leaders aimed
to morally inculcate the American-born generation with the Japanese spirit, so
too did "Japan" become important as a symbol, reference, and source of inspiration and mental discipline. Within this context Issei began to stress the
advantages of the Nisei's protracted sojourn in Japan for heritage learning.
During a time of national mobilization and aggressive expansionism, the sudden
increase of American Nisei in the archipelago prompted the empire to contem-

plate ways in which to utilize the successors of Japanese overseas development. The enterprise of transnational Nisei education therefore brought into sharp contrast the visions of the Issei and those of their homeland compatriots on questions of colonialism, national and racial identity, and citizenship. And such contradictions were condensed and crystallized in the lives of Nisei youth—now immigrants—in their ancestral land, which turned out to be so foreign to them.

Prior to the Pacific War, three types of Nisei lived in Japan. The vast majority of them were victims of circumstances, the children of people who had pulled up stakes in America and returned to Japan. In other cases, Issei sent their children for primary or secondary education in Japan and placed them in the care of grandparents and other relatives. No matter how they ended up there, these Nisei generally acclimated to the Japanese way of life quietly, while maintaining dual nationality until they lost American citizenship due to military service or other civic/social commitments to Japan, including voting. During the 1930s, various sources estimated the presence of between 10,000 and 35,000 Nisei, who were "assimilated" enough to pass as ordinary Japanese.[2] Most of these youth resided in so-called emigration prefectures in rural Japan, where their parents had originated. According to 1933 reports of the American-born population, Hiroshima, Yamaguchi, and Wakayama had the largest groups, with 4,655, 2,636, and 2,365 Nisei, respectively.[3]

The second group of Nisei consisted of men and women in higher education or in professional, white-collar occupations, numbering a few hundred. Typically university-educated, these Nisei tended to be older than other expatriates. With their command of English, as well as specialized skills and knowledge, they assumed important positions in corporations, bureaucracies, mass media, and academia in Tokyo and other major cities.[4] For them, Japan was a land of opportunities, just like the United States had been for their parents. This ironic situation resulted from the racial exclusion of the Nisei from the mainstream American economy, a condition that induced these high achievers to seek university education or employment across the Pacific.

Journalist Welly Shibata was one of these Nisei. In California, he had to work in the Issei-owned produce business while writing intermittently for the Japanese American press. In a 1932 letter to a Nisei journalist friend, this University of Washington graduate lamented: "The boss is O.K. and the work is rather easy, but my heart's not in this sort of work, as you know." Shibata asked his correspondent, "What do you think about prospects for some newspaper job in Japan?" Before long, he was aboard a transpacific steamer, and he eventually landed the English editorship of the *Osaka Mainichi*—his dream job.[5]

Charles H. Yoshii of Portland was another example. While studying at the University of Oregon, he had initially "hoped to exercise full citizenship rights in the United States" and applied for commission as a second lieutenant after completing the ROTC program. When he was denied, the dejected Yoshii called it an "official notification that the United States did not completely trust its Japanese [American] citizens." Encouraged by his parents and a family friend connected to the Japanese government, he turned his eyes to his ancestral land. Yoshii visited there twice before emigrating in 1933 to "benefit from his racial heritage to the fullest, without having to undergo the handicaps placed in his way on the Pacific Coast."[6] Once in Japan, he became the first Nisei to enroll in Tokyo Imperial University, and later worked as a college professor and English announcer for Radio Tokyo. Nisei like Yoshii and Shibata formed the core of the Japanese American expatriate community, serving as leaders and mentors for the third group.

The rest of the Nisei youngsters were so-called *ryugakusei*, high school to college-age students who crossed the Pacific alone for a few years of schooling. Though no reliable statistics are available, by the mid-1930s there might have been nearly 4,000 such students, most of them congregated in the vicinities of Tokyo and Osaka. While hundreds of these Americans attended regular institutions of secondary and higher education, many others learned basic Japanese language and culture at special schools for the foreign-born in the capital city.[7] If the Nisei in regular Japanese schools comprised the more permanent class of *ryugakusei*, many of whom would likely pursue employment in Japan or in its colonial territories after graduation, the language students consisted of Japanese Americans who would return to their native land after a few years of sojourning in their ancestral land.

As Goro Murata reported, the migration of the *ryugakusei* contingent to Japan became especially "conspicuous" in the early 1930s, because the rapid decline of the Japanese yen relative to the U.S. dollar made the scheme of Nisei study abroad financially viable for many Issei parents. The Great Depression had caused a sharp drop in exports and a massive outflow of gold from Japan. In desperation, Tokyo took the country off the gold standard and restored the embargo on gold in December 1931—a policy that led to the plunging of the yen-to-dollar exchange rate. By November 1932, the value of ¥100 had dropped by 50 percent, from $38 to $19, and it stayed below $24 during 1933. Whereas attending college in the United States would cost a student $40 to $80 a month, studying in Japan, including living expenses, only required roughly $18 to $20 a month.[8] Hence, a number of parents began to send their sons and daughters to schools in Japan instead of to American colleges, although the prevailing economic difficulty still limited this option to the leading class of well-off agriculturalists and urban entrepreneurs, and excluded the great majority of struggling tenant farmers and laborers.

Aided by favorable economic conditions, Japanese immigrant parents and leaders had a host of other reasons for sending their children to school abroad. On a pragmatic level, Issei found many advantages in transnational education, including the betterment of the Nisei's employment opportunities and the narrowing of cultural and linguistic gaps between the first and second generations. Many also saw the purposes of study abroad in terms similar to community-based language instruction at home. Immigrant parents anticipated that attending school in Japan would enhance their children's appreciation of a moral and dignified lifestyle based on Japanese ethics.[9]

ISSEI INTERNATIONALISM AND HERITAGE LEARNING

Beyond such pragmatism, the advocacy of the Nisei's study of things Japanese in their ancestral land was deeply intertwined with the development of internationalist ideals—an extension of time-honored immigrant eclecticism—in Japanese America. Mirroring aspects of larger cultural internationalism in the 1930s, the Issei's concepts of the "Pacific era" and their children as a "bridge of understanding" between the United States and Japan glamorized a future role for the Nisei beyond the borders of the American nation.[10] Following the First World War in Europe, Japanese immigrant literati came to think that the center of the world was moving from the Atlantic to the Pacific, where a higher level of civilization would take shape. With the genesis of this "Pacific civilization," they felt, history itself would soon enter into a new Pacific era, in which the United States and Japan would replace their European rivals as pivotal global powers. Not only would the two nations represent the West and East, but they would also fuse the best elements of the divided worlds. Born as American citizens with Japanese heritage, the Nisei inadvertently became saddled with the mission of facilitating this process as ambassadors between the two nations and the two worlds. Their internationalist role would concomitantly buttress their particular duties as citizens of the American state and as members of the Japanese race, while maintaining peace and harmony in the Pacific basin. To do this, the youth had to be fully informed about the countries between which they were supposed to mediate, thus creating the need for their transnational education in Japan.[11]

Based on this need, Issei leaders, like Kyutaro Abiko, initiated various educational programs for the second generation, like short-term study tours to Japan, which began in the mid-1920s, and under the spell of their constant inculcations, a number of older Nisei came to embrace the bridge concept as well.[12] For example, the Japanese Student Christian Association in North America, which included many American-born members, proclaimed in 1926:

The second generation are the living connecting links between the United States of America and Japan. As American citizens, they should be provided with the best of American ideas and trainings; while as offsprings of Japanese parentage, they should be well equipped with the best of Japanese culture and traditions . . . These, indeed, are the two wheels in their unique position in America, and neglecting one of them will result in an unbalanced future and losing race. What a remarkable future role these second generation Japanese are destined to play on the stage of the dawning Pacific Era, especially with such double background, provided they can develop their invaluable international heritage . . . Let there be respect for Japanese heritage at the basis of such internationalism.[13]

Established in 1929, the Japanese American Citizens League (JACL), a central Nisei organization on the continental United States, took this as one of its guiding principles during the ensuing decade. James Y. Sakamoto of Seattle, an early JACL leader and publisher of the first English-language newspaper dedicated to Nisei, continually espoused the bridge ideal in his *Japanese American Courier*.[14]

For many Issei, the bridge concept represented an enchanting dream, allowing them to think beyond the harsh realities of racial subordination just as the Issei pioneer thesis did. Training the second generation for its role as the international bridge permitted the immigrants to imagine something empowering, that is, the possibility of putting Japanese Americans on a par with white Americans (and thus above all other minorities) in the construction of a new global civilization. This racialized ideology of self-empowerment, grounded in their contrary social realities, compounded enthusiasm for the reclamation of their "superior" heritage and support for transnational education. Arguably, Nisei education in Japan stemmed mainly from the aspirations of the first generation in the local context of racial subordination. Although a small number of older Nisei appropriated the lofty ideal when they crossed the Pacific, most students did not participate in the decision to study abroad. Instead, the initiative was the joint effort of Issei parents and Japanese supporters, who actually facilitated and oversaw Nisei education in Japan.[15]

The "success" or "failure" of such education—from the vantage point of Issei parents and leaders—depended on how the receiving institutions in Japan were set up, who acted as the primary benefactors of and caretakers for Japanese American students, and what kind of relationship the schools maintained with the immigrant community. Because of the unique pedagogical needs of Americans of Japanese ancestry, a handful of institutions dedicated to Nisei education played a key role in transplanting the Issei's internationalist agenda.

Under the aegis of the Hompa Hongwanji Buddhist mission, the largest religious group in the Japanese immigrant community, Nichibei Home (Japanese American Home) pioneered transnational education along the lines envisioned by Issei. In 1928–1929, a Buddhist educator named Tsunemitsu Konen traveled to Hawaii and the continental United States to investigate the social conditions of Japanese residents. Having observed the Issei's strong interest in transnational education, Tsunemitsu, upon his return to Japan, lobbied for a special educational institution that could play multiple roles as "a dormitory, family, and school" for Nisei students in Tokyo. In 1930, Tsunemitsu's pet project began as a dormitory with a modest number of students who commuted to regular Japanese schools. By 1934, residents, ministers, and Issei Buddhists in America collected more than $10,000 for new school buildings to turn Nichibei Home into a genuine boarding school for Japanese American youth.[16] Until the outbreak of the war, Tsunemitsu and his wife acted as surrogate parents to a few dozen Nisei boys and several girls. In his 1935 report on Nisei schooling in Japan, the American consul characterized this endeavor as "successful" and "sensible." He wrote, "[W]ith the close relationship and personal contact between [Tsunemitsu] and the parents of the boys in the dormitory, the supervision necessary has been maintained." The consul then predicted that the institute "may very possibly develop considerably along the same lines it is now following."[17]

The pedagogical goal of this collaborative venture was to reconcile the Nisei's Americanism with their Japanese racial heritage. From the immigrant perspective, transnational education was integral to their efforts to make self-confident, capable American citizens out of the second-generation Japanese, and the success of their internationalist duty hinged first and foremost upon the maximum enhancement of their American citizenship. Faithful to his Issei patrons, Tsunemitsu crafted the Nichibei Home program around the goal of "breaking down the Nisei's racial inferiority complex." American racism, he argued, had deprived the second generation of the Japanese racial trait of "perseverance," which had enabled their parents' generation to achieve such notable economic ascendancy that jealous whites had to resort to unfair laws. Whereas the current racial status of the Japanese in America was an ironic consequence and a symbol of their "superiority," Nisei children were not cognizant of it, inheriting a state of subordination instead. Learning Japanese and experiencing modern Japan firsthand would awaken the youngsters to the fact that "being Japanese is an honorable thing," thereby reviving in them perseverance and racial pride. Borrowing the Issei's argument for the racial division of labor in society, Tsunemitsu justified his position to raise American citizens with specific racial/cultural faculties for, without them, the Nisei remained a liability to their native country, like other minorities. Racist as they were, Tsunemitsu's ideas conformed neatly with those of his Issei friends and patrons, which tied the responsibility of citizenship to racial attributes.[18]

To better achieve his objective, Tsunemitsu devised a one-year program called *Shugakudan*, or study corps. Most immigrant parents, according to him, wanted their children to learn the "essence" of Japan in the shortest period of time and at the least expense before resuming their lives in America. Posed as an alternative between the short-term study tours and full-fledged study abroad, the study corps required $220 to $250 annually—only $50 to $80 higher than the typical three-month study tours and much lower than average four-year college expenses. In order to maximize the educational effects and minimize parental concerns, the corps' members consisted of youth in their mid-teens—when they were thought to be most susceptible to new ideas and influences—who originated from the same communities in the United States. In 1937, the first study corps came from Denver, Colorado, where Tsunemitsu had personally recruited seventeen Nisei in cooperation with a local Buddhist minister.[19] In addition to frequent cultural excursions, the students learned Japanese reading, composition, conversation, and calligraphy and penmanship; Japanese morality, etiquette, and customs; Japanese history and geography; mathematics, music, and martial arts. The favorable reports of this group allowed the Buddhist educator to recruit more than fifty youngsters from various parts of the American West for the second study corps in 1939.[20]

True to immigrant internationalism, Tsunemitsu demanded that his students appreciate the meaning of heritage learning in terms of the school's anthem—the musical embodiment of the Issei's educational ideology, which the Nisei sang every morning in Japanese at Nichibei Home:

Our pride
In our veins we have the precious blood of Japanese
The nation now glittering in the world
We are Japanese American citizens
Our heart is filled with pride
So lofty is the ideal of our Study Corps
For that let us work arduously

Our mission
The bright light now shining in the East
The Pacific Era has arrived
To coalesce the cultures of the East and West
Is the duty placed upon our shoulders
So majestic is the mission of our Study Corps
For that let us study arduously.[21]

Another example of transplanted immigrant pedagogy was the Nisei department of Keisen Girls' School, which offered two-year and one-year intensive cultural immersion courses. Founded in 1935, this institute outdid Nichibei Home in its steadfast adherence to internationalism and respect for the Nisei's American citizenship, albeit in a markedly gendered way. With the goal of producing cosmopolitan Japanese women, Keisen began six years earlier under Kawai Michi on the outskirts of Tokyo. Kawai was among the most faithful supporters of Japanese in the United States. For this leading female educator, the two generations of Japanese American women—the Issei women in the 1910s and their Nisei daughters in the 1930s—were allies in her long-term politics of internationalism in Japan, in America, and beyond. As she often stated, both Issei and Nisei were "pioneers" whose "task" was "to blaze the trail for those who come after" in their own ethnic community and for international peace.[22]

Keisen's Nisei department was established in response to the pleading of Kawai's Issei friends and disciples for educational help. Her 1934 visit to California decidedly "turned [her] attention to the problems of the 'second generation' Japanese." Addressing Nisei at lecture meetings, the Christian educator declared: "Come to Japan when you can . . . and let us work together to solve your problem." No sooner had she returned to Japan than Keisen witnessed the arrival of one Nisei after another, "[s]ome I had met and some of their parents I had talked with in America."[23] Her ensuing efforts to build a special Western-style dormitory revealed a glimpse of Kawai's unflinching commitment to the welfare of her Nisei students and the second generation in general. Whereas most Japanese educators had little sympathy for the youngsters' dilemmas as an American racial minority, condescendingly treating them as Japan's pawns, Kawai was a notable exception. When "experts" in Tokyo convened a round-table discussion on Nisei education under the aegis of the Foreign Ministry, all but Kawai indulged in criticisms of the American-born, ridiculing their "outlandish ways," their "horrible, low class, boorish country style Japanese speech," and their "simple-minded chattering." One participant concluded: "The Nisei are children of low class, peasant emigrants, so what could one expect of them?" While everyone else "solemnly nodded" in the affirmative, Kawai "stood up fearlessly for the Nisei."[24]

Kawai's respect for the Nisei's American citizenship appears to have been taken as a matter of course by her students. One can detect little confusion as to their national identity in the young women's writings, which usually show tremendous enthusiasm "to understand and to appreciate the Japanese mind, culture, life, customs, and traditions" as outsiders, but not aspirations to become assimilated into them. At Keisen, the Nisei did not seek to emulate "Japaneseness" in order to become Japanese. Their heritage, according to the students, only served as "the foundation upon which they may build their future life and society" as useful citizens when they returned to the land of their birth.[25] Upon her graduation, one student commented:

> Our teachers have taught us that it was mistaken if we simply aspired to mimic the ways of the Japanese woman. Cognizant of our special position as Americans of Japanese ancestry, we must instead strive to promote the U.S.–Japan friendship. Furthermore, we must adapt the merits of the Japanese spirit to our Americanism. Back in the United States, we will dedicate ourselves to the good of our own society as the best possible citizens.[26]

Keisen's curriculum also rendered the internationalist ideal in a gendered manner. The school's instruction limited Nisei women to the feminized realm of family and culture. In lieu of history, politics, and other contemporary social issues, Keisen students learned traditional aesthetics like flower arranging and the tea ceremony, basic womanly etiquette, and the "arts" of Japanese sewing, dyeing, and cooking. Combined with basic language courses, these subjects sought to make good Japanese wives and mothers out of the young Nisei women, which harmonized perfectly with what Issei leaders had pursued in their educational programs.[27] While many community-based schools incorporated the teaching of gendered values throughout the 1930s, individual Issei and organizations made special efforts to foster domestic and feminine qualities in Nisei daughters. In Los Angeles, for example, Yonako Abiko—Kawai's close friend and long-time ally—offered immensely popular lectures, in which she taught second-generation Japanese Christians proper feminine speech and manners. In the northern California town of Alvarado, another Issei educator set up a boarding school for Nisei girls to learn a variety of Japanese housekeeping skills, so that they might "assist their [future] husbands just as their virtuous Issei mothers did."[28] Keisen's program furthered the cause of these immigrant educators and leaders in the making of ideal Japanese American womanhood. The emphasis Kawai put on this pedagogical principle is crystallized by the project of the Class of 1940: a 220-page English treatise entitled *Japanese Cooking and Etiquette.*[29]

Student compositions reveal what was taught at Keisen and how the Nisei students understood it. In her essay titled "A Nisei Philosophy," one student postulated that the duty of the second-generation women—"the products of two cultures"—would be to "lay the foundation for a happier and a more complete family life" in America. According to her, as wives, they should build Japanese American households around "the companionship and equality of the American life, and the sense of respect and duty of the Japanese." As mothers, they must "teach both languages to [their] children; also to encourage and

THE FIRST COMMENCEMENT FOR KEISEN'S
JAPANESE-AMERICAN STUDENTS, 1937

FIGURE 6.1. First Commencement for Keisen's Nisei Students, 1937
The juxtaposition of the two national flags was a common practice to illuminate the inter-
nationalism and dual qualities of Japanese Americans. Reprinted from Michi Kawai, *My
Lantern* (1939).

cultivate the different talents which [their] children may possess by giving them
the proper education." Her discussion of the Nisei's dualism focused exclusively
on family formation.[30] Later, back home, most of these women got married
and began new Japanese American households, while a few strove to share what
they had learned at Keisen with other Nisei women. One of the first graduates
even ran a sewing school for the benefit of future Nisei homemakers in Los
Angeles's Little Tokyo.

At times, what Keisen's Nisei came to envision as a result of their educational stint in Japan not only paralleled the Issei's call for racial pride but also
approximated the celebrated notion of racial/ethnic diversity as a viable form
of American nationhood. This formulation, in its structure and scheme, resembled the liberal idea of "cultural pluralism," which attempted to resist the op-
pressive imposition of Anglo assimilationism.[31] Influenced by the affirmative
recapitulations of their heritage at Keisen, the students' essays often intimated
views that transcended Anglocentric orthodoxy, extending the possibility of national inclusion even further beyond white racial boundaries. For example, the
project of the Class of 1939, published as *The Nisei: A Survey of Their Educational, Vocational, and Social Problems*, characterized "a few years of study in

Japan" as having helped to eradicate many Nisei's feelings of "inferiority" and rectified their "apologetic" attitude toward their Japanese heritage: "We must realize that all Americans are descendants of foreigners and that they are proud of their ancestry." The second-generation authors added, "The Nisei, too, have the right to feel just as proud of their own ancestry, and must do so."[32] In light of the bridge ideal, then, not only would the Nisei play a role in uniting nations in the international arena, but they would also internationalize the American nation "as the best possible citizens, cooperating with Americans of other races and learning from each other," as one Keisen graduate pledged.[33]

Despite its positive effects, Keisen's transnational education benefited only a small minority of Nisei *ryugakusei*. Like Nichibei Home, the boarding school maintained a relatively small student body, and during the seven years of its operation, only 125 Nisei attended the school.[34] These students were exceptional and considerably fortunate because, unlike most other Nisei in Japan, they largely avoided paying the wages of internationalism under the ultranationalist, militarist regime.

A CONTESTED TERRAIN: MULTIPLICITY OF THE BRIDGE CONCEPT

The idea of the Nisei as a transpacific bridge was not simply an Issei invention, nor was it meant to serve their immigrant needs only. Educators, intellectuals, and government officials of Japan took no less interest in the concept throughout the 1930s.[35] As abstract as it was, the bridge ideal offered ample room for differing interpretations, which often led to the distortion of the Issei's visions at the hands of Japan's nationalist agendas. When a few, like Tsunemitsu and Kawai, endeavored to address immigrant concerns and to defend the Nisei as American citizens, most other Japanese used Nisei education toward different, even diametrically opposite, ends. Behind the facade of the cosmopolitan bridge ideal and the common language associated with it, the Nisei's study in Japan formed another field of contestation between the perspective and logic of Japanese immigrants, embedded in their American minority experience, and imperial Japan's quest for colonial expansion. As the previous chapters have shown, Issei eclecticism and Japan's state nationalism were not necessarily mutually exclusive; Japanese immigrants often viewed Japan's ascendancy in Asia in such a way as to bolster their own ideology of racial empowerment in the American context, which motivated many parents to send their children to the racial homeland in the first place. The idea of the Nisei as a bridge of understanding, in this respect, was a complex entanglement of disparate interests, competing visions, and conflicting expectations that did not look so different prima facie.

In the early 1930s, the changing mandate of Japanese diplomacy valorized the political utility of the bridge concept, thereby garnering support from the official circles of the island empire in a manner quite unexpected from the Issei perspective. Beginning in 1931, Japan's military aggression in Manchuria rendered the bridge concept more ideological than idealistic.[36] Given the deterioration of Japan's image and the surge of anti-Japanese sentiment in the United States, the Tokyo elite found it necessary to have reliable English-speaking spokespeople for their policy. The Nisei—Japanese in their racial origin and yet American in their psychological makeup and cultural sensitivity—would be the best candidates for such a propagandist role. In the eyes of Japanese leaders, the "bridge of understanding" was equated with being apologists for Japan. And because the class specificity of transnational education meant ensuring the future leadership of Japan-educated Nisei—sons and daughters of the relatively affluent and the powerful—back in the ethnic community, the incorporation of Nisei into Japan's formal educational process was considered a form of long-term political investment for the Japanese empire. Keenly aware of Japan's intention, an American diplomat depicted Nisei education as "a good deal to Japan." He further observed:

> Upper class Japanese civilians were at first generally reluctant to associate with the sons and daughters of low born Japanese emigrants but more recently the Japanese Government and various semi-official organizations have recognized the advantage of cultivating the good opinion of these Americans of Japanese race for the purpose of spreading in the United States a favorable opinion of Japan and of Japanese policy.[37]

Beyond the politicization of the bridge concept after the Manchurian incident, Japanese officials and educators also embraced Nisei education because of its implications for the future of Japanese colonialism. They saw the education of American Nisei as an unprecedented national experiment in the relatively short history of Japan's colonial empire. Since Japanese emigration to Hawaii and the United States commenced before the exodus of Japanese subjects for other destinations, pundits often claimed that the problems of cultural retention and national allegiance concerning the foreign-born Japanese had manifested themselves in North America for the first time in Japan's modern history. Given the recent increase of the overseas population, Japanese proponents of Nisei education argued that the practical, pedagogical lessons they could garner from the experiment on the American-born would prepare them better for similar problems elsewhere, thereby shoring up Japan's quest for greater influence in the world.[38] Fundamentally, then, the Japanese interest in the bridge concept in particular, and in Nisei education in general, was fostered by the privileging of their racial (blood) ties over their citizenship status. As a

Japanese politician put it succinctly, American Nisei were preordained to be the first of the overseas "vanguards" for the cause of their racial homeland.[39]

Typical of Japanese racial thinking, a Tokyo college professor claimed that the main purpose of educating Nisei in Japan was to "activate" patriotic sentiments that had been dormant in the bosom of their racial mind due to their American upbringing. The acquisition of proper knowledge, he postulated, would infallibly drive the Nisei to collaborate with their racial homeland of their own volition in "achieving the grand national mission."[40] Albeit with diplomatic prudence, the foreign minister discussed the meaning of the undiluted lineage in similar terms:

> You American citizens of Japanese parentage are to play an increasingly important role in furthering the friendly relations between Japan and the United States . . . You owe your allegiance, of course, to the United States, the country of your birth; at the same time, you are closely bound by the ties of blood to the people of Japan, the land of your fathers. What then is more logical than that you should be expected to provide an indestructible link between our two great nations?[41]

To the Japanese elite, racial ties were innate and immutable, while citizenship was contingent and expedient. The preeminence of ancestry in their utterances articulated the baseline expectation that Nisei allegiance to the United States could be compromised, trivialized, or overridden when the call of blood became unmitigated, forceful, and too difficult to resist.[42]

The dictates of national interest, as well as a prevailing sense of sovereign rights over the foreign-born Japanese, underlay the mounting support in Japan for the institutionalization of the Nisei's schooling as a part of its national(ist) educational agenda. In 1932, the Japanese Ministry of Education issued a directive, enabling "foreign citizens of Japanese ancestry" to enroll in public elementary schools and to be "treated as Japanese citizens." Three years later, another order stipulated that "Japanese Americans" be admitted into middle schools and higher girls' schools (both equivalent to U.S. high schools), provided they received permission from the ministry.[43] With this change, 1935 marked the beginning of a state-sponsored educational enterprise that attempted to systematically import a large number of foreign students—Nisei and others—for pro-Japan inculcation. While Tokyo established a new governmental agency to facilitate this project, a number of universities and colleges started to admit into their normal academic tracks students from the Americas and Asia in hopes that they would later become the bridges between Japan and their home nations, over which the empire aspired to exert more influence.[44]

In this development, Waseda International Institute, a special division of Waseda University in Tokyo, exemplified a miscarriage of Issei internationalism, where Japan's colonialist mandate outweighed the immigrant goal of creating culturally/racially endowed U.S. citizens. Insofar as the school aimed to produce foreign students suitable for formal higher education, Nisei education at Waseda International Institute tended to be subsumed under the policy of imperial Japan from the outset. The changing composition of its students testified to Waseda's compliance with the state program. While it started out with only twenty Nisei, the institute's student body grew steadily larger and turned more diverse with additional students from Asia. In its first three years (1935–1937), students from Hawaii, the mainland United States, and Canada constituted over three-quarters of the 226 students, while non-Japanese Asians accounted for only 18 percent. By 1940, out of 195 students, the percentage of North American Nisei declined to 59 percent, while their Asian counterparts rose to nearly one-third.[45] On this change after the outbreak of the Sino-Japanese War in 1937, a schoolmaster expounded: "[I]t is particularly noticeable that yearly other foreign students [than the Nisei] are increasing rapidly. From China and Thailand have come children of state ministers. Also a very close relative of the Manchurian Emperor is, at present, studying here."[46]

The political orientation of Waseda International Institute unambiguously set the tone for its curriculum and the characteristics of its student body. At first glance, the list of subjects appears similar to Nichibei Home's, but Waseda's program was more advanced and intensive in its standard of two- to three-year college preparatory courses. The institute only accepted high school graduates or above, and a large number of the students had already completed higher education outside Japan.[47] A majority of its graduates moved on to prestigious Japanese universities and colleges. Others entered Japan's business world and the public service sector, including the Foreign Ministry and even the Man-chukuo government, after mastering Japanese language and culture.[48] Unlike their counterparts at Nichibei Home and Keisen, many of Waseda's Nisei grad-uates lived as permanent residents of Japan, destined to be swallowed up in Japan's war machine against their native country. In some cases, this literally involved their dropping of American citizenship—an idea many Issei dismissed as contradictory to the goal of Nisei education and the bridge ideal. Indeed, wary of Waseda's program from the standpoint of U.S. strategic interests, an American consular official branded it "pure [pro-Japan] propaganda."[49] And their experience at Waseda was not very different from that of thousands of Nisei students at accredited schools under the rigid control of the Japanese government.

In light of its self-serving interpretation of the bridge concept, Tokyo in-stituted an even more blatantly nationalizing scheme, recruiting Nisei for official propagandist training in the disguise of a government-sponsored scholarship program. Secretly organized in 1939, a boarding school called the Heishikan was the brainchild of Kawai Tatsuo, the Foreign Ministry's chief of the information bureau. As a former Heishikan student recalls, Kawai wanted to "train a select group of Nisei as [English-language] press attachés," who would "spearhead the promotion of U.S.-Japan friendship."[50] In reality, graduates of the school would be enlisted as full-time intelligence agents, as they were expected to serve as foreign correspondents for the state-owned Domei News Agency, join the foreign office, or work for the South Manchurian Railway. As Japanese American leftists perceptively pointed out in their criticism, ministry officials knew all too well "that nisei with their intimate knowledge of America and the English language [could] become valuable tools in spreading the gospel of fascism."[51] Some officials actually viewed the political value of the Nisei beyond the simple bilateral context. Less than two weeks before the bombing of Pearl Harbor, Kawai's subordinate compiled a classified report, in which he recommended "the use of Spanish-speaking American-born Nisei males" for "anti-American operations in Mexico and the American West" to turn Mexican and Mexican American sentiments against the Anglo ruling class.[52]

In order to solicit applications for the Heishikan from the United States and Canada, Kawai first sent letters to the principals of Japanese-language schools without disclosing the real purpose of the academy. Searching for twenty Nisei to whom the Foreign Ministry would offer full scholarships, Kawai simply requested that an eligible applicant, whether male or female, must be between twenty and thirty years old; must be a graduate of a Japanese-language school with an American high school diploma; and must pass character and background checks by the local Japanese consulate, as well as oral and written examinations administered in English and Japanese. The ministry would offer each scholarship recipient a $300 stipend to travel to Japan and, upon arrival, another $37. Quite a few Nisei found this scholarship program attractive, since, as a Heishikan graduate remembers, more than fifty people took the examination at the Los Angeles consulate. In their eyes, the program seemed a good way to escape the circumscribed life of a racial minority in America, but most failed to predict the devastating effects that attending the school would have upon their lives after December 1941. Instead of working as an international bridge for peace and friendship, they were forced to partake in the destruction of their own country.[53]

The Heishikan was a clandestine school accommodating only a handful of Nisei students, which limited its effect. In the Class of 1940, there was a total of sixteen Nisei: four from San Francisco, four (including two females) from Los Angeles, three from Honolulu, two each from Portland and Vancouver, and one from Seattle. Their age ranged from twenty-one to twenty-seven, and the majority graduated from or previously attended American colleges and universities, including the University of California, University of Hawaii, and

Northwestern College Law School. At the Heishikan, they studied Japanese, constitutional and international law, political science and economics, Chinese classics, history and geography, journalism, ethics, and calligraphy, as well as martial arts. After completing the intensive two-year program, these Nisei were required to serve in whatever capacities they were ordered for a minimum duration of three years. Members of the first graduating class were assigned to work for the Foreign Ministry, the Domei News Agency, and the *Japan Times,* while a few received overseas appointments in China, Manchukuo, and Australia.[54]

However, Japan's attempt to undermine the Nisei's Americanness did not go completely unnoticed. "Behind this type of thinking," condemned a Nisei leader in Japan, "there is a strong—should I say—nationalistic ideology to make them stronger Japanese and to utilize them . . . [for] spreading the national glory abroad." Another expatriate deplored the fact that the majority of the Japanese "could not understand the sentiment of the nisei . . . —their loyalty to America."[55] Kazumaro Buddy Uno, a well-known Nisei writer, concurred: "It is not fair for Nipponese to think the Nisei want to be 'taken back into the fold of Nippon' for they never were a part of the Nippon fold." While an average Nisei took pride in "his Nippon heritage," Uno insisted, the second generation was still "constitutionally and psychologically American. Let there be no doubts about this."[56] An Issei Buddhist minister echoed these voices of protest, underscoring the preponderance of citizenship over lineage:

> Japanese people like to discuss the problem of American Nisei, but that is utterly inappropriate . . . Our Nisei are Americans. [Nisei education] should be left in the hands of residents in America, and the people of Japan should stay out of it . . . No matter what, the second generation is destined to carve their own way as Americans, and that's how it should be. [The meddling of Japanese] is a great nuisance to the Nisei.[57]

Though a vast majority of Nisei in Japan did not complain as forcibly, nor did they revolt publicly against the Japanese rendition of transnational education, the propagandist mission under the guise of the bridge ideal failed to inspire ordinary American-born men and women. Japanese calls seem to have fallen largely on deaf ears, as most Nisei stubbornly refused to become "nationalized" by the call of blood. On the matter of the Sino-Japanese War, for example, an anonymous writer reported from Tokyo in the *Shin Sekai*, "[T]he general run of the Nisei here are wholly indifferent and passive." He categorized approximately 900 Nisei expatriates in the Tokyo area into three different groups in terms of their political stances toward Japan. The first consisted of some 200 youths, who "are in sympathy with the policy of the [Japanese] government." Another 160 Nisei generally sympathized with the suffering of the Japanese people, but they did "not agree with the views set forth by the government leaders." A majority of the Nisei in the capital city would "not care whether Japan is right or wrong—as long as they don't have to do any fighting." The Nisei reporter analyzed that the first group represented those who had become "intensively Japanized" by work situations or family associations. The intermediate members tended to have decided to make Japan their home for the time being, which sensitized them to the frustrations that the general public experienced in the exhausting war against China. The rest were mostly *ryugakusei* without significant family ties or commitment to the society in Japan. Living off the remittances from their parents in America without the worries of conscription in the Japanese military, these students simply intended to return to the United States "if things [got] too hot." The reporter's conclusion poignantly elucidated the unbridgeable gap between Tokyo leaders and most Nisei students in Japan. "They are as a rule intensely indifferent to any acts of patriotism," the *Shin Sekai* correspondent noted. "Like one student put it, 'This dying for your country is not my idea of living a long life.' "[58] How, then, did this and other American-born youth live in a country so uncongenial to them?

STRANGERS IN THE ANCESTRAL LAND

"As individuals and as a group they are more concerned with their everyday problems than with politics," reported an American diplomat in Japan.[59] Living in an unfamiliar environment often without anybody to turn to, an average Nisei expatriate grappled with the mundane challenges that derived from cultural differences, language difficulties, and homesickness. The ordinary Japanese around whom the second generation lived their daily lives knew little of their purported bridge mission. Instead, applying their own understandings of international relations, most Japanese treated the American-born with preconceived biases and stereotypes. A woman who unexpectedly found herself in Tokyo as a result of her family's relocation from southern California gave a glimpse of the common Nisei dilemma in Japan during the 1930s. She wrote to her journalist friend frankly about her encounters with militaristic Japan, her daily struggles, and her longings for American life. "It is simply terrible not being able to speak Japanese. You're an outcast, a freak, an imbecile. It certainly is an embarrassment." Complaining about how boring life was there and how every Japanese stared at her and her younger brother, the Nisei woman remembered her California life with affection. "I'm missing the Lil' [*sic*] Tokyo gang terribly. It burns me up to think that I'm missing the grand mass picnics at Luna Park, the Nisei Week, Brighton Beach and dancing at the Bon Ton in

Ocean Park. How I'd like to come back to America."[60] Countless other Nisei in Japan must have similarly felt a keen sense of loss.

Their international upbringing put most Nisei expatriates in a great quandary. On the one hand, with their belief in the immutability of race, the people of Japan pressured the American-born to act as part of them, imposing rigid cultural norms and a prescribed mode of behavior. "When in the country of their ancestors, because of their physical characteristics they are looked upon as Japanese and anything that may seem foreign about them is looked upon with a critical eye," Keisen students observed. The life of female Nisei tended to be fraught with even more troubles, because they "[were] expected to live up to the strict standards of social etiquette for Japanese women."[61] This force of relentless Japanizing was nonetheless countered by another, which classified the entire second-generation population as antisocial, even criminal. Whereas the former had its roots in the logic of blood-will-tell racism, which demoted citizenship status in questions of national belonging, the latter stemmed from a position that tended to emphasize cultural attributes—perceived or real—as signs of authenticity.

Under the militarist regime, this cultural essentialism rendered the Nisei as a synonym of "individualism" and "materialism," the concepts that symbolized the worst social ills of "foreign" origin. During the 1930s, many people in Japan, as in the United States, embraced the value polarization of things as Japanese or American. From this perspective, the behavior of a typical Nisei would look rude, unbearably disrespectful, and lacking in basic social modesty. Moreover, an American-born woman registered as shamelessly arrogant and demanding, and an American-born man as hopelessly spineless and epicurean. Rumor also had it that the second generation would frequent cafes and dance halls in Tokyo's entertainment district, enjoying extravagant lifestyles, spending money on gaudy clothes, watching decadent American movies, and consuming expensive Western food. Of course, according to the Nisei's cultural common sense, many of these recreational activities entailed nothing more than legitimate ways of socializing, but they signaled moral degradation to the nationalistic Japanese public.[62]

Several well-publicized cases of alleged Nisei malefactors reinforced the general perception of the Nisei as the embodiment of abhorred Americanism. The year 1933 witnessed some of the most notorious ones. In May, an Osaka newspaper reported the story of an eighteen-year-old Hawaiian-born woman who was discovered working as a cafe waitress, an occupation that often bordered on being an unlicensed prostitute. While this news whetted the public's curiosity about the second generation in general and reinforced an image of Nisei women's promiscuity, a rush of other newspaper accounts helped to shape a notion of Nisei criminality in the minds of the Japanese masses. Some of the examples included reports about second-generation students, like one who impregnated a dancer, while others coaxed money out of waitresses and dancers and engaged in lecherous conduct in the gay quarters. Further tainting their name was a sensationalized story of "some Nisei's involvement in an American espionage network."[63] The Nisei were not only cultural misfits; they were now public enemies inimical to national security.

In the fall of 1933, the suicide of a Nisei fugitive in a Tokyo dance hall drew extensive public attention. This man represented all of the moral transgressions that the militarist state was attempting to root out from Japanese society. Seattle-born Frank Kumagaya spent his early years in Japan until his return to California at the age of nineteen. After attending a Los Angeles high school, he went to Japan in 1931 and soon became a familiar face on the social scene in the Tokyo-Yokohama region. Wearing a shiny suit with his hair set neatly with pomade, this Nisei charmed pleasure-seeking patrons at the dance halls. Yet, in order to support his extravagant lifestyle, he also extorted money from dancers, hall managers, and even his own siblings by threatening their lives. By May 1933, the Tokyo Metropolitan Police learned of his criminal acts and proceeded to expel him from Japan. Kumagaya, however, managed to sneak back into the country from China. At that time, as a part of the cultural purification campaign, law enforcement made frequent raids on dance halls. Early in October, there was a citywide surprise raid, during which a detective caught a glimpse of Kumagaya and chased him to a restroom. The young man put up a fight, knocking down the detective, but other policemen eventually restrained him, at which time Kumagaya began coughing up blood, and he soon died. Later, the police found that the Nisei had taken poison before being caught. Tokyo newspapers sensationalized his death with details of past malfeasance and ascribed his behavior to his upbringing as a Nisei. The distorted reports described Kumagaya as having grown up among "American [Issei] ruffians" and having acquired his criminal qualities in American society, even though he actually spent most of his adolescent years in Japan. Nonetheless, the newspapers led readers to associate every Nisei with illegality and immorality.[64]

The wholesale criminalization of the Nisei by the Japanese police soon followed the Kumagaya incident. By late 1933, the problem of the American-born went beyond scandalous newspaper articles to become a real concern of the law. In order to have a comprehensive grasp of the situation, the Home Ministry ordered the prefectural police to compile statistical data on resident Nisei and to make inquiries about their organizational activities, lifestyles, and personal conduct.[65] Detectives visited apartments, boarding houses, schools, dormitories, and other places where there was a Nisei presence. Although most prefectural police found no existing or potential problems in their jurisdictions,

Tokyo pointed out instances of illegal work, a "thought problem," and other forms of less-than-satisfactory behavior among its Nisei population. The secret report, dated December 15, 1933, remarked:

> There is virtually no work for them [in Japan], so most of them attend [school] under the guise of studying Japanese by receiving remittances from their parents. Yet, some are employed by shady companies, and others are engaged in illegal activities as [unlicensed] tour guides. As they believe in so-called Americanism, they possess no sympathy for Japan. They are deficient in an understanding of the Manchurian situation, and they condemn Japan as the aggressor. They exhibit hardly any enthusiasm for studying or [other] positive activities.[66]

While the police classified some Nisei organizations as "secretive" with a hint of security risk, it also depicted one group as full of dance-hall goers and cafe patrons.

After this nationwide investigation, the Nisei became the target of greater police surveillance along with other dangerous "criminal" elements, including communists, liberals, and cosmopolitan thinkers—the groups with misguided "anti-Japanese" traits. An expatriate leader reported that "600 of the 1,000 niseis in [the] Tokyo [region] were on the so-called black-list of [the] Metropolitan Police bureau" by November 1934. How and why the police placed them on such a list must have been utterly surprising and incomprehensible for most Nisei. One woman recounted the events at a dance party held at a Nisei social club in a respectably American fashion: "[A] whole troop of policemen" raided this private gathering and interrogated the Nisei participants. After taking down their names, the police blacklisted every one of them. Frequent raids upon dance halls resulted in some Nisei being detained by the police, who often resorted to violence during interrogations.[67] The persecution of Nisei young men and women constituted a significant part of the cultural purge and purification of Japanese society under the militarist regime.

Viewed from the perspective of police and military officials, the American-reared Japanese looked increasingly like agents for foreign powers. At a 1939 "thought-control" conference, a high-ranking Ministry of Justice official briefed the attendees on three apparent patterns of foreign intelligence in Japan. Most of the activities centered around foreign diplomatic establishments and personnel, while resident aliens, such as newspaper correspondents, businesspeople, Christian ministers, and exchange students, comprised the next major element. The third pattern of foreign intelligence was to employ "Japanese" spies, including so-called dissident Koreans and Nisei. According to the official, this option would be the "ideal method of information gathering," whereas the first two presented racial and language difficulties that impeded their effectiveness.

An ordinary Japanese, however, was "so strong in his loyalty to the emperor and patriotism to the state" that the use of the native-born national would be "extremely difficult." In the case of Koreans and Nisei, they generally "lacked a national sentiment," making them suitable for the work of espionage on behalf of foreign governments.[68] The juxtaposition of Nisei and "dissident Koreans" signified the extent of official distrust, for Korean nationalists had always been considered the most treacherous elements in the Japanese empire.

Thus, from the mid-1930s, the authorities tightened up control over the American-born in Japan. The first step was to keep resident Nisei in line through supervised mobilization. An American consular report remarked on this new method: "For purposes of better surveillance the 'Nisei' have been encouraged to organize clubs. The membership, purposes and activities of the clubs are carefully watched by the police." This measure accompanied "the [imposed] study of Japanese culture" in the Nisei clubs, designed to give them "as much Japanese propaganda as they will absorb."[69] Legal and procedural changes were also put in place, which affected the immigration status of the second generation. Under the existing law, for example, a Nisei without Japanese citizenship was supposed to register at the local law enforcement office, but most had disregarded this rule without repercussions. The police now began vigorously enforcing this law, declaring that unregistered Nisei could face serious consequences, including a ban on embarkation from Japan. Officials at Yokohama and Kobe also started to require that incoming Nisei, like other foreigners, possess regular visas issued by a Japanese consulate, which represented the revoking of their special privilege based on their common racial origin.[70] At the immigration station, their political orientation drew especially close scrutiny from the Japanese authorities.

Unfortunate victims of stiffened official attitude, a Nisei couple from Washington found themselves beset by a contradiction of racial and cultural essentialisms when they arrived at Yokohama in March 1936. The second-generation man recalled that immigration officers were hostile from the outset, segregating the American-born Japanese from the rest of the arriving passengers for special inspections. Following a brief interview, an officer ordered the couple to go to a separate room, where four men stringently interrogated the Nisei husband and wife. Their questioning focused on the reason behind the man's prior decision to renounce Japanese nationality in favor of single U.S. citizenship. He ascribed it to his desire to concentrate on his theological "study" in Japan. Considering him to be a selfish draft evader, the officials angrily accused the Nisei of putting schooling ahead of a sacred obligation to the country. One official yelled, "A Japanese must always give utmost priority to his Emperor and the nation-state."[71]

Once his allegiance to the racial home was deemed dubious, the Nisei's politics became a matter of official concern. He was questioned insolently about whether he was a communist, internationalist, pacifist, or socialist. Indignant over rude treatment and groundless imputation, the man finally requested that his wife and he be admitted simply as Americans. The Japanese were so infuriated that they flatly told him to go back to the United States if he trivialized his Japanese heritage. Learning that the couple did not have the required amount of funds for entry as regular foreign visitors, a regulation that was rarely enforced, the immigration officers proceeded to send them back on the steamship, which subsequently sailed off to China and the Philippines with them. Not until repeated apologies were filed by their families in Japan did the authorities lift the ban on the Nisei's disembarkation, and they returned on the ship two weeks later.[72] The couple's ordeal did not end there, however; once in Japan, they simply joined other blacklisted American-born who were subject to police harassment and public malice. Under the banner of the bridge ideal, such schizophrenic treatment of the Nisei as both a racial property and a cultural/political menace provided the context for their struggle as strangers in their ancestral land during the 1930s.

Though life for the second generation became progressively harder in Japan, Tamotsu Murayama and a few other resident Nisei leaders seriously contemplated ways in which to keep their international identity intact. A prominent Nisei journalist and early JACL leader, Murayama was an ardent defender of the American-born Japanese and an advocate of their interests in Japan and the United States. Educated in a Japanese middle school before working as a reporter for a San Francisco vernacular press, Murayama could appreciate the Issei vision better than any other Nisei, and thus looked to reflect the bridge concept in the JACL platform in its formative years. Seeking a better career opportunity and a transpacific life, he opted to move to Japan in 1934 to work for the Domei News Agency. Faced with biases against Nisei, Murayama always admonished his junior *ryugakusei* against "careless" behavior, but he was also exasperated at groundless criticism and police harassment. His disdain for so-called Japanese experts in Nisei education ran especially deep, because he thought they caused more harm than good. In many cases, their know-it-all writings, to which the public gave considerable weight, not only reinforced existing stereotypes but also fueled social persecution. Murayama also strove to rectify misperceptions among Japanese journalists, and he was a frequent visitor to the Foreign Ministry and the police bureau in defense of Nisei.[73] In his words, it was "an endless fight to defend nisei in this part of the world." Yet, "I shall carry on as long as I stay here," vowed Murayama to his close friend James Y. Sakamoto in Seattle, "since I feel it is my duty for the nisei in America."[74]

Murayama believed that the Nisei must speak for themselves rather than let the Japanese misrepresent them.[75] The Nisei leader insisted that they create an institutional apparatus to safeguard Nisei rights in Japan and engage in a positive public-relations campaign there.[76] Established in 1937 and 1939, respectively, the Japan-America Young People's Federation (JAYPF) and the Nisei Information Service (NIS) were Murayama's brainchildren. The JAYPF brought fragmented existing Nisei organizations in Tokyo into a federated body for the purpose of representing their collective interests. Addressing the immediate concerns of the resident Nisei married to Japanese nationals, its first project pushed for the modification of the exclusion clause in the American Immigration Act, by which to enable those couples to return to the United States together.[77] In all probability, this effort took place in conjunction with what historian Izumi Hirobe calls transnational "private diplomacy" conducted by a coalition of American clergy, West Coast white business leaders, and Japanese liberals.[78] In addition to this movement, the JAYPF published a quarterly magazine titled *Pan-Pacific Youth*, which carried the latest English-language news reports and political commentaries, along with literary works "exclusively for Niseis, by Niseis."[79]

Murayama specifically tied his support for the NIS to the bridge concept. Characterizing "the nisei community in Japan" as "an extension of America," he wrote: "[I]t sound[s] very good when we say that the nisei must be the bridge of the Pacific. The leg of the Pacific Bridge was build [*sic*] in America in the name of the Japanese American Citizens League . . . and the time has come to build the other end of the leg in Japan."[80] Whereas the JAYPF's function was to unite American-born expatriates along their citizenship ties, the NIS intended to service intellectual needs for the future international bridge. First and foremost, the organization's mediating role in Japan had to begin by countering the negative images of the Nisei and the "America" that they represented in the mind of the public. Along these lines, the organization endeavored to disseminate "correct" data and facts on Nisei students by means of in-house publications and lectures to the general populace in Tokyo. By the same token, since the youngsters were to work as cultural interpreters of misunderstood Japan for the home public in America upon their return, the NIS furnished the American-born with useful English-language information on Japanese society, history, and culture. At its library, students could also read American newspapers and other materials. Additional components of its program included arranging home stays with Japanese families for Nisei *ryugakusei* and work placement for new graduates, as well as operating the Nisei Center, a social and cultural sanctuary for the second generation in Japan.[81]

In reality, Murayama's "endless fight to defend nisei" was doomed, for the two countries were fast going down the path toward a military clash. Not only were the negative qualities of the Nisei magnified in Japanese eyes, the society turned so prohibitive of anything "American" that *ryugakusei* were unable to speak English even among themselves without provoking nationalist wrath. Murayama reported a case in which a man slapped a Nisei woman on a train, enraged by her English-language conversation with another American-born student.[82] As the situation worsened for Nisei in Japan by the late 1930s, Murayama began to urge Nisei students to return to America. In his opinion, only those who had the will to dedicate themselves to United States–Japan friendship should remain in Japan. But he also emphasized that those who remained had to be serious and obstinately determined, for there was the risk of being stranded in Japan as enemy nationals.[83] He also told them that they had to be prepared to accept the fate of forfeiting U.S. citizenship to live as Japanese subjects, willingly or unwillingly, in case of war. With such a dismal outlook, an exodus of Nisei from Japan began in 1940. While the number of Japanese American visitors to Japan dropped sharply, from 189 to 11, between the third and fourth quarters of 1940, several hundred hurried back to the United States.[84] For those who failed to do so, the hardships would be harsher than Murayama's gloomy predictions. Throughout the war years, their American backgrounds made the resident Nisei the target of constant harassment and close surveillance by the police and the war-mongering public. While the Japanese military often conscripted them for its propaganda and intelligence work, epitomized in the case of "Tokyo Rose," many Nisei suffered social ostracism as likely "American spies."[85]

Even for those fortunate enough to reach the shores of California or Washington in time, distrust and rejection were all that awaited such Nisei, now lumped under the general category of "Kibei." In American society, wild accusations were raised with regard to where their political allegiance lay due to their Japanese education. The following description in a mainstream publication of the Kibei's alleged treacherousness, contrived as it was, suffices to illuminate the burden of internationalism that the group had to carry back to the United States:

> Thwarted by cruel discrimination [in America], *nisei* in large numbers return to the land of their fathers; only to find that there too they are out of place. They are disliked as "different." They may return to America full of resentment toward their own people. But if you think that the last spark of Nipponism has now been extinguished in their breasts, go to meet one as he lands in San Francisco and greet him with a laughing insult at the expense of the Japanese Emperor. Someone tried it recently; within twenty-four hours he was dead of a sword-thrust, and beside him lay the nisei, "happily dispatched" by his own hand with the same sword.[86]

As adults were burning the bridge over the Pacific, the meaning of *international* turned into the polar opposite of *national*, or the antinational, which rendered a Kibei an embodiment of the loathsome enemy, in the language of war. Marked by the imprints of Japanese culture that accentuated their racial semblance, the youngsters defied every sense of Americanism, and their national identity was questionable in the eyes of both hardcore Anglo-Saxonists and liberal cultural pluralists. To those Americans, several years of schooling were sufficient to transform Kibei into carbon copies of the fanatic Japanese soldier ready to die or kill in the interest of the divine emperor. Not surprisingly, U.S. intelligence officers and the military singled out the Nisei returnees as suspected agents of Japan for being a product of transnational education. "Such persons must be considered guilty until proven innocent beyond reasonable doubt," one intelligence expert put it unabashedly, as if an excess of foreign acculturation warranted such a blatant denial of their citizenship rights.[87] Ironically, in pursuit of a mediating role, the internationalized Nisei found themselves alienated not only from their ancestral land but also from their native country.

How, then, had their alien parents maneuvered between the conflicting forces of the two countries for the decade prior to the nations' final clash? For Japanese immigrants, nationalism ironically provided the ways to express their diasporic imagination relative to their homeland and to make sense of their minority life in the United States; it also allowed them to maintain a delicate balance between a return to their racial heritage and their movement into American national life.

Part IV

Complexities of Immigrant Nationalism

7

Helping Japan, Helping Ourselves

The Meaning of Issei Patriotism

The decade of the 1930s ushered in the ascendancy of militarism in Japan and a corresponding surge of nationalism in the Japanese immigrant community. The ideology of imperial Japan affected overseas Japanese, including many Issei and Nisei in the United States, by intensifying nationalistic connections to their country of origin or ancestry. Though the political developments in Japan doubtless changed how the immigrants saw their native land, many aspects of Issei nationalism still remain largely unclarified. Standard interpretations draw little distinction between the nationalism of those still living in the homeland and that of overseas Japanese. The U.S. government, which decided Japanese residents were a security risk and placed them in segregated camps during the Pacific War, inarguably held such a view, and so did many postwar Japanese Americans, who had been led to inherit it through the ideological disciplining that continued even after the war. Seldom has the field of Japanese American history seen a serious discussion of the immigrant politics generated by their transnational ties during the 1930s.

Recently, some historians have begun to take up the question of Issei nationalism, offering new insights that challenge the notion of divided loyalty. Focusing on the impact of racial exclusion, Yuji Ichioka argues that the accumulated Issei anger manifested itself as a patriotic identification with Japan during the late 1930s. Brian M. Hayashi points out a correlation between the class and intellectual backgrounds of Japanese American Christians and their homeland ties. Underlying the point that Issei, like anyone else, "quite naturally loved the land of their birth and were proud of Japan's emergence as a world power," John J. Stephan compares their nationalism to a child's love for the parents.[1]

Indeed, seen from the larger perspective of American immigration history, Issei nationalism offered no unique case. From the late nineteenth century through the early twentieth century, Irish, Polish, and Jewish immigrants sustained strong ties to political projects and causes in their homelands. Korean nationalists, Chinese republicans, and Asian Indian anticolonialists turned their diasporic communities in the United States into key sources of support for national liberation.[2] American historians are generally sympathetic in their assessment of these movements, for the national liberationist motifs fit the ideological tenets of the United States as the land of the free and a haven for the oppressed. Only when their country of origin emerges as an antagonist to the adopted country is immigrant nationalism stigmatized in hindsight. During America's major foreign military engagements, German, Italian, and Japanese immigrants most notably fell into this historiographical trap.[3] In an effort to free our historical consciousness from this nationalist lens, this chapter treats Issei patriotic politics as one aspect of their complex transnational imagination and as a reflection of their restricted lives as a racial minority, instead of as evidence of their alleged anti-Americanism.

The origin of modern Issei nationalism can be traced to the rise of Japanese militarism in Manchuria in the early 1930s. This new geopolitical development in East Asia drastically transformed the hitherto estranged relationship between the empire and the immigrant community after 1924. For policy makers in Japan, Japanese residents in the United States became politically relevant again in the context of the growing tension with Anglo-American powers. After the establishment of a puppet Manchukuo in 1932, imperial Japan and the Issei community served each other's interests and goals even though these were fundamentally in conflict. The rise of Japanese immigrant patriotism, and Japan's attempt to exploit it for geopolitical purposes, did not result in the metamorphosis of the Issei into a replica of the Japanese militarist or the ultranationalist extremist, as anti-Japanese agitators often claimed. Instead, Issei patriotism inaugurated another phase of the immigrant-state partnership where immigrant dreams and Japan's state mandate converged in complex ways.

MONETARY AND MATERIAL SUPPORT FOR JAPAN

The news reports of the clash between the Imperial Japanese Army and the Chinese Nationalist Forces on September 18, 1931, initially elicited little reaction from Japanese immigrants. The *Nichibei Shimbun* calmly called for "coopera-tion" and a "diplomatic solution" between the two Asian nations instead of military aggression. It never discussed the direct impact that the event might have on the lives of ordinary Japanese in America. Another newspaper observed that most Issei were "uninterested" in the East Asian crisis.[4] The vernacular press reported the incident as one of many skirmishes that had sporadically occurred between the Japanese and Chinese forces since the 1920s. Nonetheless, as Japan escalated military action in northern China after October, immigrant attitudes changed. The end of the crisis now seemed distant, and the severe winter in Manchuria was about to set in. Reports of hardships tormenting Japanese soldiers began to appear in the Issei press. The masses of Japan, ac-cording to the wire news, engaged in patriotic campaigns to collect money, care packages or "comfort bags" (*imon bukuro*), and other relief materials for the soldiers in Manchuria and their families left behind in Japan. It is in this context that many Issei were propelled to show their "gratitude" for their fellow coun-trymen at the war front.[5]

Along with the shifting tone of the vernacular press, a personal plea for support made by a leader of the Patriotic Women's Society in Japan inspired a number of self-styled immigrant patriots. In response to the call for the collec-tion of comfort bags in America, many immigrant organizations, especially women's clubs, launched patriotic campaigns throughout the Pacific Coast states. In southern California, the Federation of the Southern California Japa-nese Women's Associations announced its plan to send 5,000 comfort bags to Manchuria. Within four days, the Japanese farmers of Venice donated more than $500, which translated into 1,500 comfort bags just from this one small farm community. To this, a Los Angeles Buddhist women's association added another 1,000 bags; produce market youths 1,800; and a local farmers' league 500 more.[6] Meanwhile, a *Nichibei Shimbun* editorial urged its northern Cali-fornia readers to carry out their own campaigns, arguing that they, as members of the Japanese nation, also had an obligation to help their compatriots in need.[7] In Walnut Grove, the women's association hastily collected 135 comfort bags with donated "comfort money" of $25. The local Buddhist women's group also donated six boxes full of care packages.[8] Containing goods worth twenty-five to fifty cents, each package typically included cigarettes, underwear, razors, candy, talismans, and a "comfort letter."

The Issei's support was contingent on their perception of the extent to which their homeland was in trouble. Their behavior was not unique in the history of the Japanese in America. When Japan first fought China in 1894 and then Russia a decade later, many Issei had given similar support for Japan's war efforts. In 1904, for example, San Francisco's Japanese donated approximately $100,000 to their native country.[9] Moreover, sending comfort bags to soldiers was no different from sending care packages or donations to victims of natural disasters, which the Issei had always done for their compatriots. In light of this, it was only natural that the sudden patriotic fever lasted only a few months in the winter of 1931–1932, for the open conflict between Japan and China quickly came to a halt. As long as the war required their native land to exhaust its resources, Japanese immigrants, like many other immigrant groups in the United States, took it for granted that overseas residents were obligated to render as much material support as they could. As the press often argued, Japan, after all, was still their country of citizenship.[10]

Following the Marco Polo Bridge incident of July 7, 1937, the full-fledged war between Japan and China led to similar calls for national duty. About a week after the beginning of the battle, the Issei press started to report on how unified the people of Japan were behind the imperial forces. In no time, groups of imperial army veterans spearheaded collection activities in San Francisco and Sacramento. On July 20, the Japanese Association of San Francisco and representatives from the *Nichibei Shimbun* and the *Shin Sekai* discussed how to coordinate a patriotic effort in northern California. They agreed to launch a massive comfort bag collection campaign with the sponsorship of local Japanese associations and asked the Nippon Yusen Shipping Company to provide free transport of the donations from San Francisco to Japan, a nationalist proposition that the Japanese firm could not refuse.[11]

In southern California, major community organizations responded to this crisis by early August. The Japanese Association of Los Angeles decided to focus on the collection of monetary donations, a move that resulted in the formation of an emergency committee with the local Japanese Chamber of Commerce. The joint agency swiftly produced $63,900 for the Japanese military. While the Federation of the Southern California Japanese Women's Associations solicited comfort bags from female Issei and Nisei, Japanese residents of the Pasadena area discharged their patriotic service in a unique way. Setting the goal of presenting the Japanese armed forces with warplanes, a voluntary group managed to remit enough funds for an army liaison aircraft, which was later named for the group.[12] Meanwhile, the Japanese of Seattle forwarded twenty-five tons of used clothing and rugs, as well as bandages worth more than $6,500 for army hospitals in China.[13] Even in the far-flung settlement of Ogden, Utah, the local Japanese association sent 933 comfort bags by raising $72 early in September. By the end of the month, 142 area residents made additional donations of $1,723; more than half of the 272 households in Ogden participated in this campaign.[14] Since the fierce and brutal war went on with no end in sight, the intensity and longevity of the Issei's patriotic drives distinguished this movement from its 1931 counterpart.

Japanese immigrant patriotism, however, did not simply emanate from

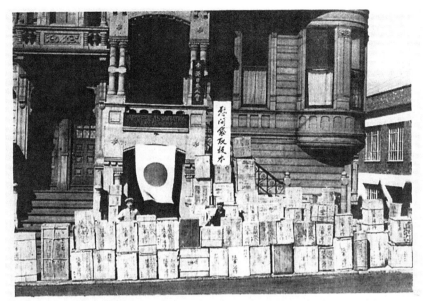

＝一九三七北支事變出征將士慰問袋（一般募集）風國發途の直前＝
＝在米本日人會場前に於て＝

FIGURE 7.1. Boxes of Care Packages en route to Japan, San Francisco, ca. 1937
Piled up in front of the Japanese Association of San Francisco building, these boxes contained care packages, or *imon bukuro*, for Japanese soldiers on the China front. Since the early twentieth century, the collection of relief materials and funds for their homeland in crisis had been a routine practice in the Japanese immigrant community. Reprinted from Zaibei Nihonjinkai, *Zaibei Nihonjinshi* (1940).

emotional attachment to Japan or reaction to its perceived crisis. It mirrored an ongoing power struggle within the ethnic community, and behind their activities lay the interacting forces of competition and social pressure. Power relations and community politics generally revolved around various cultural and social advantages, or capitals, that the immigrant elite possessed, which included education, material wealth, class background, and prefectural origin.[15] Built upon the Issei's nationalistic common sense that support for Japan was the right thing to do, it became an imperative after July 1937 for one to partake in patriotic campaigns in order to remain a legitimate member of the ethnic and national community. The extent of one's contribution, or the lack thereof, now signified the degree of one's authenticity as a Japanese, which enabled individuals to either elevate or devalue their social position within a community or an organization. In theoretical terms, patriotic activities arose as a new social capital, around which an aspect of power struggle and position-taking evolved. The

Sino-Japanese War produced a common field of contestation for community leadership, where most individual Issei, and organizations, could gauge—and agree upon—their mutual worth in terms of their demonstrated patriotic identification with Japan.[16]

This nationalistic frenzy pitted individuals against individuals, organizations against organizations, and even communities against communities.[17] Columns of newspaper space were dedicated to listing the names of patriotic donors with specific dollar amounts in each community—a practice initiated by the *Nichibei Shimbun* in August 1937 and mimicked by other major Japanese papers. Local correspondents sent in the donors' lists for Japanese settlements up and down the Pacific Coast, and newspapers singled out those who made large contributions in special reports. In the competitive atmosphere, sponsoring organizations often split their members into squads of solicitors and dispatched them to collect money from other residents in the vicinity. In Portland, for instance, the local Japanese association divided its jurisdiction into thirteen districts, according to an FBI agent: "Three men in each district are designated as collectors of the money, one doing the talking, the second the actual taking of the money, and the third making the record of the amount donated."[18] Anyone who hesitated to comply with the donation "request" exposed himself to the possibility of being criticized in print as a "selfish tightwad" or even as a "traitor."[19] In this way, immigrant elites vying for power and status in the community exploited the Issei's emotional reaction to Japan's crisis, while putting pressure on the indifferent or the reluctant. Taken together, the forces of competition and coercion collaborated to help generate what looked like feverish immigrant patriotism.

The inflated meaning of support for Japan also engendered a transnational competition—another factor that fueled the practices of nationalist contribution in the ethnic community. Ever obsessed with their self-image as the pioneers of racial development abroad, many Issei expressed their desire that the homeland acknowledge their patriotism as second to none. The vernacular Issei press on the West Coast frequently printed the amounts of donations from outside Japan with special emphases on their own preponderance in dollar (or yen) terms. The imperial navy's official report of the first-year aggregate after the Marco Polo Bridge incident, for example, revealed that Japanese in the continental United States were responsible for gifts of $97,200, or 34 percent of the total $286,600 from all of the overseas Japanese. Hawaii came in a distant second with $67,200; Manchuria and China $59,600; Southeast Asia and Micronesia $34,200; and Latin America only $17,400. Many Issei took great pride in the fact that this rank order remained the same before 1941.[20]

In the context of grassroots community politics, nationalist competition enabled a younger group of immigrant men, as well as immigrant women, to play a particularly prominent role in the area of patriotic fund-raising. These Issei tended to have little influence in the organizations controlled by the old immigrant male elite. The prominence of women in collecting comfort bags and relief funds exemplified this dimension of patriotic activities as intraethnic power struggle. Likewise, the Heimushakai, an association of Issei men of draftable age (twenty to forty-two years old) who had deferred their Japanese military service due to their residence in America, was another product, as well as a major source, of nationalist competition and pressure in many Japanese settlements. By monopolizing the new social capital of patriotic contribution, the Heimushakai brought together younger immigrant males for distinction within Japanese immigrant society. Reading every day about compatriots of their generation fighting for the homeland on the battlefield, they felt guilty about "not [being] able to sacrifice [their lives] for the National Cause."[21] According to its mission statement:

> Since we were born in glorious Japan we are under the obligation and have the full responsibility of participating in the military service and [of] tak[ing] our place in the front line of national defense. We are unable to meet such responsibilities solely because we happen to be here in America. Once we shift our thoughts to the fighting Japanese soldiers we are unable to sit by and watch their hardships, but should and must do something. Therefore, on August 21, we called you together to organize this association and a resolution was passed to choose the best method to send the Japanese soldiers relief donations.[22]

Impelled by their sense of guilt, Heimushakai members found for themselves a special niche in patriotic fundraising at the "front line" of the nationalist movement in America. Taking charge of a donation drive gave younger Issei a rare opportunity to claim leadership in this aspect of community affairs. While the remittances from other groups quickly waned toward the last months of 1937, the Heimushakai implemented a "long-term contribution program," whereby members pledged to offer monthly dues of $1 for as long as the war in China lasted.[23] For example, the intermountain Heimushakai branch in Ogden collected nearly $300 during the month of December 1937 alone. In the meantime, the local Japanese association produced less than $160 for the three-month period between September and December.[24] To keep the inflow of money from nonmembers, Heimushakai Issei also employed, as described by a Japanese diplomat, "strong-arm tactics to coerce [them] into making donations," while rivaling each other in the amount of funds they raised. Furthermore, the organization targeted Japanese communities without a branch office and pressured them to establish one.[25] One year after the inception of its headquarters in San Francisco, there were already more than sixty Heimushakai chapters with 6,000 members throughout California and other Western states. By 1940, the number of offices and the aggregate membership further increased to eighty-two and 10,000, respectively.[26]

Although generally they were "uncertain as to how to think" or wished to "have nothing to do with the present difficulties in Japan and China," the atmosphere of hyperpatriotism induced Nisei adolescents and young adults to participate momentarily in the competition for distinction as well.[27] In December 1937, a group of leading American-born youth formed a Nisei Sincerity Society in Salt Lake City, Utah, under the leadership of Mike Masaoka, a future national leader of the Japanese American Citizens League. According to a newspaper announcement, the society set a goal of raising a military relief fund for the Japan Red Cross by collecting $1 from each Nisei of high school age or above in the area. Observing the patriotic craze of the first generation, the founders reportedly felt compelled to "make contributions to the parents' homeland." To involve as many Nisei as possible, Masaoka urged local Issei to advise their sons and daughters to cooperate with his pro-Japan campaign. The society also held a charity Christmas and roller-skating party under the official sponsorship of the local JACL chapter, for which its founders simultaneously served as leaders. All of the proceeds of the party went to the relief fund, while every Nisei donor received a "sincerity badge" as recognition.[28] Several months later, Long Beach Nisei formed a similar fundraising organization called the Nisei Patriotic Society, while in Los Angeles, there was a Patriotic Girls Society.[29]

Competition, coercion, and social pressure in Japanese immigrant patriotism masked the fact that a number of ordinary Issei might not have taken part in the movements on their own. There were sporadic reports of the Issei's reluctance, unwillingness, and even outright refusal to make donations. In June 1938, a group of Issei and Nisei communists also made two important observations; first, "the Japanese in America have been less and less eager to cooperate with fund raising for the military." Second, "having been fed up with the war, many of them now hope for an early conclusion of the conflict, albeit from a very passive [selfish] standpoint."[30] The *Doho*, their organ, concentrated on the problem of "forced contributions" as a way to win the support of the immigrant masses. Interested in penetrating into what they regarded as the conservative Issei community, the radicals found it more effective to address such "mundane" issues important to ordinary residents rather than chanting abstract theoretical slogans. Indeed, as the war became prolonged with no end in sight, forced contributions likely emerged as a matter of concealed discontent among a number of Japanese residents who had little or no stake in an intraethnic power struggle.

CAMPAIGN OF EDUCATION AND PEOPLE'S DIPLOMACY

If the Issei's direct material support for Japan characterized the early expressions of their patriotism following the Manchurian incident of July 1931 and the Marco Polo Bridge incident of September 1937, pro-Japan propaganda formed the locus of sustained Japanese immigrant action for most of the war years. Not merely reflective of their diasporic attachment to the faraway homeland, the publicity effort saliently exhibited a central theme of Japanese immigrant patriotism—the need to preserve their corporate community through the defense of Japan. The war in China created twin threats to the livelihood of Japanese America: white American enmity and Chinese American boycott. In politico-economic terms, Japan's dominance of the Manchurian region undermined the interests of other imperialist powers in maintaining the Open China policy, a situation that estranged the Asian empire from the international community. In particular, the founding of Japan's puppet Manchukuo in 1932 antagonized the West so much that the League of Nations almost unanimously condemned Tokyo. The United States, too, stood firmly against the Japanese military action in China, and anti-Japan sentiments spread in domestic public discourse. In the Pacific Coast states, as in other parts of the world, Chinese residents waged an extensive boycott against Japanese-owned businesses and interests, an action that white labor unions and leftists supported through organized picketing and public demonstrations around Japantowns and Little Tokyos. When the problem reached critical proportions during the winter of 1932, Japanese immigrants began pro-Japan publicity efforts, or what they called a "campaign of education," as a self-protective measure.

In partnership with the Japanese consulates, many Issei took on new roles as agents of the so-called people's diplomacy (*kokumin gaiko*).[31] An extension of a Wilsonian vision akin to the bridge concept, that notion envisioned that Japanese immigrants, as popular diplomats, would spearhead the promotion of U.S.–Japan friendship and peace as well as interracial harmony. Diplomacy now called for more than power politics based on military might and economics, for "people" had become an important part of the political landscape in the post–World War I years. According to this democratic theory, each and every one of the Japanese in America was entrusted with the mission of educating white Americans about Japan and the "truth" about the East Asian situation. With scarcely any interest in or knowledge about Asia, Issei reasoned, average white citizens easily fell prey to preposterous Chinese propaganda. If Japanese residents explained Japan's political position to ordinary Americans, they would be able to reach the misguided public and improve its view of the Japanese people, including Japanese Americans. Immigrant newspapers argued that this had to take priority over any other patriotic activities, since defeating Chinese propaganda and the boycott would safeguard Japanese interests in the United States in addition to benefiting Japan's diplomatic effort.[32] Helping Japan thus became tantamount to helping themselves.

In 1932, Japanese immigrant leaders, especially in urban areas where the Chinese boycott was felt most severely, first mobilized to speak for Japan. To counter anti-Japanese propaganda, Issei leaders distributed pro-Japan pamphlets and leaflets. In San Francisco, the local Japanese Chamber of Commerce printed 10,000 copies of The Shanghai Incident and Its Fact for local distribution in early 1932. During the ensuing months, Issei leaders compiled five other publications in cooperation with the Japanese consulate.[33] Furthermore, they turned their efforts toward making ordinary immigrants into "popular diplomats." The March 7, 1932, issue of the Shin Sekai printed a special English edition, which offered formal Japanese government statements, designed to provide its readers with effective public relations material.[34] About three weeks later, the Nichibei Shimbun put out a similar but more detailed English supplement titled "Symposium on the Far Eastern Crisis." Intended to justify Japan's military deployment as an act of self-defense and, more important, to stir up public aversion to the Chinese action, this eight-page document outlined alleged Chinese atrocities against Japanese civilians and their inability to govern themselves and emphasized the menacing effects on American workers and consumers of the Chinese boycott against Japanese imports. Both newspapers urged Issei readers to "present these supplements personally to their American friends and neighbors" and to make heartfelt explications no matter how bad their English might be.[35]

This version of Japanese immigrant patriotism was most evident in Walnut Grove, California, where the entire ethnic economy rested on the support of the local white elite. As in other places, the local branch of the Chinese Nationalist party spread anti-Japanese propaganda and staged an extensive boycott, which, coupled with the critical media coverage, instilled ill feelings toward Japan and the Japanese in local white land owners.[36] This situation drove local Issei farmers to seek to recapture white sympathy in order to maintain their local business interests. Beginning in March 1932, Walnut Grove immigrant leaders engaged in counterpropaganda by distributing copies of The Shanghai Incident and Its Fact. The local Japanese association also arranged for a Japanese consular member to give a speech in English to elite land owners and businespeople, where he presented the official explanations of the political situation.[37]

The wives of the white leaders were targeted by Walnut Grove Issei as well. Since they seldom attended formal political meetings, the Japanese community set up a special program for white females. Issei men asked their wives to sponsor a cultural event, to which they invited nearly fifty leading white women. Dubbed "Japan Night," it featured Japanese music and traditional dances by Nisei girls, followed by a political speech by the consular official. This program successfully lured unsuspecting white women to pro-Japan propaganda. A Walnut Grove Japanese leader claimed that these public relations activities enabled them to reinforce a "favorable" image of Japanese people in the area, thus protecting their pivotal relationship with landed whites.[38]

Not only did Japanese diplomats approve the idea of people's diplomacy, but they also wholeheartedly supported the Issei's publicity role as a useful supplement to the official propaganda program. As Japan had suffered from a depression and a chronic shortage of foreign currency during the 1930s, it could not afford to lose its exports to the United States as a result of the boycott. In order to curry favor with the American public, Japanese diplomats and consular workers barnstormed throughout California.[39] As extensive as it was, the official propaganda campaign still fell short, and Tokyo's agents felt that only local Japanese residents could fill the void. Since the official endeavor did not reach the vast majority of the American public, immigrants were in the best position to reach out to ordinary and especially rural individuals, as in Walnut Grove. In addition to being dispersed all over the American West, Japanese immigrants and their children were also strategically located within a specific stratum of American society. The Seattle consul candidly admitted that his message did not permeate to Americans of the "lower class," among whom anti-Japanese propaganda from the Chinese and leftists had taken a strong hold. Local Japanese should carry out this work, he argued, for it was these "immigrants" who dealt with common laborers and other "lower-class" citizens in their daily interactions.[40]

This diplomat had the immigrant leadership prepare a leaflet in language simple enough for ordinary people to understand. Issei small-business owners handed out leaflets to their customers, while laborers passed them to coworkers and employers. Christians distributed leaflets to white churchgoers, and Nisei schoolchildren gave them to classmates and teachers.[41] In this way, the Japanese consulates brought Japanese immigrants, as well as their American-born children, into the official propaganda apparatus in the United States. Most Issei did not give serious thought to the long-term implications of such partnership, since for the time being it served their primary agenda of self-preservation and survival as a deprived minority in America.

In this official-immigrant nexus, the Japanese associations, especially the regional headquarters in Seattle, Portland, San Francisco, and Los Angeles, restored their close working relationships with Japanese diplomats and regained their past prominence in the immigrant community. After the termination of Japanese immigration in 1924 had deprived them of key administrative functions, the Japanese consulates had abruptly severed their community ties, and every Japanese association had suffered severely from shrinking membership and operational budgets.[42] With the Manchurian crisis, diplomats found a new use for the Japanese associations in their propaganda program.[43] In 1933, the Los Angeles consul requested permission to formally subsidize the Japanese associations, contending that "the satisfactory enlightenment of Americans [on East Asian affairs], which is an extremely difficult task, cannot be fully achieved because of the current shortage of the personnel." Acknowledging the Issei's spontaneous endeavors during the previous year, the diplomat recommended to Tokyo that it "guide the Japanese associations in the right direction and integrate them into our general cultural edification project."[44] The Foreign Ministry accepted this proposal. Just as the delegated endorsement rights had in the 1910s, the new propagandist role revived the Japanese associations in the 1930s, marking the second phase of the official-immigrant collaboration.

Until July 1937, this partnership chiefly took the form of patriotic education among Issei and Nisei. With the help of the Japanese consulates, immigrant leaders endeavored to turn the residents into capable spokespersons, or popular diplomats. They first raised the issue of training residents to provide model answers to the Manchurian question. In response to the Issei's requests, the consulates dispatched representatives to rural communities for special lectures at regular intervals.[45] Pro-Japan educational efforts targeted Nisei most emphatically. Many immigrant leaders shared with Japanese officials the belief that American-born youngsters were the best publicists à la the "bridge of understanding," because unlike their parents they could fluently speak English and understand American ways of thinking.[46] Immigrant leaders agreed that many Nisei also realized the need for education about Japan and East Asia, because classmates and teachers at public schools often confronted them as if they were representatives of Japan.[47] Increasingly, members of the second generation were expected to act not simply as cultural interpreters, but as Japan's defense attorneys, mainly in defense of their position in America.

Yet, the Nisei still suffered from a serious deficiency, since they lacked practical knowledge of Japanese history and society, as well as a grasp of international relations in East Asia. Protracted educational sojourns in Japan offered one solution to the challenge, but these were not widely available to the majority of the American-born children. Issei leaders frequently furnished English-language forums for their study of Japanese history and East Asian affairs by consular staff members or English-speaking Issei.[48] Starting in the mid-1930s, many Issei educators also came to incorporate the subject of East Asian politics into Japanese-language instruction. A sudden curriculum change at the Walnut Grove academy was a case in point. From 1933 to 1941, the Issei principal taught special summer classes on Japanese history and philosophy. As soon as full-scale

MORE OF THIS SUNSHINE IN 1937–WE HOPE!

✦ *FIRST PRIZE CARTOON—By Frank Taira of San Francisco*

FIGURE 7.2. New Role for Japanese Americans in US–Japan Amity and Interracial Harmony, 1937
First-prize winner of a cartoon contest, this illustration encapsulates the Issei's idea of "people's diplomacy." The traditional culture of Japan, as indicated in this image, always constituted a significant part of their pro-Japan publicity efforts. Reprinted from *Shin Sekai* (New World, San Francisco), Jan. 1, 1937.

war broke out between Japan and China in 1937, the school offered intensive education on the historical outlines of the Sino-Japanese relationship, the socioideological systems of the two nations, and Japan's policy in Asia.[49]

Japanese composition was a popular method of "enlightening" the second-generation adolescents on the China question. The practice entailed not only language learning but also ideological training, as it required students to think and express their ideas in their own words. With this in mind, the Los Angeles Japanese consulate stepped forward to sponsor a Japanese composition and oratorical contest in 1933. Themes for the compositions were announced on the spot, and Nisei participants, divided into various age groups, were given two hours to write their essays without the help of a teacher or dictionary. Thirteen students of the intermediate level (fifteen to nineteen years old) tackled the most ideologically charged theme, "The Pacific Era and Japanese American Citizens." The compositions of the prize winners, though not representative of ordinary second-generation youth, revealed that the Issei's message had been received, at least by some Nisei. All winners stressed that it was their generational mission, as ethnic Japanese and as American citizens, to enhance "Japanese-American friendship by dispelling the prevailing ignorance of [white] Americans."[50] This contest became an annual tradition in southern California, although the consulate transferred its sponsorship to Japanese immigrant educators in 1935, probably out of concern about a possible attack from white exclusionists for meddling in the education of Nisei.

Many schools employed the same pedagogical methods in daily instruction. The Compton Japanese School was very active in using Japanese compositions. In late 1937, teachers assigned students of the sixth to twelfth grades to write short essays on the Sino-Japanese War, which ranged from stories of their encounters with anti-Japanese sentiments held by "ill informed" public-school teachers and peers to the familiar thesis of their generational mission. Reflecting what had been ingrained in Nisei pupils, their compositions contained expressions of racial pride and patriotic feeling toward Japan that always aligned with their sense of duty as American citizens. A typical example, entitled "My Thoughts on the Sino-Japanese Crisis," read in Japanese:

> Many of us, the Nisei, are not sure what position to take on the recent Sino-Japanese crisis. Regrettably, I myself do not know much about the truth because I have not had a chance to attend a lecture [on the subject]. Yet, I know that we all have to learn why Japan must fight China despite the comfort that a neutral stance may offer to us . . . Since we are the Nisei, one may argue that we should have the same opinions as other Americans do. But we cannot help hoping for Japan's victory because we share the same blood with my parents . . . We shall do our best to understand the truth of the crisis as well as possible, and we shall all try to inform Americans of the righteous Japanese position and prevent further damage on Japanese-American relations.[51]

The school later compiled a special anthology that contained sixty-five essays of this sort.

The Reverend Takeshi Ban, a Los Angeles Christian educator, devised the most innovative program for the patriotic education of ordinary Issei and Nisei youngsters. A few months after the Manchurian incident in 1931, he founded the Pacific Society of Religious Education (Taiheiyo Bunka Kyoikukai) and conducted educational tours annually, which combined the presentation of imported Japanese films with cultural and political lectures.[52] The reverend's tour involved visits to Japanese-language schools, churches, association halls, farm coops, lumber mills, mining camps, and fishing villages, extending north to the Pacific Northwest and east to the Rocky Mountain states. In late March 1934, for example, Ban embarked on a nine-month tour that went from Los Angeles to central California, then back to southern California, and to Arizona, Nevada, Utah, Colorado, Wyoming, and Nebraska. Next, the caravan moved westward to Idaho, Washington, Oregon, and finally back to California. He again traversed the farming districts of the Sacramento–San Joaquin Valley before finally returning to Los Angeles for the Christmas and New Year holidays.[53]

Because of the popularity of his Japanese movies, Reverend Ban could reach more Japanese residents with his message than could any other lectures or newspapers. In many Japanese communities, his visit attracted several hundred people, including members of both the first and second generations. A total of 3,400 attended his five-day program in Seattle and several hundred had to be turned away. In rural settlements, where people were much less likely to have access to imported Japanese films, his program proved especially popular. Even in small communities like Pocatello, Idaho, and Cheyenne, Wyoming, approximately 150 and 70 people, respectively, attended Ban's programs, even though they had only 199 and 114 Japanese residents. From March 1933 to September 1934, Ban gave 257 lectures to a cumulative total of 91,095 Issei and Nisei throughout the Western states, nearly 70 percent of the 1930 total Japanese population.[54]

Ban's success partially rested on the shrewd arrangement and practical execution of his program, whose motto was "education through motion pictures." With an eye toward fostering the Nisei's understanding of Japan and its culture, his selection of motion pictures revolved around those espousing traditional Japanese morality and martial virtues, which served as "visual textbooks."[55] Toward the latter half of the 1930s, war-related movies were added to his list of feature films. While *Captain Nishizumi* dealt with "the bravery and the daring" of individual soldiers, other titles, like *Young Pirate* and *Five Scouts*, demonstrated "the might of the Japanese Army and Navy." The escalating war in Asia also prompted the Christian educator to try to familiarize the Nisei and Issei with Japan's side of the story by showing imported news films.[56] Typically, his lengthy lecture supplemented these films with a skewed interpretation of the ingrained political messages, making them relevant to the specific circumstances of Japanese America. The visual representations of Japan's East Asian politics and Ban's rendition of their meanings collaborated to maximize the effect of the propagandist education, especially among the less informed masses of rural Issei and Nisei.

Yet, the reverend also knew all too well that the Japanese films were the main attraction for most people. Insofar as the East Asian situation had no direct bearing on their daily lives and caused little apparent damage to Japan, not many residents would have been motivated to attend events of a purely academic or political nature on their work or school nights. In order to bring them to his didactic talks, he therefore characterized his program as unadulterated entertainment. At a typical program, however, Ban's lecture preceded the movies, so that even uninterested audiences would have to listen to what he had to say first about the Sino-Japanese conflict and the "missions" of Issei and especially Nisei.[57] Like Ban's example, organized by elite Issei, many other similar activities of community "entertainment" during the 1930s were geared toward the training of popular diplomats.

The Issei's commitment to people's diplomacy also led to an institutionalization of the educational campaign. Faced with the difficulty of countering the massive flow of hostile information from American and Chinese sources, Japanese diplomats advocated setting up permanent propaganda apparatuses within the United States.[58] The Seattle consul first worked with local Issei businesspeople, Nisei leaders, and sympathetic white Americans in the establishment of the Committee on Pacific Information (CPI) in 1932. Under the facade of a "genuine American [cultural] organization," Ashley E. Holden, the president of the local Japan Society, and James Y. Sakamoto, a Nisei newspaper publisher, coordinated the CPI's day-to-day operations, which targeted secondary school students and teachers. Using its Nisei members as cultural ambassadors, the CPI attempted to disseminate positive images of Japan in classrooms and similar contexts. Sakamoto's *Japanese American Courier* played the role of its house organ, and even after the organization became defunct, the newspaper continued to work in tandem with the consular-Issei publicity program.[59]

In Los Angeles, local Issei elites took the initiative in assembling a public relations apparatus. In 1935, the regional Japanese association headquarters first formed an "information bureau," which successfully obtained financial assistance from Tokyo. In 1937, nominating the Los Angeles consul as its honorary president, the bureau reorganized itself ostensibly into an independent institute of cultural education.[60] For the new Japanese Cultural Center of Southern California (Nihon Bunka Kyokai), the consul elucidated this fundamental aim:

> Now our homeland is facing the unprecedented national crisis with the entire nation united in pursuit of peace in the Orient. Yet, there are still many Americans who criticize Japan's East Asian policy due to their mis-

understanding of Japan and the Japanese. This situation requires us to show them our proud culture that has a history of 3,000 years, and help the nations of the world to appreciate our real worth.[61]

In cooperation with a state-run agency of cultural diplomacy in Tokyo, the JCCSC functioned until 1941 as the regional distribution center for documentary films, printed materials, musical entertainment and performances, exhibitions, and public lectures on Japanese society and traditions aimed at white audiences.[62]

Through the center, local Issei leaders attempted to engage the most "apolitical" resources in the ethnic community: culture and women. The culture of Old Japan, which appeared to be detached from the present, offered them an effective means of propaganda, since it could lower Americans' guard against things Japanese. Furthermore, as the case of Walnut Grove Japanese suggested, the use of culture for political ends carried certain gender ramifications. Culture conventionally belonged in the female domain, whereas politics was associated with men. Japanese culture was even more feminized compared to its Western counterparts, given the "Orientalization" of the East. Indeed, for the average American, a woman clad in a *kimono* was the exotic embodiment of traditional Japanese culture (and its "history of 3,000 years"), and her attractiveness could be embraced in spite of the current state of affairs between the two countries.[63]

The JCCSC not only exploited gendered distinctions between culture and politics, as well as between the past and the present, but it combined those binaries systematically so that the tradition of the Orient would serve the interests of imperial Japan. Showcasing various types of age-old feminine culture, like folk dancing, singing, string music, the tea ceremony, and flower arrangement, the center mobilized many immigrant and second-generation women to perform at cultural events. The ultimate message of their exotic performances, however, was not an aesthetic appreciation of cultural diversity, but it was what the Japanese consul called the "real worth" of modern Japan. For this, the organization was equipped with a special lecture bureau staffed by English-speaking men, who would give political life to its cultural programs. While women gave visual presentations of traditional cultural practices, male lecturers would elaborate on their contemporary meanings, relating them to geopolitics when appropriate.[64]

The preparations during the interwar years—namely, the campaign of education for Issei and Nisei residents and the institutionalization of propaganda machines—ensured better-orchestrated measures following the Marco Polo Bridge incident of 1937. This time, Japanese leaders acted, rather than reacted, fast enough to keep abreast of their Chinese rivals in the public relations effort. During the 1931–1932 crisis, they had learned firsthand what hostile publicity about Japan could do to their community, economy, and collective image. The Issei's initial response was to garner monetary and material support for Japan, but the leading community organizations swiftly adjusted the direction of the movement, leaving fundraising to specialized groups like the Heimushakai. Japanese diplomats unreservedly endorsed the Issei's shift in focus, successfully convincing immigrant leaders to form "emergency committees" in Los Angeles, San Francisco, Seattle, Portland, and New York solely for publicity purposes. Combined with the existing propaganda apparatuses, these committees put out pro-Japan material for white consumption, while the Japanese embassy and consulates "engineered the overall scheme and manipulated it from behind the scene," according to the general state policy for worldwide war propaganda.[65]

In Los Angeles, an emergency committee was established in late September with the joint leadership of the regional Japanese association headquarters, the local association, and the chamber of commerce, which agreed to launch a four-tiered program. First, the committee printed 20,000 copies of English pamphlets and 100,000 leaflets for wide distribution. Like the 1932 pamphlets, these documents explicated the official position of the Japanese government and projected the picture of a "righteous" Japan fighting for "peace and order" in East Asia. Second, the committee purchased time slots on local radio stations to appeal to the American public. Third, it lobbied the American press to publish articles and reports favorable to Japan. Finally, Issei leaders attempted to influence the opinion of white business and social leaders through formal parties, social events, and other gatherings, as well as special lectures. At the same time, they advised all residents to work as popular diplomats rather than continuing to collect donations.[66]

Even without being told, many immigrants spontaneously assumed ambassadorial roles in order to safeguard their individual livelihoods. This was especially manifest among those whose businesses relied mainly on the patronage of white Americans. Critically positioned at the intermediary point between white citizens and other Japanese residents, these Issei could sense the changing current of public opinion faster than anyone else and were the first to suffer the negative consequences. Thus, many embraced the concept of people's diplomacy, using it to stabilize their relationships with white customers and to defend their economic interests. A close reading of the monthly newsletters published by a gardeners' association in southern California provides a glimpse into such a grassroots publicity effort. In the first issue after the outbreak of the all-out war, dated August 10, 1937, an Issei gardener noted that those in the business had already experienced intensified questioning about the East Asian crisis from their clients. As the author stressed, they had to maintain a careful but resolute attitude, because how they responded to the public would have serious ramifications for the future development of American perceptions of the Japanese in general. In order to improve white attitudes, the writer recommended that his fellow gardeners "emphasize that Japan's government, its people, and the Japanese residents in America unanimously agree to seek a peaceful solution."[67] In the ensuing months, alarming reports of abrupt dismissals by employers appeared in the pages of the newsletters, resulting in an ever-heightening sense of crisis among the area's Issei gardeners. As soon as the Japanese Association of Los Angeles compiled English pamphlets, they armed themselves with the material to present Japan's position to their employers.[68]

Despite the spread of the grassroots movement, the continuing donations of money and goods to the Japanese military posed a practical problem for the emergency committees, since many residents allocated their limited resources to this cause rather than to the pro-Japan publicity campaign. This was especially true in the Los Angeles area, where a number of major relief and fundraising drives were simultaneously in progress. Moreover, southern California had only a few Heimushakai, a unique situation that left the local Japanese associations responsible for collection activities. Thus, while the emergency committees of New York and San Francisco built up reserves of $100,000 and $50,000, respectively, by the summer of 1938, their Los Angeles counterpart failed to secure even $5,000 for its publicity program.[69]

To steer popular sentiments, guidance had to come from a high-level official in Japan who could dictate what "true patriots" ought to do. On July 10, 1938, the Los Angeles consul advised Tokyo to reorient Issei nationalism toward the general cause of people's diplomacy. He recommended that either the prime minister or the foreign minister announce that "while it was laudable for overseas Japanese to contribute money to Japan's war effort, it was by far better for them to use such funds to educate the citizens of their [adopted] country about Japan's policy."[70] A month later, the Foreign Ministry issued an informal statement that repeated this recommendation. The spokesperson called it the Issei's "special privilege" to be able to work for the "enlightenment" of Americans about Japan and for the preservation of friendly Japanese-American relations, duties that must take precedence over other forms of patriotic activities in the United States. Tokyo argued that Japanese immigrants could remain "true patriots" only as long as they dedicated themselves to the public relations task—an argument that the Issei elite tacitly welcomed but that members of patriotic relief organizations found insulting.[71]

While the immigrant generation had difficulty balancing the pressure for patriotic donations and the call for people's diplomacy, many Nisei took it upon themselves to combat the rising tide of anti-Japanese agitation by conducting English-language public lectures. "The first to suffer from anti-Japanese propaganda," Larry Tajiri of the *Nichibei Shimbun* explained, "have been ironically enough the American citizens of Japanese ancestry. We believe it is to be for the interests of these nisei that they be able to justify Japan's objectives [in China]."[72]

Because their Issei elders were especially ineffective in publicity campaigns, Los Angeles Nisei were most active in the distribution of pro-Japanese views to the public. In October 1937, leaders of the local JACL proposed to form within the Japanese Association of Los Angeles the English Speakers' Bureau, which later became the independent Far Eastern Research Institute.[73] Discussing the negative impact of "the economic boycott and [the] numerous incidents of violence" against Nisei children, Kay Sugahara, a central figure in the institute, outlined multiple benefits of their publicity efforts:

> I believe our action in this matter might well be justified from the American standpoint, in that Americans have always been interested in knowing the true facts of every case and always believed in fair play. It will [also] be justified from the nisei standpoint as it will ease the hardships that they have to bear in the face of the malicious propaganda and may cause the public locally to see us in the proper light. It will be [further] beneficial in our dealings with [the] Issei in that we will be doing them and their country a service by explaining to the American public the reason and justification for the conflict in the Orient.[74]

The core members of the Far Eastern Research Institute made their rounds throughout southern California, giving some sixty public lectures to white Americans during its initial six months.[75] Sugahara's commentary, which was broadcast in Los Angeles and San Francisco in November, provides a window into what they likely talked about. Entitled "Boycott—Boon or Boomerang?" the speech claimed that the available war information was "largely propaganda" originating from the Chinese, which deceived many Americans into sympathizing with the boycott of Japanese goods. The Nisei then elaborated how the boycott would harm the lives of the average American citizen, consumer, and merchant. The boycott of raw silk from Japan, for example, would displace both American traders and factory workers; Japan's expected retaliatory boycott of American goods was likely to cause turmoil in various sectors of the American economy, affecting "millions of our citizens . . . directly or indirectly dependent upon these import and export items." As an American citizen, Sugahara also stressed how it was unfair and un-American to make Japanese residents suffer for something for which they were not responsible. In reference to his fellow Nisei, the Los Angeles JACL leader noted: "They are not aggressive. They are not warlike. In fact they are the most peaceful and law abiding group in their respective communities . . . But the full weight of the boycott falls upon them." Sugahara concluded that the anti-Japan boycott had not "been a boon, but a boomerang," because it inflicted unjustifiable economic damage on Americans in general, and did grave injustice to Japanese Americans in particular.[76] Obviously, it was not loyalty to Japan but the concern for Issei parents and their own status as American citizens that was the foundation of these Nisei's pro-Japan activity, as well as the larger immigrant effort of people's diplomacy.

FROM JAPANESE PATRIOTISM TO AMERICANISM

At the end of the 1930s, war fears loomed ever larger in the Pacific, prompting the reorientation of Japanese immigrant patriotism. In July 1939, the American government notified Tokyo of its intention to abrogate the commercial treaty six months later. In October 1940, shortly after Japan concluded the tripartite military alliance with the European Axis powers, the United States declared an embargo on scrap metal exports, which was followed in July 1941 by a presidential order to freeze Japanese assets in the United States. Meanwhile, the FBI and military authorities increased surveillance on the Japanese community, scrutinizing its past patriotic contributions and propaganda for Japan.[77] Although these developments did not necessarily thwart Issei's nationalistic identification with their native country, most were compelled to reckon seriously with the ramifications of their transnational ties, were more cautious in expressing them publicly, and eventually decided to terminate their pro-Japan activities altogether.[78] It did not take immigrants long to figure out that their eclecticism was no longer tenable and could even ruin their livelihood, safety, and place in a war-mongering America.

During the early months of 1941, a voluntary dissolution of patriotic organizations and fundraising agencies ensued. As a Heimushakai branch in Fresno explained:

> At first, it was only China that Japan was at war with, which made it natural for us to collect donations. We had no reason to hesitate . . . Yet, now that Japan and the United States are on a collision course in this rapidly changing world, . . . a fund-raising drive that aims at benefiting Japan will mislead Americans to think as if we, especially the Nisei, have divided loyalties, or even worse, single allegiance to Japan.[79]

Once the epitome of this minority's incessant obsession with self-preservation, the Issei's patriotic attachment to Japan now posed a major threat to their ethnic survival. In accordance with the new political challenges, Issei abruptly ended their partnerships with the Japanese consulates and scrambled to supplant Japanese patriotism with a profession of undivided American loyalty.[80]

Japanese immigrant leaders built on the existing notion of people's diplomacy and further elevated the meaning of pursuing white-Japanese friendship.

The emergency committees of the Japanese associations, which had previously functioned as public relations agents for Japan, transformed themselves into facilitators of Americanism among Issei residents. Los Angeles took the lead in this, offering multifaceted programs that benefited Japanese residents throughout the West.[81] When the ill-fated diplomatic tug-of-war commenced between the two governments in April 1941, the Los Angeles Issei-Nisei joint leadership compiled a twenty-page bilingual booklet titled *Americanism* and distributed it to Japanese households throughout the region. It contained the Pledge of Allegiance to the American flag, the Declaration of Independence, the Bill of Rights, and the following statement:

> We, the Japanese residents of Southern California, have faith in America. The United States protects our personal security and property. We appreciate, admire and respect the American Government . . . America is our home. Here, we live as permanent residents. Here, we bring up and educate our children in the hope that they may become good Americans . . . Today, we realize that America faces a national crisis. We know that National Unity is absolutely necessary for the preservation of American democracy. In view of the foregoing, we feel that it is our duty and privilege to support American ideals and principles.[82]

In the new context of growing U.S.–Japan estrangement, the "political language of Americanism," as historian Gary Gerstle astutely calls it, offered Issei leaders yet another way of articulating their undeviating demand for national inclusion and of thrusting their ever-malleable identities into the public discourses of the ethnic community and the larger society.[83] Couched in such Americanist language, the 1941 booklet outlined "ten commandments" for Japanese residents, which told them to obey American laws and ideals; cooperate with the authorities; contribute to the American way of life; foster friendship with all Americans; and show an appreciation for the United States in their daily conduct. No trace of the dualism of the past could be detected in this political document.

The Issei's historical discourse, which had always accounted for the ebbs and flows of complex immigrant sentiments toward their native and adopted lands, followed the general shift from the transnational to the national. The regional Japanese association headquarters in Los Angeles took up the laborious task of translating parts of *Zaibei Nihonjinshi*—an official history of the Japanese in America—specifically for white American consumption in order to fight xenophobic agitation. Yet, Japan now ceased to serve as a useful reference point, because it constituted the very cause of the suspicion and rejection that Japanese Americans were experiencing in the land of their residence. The commissioned translation drew selectively from *Zaibei Nihonjinshi* and focused solely on the

American nature of Issei pioneers. Citing their accomplishments in California agriculture, the unpublished manuscript made no causal reference to their Japanese heritage:

> [T]hese facts . . . are living testimonies for the tremendous success of the immigrant Japanese in America, and vividly show to what extent they have become an integral part of the nation in her agricultural life alone. Their achievements in this line of endeavor are more remarkable when you stop to think of their brief but colorful history in the United States, or more specifically in the state of California, a history full of hardships, miseries, persecutions, failures, and successes, a history that could have happened only in America and that now forms an exciting chapter in the history of the great nation. Yes, these Japanese farmers, too, are ranking pioneers of America . . . Japanese pioneers have played a fine role in building the great country—the United States of America.[84]

This pro-American inflection was coupled with brand-new material to further that point. For instance, the manuscript quotes "a few words of Gongoro Nakamura," which purportedly "exemplify the 'American' spirit of the average Japanese pioneer who has lived most of his life in this, his adopted country." Nakamura, a Los Angeles leader, reportedly proclaimed: "Today, although various laws compel me to be an alien ineligible to citizenship, I believe in the United States of America, I believe in her traditions, ideals and institutions, and I believe it is my duty and privilege to serve her, if need be, with my life!"[85]

While engaging in the refashioning of their monolithic identity as loyal Americans, Japanese immigrant leaders resorted to the ultimate people's diplomacy, turning themselves into agents of direct negotiation with the American state. Between late October and early November 1941, two representatives, Gongoro Nakamura and Togo Tanaka, a senior Nisei, traveled from Los Angeles to Washington, D.C., to convey the heartfelt plea of Japanese residents for "fair treatment" in case of war. After meeting Attorney General Francis Biddle and First Lady Eleanor Roosevelt, they also got a California congressman to read a declaration of Japanese immigrant Americanism in the House of Representatives. This political lobbying enabled the Japanese community to communicate their wishes and demands directly to the U.S. government. Washington officials and other dignitaries "assured" Japanese Americans of due process and equal protection, as long as they remained law-abiding residents—a promise on which Biddle reneged under the intense pressure of the military a few months later.[86] Yet, at least for the time being, Americanism seemed to have paid off in the eyes of Issei leaders.

Japanese immigrant Americanism crystallized their desperate quest for acceptance and survival in American society on the eve of the Pacific War. Their sudden 180-degree turn from Japanese patriotism to American loyalty in early 1941 was necessitated by geopolitics and domestic social relations, in which any support for Japan became tantamount to disloyalty toward the United States. As the dichotomy between Chinese and Japanese under the local and international circumstances gave way to one between the United States and Japan, the Japanese immigrant community could defend itself only by identifying with its country of residence while distancing from its native state. The Issei's public expression of national allegiance was situational, but their chief concern stayed consistent. The idea of people's diplomacy derived from the multiple positionality of the Issei, caught between the two nation-states that articulated and enforced the terms of their existence, within the white-dominated racial order of the West that restricted their life chances, and in contestation with other minorities for limited resources on the borderland. Not only did the profession of their patriotic feelings—Japanese or American—divulge the complexity of the social spaces where this immigrant group lived, but the Issei's Japanese patriotism defies conventional interpretations that tend to view their social and intellectual practices from the lens of the national binary. In the same vein, their oscillation between Japan and the United States was congruent with their eclectic way of thinking, which manifested itself in differing forms in varied situations throughout the 1930s.

But patriotic activities explain only one aspect of the Japanese immigrant nationalism of the decade. Local interethnic strife served as a hotbed for another form of Issei nationalism, which did not necessarily entail outright patriotic identification with their native or adopted countries. That nationalism concentrated on their own community, configuring and reconfiguring its corporate identity in accordance primarily with the logic of multilayered race relations in the American West.

8

Ethnic Nationalism and Racial Struggle

Interethnic Relations in the California Delta

On the evening of February 8, 1930, Japanese in Stockton, California, were stunned when Filipinos boycotted their businesses, causing a virtual shutdown that lasted almost two months. According to the local Japanese press, this clash between two ethnic groups resulted from "a personal affair"—the secret marriage of a Nisei woman and a Filipino laborer.[1] The woman's father had strongly opposed the marriage, telling her that "racial and cultural differences" between Japanese and Filipinos doomed the relationship. She soon left her Filipino husband, an action that he, his friends, and his relatives blamed on the entire Japanese community for allegedly believing that "the Filipinos [were] inferior."[2] Infuriated, Filipinos called a "sympathy boycott."

As the boycott dragged on for a second week and merchants' losses escalated, frustrated Issei residents came to see the conflict as a "war" between the "races," a perception reinforced by news reports in the vernacular press. A Stockton correspondent of the *Nichibei Shimbun* reported that Filipino store owners, doctors, and newspaper executives actively supported the boycott. The Filipino community, he wrote, "seems to have learned the weakness of the Japanese."[3] Most Japanese businesses in the delta, especially restaurants, pool halls, grocery and general merchandise stores, and soda fountains, relied heavily on the Filipino trade. The Issei proprietors feared that Filipinos might develop an ethnic entrepreneurship of their own and patronize their fellow merchants instead of Japanese establishments.[4] To avoid such a development, Japanese community newspapers urged all Japanese in Stockton to withstand this boycott at any cost.

Issei businesspeople moved quickly to diversify their customer base. To reduce their reliance on Filipinos, merchants decided to bring Mexican laborers into the San Joaquin delta. In mid-March, a special committee, formed from within the local Japanese association, dispatched representatives to urge Japanese farmers in the outlying areas to hire Mexicans. Mexican workers, they counseled, would stabilize Japanese agriculture because they were more "docile" and "better" than Filipinos, who had already struck against farmers elsewhere in California. Although the plan was abandoned when the boycott ended in April, what Issei called "Japanese consciousness" continued to run high in the delta.[5] The emotional response of Issei to the Filipino boycott merely presaged an ever-growing nationalism spurred by local interethnic conflict, which went beyond identification with the Japanese state.

This chapter explores how immigrants' identity and nationalism developed out of the conflict between Japanese and Filipinos in the San Joaquin River delta during the 1930s. Focusing on the local expression of immigrant nationalism, what I call *ethnic nationalism*, it argues that their "Japanese consciousness" was primarily a product of American social relations, which shaped their interests and directly affected their daily livelihoods. The Issei's ethnic nationalism resulted as much—if not more—from an image of a collective enemy and a sense of shared interests in the delta as from events in Asia or anger against racist society. Regionally prescribed experiences prompted the Japanese residents to forge unity within a community in an effort to overcome adverse social conditions, both perceived and real. These developments subsequently engendered a localized concept of "race" and an identity of the racialized ethnic body, that were rooted in their lives of struggle within a racial hierarchy in the delta.[6] Yet, importantly, the Issei's localized concerns did not cancel out their state nationalism. They conflated state and ethnic dimensions in their nationalism, imagining a national identity with Japan, on the one hand, and inventing a regional identity as delta Japanese, on the other.[7] Such conflation was possible primarily because Japanese immigrants had already formulated the idea of overseas development. This diasporic perspective saw their ethnic community and homeland as parts of a common endeavor, thereby intricately interweaving racialized local identity and transborder nationalism.

EMERGENCE OF INTERETHNIC CONFLICT

The Issei's ethnic nationalism developed in the San Joaquin delta from a series of clashes between Japanese and Filipinos throughout the 1930s. The decade commenced with the Filipino boycott, which marked a watershed in interethnic relations. Issei residents began to perceive their relationship with Filipinos in racial more than in economic terms, although the two were always intertwined. Underlying the rise of racial discourse was the rapid transformation of the local agricultural labor market in the last half of the 1920s, when Filipinos became an integral part of the Japanese immigrant economy. The Japanese dependence on Filipinos derived mainly from state and federal discriminatory legislation that drastically affected the Issei socioeconomic position. In the San Joaquin delta, the pattern of interethnic relations was characterized by a process of replacement and succession. Surrounded by the San Joaquin and Sacramento rivers, the region was an agricultural center in which a handful of wealthy white landlords used different groups of Asian tenant farmers and laborers in succession—the Chinese until the turn of the century, then Japanese, and finally Filipinos.[8] Starting with the Chinese Exclusion Act of 1882, anti-immigrant legislation always played a pivotal role in this transition. The 1920 Alien Land Law reduced many Issei farmers to hired foremen, while compelling others to give up farming altogether. The Immigration Act of 1924 then terminated the new supply of labor from Japan and opened the way for Filipino laborers as replacements. As colonized U.S. nationals, Filipino immigrants were exempt from the law and quickly filled the labor vacuum in the Western states. Japanese farmers came to depend on the "cheap but valuable [Filipino] labor" that they perceived would carry them through the Depression, while Japanese commercial establishments catered to Filipinos for their own survival.[9]

In the eyes of Issei, who were fully aware of the ramifications of such a change in the delta, the 1930 boycott signified Filipinos' attempt to accelerate the process of replacement and succession. Of course, as the *Nichibei Shimbun* correspondent reported, some Issei recognized at first that Filipinos waged the boycott specifically against Japanese merchants, not against all Japanese, and that the Filipino business sector was at the helm, seeking to profit from the situation. Nevertheless, a majority of Issei residents interpreted the boycott as a collective racial challenge by the Filipino population, one that appeared to threaten not only their survival but also a smooth transition to a Nisei era. In the Japanese community, mass meetings and the vernacular press further propagated such an interpretation and helped to ignite ethnic nationalism. With the veiled threat of social ostracism and persecution, the delta's Issei leaders demanded that all community members try to keep Filipinos under Japanese control.[10] Here, the racial rhetoric overshadowed the economic dimension of the conflict.

The 1930 incident also awakened the Japanese community to what was called the "racial menace" of Filipinos, which continued to haunt them until Pearl Harbor. To the dismay of Issei, it appeared that the root of the incident—

a marriage between a Nisei woman and a Filipino man—foreshadowed more "interracial" unions. Many Nisei reached adulthood in the 1930s, and their parents believed that male Filipino laborers posed a serious threat to the chastity of Nisei women. According to Japanese newspapers, Filipino men were trying to "seduce" Nisei women, for few Filipina women lived in the delta.[11] Besides, many Issei parents dreaded the "sexual laxness" and "uncontrollability" of young Nisei, which they usually attributed to negative "American" influences. Fearing the recurrence of Japanese-Filipino marriages, a local reporter of the *Shin Sekai* warned the community shortly after the boycott: "This incident [marriage], I often hear, points to the fact that many more problems like this have already 'struck root' and are about to 'put forth buds.' It is our responsibility—parents, social leaders, and community at large—to make sure to raise our children properly [so as to avoid interracial marriage]."[12] Filipino laborers, albeit indispensable for local ethnic agriculture, now represented a racial peril to Nisei young people—the successors of Japanese development in the delta.

Japanese immigrants worried about intermarriage because it signified Filipino "contamination" of their "pure" bloodline. This racial doctrine derived partially from the racism of imperial Japan, which sought to dominate "backward" races in Asia. During the years of militaristic aggression in Asia, a number of government officials and intellectuals expressed faith in the purity of blood, and they frequently admonished imperial subjects against miscegenation with the dominated, on the grounds that it would "destroy the 'national spirit' of the Yamato race" and spoil their racial superiority.[13] These ideas crossed the Pacific through imported Japanese publications, lectures by writers and scholars from Japan, and frequent visits by Issei to their native villages in Japan. Other perspectives on racial mixing coexisted in imperial Japan, however. As recent Japanese-language scholarship on race and nation points out, intermarriage between Japanese and colonized Koreans and Taiwanese was encouraged rather than discouraged after the early 1920s by Japanese assimilation policy. To rationalize a colonial social structure that required the inclusion of newly dominated populations into the Japanese nation, bureaucrats and other ideologues who favored assimilation propagated the notion of the Japanese race as a hybrid, consisting of Korean, Chinese, Ainu, Okinawan, Micronesian, and core imperial elements.[14] While Issei were grappling with emerging racial problems, in Japan itself the discourse on racial hybridity was actually as influential as the racial purity argument. Why, then, did the latter predominate in the American West?

Issei leaders both adopted and adapted the racial purity position because it best fit the sociohistorical context in which immigrants found themselves after the mid-1920s. In the American West, where they had been subjected to a series of discriminatory laws as aliens ineligible for citizenship, Issei envisaged a better future not during their own lifetimes but during their children's. They believed that U.S. citizenship would allow Nisei to restore what they saw as the golden age of the Japanese community prior to 1920. Such a view was grounded solely in their belief in the purported superiority of the Japanese race. Without state military apparatuses to create the actual situation of Japanese supremacy over Filipinos and other "lesser" groups, the protection of racial purity was defined as *the* precondition, albeit not the guarantee, for a Nisei victory in racial competition and for future prosperity. In no uncertain terms did immigrant leaders stress over and over the enormous implications of racial transgressions for the future of Japanese Americans. For example, a *Nichibei Shimbun* editorial prophesied:

> The Japanese race, possessing superior racial traits unparalleled in the world, are destined for ceaseless development and prosperity. On the other hand, those people [Filipinos], whose homeland contents itself with being a third-class nation, . . . would see nothing but poverty and misery in their lives. If their lazy blood becomes part of the Japanese race through interracial marriage, it would eventually offset the racial superiority of the Japanese. . . . Racial purity is a precondition for the welfare of the second generation.[15]

What is clear in this line of reasoning is the sharp contrast between the Japanese race/state and the colonized Filipinos and their dominated homeland—a contrast reflected in Issei views of Filipinos in the delta. The theory of overseas development played a major role in this juxtaposition. Embracing both the state and overseas communities as intertwined components of "the Japanese race . . . destined for ceaseless development and prosperity," the concept enabled Issei to imagine race relations in the delta as a manifestation of the hierarchical power relations of nation-states. As Japan enjoyed supremacy over all other Asian nations, so the Japanese in the delta should keep Filipinos and other "third-class" races in a subordinate position. Of course, the Issei left whites out of this picture, for they represented the real power in the delta and in the United States at large.

White American racism further strengthened Issei repugnance for intermarriage. Based on bourgeois liberalism and the fictive racial hierarchy of eighteenth-century Europe, Anglo-American racial ideology defined *miscegenation* as causing the degeneration of race, nation, and class in scientific terms. In order to prevent such a crisis, managing the sexuality of children was considered crucial not just for personal well-being but for society as well. In California, as in other states, interracial unions were legally banned, and "mixed-blood" children were excluded from the ruling circle of the white race.[16] This white ideology, which articulated and enforced fundamental social norms in the American West, gave Issei an objective justification for their own views. Like white Americans, Japanese immigrants stressed the value of child rearing and the need to protect the chastity of their daughters from "inferior" races, but they also linked these conditions to the survival of their race in the United States.

Indeed, the prescribed notion of motherhood worked hand in hand in the fusion of the two racisms, making Nisei women especially accountable for maintaining and extending the legitimate lineage to ensuing generations of Japanese Americans. Tying their survivalist concern to the national tradition, a *Nichibei Shimbun* commentator succinctly summed up Issei's eclectic thinking. "Read the history of the Japanese race," the writer urged Nisei girls, "because every page [of that history], from Amaterasu [the mythical sun goddess] on the first page to your [Issei] mothers on the current, represents the ongoing transfer of the [pure racial] blood from one Japanese woman to another."[17] For the goal of antimiscegenation, the scientific racism of white America and the racist mythology of imperial Japan were indispensable partners.

In disciplining Nisei behavior, the immigrant print media actively disseminated a hegemonic discourse on racial purity, reporting many "tragedies" of Japanese-Filipino unions and romances throughout the 1930s. Offering cautionary tales that Issei parents and teachers could utilize in family education and classroom lessons, those stories highlighted that not only could interethnic marriages never be tolerated by Japanese communities but they would ineluctably end up ruining the lives of individual Nisei women. For example, one Seattle Nisei was reportedly "disowned" by her parents due to her marriage to a Filipino man. When she became gravely ill, she was taken to a Japanese hospital, but she refused to disclose her identity to hospital staff because she felt so "ashamed" about her past racial transgression, a mistake that could not be mended.[18] Designed to appeal directly to the second-generation youth, similar subjects also appeared in the English sections of the vernacular papers. In her reply to a reader's question about interethnic romance, a columnist named "Lady Nisei" advised the adolescent about the danger associated with Filipino men. She wrote, "Filipinos are clever, persistent, and sometimes attractive to women. But when the aura of romance fades, nine times out of ten Nisei girls who marry them are appalled by the hugeness of their mistakes, and by their great disillusionment. Today's innocent acquaintanceship may tomorrow become an irrevocable tragedy."[19] Thus, the Nisei, especially females, were not allowed to encounter other groups as free individuals but only as a racialized people whose utmost responsibility was to their compatriots and the collective future.

Following the 1930 boycott, the issue of race occupied the central position in Japanese attitudes toward Filipinos. The contrast between the economic value of Filipino labor and the racial peril Filipino men represented became widely discussed topics, and Issei contemplated how to exploit the former while circumventing the latter. Essays written by Issei readers for a 1933 *Nichibei Shimbun* contest on the topic of "the expansion of Filipino influences and our preparation" reveal these unsettling concerns. The winning essays were selected by immigrant leaders for their content, and the assertions in them represented orthodoxy in the Japanese community. Characterizing their relationship with Filipinos as a "race war," the writers' main theses were strikingly similar: first, the Nisei mission to win a total victory in their competition with Filipinos, and second, the Issei duty to lay the economic foundation for that final battle. One prize winner, a Stockton immigrant, writing specifically of the delta situation, analyzed the dangerous trend of Filipino settlement (as opposed to migratory labor) on area farms and of Filipino encroachment into small businesses. In his opinion, such changes hindered the development of the Japanese community, and it was necessary for "all our Japanese brethren to mobilize" against them. To protect Japanese farming and commerce, he insisted that Japanese laborers be used for long-term farm work and that Issei farmers and merchants expand their capital base. Until Nisei could finally "expel" them from the delta, Filipinos must always be harmless workers and customers, never contenders or equals.[20] These viewpoints expressed a consensus in the delta.

The Issei quest to gain the upper hand over Filipinos, which gave shape to the delta's Japanese identity, accounted for an aspect of an ongoing "war of maneuver" in local race relations.[21] Under white hegemony, subordinate groups were prone to view each other as standing in the way of their respective survival rather than sharing a common destiny. Racial struggles often took place over limited material and cultural resources in the society. Because the ruling group arbitrarily determined the distribution of them, the minorities had to maneuver within the basic structure of the white regime rather than disrupting it. In the 1930s, beset by Filipino economic encroachments, leading elements of the delta Japanese, too, felt it necessary to rally the entire ethnic community in defense of the niches that they had established within the regional racial order. And when a mass of militant Filipino laborers directly challenged the integrity of the Japanese ethnic economy in the delta after the mid-1930s, Issei antagonisms intensified even further, and a series of confrontations ensued. Through ethnic nationalism, the residents revealed their consent to the local system of racial rule that had accommodated what they considered to be key Japanese interests, as well as a racial ideology that placed them above Filipinos.

RACE, CLASS, AND JAPANESE IDENTITY IN THE DELTA

From 1936 to 1941, a second round of conflict occurred between Issei farmers and merchants on one side and Filipino laborers on the other.[22] In late November 1936, the San Joaquin delta experienced the first major Filipino strike, which targeted Japanese celery growers and their white landlords. When nearly 1,500 Filipino field hands walked out, demanding a 30 to 40 percent raise in hourly wages, 150 percent overtime pay, and the recognition of their union, Japanese growers, who constituted approximately three-quarters of the celery producers in the area, recruited hundreds of younger Issei laborers as scabs with the help of Japanese merchants in Stockton. Castigating all Japanese as "traitorous" to the working-class cause, the outraged union retaliated by staging an anti-Japanese boycott. In turn, Japanese leaders viewed the boycott as another Filipino assault on their community.[23] As in 1930, the two groups were again in a "race war."

The Issei response to the labor union reflected the status of the Japanese community in the local hierarchy of race and class, especially in relationship to the propertied white elite. Land prices in the delta were extremely high, and only a handful of affluent whites owned land and exerted influence in the local society. As leading entrepreneurs in a California agribusiness center, a majority of these landlords simultaneously ran shipping and marketing companies or were closely linked with canneries and wholesale merchants. In exchange for financial assistance, landlords usually bound tenant farmers to sell crops at prices they arbitrarily set; deducted commissions, transportation fees, and crate costs; and even prescribed the wage scales according to which growers managed farm operations. Controlling every facet of the local political economy, these men occupied the top tier of the delta's race and class hierarchy.[24]

Subordinate to the white landlords were Japanese immigrants employed in various agricultural capacities. Prior to the 1920s, white elites saw Japanese tenants as economically necessary, albeit culturally undesirable, because they could recruit and supervise Japanese farm laborers who did not understand English well. The use of Issei tenants and merchants resulted in an efficient system of farm labor recruitment that involved all segments of the ethnic community with the farmers at the core.[25] If a laborer wanted a farm job in the delta, he had only to go to a local Japanese merchant, who then referred him to a farm in the vicinity. In the 1920s, Filipinos entered at the bottom of the hierarchy, replacing older Issei laborers. The newcomers were hired under the existing recruitment system, leaving it intact for the time being. Nonetheless, the near-extinction of the Japanese labor force in the delta, a product of Japanese exclusion and the aging of remaining immigrant laborers, eliminated the advantage of Japanese tenancy for white landlords. Without landlord support,

Issei knew that the entire ethnic economy would collapse. All classes of Japanese immigrants—farmers, merchants, and laborers—were obsessed with how white elites perceived them.

The delta racial hierarchy had two consequences. First, it allowed the development of Issei nationalism only within the limited spectrum of the farming and merchant classes. Theoretically, various contesting groups and classes in the Japanese community could have articulated their own versions of ethnic nationalism for their specific goals.[26] In the delta, however, both the perceived and the objective conditions informed Issei of the unlikelihood of their racial survival without the continuation of the leading occupational groups of farmers and merchants, which laid the foundation for class-based Issei nationalism. No other goal than protecting and preserving Japanese farming and commerce was tolerated, with dire consequences for Japanese labor activism. In the delta, the range of Japanese ethnic nationalism and identity was narrow, since it was predicated upon the dictates of the material concerns of the two particular groups.

The second consequence of the racial hierarchy was the oversimplification of race and class relations in the perceptions of Japanese in the delta. Issei essentialized the local white population to include only landlords and other elites. Since many white laborers and tenant farmers did not fit the Japanese definition of the white race, a fictive image of white homogeneity was constructed. Likewise, Filipinos were racialized in such a way as to be identified summarily with anti-Japanese union members, despite the fact that there were many nonunion laborers and entrepreneurs as well. The internal diversity of Japanese residents similarly suffered the effects of homogenization, for the community was represented as a unified body that upheld only the interests and goals of the leading classes of male farmers and merchants. As a result, Japanese residents envisioned a simple, three-tiered, overlapping race and class hierarchy, where white elites, Japanese entrepreneurs, and Filipino union laborers formed the pyramid in descending order. Although one's class position tended to correspond with one's race in delta society, this order was half true at best, because it disallowed class diversity within each racial group. Yet, importantly, this vision of social relations enabled Japanese to formulate a racial ideology that they expressed in their ethnic nationalism. This ideology informed them how to distinguish an enemy race from a benefactor race and taught the victims of racism to oppress another racial minority. For the survival of their own race, Issei appropriated the ruling ideology of white supremacy as their own and endeavored to turn perceived social relations into real ones.[27]

Ultimately, interethnic conflict became a question of the Issei's rightful position under white hegemony. Since only white elites could determine the legitimacy of Japanese "superiority" to Filipinos in the delta, fighting Filipino laborers had a dual meaning for Issei. It meant not only defending their own economic interests but also demonstrating their submission to the landlords— symbolizing Issei allegiance to the established order that constituted the core of their racial identity. In other words, in their racial struggle, Japanese immigrants sought to parade before landlords both their economic profitability as employees and their racial desirability as loyal servants. Under the white-controlled political economy of the delta, only such an action could ensure the Issei's fragile position.[28]

Indeed, in the midst of the 1936 strike, the *Nichibei Shimbun* posited that their anti-union effort offered proof of "Japanese loyalty to delta agriculture." Since Japanese as a group "represented [white] capitalists in charge of all the farm work ranging from seedling to harvest," their interests always lay with the landlords. In this sense, even farm laborers in the fields were considered to be proxies of whites.[29] Issei field hands defined their economic status less in class terms than in racial terms, for racial solidarity as Japanese superseded class identity as laborers. Insofar as they acted on the principle of intraethnic cooperation by serving as strikebreakers, the laboring Issei, too, internalized this racial identity. Hence, it was no mystery that they were "traitorous" to the working-class cause, as the union insisted. A Stockton Japanese reporter boasted that nothing—not even higher pay—was more valuable than the "white landowners' trust" that the delta's Japanese residents had earned through this struggle.[30]

What began in 1936 recurred in a series of labor disputes in subsequent years. The next clash took place during the celery harvest in late November 1939. About 2,500 Filipino workers, who had organized the Filipino Agricultural Laborers' Association (FALA) several months before, quit working altogether, paralyzing the delta's celery industry. Joining them were members of the United Cannery, Agricultural, Packing and Allied Workers of America (UCAPAWA, part of the Congress of Industrial Organizations) Local 20 and other laborers, including 150 Japanese. This multiracial union demanded a uniform wage increase of five cents an hour, which employers flatly rejected. The strikers promptly set up picket lines.[31] The situation lasted until December 1, when landlords acknowledged the FALA as a bargaining agent for the celery workers and granted raises.

Initially, this strike looked like a successful case of interethnic working-class unity since it included many Japanese workers. That was the very goal of the UCAPAWA, as the union appointed a Nisei agent, Louis Yamamoto, to organize Japanese workers prior to and during the strike. Here, we find a brief moment of an alternative ethnic identity based on the concerns of Japanese labor that could have come to terms with rigid divides between Filipinos and them. However, that possibility soon proved elusive. Under the call of blood ties, Japanese workers were the first to return to the fields, while others continued to picket. Observing the quick collapse of interethnic unity and Japanese labor organization, Yamamoto lamented:

> During the first days of the strike, the Japanese workers walked out with 1,500 Filipinos, [white] American[s], Mexican[s] and Hindus [*sic*]. But through various pressures and influences they were forced to go back to work. . . . Their ranks were completely dominated by contractors; and they lacked knowledge of what true unionism and labor solidarity mean. . . . Generally throughout the strike area, due to lack of leadership, most Japanese went back to work within a few days.[32]

This Nisei communist added that Issei employers intimidated the workers into defying the strike and scabbing on their comrades. Eventually, only thirty Japanese stayed on the picket line with the other strikers.

Although Yamamoto blamed the failure on the laborers' lack of class consciousness and the farmers' intimidation, many Issei laborers were acting according to their own racial ideology more than reacting to external forces. Japanese newspaper reports provide a glimpse into how unsympathetic the laborers were to the strike. They were so willing to work that, in a very short period, Issei merchants recruited hundreds of Japanese strikebreakers, which allowed most farmers to continue the harvest and keep two of eight packing facilities in full operation during the five-day tie-up. An Issei reporter who visited the celery farming district depicted a busy Japanese farm as "a peaceful paradise between a grower and laborers." When he asked Issei scabs about the ongoing strike, they cast ridicule upon the strikers, "looking dubious" of their intentions.[33]

The racial ideology was reflected in the reaction of Issei growers and merchants as well. Despite the initial walkout of 150 Japanese laborers, the growers and merchants found no sense of Japanese unity with Filipino strikers, and they reduced every issue to the Filipino "racial menace." In their opinion, Japanese workers had been "forced to do so [walk out] by force of circumstances," and it was therefore "an involuntary strike." The Japanese "strikers" stayed away from the farms only because of "a desire to prevent any violence."[34] The walkout was unjustifiable, and all the blame rested on "Filipino laborers [who] are heading the strike," because their selfishness had led to such a disastrous situation. According to the *Nichibei Shimbun*, Filipino laborers had been treated very well, in fact being paid 20 percent more than other ethnic groups. Japanese residents did not understand why the laborers walked out despite such favored treatment, and the reporter added that many Issei were even feeling "piteous for the Filipino race that is incapable of fair judgment."[35] From the Japanese perspective, the strike was merely a continuation of the Filipino threat that had plagued them since 1930. It was only natural for Issei—and imperative for their racialized ethnic identity—to engage in anti-union activities.

Filipinos retaliated with a boycott of Japanese businesses. On November 30, 1939, exactly a week after the beginning of the dispute, a group of strikers appeared in Japantown with anti-Japanese placards. They forcibly dragged Filipino customers out of Japanese stores and talked others out of patronizing them. Escalating day by day, this boycott paralyzed local Japanese commerce by impinging on the businesses' crucial year-end sales. Although the FALA claimed no responsibility for the boycott, its officials composed the leadership.[36] Interethnic relations deteriorated rapidly.

The Japanese employed a threefold strategy to fight the boycott and the union. First, they collaborated with local law enforcement officials to root out picketing in front of stores. Tied to the white establishment, the police and the courts were eager to help out the "loyal servants" and punish the defiant "troublemakers." In the middle of December, detectives started to patrol Japantown and watch for illegal interference with businesses. On December 24, the FALA treasurer was arrested, along with three other Filipinos, for violating a city ordinance prohibiting loitering and blocking the sidewalk. Japanese residents alleged that his kind represented "vagrant gangs who [were] obstructing our commercial activities."[37] They were happy to see such troublemakers taken away. Meanwhile, Japanese eliminated their own traitorous element—specifically, Louis Yamamoto, who was considered a quasi-Filipino due to his involvement in union activities—by secretly informing the police of his whereabouts. Three days after the arrest of the four Filipinos, Yamamoto was prosecuted on a vagrancy charge. At the trial, Yamamoto's public defender, a Stockton Nisei, "did not defend" him at all, so he had a communist lawyer from the International Labor Defense come from San Francisco to assist him. Receiving a court order to stay out of San Joaquin County for two years, Yamamoto, whom the *Nichibei Shimbun* correspondent portrayed spitefully as "a devilish hoodlum," soon departed, leaving behind a wasteland for Japanese labor activism.[38]

The second measure to break the Filipino union was the early recruitment of nonstriking laborers for the coming asparagus season. In January 1940, the Japanese community formed a special committee of boardinghouse owners and other leading merchants, who put job advertisements in the vernacular newspapers to attract Japanese laborers from outside the delta region. Issei community leaders sounded out white landlords and growers about an increase in Japanese employment on their farms, which resulted in many job offers. Local newspaper correspondents reported every step of the community effort, noting that "landowners have reaffirmed the notion of loyal, obedient, and troubleless Japanese laborers." The reporters also stressed the important role of second-generation youths—especially Japan-educated Kibei—in taking over the labor market from Filipino union workers. In all, this orchestrated effort created more than 500 new positions for "peaceful" Japanese field hands.[39]

Third, the Japanese attempted to divide the Filipino community by collaborating with the Filipino Federation of America (FFA), a rival organization of the FALA in Stockton. This alliance was built on a mutual interest in undermining the organizational base of the Filipino union. The FFA was a semireligious social movement organized in Los Angeles in 1925 by charismatic leader Hilario Camino Moncado. In the 1920s, his popularity spread rapidly, and branches were established throughout California and Hawaii. The Stockton branch of the FFA was set up around 1928 and quickly extended its influence among farm laborers through Christian-based moral reform activities, including crusades against gambling, smoking, drinking, and patronizing taxi-dance halls.[40] With the rise of the FALA in the late 1930s, the FFA saw its membership decline and its authority weaken, which made it more willing to collaborate with the Japanese community. Since Moncado stressed the principles of loyalty and hard work relating to labor issues, Japanese leaders found his federation the best partner in their fight against the FALA.[41] Many FFA members served as strikebreakers and worked alongside Japanese.

In the Japanese-FFA alliance, a rupture can be seen in the monolithic image of Filipinos as the archenemy, which Issei had created during the early 1930s. When they collaborated with Japanese, Moncado's men did not fit that image. Yet, what Filipinoness fundamentally signified changed little, if at all, in the Japanese racial ideology. As long as the FALA continued to challenge Japanese agricultural and commercial interests, the image of Filipinos as the enemy remained intact; Moncado's men thus were not authentic Filipinos.[42] For this reason Japanese usually referred to them with qualifiers, such as "peaceful Filipinos," "good Filipinos," or "federation workers."

A Japanese American woman, Kay Morimoto, played a crucial role in forging this alliance. Born on the Hawaiian island of Maui in 1907, she had close contact with local white elites, since she was a well-known semiprofessional golfer in the state and her dentist husband was a leader of the Japanese American Citizens League chapter in Stockton. At first asked by some Issei merchants to help them recruit nonunion Filipinos, she soon became a self-appointed spokesperson for the Japanese community, which Issei leaders tacitly approved. In addition to her personal connections, being a female Nisei put Morimoto in the best position to represent Japanese immigrants in relation to whites and nonunion Filipinos. The traditional notion of femininity—nonpolitical, nonthreatening, and incapable of scheming—rendered her far more effective at public relations than any man.[43] Her plea for help could buy sympathy from white landlords, while making Filipino union members look nefarious should they torment a "weak" woman. Moreover, since the male-dominated social structure prevented women from being taken seriously as equals, both whites and federation members probably lowered their guards and were more relaxed in dealing with her than with male Issei leaders. Ironically, her image of helplessness gave significant influence to the Nisei woman.

Since the racial struggle revolved around the question of the two groups' relative attractiveness to the white elite, Morimoto concentrated her efforts on winning landlord support for the anti-union alliance. When agribusiness leaders held a mass meeting to discuss how to deal with an expected strike during the 1940 asparagus season, she attended without invitation and declared that the Japanese community could offer alternative Filipino labor as well as their own. She also repeatedly visited the asparagus farms and talked to white landlords and growers individually. Consequently, federation members replaced most FALA asparagus cutters in the area. To minimize a potential labor dispute and to benefit her own people, Morimoto also supplied exclusively Japanese laborers for asparagus-packing facilities, where the work was easier and more lucrative than field work.[44] With a few thousand members, the FALA was still powerful, but the union nonetheless lost hundreds of jobs in the asparagus industry to the Japanese. Morimoto's activity was so effective that the FALA could not even initiate a walkout until the end of the asparagus season in June.

The FALA viewed the situation as a life-and-death matter. With the growing success of the Japanese pleas to the white population, the union was most concerned about damaging the white perception of Filipinos. Like the Japanese, union leaders sought the sympathy of landlords by stressing their desirability as a people and a race. Despite labor disputes, Filipinos insisted how much they cared about whites' economic interests and prosperity. According to the *Philippine Journal*, the union organ, the previous asparagus season was a case in point. Explaining why there had been no labor dispute then, the newspaper claimed: "[T]he FALA could have forced the rehiring of the displaced workers, but in the interest of the farmers [landlords] who would suffer tremendous losses in case of a tieup . . . the FALA let the matter drop."[45] In another "open letter" to white landlords, the journal attributed the origin of past labor disputes to the "meddling" of Japanese merchants and farmers or to "extraneous interests which have for their aim the exploitation of Filipinos."[46]

The union also attempted to illustrate the "good" character of Filipinos and the "sinister" nature of Japanese by juxtaposing the local racial struggle with international politics. With the deterioration of U.S.–Japan relations in mind, the FALA appealed to rising antagonism toward Japan among white Americans. Filipinos characterized themselves as loyal American nationals, who "would only be too willing to take up arms at any time in her [the United States'] defense."[47] They also contended that the FALA had official backing from the Philippine government, which was under U.S. control, so that it would not dare to criticize the American system and its democratic ideals.

By contrast, the union cast Japanese as anti-American, since they were aliens from an undemocratic homeland. When Moncado told a reporter from the white-run *Stockton Record* that Filipinos would seek help from Japan to fight for their freedom if the United States failed to grant independent status to the Philippines in 1944 as promised, union leaders bitterly denounced him as disloyal to America. One FALA official was quoted in the same newspaper as saying that Moncado's statement revealed "a new angle" that "must come from certain foreign friends."[48] In this dispute, antilabor Filipinos, friendly to both Japan and the delta's Japanese aliens, were portrayed as the very opposite of union Filipinos, that is, loyal American nationals. This contrast greatly worried Issei lest white residents mistake them for anti-American conspirators. The trust of their patrons was at stake.[49]

Japanese fought just as vigorously to win whites to their side. A few months before the next celery season, Morimoto started to sound out landlords about increasing the employment of Japanese and FFA workers. In early August, at a meeting of the San Joaquin County Farm Bureau directors, she denounced FALA's strong inclination toward labor militancy and emphasized that "there is another group among the Filipinos which wants to work and is willing to accept reasonable hour and wage schedules."[50] Her plea for peace in the ranks of Filipino labor, she pronounced, was in the interests of both the white and Japanese communities. In order to free local agriculture from its labor woes, Morimoto requested that the farm bureau give formal sanction and financial aid to her efforts. Although no concrete action was taken, the news made it into the local English-language newspaper, generating positive reaction and sympathy from white residents.[51] Despite Issei concern, landlords still appreciated the value that the Japanese community offered to them: the economic advantage of using Japanese tenants and laborers, as well as the symbolism of their loyalty and submission to the established order.

Finding more of its members displaced from the celery fields even before the beginning of the harvest in late October 1940, the FALA resorted to drastic action to take back lost jobs. As early as mid-October, the union announced that it would seek a closed shop in the delta's celery industry. The demand concentrated solely on the exclusion of Japanese and nonunion Filipinos, whom they often termed "pro-Japanese traitors," without even mentioning wage increases. One month later, union officials petitioned for a charter with the American Federation of Labor (AFL), so that they could avail themselves of more effective tactics than picketing. Presented with the charter on November 20, 1940, the FALA, now renamed the Federated Agricultural Laborers' Association, immediately issued an ultimatum: either the employers would agree to a closed shop and the reinstatement of displaced FALA members, or the union would call for a nationwide hot cargo (refusal to handle the crop) initiative in cooperation with the AFL Teamsters Union.[52]

Issei merchants and farmers joined together with white landlords and shippers, and their alliance was stronger than ever before. The FALA's demand for a closed shop threatened the economic survival of the entire Japanese community. Should it become a reality, every Japanese would lose out; given grim market conditions, a farmer would go bankrupt, while a laborer would go adrift without a job. Japanese farmers did not exaggerate when they declared that they would quit celery production if the closed shop materialized. Merchants would eventually suffer, too, because they faced intense competition from union-affiliated Filipino businesses.[53] Thus, the recruitment of strikebreakers intensified, along with other forms of harassment, including the eviction of union Filipinos from Japanese-owned or -leased buildings. The FALA president, local physician Macario Bautista, fell victim to this tactic. After the eviction, his former office was leased to none other than the rival FFA for the recruitment of nonunion Filipinos.[54]

Fervent in their anti-union activities, white elites held the Japanese in high esteem and openly praised their "loyalty." One agribusiness president averred that, rather than "sign that [closed-shop] contract, I'll first raise a Japanese flag on my packing houses and will never hire one Filipino as long as I live."[55] Encouraged by Japanese efforts, eight out of eleven major shipper-growers flatly refused the FALA's demand, stating that they had secured enough labor through Morimoto, while the other three retained FALA workers pending further negotiations. Meanwhile, displaced FALA members could do nothing but picket—or, rather, simply stand—while the Japanese and Moncado's people busily engaged in strikebreaking work.[56]

Consequently, the overall composition of the celery labor market changed in favor of Japanese workers. According to a *Nichibei Shimbun* reporter, the number of Japanese workers in packing sheds rose fivefold from the 1939 season, while that of FALA members dropped dramatically. Out of the nine packing sheds, six had 292 Japanese and 117 federation workers in their facilities; there were only 197 union members working in the other three sheds, more than 500 fewer than in 1939. Since there were two other packing sheds that employed Japanese exclusively, the total number of Japanese packers in the delta reached 400. Moreover, about 90 percent of field workers were said to be Japanese, due to the strikebreaking of the previous year. All in all, Japanese workers totaled 787, while Filipino workers decreased from about 2,700 to 851, the majority of whom were probably federation workers in 1940.[57]

From the Issei perspective, this situation represented a turning point in the racial struggle in the delta. Because young Nisei—mostly Kibei—constituted 80 percent of the Japanese labor force in the fall of 1940, the day when American-born Japanese would finally expel Filipinos from the delta appeared to be nearing.[58] Seemingly underscoring the success of the Return-to-America campaign, this development reinforced Issei belief that the second generation would once again monopolize the labor market and bring back the golden age of Japanese agriculture that their immigrant parents had enjoyed during the 1910s. Meanwhile, about 300 local Nisei—mostly sons of Issei farmers—had already formed the Nisei Farmers' League of Stockton for the purpose of promoting Japanese agricultural interests along the line of the statewide Back-to-the-Farm movement. As the Nisei Farmers' League enjoyed full support from the white-controlled Stockton Vegetable Growers Association and the Farm Bureau of Stockton, the youngsters were on their way to taking over the Issei proxy for white agribusiness.[59] The historical dynamic of replacement and succession was now working in favor of the Japanese.

Japanese leaders resolved to protect the labor advantage that they had recovered from Filipinos. Issei were still concerned about Filipinos' dogged demand for a closed-shop contract, which could oust all nonunion Japanese from local agriculture. When white AFL officials urged Japanese to join the new FALA, now a multiethnic federated union, some Japanese leaders seriously contemplated the option. Yet, at the meeting of Issei labor representatives and contractors, the majority opinion of "capital-labor cooperation" quickly overrode this option, because they agreed that the issue was not class strife but racial "war" for hegemony in the field—or, more precisely, for a proper place in the racially stratified political economy of the delta.[60] In order to confront the powerful Filipino-AFL alliance, Issei leaders decided to set up their own "labor" union.[61]

After the end of the celery harvest, on December 30, 1940, the California Farm Labor Union (CFLU) was formally established with an initial membership of 500 Japanese. Although dubbed a "labor union," this organization stood against the working-class movement, as it pursued "the mutual prosperity of farmers and laborers." A product of the Issei's ethnic nationalism, the CFLU aimed to mobilize all strata of the Japanese agricultural population in the delta under its umbrella. The official statement of purpose revealed its racial ideology and firm belief in the concept of racial struggle with strong undertones of Social Darwinism:

> The welfare of the Japanese race is predicated upon the development of a healthy economy. . . . Today is the age of struggle for survival. Many [ethnic] unions have emerged to defend their own interests. . . . The [1940] celery strike could have developed into a serious threat that might

have overturned our vested position [in agriculture] had it been left unchecked. Only in our cooperation does the solution lie. We are now
faced with the grave crisis to our economy. When we think about the
coming era of our successors, the Nisei, we shall all realize that we must
live up to the grand ideal of our race [the development of the Japanese
in America] notwithstanding personal differences. We urge you to join
the union![62]

The actual membership of the union mirrored the ideology of pan-Japanese
unity and racial development. Its president and treasurer were prominent farmers, and the union headquarters was located on one of their farms. The rest of
the leadership, it seems, consisted of a mixture of farmers, merchants, and
laborers drawn from both the first and second generations, many of whom had
also been involved in the Nisei Farmers' League. A majority of lay members
were Issei and Nisei celery workers who had replaced FALA members.[63] For
the coming asparagus season, the Japanese union ambitiously sought to expand
its base by incorporating 500 more laborers.

The formation of the CFLU also symbolized the unshaken Issei loyalty to
the established order. This union embodied the traditional alliance among white
elite, Japanese farmers and merchants, and Japanese laborers, which had shored
up the delta's agricultural economy since the 1910s.[64] Its membership of several
hundred recruited candidates for strikebreaking on whom white landlords could
rely at any time. Nothing was more beneficial than this pool of ready-to-use
scabs in the center of a militant Filipino labor movement.

With the unionization of anti–working-class Japanese, the Issei struggle for
their rightful position in the delta reached new heights. Starting in February
1941, the CFLU launched a campaign to counter the FALA's demand for a
closed shop in the asparagus industry. At a special meeting, asparagus subcon-
tractors and labor leaders were reminded that what was at stake was not only
jobs but the future of the Japanese community and race in the United States.
They collaborated with the union to distribute more than 2,000 Japanese laborers to packing facilities throughout the delta region, nearly monopolizing
that line of work. Along with federation Filipinos, a few hundred others also
encroached upon the FALA's stronghold of field work. In the end, it was reported that the delta's asparagus farms employed more than three-quarters of
the migratory Japanese laborers in northern and central California during the
1941 season.[65]

The new labor market conditions in the celery and asparagus industries
presaged the death of the FALA. A new strike, called at the beginning of April
1941, failed to spread, except for some tie-ups in limited areas. Under the auspices of the Associated Farmers, a conservative organization of agribusiness

leaders in the state, white landlords quickly built a united front against Filipino union members, and the harvest continued with available Japanese and anti-union Filipino labor. As a result, the unity of the FALA rapidly crumbled. To make matters worse, the AFL Cannery Workers' Union, which struck when the canning of asparagus commenced, left the FALA out of its agreement with the canneries and growers. Betrayed by their white comrades, many Filipino union members turned their backs and returned to work, which led to the virtual demise of the FALA by late May.[66] Interpreting this situation as their decisive triumph in the racial struggle, the delta's Japanese enjoyed the "peaceful paradise between grower[s] and laborers" and celebrated their alliance with white elites for a few more months. Although U.S.–Japan relations rapidly deteriorated, many Issei still had reasons to anticipate a brighter future for their community, until that fateful day when their homeland callously dashed the dream of racial development.

ETHNIC NATIONALISM AS CLASS UNCONSCIOUSNESS

The racial ideology of Japanese immigrants in the delta, expressed in Issei ethnic nationalism, constructed the Japanese community through a denial of internal diversities. In the process, nationalism valorized the interests of male Issei farmers and merchants, who formulated a class-based ethnic identity. Just like the politics of history making, Japaneseness in the delta was defined by the needs of these leading groups. Whether farmers or laborers, men or women, first generation or second generation, all Japanese were expected to act to enhance the interests of Japanese agriculture and commerce and to "live up to the grand ideal of [their] race."[67] Issei essentialized the concept of race to the extent that they considered it as the one and only truth in social relations. In their eyes, every conflict that they had with Filipinos—interethnic marriage, commercial competition, and labor disputes—registered as a conflict of race that involved every member of the community. There was little room for forms of interethnic relations other than "racial struggle." The expulsion from Stockton of Louis Yamamoto, who attempted to pit Japanese laborers against farmers, underscored the class-specific nature of Issei nationalism. Likewise, the failure of a marriage between a Nisei woman and a Filipino man exemplified how Issei entrepreneurs arrested another heterodox form of interethnic relations from developing into a counterforce to the racial integrity of the community.

To understand fully how Japanese saw matters and acted, it is necessary to place their nationalism in the context of the white-controlled political economy in the San Joaquin delta rather than simply conclude that nationalism was a way to identify with Japan. The hostile interactions between Japanese and Filipinos resulted from the logic of a system of racially constituted power relations. First and foremost, the social hierarchy created a situation of Japanese dependence upon local white elites. In terms of both class and race, Japanese were relegated to a subordinate position after the early 1920s. The system only allowed them to work in very specific and limited capacities, where their labor chiefly profited the white ruling class. In this context, Issei farmers and merchants were aware that, as a group, they were dispensable if replacements were available. With the influx of Filipino immigrants, they discerned a real danger. Filipinos first took over the labor market and then threatened to destroy Japanese farming and commerce by launching hostile strikes. Japanese immigrants, especially community leaders, feared that Filipinos might persuade whites of the advantage of replacing Japanese altogether with a new group. With the rising sense of urgency in Issei minds, the rhetoric of race overlapped with that of class, obscured it, and finally replaced it. It then engendered an essentialist mode of thought that interpreted every social situation in terms of race. Throughout this process, ethnic nationalism marshaled disparate ideas into a coherent ideology.

The notion of "class unconsciousness" succinctly explains the nature of the Japanese racial ideology.[68] It refers to the misrecognition of one's class position in society as natural. Indeed, the Japanese of the delta accepted the racially stratified class hierarchy as natural. They showed little desire to challenge or even question white hegemony and their own subordination—at least for the time being. By the same token, they also took their racial superiority to and class dominance over Filipinos as natural. In light of this class unconsciousness, the Issei decision to fight militant Filipino laborers meant protecting the "natural" order of existing power relations. Interethnic conflict thus created a no-win situation for everyone but the ruling class. The nationalism that arose operated as a form of social control rather than of social resistance in the delta, for the local structure disallowed the emergence of heterodox ethnic identities, such as a labor-based Japanese identity. Problems of class exploitation and other social injustices within their community were set aside in the name of the larger interests of the Japanese race in America.

While the ethnic nationalism of Japanese immigrants was rooted in their delta experiences, it also reflected international developments. Through the concept of overseas development, elements of Japanese colonialism and imperial racism crept into Issei racial discourse, in which local race relations overlapped with the power relations of nation-states. Subsequently, the delta's Japanese community often resembled a miniature Japanese state, and its relationship with Filipinos mirrored a hierarchical order between a colonial empire and a "third-class" nation. The construction of a delta-Japanese identity also involved an Issei attempt to make sense of local affairs in terms of international situations—

a sort of transnational imagination. In California and other Western states, combined local and international forces provided the background for a distorted mode of interethnic interactions among Asian immigrant groups, based on animosity and suspicion rather than on amity and cooperation.[69] And when there was outright conflict, it frequently fostered the development of ethnic nationalism—an immigrant nationalism far more complex than notions of patriotic identity with a native land.

In the delta, as in other parts of the American West, the end of ethnic nationalism paralleled the disappearance of shared interests and the sudden reversal of interethnic relations after the Japanese attack on Pearl Harbor. The new development in geopolitics engrossed the local society thoroughly, changing the places of Japanese and Filipino immigrants in the racial hierarchy. Whites associated Japanese residents with the enemy across the Pacific, and the mounting suspicion of Issei treachery in America marred their track record of steadfast allegiance to the existing order. The rupture between white elites and Japanese middlemen paved the way for the ascent of Filipinos and other minorities. As Issei farmers found their leases terminated by landlords and as merchants lost customers, the ethnic community, as imagined and defended by the people, was effectively eliminated from the local political economy, even before the actual removal of Japanese residents from the West Coast.[70] Along with the community, their identity as delta Japanese, as well as the ethnic nationalism that supported it, likewise drowned in the whirlpool of war hate and intolerance.

Epilogue

Wartime Racisms, State Nationalisms, and the Collapse of Immigrant Transnationalism

"East is East, and West is West." With this statement the narrator of *Little Tokyo USA*, a 1942 Hollywood film, began the story of an alleged Nisei espionage ring, which commanded "a vast army of volunteer spies steeped in the tradition of their homeland" while "complacent America literally slept at the switch."[1] Unified behind these Oriental traitors was the entire ethnic community, which conspired to aid a Japanese invasion along the Western seaboard. Corresponding with the official military policy of mass "evacuation" that commenced in the spring of 1942, the movie justified the incarceration of all Japanese residents for national defense on the simple premise of the eternal East-West divide that mere acculturation or the possession of citizenship would not leap. Exactly thirty years after Jizaemon Tateishi, an Issei University of Southern California student, had challenged the idea of such polarities, America finally declared, once and for all, that being Japanese was antithetical to being American in every possible sense and thus "never the twain shall meet." Riichiro Hoashi's call for "transcend[ing] the narrow bound of nationality and race" proved to be just as vain, for the U.S. government and society subsequently treated the Japanese race—long-time resident aliens and native-born citizens alike—as untrustworthy and their loyalty, if existent at all, as indiscernible.

The Pacific War disallowed the kind of *inter-national* flexibility that Japanese immigrants had enjoyed in the interstices between the two nation-states for the preceding decades. What took place after December 7, 1941, was an amalgamation of nationalism and racism, which culminated in a complete polarization between things Japanese and things American in each warring state. The conflation of the national and the racial in the American public discourse deprived Japanese immigrants of access to the ruling ideology. In the intersections of nationalizing racism and racializing nationalism, the universality of exclusionist politics prevailed against the Japanese, enabling white racism to function as a super–American nationalism that drastically shrank the boundaries of nationality and resulted in the total repudiation of the Issei and Nisei on the West Coast.[2] Hence came Lieutenant General John L. DeWitt's casual suspension of Japanese American citizenship rights: "The Japanese race is an enemy race and while many second and third generation Japanese born on the United States soil, possessed of United States citizenship, have become 'Americanized,' their racial strains are undiluted."[3] On February 19, 1942, just a week after this "final recommendation," President Franklin D. Roosevelt authorized the removal of nearly 120,000 Japanese Americans from the Pacific Coast states and parts of Arizona. Although Yale law professor Eugene Rostow later characterized this episode as "our worst wartime mistake," it was not a mistake at all. The Japanese American incarceration signified a historical moment when the cultural, racial, and national Otherness of the Asian was most lucidly articulated, most undisputed, and most resolutely dealt with by the American citizenry and state.[4]

In a series of events that occurred between 1942 and 1945, Japanese immigrants found their eclectic social orientations denied thoroughly. With the administration of the infamous loyalty questionnaires in the internment camps, the possibility of public self-expression was limited to a futile show of unqualified Americanism or an angry declaration of pro-Japan fanaticism.[5] No longer was it tenable for Issei and Nisei to openly fancy Japanese American compatibility or their mediating roles in the Pacific, because, as historian John W. Dower notes, neither Japanese nor American wartime discourse "offer[ed] much ground for the recognition of common traits, comparable acts, or compatible aspirations."[6]

The war hammered the last nail in the coffin of Issei transnational history—one that had already become increasingly "American" before Pearl Harbor. The collective world view that had inspired Issei to search for a pioneer past and strive for a better future vanished with the collapse of the Japanese settlement communities and industries in the American West—tangible markers of racial development. In a *haiku* poem, which offered a rare type of uncensored expression during incarceration, one Issei condensed a stuporous sense of ending into seventeen Japanese syllables:[7]

The futile sweat
Our many years in America are wasted.[8]

Another poem conveys the betrayal of history:

The foundation of our permanent settlement
The current crisis has spoiled it.[9]

Not only did their history appear to have come to a terminus, but Japanese immigrant pioneers also had nothing to pass on to their successors. By 1941, most immigrant men were in their sixties, and women were in their forties to fifties. As the Japanese often characterized it, the "winter" phase of their lives was supposed to be uneventful and yet full of hope for the springtime of a Nisei era. According to a former Los Angeles resident, no such future was in sight in wartime America:

Our immigrant history in its last pages
In confinement we are in hibernation.[10]

But the demise of transnational immigrant history was not the end of Japanese American history. While many Issei lamented the loss of their proud past or silently buried it, the wartime ascendancy of American nationalism coerced many Japanese Americans into engaging in different social practices and adopting different identities. How the postwar phase of Japanese American history unfolded diverged from the Issei's original designs. Under the War Relocation Authority (WRA) policy, the leadership of the community fell into the hands of the second generation, notably senior members of the Japanese American Citizens League (JACL). Along the line of the WRA-JACL collaboration, integration into mainstream society, rather than racial development, became the central concern of the ethnic community in the wake of the internment.[11] On January 2, 1945, the WRA started to release Japanese internees, except for those deemed disloyal, to any destination on the mainland United States, including the West Coast states. At the end of 1945, the WRA shut down all the camps except the Tule Lake segregation center for the disloyal. Stripped of social authority, elderly Issei were dependent on their sons and daughters, who, in historian David Yoo's words, "carried the responsibility of caring for their parents, their own budding families, and for establishing new careers."[12] With the steady breakdown of occupational barriers and enhanced educational opportunities in postwar America, the entry of many Nisei into the society's main institutions and middle-class lives progressed to the extent that the people, by the mid-1960s, came to be hailed as "a model minority," even characterized as "out-whiting" whites.[13]

In an attempt to explain this course of development, a new master narrative replaced the prewar historical discourse with one highlighting the agency of the second generation under the collaborative efforts of senior Nisei, their white sympathizers, and government authorities. Centering on loyal Nisei servicemen and visionary JACL male leaders, the new history reduced the immigrant experience to a preface to the main story of "Americans with Japanese faces"— the heroes of history without whose "record of unswerving loyalty, Japanese Americans, and other minorities," could not have been "enjoying unrestricted citizenship rights" in postwar America.[14] Most emblematic of the Nisei's discursive takeover was the construction of the massive *Monument for Patriotic Martyrs*, erected on behalf of the Nisei GIs killed in action, which literally dwarfed the 1937 memorial to Issei pioneers in the same Los Angeles Japanese cemetery. With no reference to their ethnicity, General Dwight D. Eisenhower's epitaph on the memorial simply salutes "those who . . . gave their lives that this country, beset by its enemies, might win out of their sacrifice, victory and peace," thereby illuminating the Nisei's undiluted Americanism. Accompanied by this generational bias in history, the ascent of unmodified U.S. nationalism in the Cold War era further encouraged the genesis of a narrative with a mononational framework, as suggested in the unabashed celebration of the Nisei's patriotism.[15] Subsequently, this discursive domestication made the postwar historical construction and identity formation coterminous with what professional Asian American historians began to call, after the late 1960s, a story of Americans "from a different shore."

The casualties of a domesticated Japanese American history include the whole history of the entanglements between Issei/Nisei and Japan. In the face of lingering anti-Japanese sentiments that refused to distinguish between Japanese Americans and the people of Japan, their racial "home" continued to disrupt the lives of Japanese Americans even after the war. Furthermore, the total triumph of "American democracy" over "Japanese militarism," as well as the undying effects of wartime ideological disciplining, have led many Nisei— and Issei—into purging the memories of their engagement with imperial Japan and even retroactively claiming an opposition to its militaristic aggression.[16] The rehabilitated, often fabricated image of the superpatriotic Japanese American was accompanied by the forgetting and distorting of a transnational past, whose legacy has persisted until now in the form of historical unconsciousness among Sansei, the third generation.

In 1957, Bill Hosokawa, a prominent Nisei journalist who wrote four of the most influential postwar master narratives, printed a manifesto about the Nisei's abandonment of transnationalism. In it, the JACL leader traced the origins of the prewar bridge concept to "idealists and do-gooders on both side of the ocean," and to Issei, whose "dreams could not stand up under the realism of power politics." Hosokawa asserted, "But if the Nisei flopped as bridges,

FIGURE E.1. Six Nisei Veterans Association members stand in front of the Nisei Veterans Memorial Monument in Evergreen Cemetery, Los Angeles, 1949.
This thirty-two-feet tower was built on the same cemetery, where the smaller Issei memorial had stood since 1937. The difference in size symbolizes the preponderance of the story of Nisei patriots over that of Issei pioneers in the postwar years. Gift of Luis Aihara and Kiyo Maruyama. Courtesy of the Japanese American National Museum, Los Angeles (97.79.2).

their faith in their country was justified" because "today their acceptance as Americans is complete and their position in their native land is secure." As if ignoring his own struggle as the editor in chief of a Japan-sponsored, Singapore newspaper in the not-so-distant past, the Nisei writer dismissed the transnationality of the Japanese American experience as having no relevance to their collective identity—one forged solely in the context of the wartime internment and military service.[17] Nor did Mike Masaoka, another JACL leader, ever discuss his leadership role in the Nisei Sincerity Society of Salt Lake City, which collected donations for the Japanese army in late 1937. As the cost of such self-denials, ambiguities and intricacies in the stories of this borderland minority have long remained beyond the pale of our nationalized knowledge.

This book has explored the complexity of transnational thinking and practices among Japanese immigrants on the borderland of the American West. Caught in the interstices of competing powers and ideas, Issei actively negotiated, engaged, and often collaborated with both white America and imperial Japan.[18] Their ability to make claims on the grounds of their ethnicity/nationality as "the Japanese in America" rested with the nuances and contradictions between the ideologies of the two regimes. Although drawing on common modernist knowledge, the assumptions of the American and Japanese states never completely overlapped, creating the space where Issei could forge their own interpretations and self-definitions. In order to assert their dualistic positionality, interests, and identities, Japanese immigrants were often able to navigate through the two state ideologies, not only by turning one against the other but also by conveniently fusing aspects of them.

Based on the experience of the Japanese in America, the orthodox immigrant paradigm of American history, which assumes the one-dimensional relationality of the native-born citizen and the foreign-born alien, needs to be reconsidered. In pursuit of the goal of turning into a full-fledged American, it imposes on the immigrant a total rupture between his life before emigration and his life in the New World. Studies on U.S. migration have largely neglected people's history before immigration and have also dismissed the ties that immigrants stubbornly sustained to their homelands as obstacles in the process of linear assimilation or democratic integration into their adopted nation, that is, "Americanization." Yet, the example of Japanese immigrant practices underlines what new immigration historians have come to advocate recently: the need for alternatives to national histories in understanding immigrant lives. Operating in this emerging "historiographical no-man's-land, claimed by no nation-state and dominated by no one national myth," this book has offered a transnational rendition of Japanese immigrant history as a total experience, not simply as an American experience.[19]

The entanglements of imperial Japanese racism and white American racism occupied a focal point of Issei's total experience as a borderland minority. Under the coercion and interpellation of those hegemonic discourses, which were not necessarily incommensurate, Japanese immigrant transnationalism fundamentally failed to overcome the confines of the essentialist categories of the two regimes. For this reason many Issei uncritically embraced aspects of both racisms in their quest for inclusion into the American national society and culture while maintaining ties to their racial homeland. Whether to re-form the immigrant masses, to produce a collective vision for the Nisei era, or to defend the community against racial "enemies," Issei leaders tended to imagine hierarchical relations between the Japanese and other minorities, as well as parallels between the Japanese and whites. While it reproduced the dominant racist practices among them, such eclectic thinking still allowed Japanese immigrants to insist on their authenticity as frontier Americans and imperial Japanese, despite the contrary exclusionist claim of their unassimilability.

Viewed from an inter-National perspective, the racial formation of Japanese immigrants did not take place unilaterally, but multilaterally. In the years before the Pacific War, Issei were simultaneously "racially formed [racialized]" and "racially forming [racializing]" under the influence of the competing racisms.[20] Drawing on the duality of such immigrant experiences, this book has broadened the scope of inquiry about American race relations. First, an analysis of the Issei's racial formations requires displacing a Eurocentric lens that renders Japanese immigrants as mere objects of white racial projects. Contrarily, the Issei had propensities to play along with exclusionist politics, not because they were helpless without choices, but because their own Orientalist beliefs drove them to seek the privilege of whiteness as their entitlement as well. Hardly could one have untangled the multiplicity of racial formations but for consideration of the ideological baggage many Issei carried from their racial homeland.

Although the white racial project constantly endeavored to prescribe differences along (pseudo)biological lines, this book has highlighted a methodological need to treat Japanese immigrants as a distinctive racial category. Not only does this approach question the conventional paradigm of black-white relations, which automatically relegates others to an accessory to blackness, but it also challenges the hitherto accepted use of "Asian" as a single analytical unit in studies in American race relations.[21] Because the Japanese in America were not only racialized by a dominant white core but constantly racialized themselves on their own terms against their Asian neighbors and other minorities, they deserve to be seen as forming a separate race in the context of multilateral social relations.[22] Elite Issei's struggle against Sinification, their formulation of the Issei pioneer thesis, and the community-wide effort to hold Filipino laborers in check—all underscored dimensions of racial formation that Japanese immigrants experienced relative to their fellow Asians despite, or perhaps because of, the interventions of the hegemonic white racial project.

It is nonetheless important to note that these instances of racialization revolved around not merely skin color or moral capacity but the ultimate question of national belonging, that is, who held a rightful place in America's national community. In this sense, just as the ruling Anglo elite did through their exclusionary politics, Issei also practiced in quest of acceptance and inclusion what historian Gary Gerstle calls the "racial nationalism that conceives of America in ethnoracial terms" against other minorities.[23] A study of the Japanese immigrant experience—and for that matter, all immigrant groups—beckons to the coupling of race and nation as equally important, mutually reinforcing, and often integrated, analytical entities.

My analysis has complicated the critical nexus between racism and nationalism in the experience of this borderland minority. Race could undermine the integrity and cohesiveness of nation, and yet, nation, due to its multiple constituents, could counteract the purism that race always sought to embellish.[24] In a transnational context, Issei found the crevices between race and nation magnified even further, since the competing definitions of the two categories from Japan and the United States widened and disfigured the interstices or shades of meaning, and they continued to drift without real acceptance from either nation-state. When Issei sent Nisei to Japan for transnational education, for example, the presence of American citizens of Japanese ancestry confounded the Japanese nation-state. The Issei's vision of the Nisei as Americans par excellence did not mesh well with the way in which many Japanese took for granted the reversion of their overseas compatriots to the racial homeland. Yet, the fact that the Nisei were of Japanese origin in and of itself did not automatically secure them a legitimate presence in Japan on account of their nationality status and cultural state. Similar ambiguities persisted on the other side of the Pacific before 1942. America's civic, nationalist notion of nationhood was theoretically devoid of racial specificity as far as native-borns were concerned. Thus, under the mandate of the Fourteenth Amendment, the American state had to retain the Nisei despite the racial nationalist desire to disown them.[25] While the volatility of their national belonging ironically provided room for the Issei's simultaneous engagement with both countries, it also enabled them to envisage the likeness between Japanese and white Americans without disturbing the purity of race pursued by each regime.

To counteract the single national focus that still dominates the field of Asian American history, this book has delved into some neglected practices of immigrant transnationalism. Whether they were members of the first generation or the second generation, a significant number of historical agents have been omitted from intellectual inquiry and interpretation as personae non gratae in history, and the images of other Japanese Americans are flattened nonsensically according to postwar orthodoxy.[26] Instead of simply glorifying (or dismissing) them, our historical knowledge should recognize the human complexities that the likes of Bill Hosokawa and Mike Masaoka embodied beyond their emphasis on one-dimensional patriotism. Moreover, forgotten Issei, like Yoichi Toga and Shiro Fujioka, as well as ostracized Kibei returnees and resident Nisei in Japan, should be accorded a full appreciation of their dilemmas and ambivalence in Japanese American history. The usual narrative of a multicultural America does not suffice to tell all of their stories beyond the conventional dichotomies of the "loyal" versus the "disloyal," of "citizens" versus "aliens," or of "heroes" versus "villains," since the discourse on diversity still primarily operates in a domestic context that celebrates a particular form of American nationhood and society. Framing the total experience of Japanese immigrants and their children in an international context is just as crucial as understanding their unfaltering Americanness as a paradigm of U.S. multiculturalism.[27] This book offers an example of such a new approach, one that will pave the way to more nuanced studies of Asian Americans and U.S. (im)migration history.

Notes

INTRODUCTION

1. J. Tateishi, "Some Aspects of Japanese Traits," *Japanese El Rodeo* 1 (June 15, 1912): 10, 11. This is from the English section of *Nanka gakusō*, a yearbook published by the Japanese Student Association of the University of Southern California.

2. Riichiro Hoashi, "Cosmopolitanism," ibid., 15.

3. Willard Price, *Children of the Rising Sun* (New York: Reynal & Hitchcock, 1938), 279–280, 292.

4. Shūgiin, *Teikoku Gikai Shūgiin Iinkaigiroku: Shōwa-hen*, vol. 85 (1937–1938) (Tokyo: Tokyo Daigaku Shuppan, 1995), 72.

5. Sucheng Chan, "European and Asian Immigration into the United States in Comparative Perspective, 1820s to 1920s," in *Immigration Reconsidered: History, Sociology, and Politics*, ed. Virginia Yans-McLaughlin (New York: Oxford University Press, 1990), 38. See also Henry Yu, "On a Stage Built by Others: Creating an Intellectual History of Asian Americans," *Amerasia Journal* 26 (2000): 152–158, esp. 158. Recently, with the concepts of diaspora and postcolonialism, historians of Chinese Americans and Filipino Americans have produced notable studies of transnational community and family formations before World War II. See Yong Chen, *Chinese San Francisco, 1850–1943: A Trans-Pacific Community* (Stanford, Calif.: Stanford University Press, 2000); Madeline Y. Hsu, *Dreaming of Gold, Dreaming of Home: Transnationalism and Migration between the United States and South China, 1882–1943* (Stanford, Calif.: Stanford University Press, 2000); Au-

gusto Fauni Espiritu, "Expatriate Affirmations: The Performance of Nationalism and Patronage in Filipino American Intellectual Life" (Ph.D. diss., University of California, Los Angeles, 2000); and Arleen Garcia de Vera, "Constituting Community: A Study of Nationalism, Colonialism, Gender, and Identity among Filipinos in California, 1919–1946" (Ph.D. diss., University of California, Los Angeles, 2002).

6. On nationalized immigrant histories, see Donna R. Gabaccia, "Is Everywhere Nowhere? Nomads, Nations, and the Immigrant Paradigm of United States History," *Journal of American History* 86 (December 1999): 1115–1134. See also David Thelen, "The Nation and Beyond: Transnational Perspectives on United States History," *Journal of American History* 86 (December 1999): 967–968, 970, 973–974. Possible models for a cross-national study of Japanese immigrants include Dino Cinel, *From Italy to San Francisco: The Immigrant Experience* (Stanford, Calif.: Stanford University Press, 1982); and George J. Sánchez, *Becoming Mexican American: Ethnicity, Culture, and Identity in Chicano Los Angeles, 1900–1945* (New York: Oxford University Press, 1993). Demonstrating the fluidity and circularity of Italian and Mexican migration, respectively, these works look into the transnationality of the ideas, practices, and social relations within these immigrant groups. There is not yet an equivalent work in the field of Japanese immigrant history, although a few studies do address cross-national issues. Among these works are Yuji Ichioka, *The Issei: The World of the First Generation Japanese Immigrants, 1885–1924* (New York: Free Press, 1988); Brian Masaru Hayashi, *"For the Sake of Our Japanese Brethren": Assimilation, Nationalism, and Protestantism among the Japanese of Los Angeles, 1895–1942* (Stanford, Calif.: Stanford University Press, 1995); John J. Stephan, *Hawaii under the Rising Sun: Japan's Plans for Conquest after Pearl Harbor* (Honolulu: University of Hawaii Press, 1984); Mitziko Sawada, *Tokyo Life, New York Dreams: Urban Japanese Visions of America, 1890–1924* (Berkeley: University of California Press, 1996); Masayo Umezawa Duus, *The Japanese Conspiracy: The Oahu Sugar Strike of 1920*, trans. Beth Cary and ed. Peter Duus (Berkeley: University of California Press, 1999); and Hiromi Monobe, "Shaping an Ethnic Leadership: Takie Okumura and the 'Americanization' of the Nisei in Hawai'i, 1919–1945" (Ph.D. diss., University of Hawaii, Manoa, 2004).

7. Nina Glick Schiller, Linda Basch, and Cristina Blanc-Szanton, "Transnationalism: A New Analytical Framework for Understanding Migration," in *Towards a Transnational Perspective on Migration: Race, Class, Ethnicity, and Nationalism Reconsidered*, ed. Nina Glick Schiller et al. (New York: New York Academy of Sciences, 1992), 19; and David Palumbo-Liu, *Asian/American: Historical Crossings of a Racial Frontier* (Stanford, Calif.: Stanford University Press, 1999), 343–344. Currently in the field of cultural theories, denationalization seems to be in full bloom. Yet, as far as the issue of national(ist) perspective is concerned, what is important for historians is not so much theorizing as sound empirical research. Methodologically, to go beyond a mononational perspective takes much more than simple theorization and argumentation. In the case of Japanese immigrants, researchers must have a substantive understanding of actual events and concrete

forces, both in Japan and the United States, as well as within their communities, that influenced the ideas and practices of the Issei. From the vantage point of historians who value the meaning of empirical research, Gordon Chang and Yuji Ichioka comment critically on what appears to be the "overgrowth" of theories that have obscured the importance of careful investigations into primary sources. See Gordon Chang, "History and Postmodernism," *Amerasia Journal* 21 (1995): 89–93; and Yuji Ichioka, "A Historian by Happenstance," *Amerasia Journal* 26 (2000): 48–49. For a useful critique of excessive or uncritical denationalization, see also Sau-Ling C. Wong, "Denationalization Reconsidered: Asian American Cultural Criticism at a Theoretical Crossroads," *Amerasia Journal* 21 (1995): 1–27. Aside from abstract theorization, one positive trend in the denationalization of Asian American history is to seek meaningful bridges with Asian studies without becoming coopted by or subordinate to it. Recent revisionism in Japanese American history is part and parcel of this movement. Shirley Hune, "Asian American Studies and Asian Studies: Boundaries and Borderlands of Ethnic Studies and Area Studies," in *Color-Line to Borderlands: The Matrix of American Ethnic Studies*, ed. Johnnella E. Butler (Seattle: University of Washington Press, 2001), 227–239.

8. See Schiller, Basch, and Blanc-Szanton, "Toward a Definition of Transnationalism," 8–11; and Michelle A. Stephens, "Black Transnationalism and the Politics of National Identity: West Indian Intellectuals in Harlem in the Age of War and Revolution," *American Quarterly* 50 (September 1998): 592–593.

9. See, for example, Arjun Appadurai, "Disjuncture and Difference in the Global Culture Economy," *Theory, Culture, and Society* 7 (1990): 295–310; Arjun Appadurai, *Modernity at Large: Cultural Dimensions of Globalization* (Minneapolis: University of Minnesota Press, 1996); and Ulf Hannerz, *Transnational Connections* (New York: Routledge, 1996). Commonly embraced by theorists of this school, *diaspora* is another slippery term that I am cautious about using in my study. While it is often employed interchangeably with *transnationalism* in a casual manner, some scholars, like William Safran, maintain that the conditions of diaspora must resemble, if not overlap, the prototypical Jewish model. Others, like Stuart Hall, posit that it is "a conception of identity which lives through, not despite, difference." James Clifford focuses on the connections and networks among communities of a population dispersed beyond national borders or territories. In light of the diverse definitions and interpretations, Steven Vertovec categorizes diaspora into three types: social form and relationships, type of consciousness (identity based on a sense of multilocality), and mode of cultural production (usually tied to global capitalism). In any form of diaspora, the homeland (state) is usually treated only as a locus of collective memory and imagination instead of as a source of tangible power or control. This is where my definition of *transnationalism* differs significantly from the notions of diaspora. See William Safran, "Diasporas in Modern Societies: Myths of Homeland and Return," *Diaspora* 1 (1991): 83–99; Stuart Hall, "Cultural Identity and Diaspora," in *Identity: Community, Culture, Difference*, ed. J. Rutherford (London:

Lawrence, 1990), 222–237; James Clifford, "Diaspora," *Cultural Anthropology* 9 (1994): 302–338; and Steven Vertovec, "Three Meanings of 'Diaspora,' Exemplified among South Asian Religions," *Diaspora* 6 (1997): 277–299.

10. The most systematic study of Asian immigrant experiences according to a world-systems perspective is Edna Bonacich and Lucie Chang, eds., *Labor Immigration under Capitalism: Asian Workers in the United States before World War II* (Berkeley: University of California Press, 1984).

11. The Issei's adaptation to and adoption of racisms from the two hegemonic sources correspond with David Theo Goldberg's observation that a racial subject experiences the simultaneous processes of "the racially formed (racialized) and the racially forming (racializing)." See Goldberg's introduction to *Anatomy of Racism*, ed. David Theo Goldberg (Minneapolis: University of Minnesota Press, 1990), xii.

12. Luis Eduardo Guarnizo and Michael Peter Smith, "The Locations of Transnationalism," in *Transnationalism from Below*, ed. Michael Smith and Luis Eduardo Guarnizo (New Brunswick, N.J.: Transaction, 1998), 12–13.

13. Michael Omi and Howard Winant, *Racial Formation in the United States: From the 1960s to the 1990s* (New York: Routledge, 1994), 56, 60. David Theo Goldberg defines *racial formation processes* as "the transformation over time in what gets to count as a race, how racial membership is determined, and what sorts of exclusion this entails." See Goldberg, *Anatomy of Racism*, xii.

14. Ichioka, *Issei*, 1–2.

15. On gender and race, see Evelyn Nakano Glenn, *Unequal Freedom: How Race and Gender Shaped American Citizenship and Labor* (Cambridge, Mass.: Harvard University Press, 2002), 6–7.

16. On this point, see Arif Dirlik, "Asians on the Rim: Transnational Capital and Local Community in the Making of Contemporary Asian America," *Amerasia Journal* 22 (Winter 1996): 1–24.

17. On the ideas of "habitus," "capital," and "struggle" in a given social field, upon which I draw here, see Pierre Bourdieu, *The Logic of Practice* (Stanford, Calif.: Stanford University Press, 1990), 42–69, 80–97, 135–141; and Pierre Bourdieu, *In Other Words* (Stanford, Calif.: Stanford University Press, 1990), 87–93, 122–139.

18. In constructing a narrative around the Issei's agency, I follow the call by Roger Daniels and Yuji Ichioka for placing a primary focus on the excluded, rather than the excluders, in historical analysis. See Roger Daniels, "Westerners from the East: Oriental Immigrants Reappraised," *Pacific Historical Review* 35 (November 1966): 373–384; Roger Daniels, "American Historians and East Asian Immigrants," *Pacific Historical Review* 43 (November 1974): 449–472; and Yuji Ichioka et al., "Introduction," in *A Buried Past: An Annotated Bibliography of the Japanese American Research Project Collection*, ed. Yuji Ichioka et al. (Berkeley: University of California Press, 1974), 3–11, esp. 11.

19. Roger Daniels, *The Politics of Prejudice: The Anti-Japanese Movement in California and the Struggle for Japanese Exclusion* (Berkeley: University of California Press, 1962); Gary Okihiro, *Cane Fires: The Anti-Japanese Movement in Hawaii*,

1865–1945 (Philadelphia, Pa.: Temple University Press, 1991); and Ichioka, *Issei*. On the development of this historiography, see Eiichiro Azuma and Arif Dirlik, "Editors' Introduction: Yuji Ichioka and *Before Internment* in Japanese American Historiography," in Yuji Ichioka, *Before Internment: Essays in Prewar Japanese-American History* (Stanford, Calif.: Stanford University Press, forthcoming).

20. See Ichioka, *Issei*; Sawada, *Tokyo Life*; and Franklin Odo, *No Sword to Bury: Japanese Americans in Hawai'i during World War II* (Philadelphia, Pa.: Temple University Press, 2004), 11–14.

21. On key conceptual categories, including "frontier" and "borderland," see Jeremy Adelman and Stephen Aaron, "From Borderlands to Borders: Empires, Nation-States, and the Peoples in Between in North American History," *American Historical Review* 104 (June 1999): 814–841, esp. 814–816. On the nexus between immigration exclusion and U.S. expansionism, see Matthew Frye Jacobson, *Barbarian Virtues: The United States Encounters Foreign Peoples at Home and Abroad, 1876–1917* (New York: Hill and Wang, 2000), 179–259. On Japan's eastward expansionism, see Akira Iriye, *Pacific Estrangement: Japanese and American Expansion, 1897–1911* (Cambridge, Mass.: Harvard University Press, 1972); and Shumpei Okamoto, "Meiji Imperialism: Pacific Emigration or Continental Expansionism?" in *Japan Examined: Perspectives on Modern Japanese History*, ed. Harry Wray and Hilary Conroy (Honolulu: University of Hawaii Press, 1983), 141–148.

22. Tomás Almaguer, *Racial Fault Lines: The Historical Origins of White Supremacy in California* (Berkeley: University of California Press, 1994), 1–16.

23. For example, see Patricia Nelson Limerick, *The Legacy of Conquest: The Unbroken Past of the American West* (New York: Norton, 1987).

24. Gabaccia, "Is Everywhere Nowhere?" 1115, 1128. Representative works on Japanese Americans that draw on the immigrant paradigm are Bill Hosokawa, *Nisei, the Quiet Americans: The Story of a People* (New York: Morrow, 1969); and Robert A. Wilson and Bill Hosokawa, *East to America: A History of the Japanese in the United States* (New York: Morrow, 1980).

25. On the contemporary analysis of Nisei "problems" according to this paradigm, see Edward K. Strong, Jr., *The Second-Generation Japanese Problem* (Stanford, Calif.: Stanford University Press, 1934). On the liberal racial thinking that rendered the second generation as the marginal man, see Henry Yu, *Thinking Orientals: Migration, Contact, and Exoticism in Modern America* (New York: Oxford University Press, 2001).

26. See Lon Kurashige, "The Problem of Biculturalism: Japanese American Identity and Festival," *Journal of American History* 86 (March 2000): 1632–1654; Eiichiro Azuma, "Racial Struggle, Immigrant Nationalism and Ethnic Identity: Japanese and Filipinos in the California Delta, 1930–1941," *Pacific Historical Review* 67 (May 1998): 163–199; Yuji Ichioka, "A Study in Dualism: James Yoshinori Sakamoto and the *Japanese American Courier*, 1928–1942," *Amerasia Journal* 13 (1986–1987): 49–81, and "Japanese Immigrant Nationalism: The Issei and the Sino-Japanese War, 1937–1941," *California History* 69 (Fall 1990): 260–275; Hayashi, *"For the Sake of Our Japanese Brethren"*; Valerie J. Matsumoto, "Desperately

Seeking 'Deirdre': Gender Roles, Multicultural Relations, and Nisei Women Writers of the 1930s," *Frontier* 12 (1991): 19–32; Valerie J. Matsumoto, "Redefining Expectations: Nisei Women in the 1930s," *California History* 73 (Spring 1994): 45–53, 88; Stephan, *Hawaii under the Rising Sun*, 23–40; Jere Takahashi, *Nisei/Sansei: Shifting Japanese American Identities and Politics* (Philadelphia, Pa.: Temple University Press, 1997); David K. Yoo, *Growing Up Nisei: Race, Generation, and Culture among Japanese Americans of California, 1924–1949* (Urbana: University of Illinois Press, 2000); and Eriko Yamamoto, "Cheers for Japanese Athletes: The 1932 Los Angeles Olympics and the Japanese American Community," *Pacific Historical Review* 69 (August 2000): 399–430.

27. On this point, see also Ichioka, *Before Internment*, esp. the author's "Introduction."

28. It is to be noted that the use of vernacular sources creates problems of its own, namely, the practical difficulty of collecting the perspectives of Issei laborers and women, who seldom made imprints on the historical documents available at archives, libraries, and museums. Knowledge production, as in any society, was the monopoly of male intellectuals and social elites in the immigrant world. I have made my best effort to incorporate the visions and experiences of those marginalized Issei by deliberating on their reported actions, notable inactions, and the sparse documents left behind by them.

29. Guarnizo and Smith, "The Locations of Transnationalism," 4–6.

30. On black transnationalism, see Paul Gilroy, *The Black Atlantic: Modernity and Double Consciousness* (Cambridge, Mass.: Harvard University Press, 1993); and also Robin D. G. Kelly, "But a Local Phase of a World Problem: Black History's Global Vision, 1883–1950," *Journal of American History* 86 (December 1999): 1045–1077.

CHAPTER 1

1. Zentarō Ōtsuka, *Nichibei gaikōron* (Tokyo: Sagamiya Shoten, 1910), 130–131.

2. Ibid.

3. Peter Duus, *The Abacus and the Sword: The Japanese Penetration of Korea, 1895–1910* (Berkeley: University of California Press, 1995), 2.

4. Ibid., 1–23. On the nature of Japanese imperialism, see Ramon H. Myers and Mark R. Peattie, eds., *The Japanese Colonial Empire, 1895–1945* (Princeton, N.J.: Princeton University Press, 1984), 6–15.

5. Louise Young, *Japan's Total Empire: Manchuria and the Culture of Wartime Imperialism* (Berkeley: University of California Press, 1998), 22–24.

6. See Fumiko Fujita, *American Pioneers and the Japanese Frontier: American Experts in Nineteenth-Century Japan* (Westport, Conn.: Greenwood, 1994).

7. Young, *Japan's Total Empire*, 311–312.

8. On Asian labor migration into the American West, see Edna Bonacich, "Asian Labor in the Development of California and Hawaii," in *Labor Immigration un-*

der Capitalism: Asian Workers in the United States before World War II, ed. Edna Bonacich and Lucie Cheng (Berkeley: University of California Press, 1984), 130–185. For a general history of labor emigration from Japan, see Eiichiro Azuma, "Historical Overview of Japanese Emigration, 1868–2000," in *Encyclopedia of Japanese Descendants in the Americas: An Illustrated History of the Nikkei*, ed. Akemi Kikumura-Yano (Walnut Creek, Calif.: AltaMira, 2002), 32–48.

9. The contradictory nature of Japanese expansionism was manifested in that, throughout the history of imperial Japan, its territorial aggrandizement and the transplanting of surplus labor took place simultaneously. For example, many Japanese, including the Okinawan underclass, worked as cheap labor at sugar plantations in the Mariana Islands and in the mining and fishing industries of Japanese-occupied Micronesia. See Mark R. Peattie, *Nan'yo: The Rise and Fall of the Japanese in Micronesia, 1885–1945* (Honolulu: University of Hawaii Press, 1988), 118–129.

10. On this topic, see Carol Gluck, *Japan's Modern Myths: Ideology in the Late Meiji Period* (Princeton, N.J.: Princeton University Press, 1985); and Takashi Fujitani, *Splendid Monarchy: Power and Pageantry in Modern Japan* (Berkeley: University of California Press, 1996).

11. On Fukuzawa, see Carmen Blacker, *The Japanese Enlightenment: A Study of the Writings of Fukuzawa Yukichi* (Cambridge: Cambridge University Press, 1964); and Albert Craig, "Fukuzawa Yukichi: The Political Foundations of Meiji Nationalism," in *Political Development in Modern Japan*, ed. Robert E. Ward (Princeton, N.J.: Princeton University Press, 1973), 99–148.

12. Fukuzawa Yukichi, "Ijūron no ben," *FYZ* 9 (Tokyo: Iwanami Shoten, 1932): 459–460. See also Fukuzawa, "Kuni o fukyō suru wa bōeki o seidai ni suruni ari," *FYZ* 9 (Tokyo: Iwanami Shoten, 1932):351–353; and Fukuzawa, "Fukoku-saku," *FYZ* 10 (Tokyo: Iwanami Shoten, 1932):248–250.

13. Fukuzawa, "Aete kokyō o sare," *FYZ* 9:525–526.

14. Fukuzawa, "Beikoku wa shishi no seisho nari," *FYZ* 9:444; and Germaine A. Hoston, "The State, Modernity, and the Fate of Liberalism in Prewar Japan," *Journal of Asian Studies* 51 (May 1992): 298.

15. Eiichiro Azuma, "Interstitial Lives: Race, Community, and History among Japanese Immigrants Caught between Japan and the United States, 1885–1941" (Ph.D. diss., University of California, Los Angeles, 2000), 27–29; Shōzō Mizutani, *Nyūyōku Nihonjin hattenshi* (New York: Nyūyōku Nihonjinkai, 1921), 60–68, 320–322, 726–728; and Ishikawa Kanmei, *Fukuzawa Yukichi den* (Tokyo: Iwanami Shoten, 1932), 2:807–818.

16. Shakuma Washizu, "Rekishi inmetsu no tan," 77–78, *Nichibei Shimbun*, June 24, 25, 1922; and Yuji Ichioka, *The Issei: The World of the First Generation Japanese Immigrants, 1885–1924* (New York: Free Press, 1988), 10–11.

17. Ishikawa, *Fukuzawa Yukichi den*, 2:211.

18. Goichi Yamane, *Saikin tobei annai* (Tokyo: Tobei Zasshisha, 1906), 1.

19. A number of Japanese corporate leaders once lived in the United States. Following their teacher's advice, two of Keiō's Class of 1885 went to California upon

graduation with the aim of learning American business practices. After returning to Japan in 1887, Mutō Sanji worked his way through the Japanese business world to head Kanebō, a major cotton-spinning firm. Mutō's California companion, Wada Toyoji, similarly rose up to become the head of Fujibō, another cotton-spinning company. See Mutō Sanji, *Mutō Sanji zenshu* (Tokyo: Shinjusha, 1963), 1:21–38; and Ichioka, *Issei*, 12.

20. Affiliated with a society called Seikyōsha, many advocates of Japanese-style manifest destiny were young political activists and intellectuals, identified usually as "Meiji nationalists" or "Japanists." On this group, see Kenneth B. Pyle, *The New Generation in Meiji Japan: Problems in Cultural Identity, 1885–1895* (Stanford, Calif.: Stanford University Press, 1969), 99–102; and Nakanome Tōru, *Seikyōsha no kenkyū* (Tokyo: Fuyō Shobō Shuppan, 1998), 11–38.

21. Akira Iriye, *Pacific Estrangement: Japanese and American Expansion, 1897–1911* (Cambridge, Mass.: Harvard University Press, 1972), 131. Here, Iriye speaks of the post–Russo-Japanese War period, but this current of thought was powerful from the late 1880s. Historian Shumpei Okamoto also shows that "Pacific emigration" remained a part of Japanese imperialism until the eve of the First World War. Shumpei Okamoto, "Meiji Imperialism: Pacific Emigration or Continental Expansionism?" in *Japan Examined: Perspectives on Modern Japanese History*, ed. Harry Wray and Hilary Conroy (Honolulu: University of Hawaii Press, 1983), 141–148.

22. See Peattie, *Nan'yo*, 1–61; Young, *Japan's Total Empire*, 310–318; and Azuma, "Interstitial Lives," 32–34.

23. Shūyū Sanjin and Kumajirō Ishida, *Kitare Nihonjin* (Tokyo: Kaishindō, 1887), 5–6.

24. On American manifest destiny, see Reginald Horsman, *Race and Manifest Destiny* (Cambridge, Mass.: Harvard University Press, 1981), 272–297. Some Issei expansionists abandoned their dream of erecting a "second Japan" in the Western frontier when white Americans extended their dominance through the eastern half of the Pacific with the overthrow of the Hawaiian monarchy in 1893. Key members of the Japanese Patriotic League and the Expeditionary Society, both in San Francisco, subsequently returned to Japan and sought better colonialist opportunities elsewhere. Others shifted their attention from North America to Latin America, envisioning using the American West as a way station to the less developed frontiers. In 1898, a San Francisco Japanese monthly—*Sōkō no shiori*—discussed the idea of expanding into Mexico and South America. The journal apparently had a close connection to a group of Issei literati who regularly met to "study the conditions of Mexico and South America." See Azuma, "Interstitial Lives," 37–45.

25. On the activities of Japanese labor contractors in the West, see Ichioka, *Issei*, 57–62. Immigrant chronicles credit these labor contractors with the initial development of what would be known as "hubs" of Issei farming in California. See Zaibei Nihonjinkai, *Zaibei Nihonjinshi* (San Francisco: Zaibei Nihonjinkai, 1940),

39–45; and Shakuma Washizu, "Wagahai no Beikoku seikatsu," *Nichibei Shimbun,* December 7, 1924.

26. Shinzaburō Ban, "Ban Shinzaburō kun no Hokubei dan," *SKH* 12 (April 21, 1894): 45–46. See also Shinzaburō Ban, "Yo wa Beikoku nite yonsen no dōhō to tomoni sūko no tetsudō o shisetsu shitari," *Jitsugyō no Nihon* 12 (August 1, 1909): 23–34; Ōfu Inshi, *Zaibei seikō no Nihonjin* (Tokyo: Hōbunkan, 1904), 137–156; and Ichioka, *Issei,* 58–59, 61.

27. Rafu Shimpōsha, *Rafu nenkan* (Los Angeles: Rafu Shimpōsha, 1907), 1:54–55, 76, in box 359, JARP; and Beikoku Shokusan Gaisha, "Hokubei Kashū Yamato Shokuminchi jijō," c. 1906, 1–3, in folder 4, box 34, Abiko Family Papers, JARP. On Abiko and the Yamato Colony, see also Ichioka, *Issei,* 146–150; Kesa Noda, *Yamato Colony* (Livingston, Calif.: Livingston-Merced JACL Chapter, 1981), 1–15; and Valerie J. Matsumoto, *Farming the Home Place: A Japanese American Community in California, 1919–1982* (Ithaca, N.Y.: Cornell University Press, 1993), 38–42. Historical studies of the Yamato Colony only discuss Abiko's project in the context of a general shift in Issei mentality from sojourning to permanent settlement, but what is neglected in the literature is a crucial nexus between his ideal of permanent settlement and immigrant expansionism. In the manifesto for the Livingston project, Abiko and his associates offered their definition of peaceful expansionism. Instead of "something predatory," their colonization of California land would respect the integrity of the American political system and social structure, under which Japanese residents would strive solely for "prosperity and happiness" through independent farming, just as did white settlers.

28. Shinkichirō Shima, diary, c. 1901, in folder 2, box 136, JARP.

29. Earl H. Kinmonth, *The Self-Made Man in Meiji Japanese Thought: From Samurai to Salary Man* (Berkeley: University of California Press, 1981), 158–160, 262–271; Mitziko Sawada, *Tokyo Life, New York Dreams: Urban Japanese Visions of America, 1890–1924* (Berkeley: University of California Press, 1996), 87–115; and Tachikawa Kenji, "Meiji kōhanki no tobei netsu," *Shirin* 69 (May 1986): 86–91.

30. Hyman Kublin, *Asian Revolutionary: The Life of Sen Katayama* (Princeton, N.J.: Princeton University Press, 1964), 47–156; and Sawada, *Tokyo Life,* 126–127.

31. Sawada, *Tokyo Life,* 120–121; Tachikawa Kenji, "Shimanuki Hyōdayū to Rikkōkai," *Shirin* 72 (January 1989): 110–123; and Ichioka, *Issei,* 12–13.

32. Kinmonth, *The Self-Made Man,* 178–187, 194–195.

33. Shimanuki Hyōdayū, *Tobei annai taizen* (Tokyo: Chūyōdō, 1901), 13–17; Katayama Sen, *Tobei annai* (Tokyo: Rōdō Shimbunsha, 1901), 4–5; and Katayama Sen, *Tobei no hiketsu* (Tokyo: Tobei Kyōkai, 1906), 17–23. See also Sawada, *Tokyo Life,* 140–142; and Tachikawa, "Meiji kōhanki no tobei netsu," 91–96.

34. Shimanuki, *Tobei annai taizen,* 4–7.

35. Sawada, *Tokyo Life,* 140.

36. Ichioka, *Issei,* 28. While often assuming subordinate positions to the elite cohorts of international traders and expansionist entrepreneurs in urban centers, student-immigrants seemed to have been instrumental in forming community organiza-

tions, farmers' cooperatives, business associations, and the like in smaller Japanese settlements. Not only could they speak English due to their American education, but they were also familiar with the social and legal system and could serve as intermediaries between whites and ordinary Issei. Whereas urban Issei of upper-class origin could—and often did—return to Japan later to enjoy the social standing and prestige that their pedigree ensured, it was less likely that student-immigrants were able to live comfortably in the rigidly stratified Japanese society. Consequently, many former students remained in America. My survey of selected samples reveals that, during the 1930s, most grassroots community leaders were of this particular group.

37. Doi Yatarō, *Yamaguchi-ken Ōshima-gun Hawai iminshi* (Tokuyama, Yamaguchi: Matsuno Shoten, 1980), 114, 122.

38. Yokokawa Jihei, "Hyakushō no mitaru Beikoku to Nihon," *Amerika* 12 (January 1908): 15.

39. Ideological formation, and the nation-making contingent upon it, were never simply one-directional, top-down processes, for the masses intervened through protest and compliance. In Carol Gluck's assessment, it was "[f]rom the 1880s through the first fifteen years of the twentieth century [that] Japanese sought first to conceive and then inculcate an ideology suitable for modern Japan." Historian Andrew Gordon, on the other hand, locates a watershed around 1905, by when a tangible consciousness of being imperial subjects had emerged among the "formerly parochial, apolitical people" of Japan. Gordon's focus rests with the urban masses, and it seems more likely that a clear sense of national membership took shape in the rural population later than 1905, as Gluck suggests. Compulsory national education, for example, remained short of being "universal" until the turn of the century. Even two decades after the inception of a national education system in 1872, elementary school enrollment continued to stagnate at around 60 percent. Not until 1906 did it reach 98 percent nationally. Likewise, conscription, introduced in 1873, started to play a major role in the formation of the national mind only after Japan experienced two major foreign wars. See Gluck, *Japan's Modern Myths*, 3; and Andrew Gordon, *Labor and Imperial Democracy in Prewar Japan* (Berkeley: University of California Press, 1991), 5–9, 15–19.

40. Gluck, *Japan's Modern Myths*, 206. See also Kinmonth, *The Self-Made Man*, 1–8.

41. Kinmonth, *The Self-Made Man*, 241–276.

42. Ichioka, *Issei*, 43. On this group of Japanese immigrants, see also Hilary Conroy, *The Japanese Frontier in Hawaii, 1868–1898* (Berkeley: University of California Press, 1953), 81–89; and Alan Takeo Moriyama, *Imingaisha: Japanese Emigration Companies and Hawaii, 1894–1908* (Honolulu: University of Hawaii Press, 1985), 67–73, 81–84, 105–110.

43. Sakae Morita, *Hawai Nihonjin hattenshi* (Waipahu, Hawaii: Shin'eikan, 1915), 143–144.

44. Ichioka, *Issei*, 41.

45. See Kodama Masaaki, *Nihon iminshi kenkyū josetsu* (Hiroshima: Keisuisha, 1992), 66–67; and Azuma, "Interstitial Lives," 58–61.
46. Ishikawa Tomonori, *Nihon imin no chirigakuteki kenkyū* (Ginowan, Okinawa: Yōju Shorin, 1997), 264–270; and Kodama, *Nihon iminshi,* 158–162.
47. Ichioka, *Issei,* 42–43. On the general conditions of rural Japan in the early 1880s, see Roger Bowen, *Rebellion and Democracy in Meiji Japan: A Study of Commoners in the Popular Rights Movement* (Berkeley: University of California Press, 1980), 8–30, 49–66.
48. According to Kodama, in many Hiroshima villages, there were four times more applicants than spaces for contract laborers in 1889–1890. Competition was therefore fierce. Mitziko Sawada analyzes the general government policy to stop the emigration of the "undesirables"—a policy that worked against *burakumin* outcasts, Okinawans, and the destitute in general. See Kodama, *Nihon iminshi,* 51; and Sawada, *Tokyo Life,* 41–56.
49. On the role of village headmen in the recruitment of contract laborers, see Kodama, *Nihon iminshi,* 124–125; and Azuma, "Interstitial Lives," 63–64.
50. Senda to Asada, January 12, 1889, NJHD, DRO.
51. See reports by the governors of Okayama and Wakayama, January–February 1889, ibid.
52. Kodama, *Nihon iminshi,* 172, 174.
53. See Samuel L. Popkin, *The Rational Peasant: The Political Economy of Rural Society in Vietnam* (Berkeley: University of California Press, 1979), 18–19; and also James C. Scott, *The Moral Economy of the Peasant: Rebellion and Subsistence in Southeast Asia* (New Haven, Conn.: Yale University Press, 1976), 1–12, 26–27. By inserting the case of rural Japanese emigrants into the debate between the two schools of thought on peasant practice, I am compelled to qualify my comparisons with this cautionary note. Instead of taking sides with either (fixed) theoretical position, it is crucial to look into the shifting socioeconomic situation which enabled an individual or a class of people to see, or disabled them from seeing, the ranges of possible action in a given moment. From this standpoint, as I have explained in the case of some emigrants, a "moral peasant" could turn into a "rational peasant" when circumstances changed.
54. I arrived at the figure on the basis of the aggregate total (131,760) of the passports issued to Japanese for the two destinations during the fourteen-year period, excluding 40,230 individuals who used the service of emigration companies between 1894 and 1900 and hence most likely were contract laborers. See Kokusai Kyōryoku Jigyōdan, *Kaigai ijū tōkei* (Tokyo: Kokusai Kyōryoku Jigyōdan, 1994), 127; and Ichioka, *Issei,* 51–52.
55. Kodama, *Nihon iminshi,* 547–551.
56. Ichioka, *Issei,* 46, 65.
57. Ibid., 64–69.
58. Ibid., 52.
59. Kodama, *Nihon iminshi,* 524. On fraudulent passport applications, see also

Azuma, "Interstitial Lives," 74–75. Catering to the need of those emigrants, a few guidebooks were published to coach them at how to get around administrative restrictions with detailed explanations of loopholes. See, for example, Zaibei Kazan and Chikuyō Kimura, *Shin tobei annai* (Tokyo: Seikōdō, 1906).

60. Azuma, "Interstitial Lives," 75; Bangaku Mizutani, *Hokubei Aichi kenjinshi* (Sacramento, Calif.: Aichi Kenjinkai, 1920), 264–270; and Jesús K. Akachi et al., "Japanese Mexican Historical Overview," in *Encyclopedia of Japanese Descendants in the Americas*, 206–210.

61. From the late 1890s, many young men of prime draftable age (seventeen to twenty-one) went to the United States to avoid military service despite government restrictions. See Azuma, "Interstitial Lives," 75–79; and also Yamato Ichihashi, *Japanese in the United States* (Stanford, Calif.: Stanford University Press, 1932), 87–88.

CHAPTER 2

1. Kōichirō Masuda, "Kaigai ni okeru Nihon shūgyōfu," *Nihonjin* 15 (July 18, 1894): 29.

2. Kahoku to Aoki, June 4, 1889, ZHJT 1, DRO.

3. Tateno to Aoki, April 30, 1891, ZHJT 1; Chinda to Hayashi, September 15, 1891, ZHJT 1; and Gaimushō, *NGB* 24 (1952): 487, 491.

4. Between 1892 and 1900, Japanese immigrant newspapers frequently filled the void of a viable community leadership by acting as the chief agent of social discipline. In 1899, for example, a group of Portland residents started the first local Japanese mimeographed periodical, the *Japonica Portland*, in order to prevent the "invasion of pimps and prostitutes from Vancouver, Canada." See *Shin Sekai*, December 22, 1899; and Kōjirō Takeuchi, *Beikoku Seihokubu Nihon iminshi* (Seattle, Wash.: Taihoku Nippōsha, 1929), 538. In San Francisco, the vernacular press emerged with similar purposes. The first major newspaper, the *Shin Sekai*, began publishing in 1894, the *Sōkō Nippon Shinbun* in 1897, and the *Hokubei Nippō* in 1898; the latter two merged into the *Nichibei Shimbun* in 1899. Using imported type-sets, these newspapers dramatically expanded printing capacities and hence circulation in comparison to the mimeographed competitors, and the *Shin Sekai* and the *Nichibei Shimbun* reigned over Japanese immigrant society in northern and central California. On the press-led antiprostitution campaign, see *Shin Sekai*, February 26–March 5, 29, 1900. For an early history of Japanese immigrant newspapers, consult Yuji Ichioka, *The Issei: The World of the First Generation Japanese Immigrants, 1885–1924* (New York: Free Press, 1988), 19–22.

5. San Francisco *Bulletin*, May 4, 1892.

6. On this Japanese-style Orientalism, see Kimitada Miwa, "Fukuzawa Yukichi's 'Departure from Asia': A Prelude to the Sino-Japanese War," in *Japan's Modern Century*, ed. Edmund Skrzypszak (Tokyo: Sophia University Press, 1968), 1–26;

and see Stephan Tanaka, *Japan's Orient: Rendering Pasts into History* (Berkeley: University of California Press, 1993).

7. Setsu Nagasawa, "Sōkō oyobi sono kinpen ni okeru sanzen no dōhō," *Ajia* 29 (January 11, 1892): 4; Seichirō Akamine, *Beikoku ima fushigi* (Tokyo: Jitsugakusha Eigakkō, 1886), 43–50; and "Zaibei no Shinajin," *Dai-Jūkyū seiki* 20 (July 13, 1888). See also Sakata Yasuo, "Datsua no shishi to tozasareta Hakusekijin no rakuen," in *Beikoku shoki no Nihongo shinbun*, ed. Tamura Norio and Shiramizu Shigehiko (Tokyo: Keisō Shobō, 1986), 47–193.

8. "Zaibei Nihon minzoku ron," *Aikoku* 27 (April 29, 1892). See also Ichioka, *Issei*, 191. Chinese immigrants, on their part, harbored ill feelings toward the Japanese due to their "racism." Yong Chen, *Chinese San Francisco, 1850–1943: A Trans-Pacific Community* (Stanford, Calif.: Stanford University Press, 2000), 200–201.

9. Kahoku to Aoki, June 4, 1889, and Kitō to Hayashi, June 23, 1892, both in ZHJT 2. According to Nayan Shah, the Chinese business elite similarly distinguished themselves—as "respectable Chinese residents"—from the laboring masses when white San Franciscans attacked their community. Like their Issei counterparts, the merchants also blamed brothels and gambling dens for causing anti-Chinese agitation. Nayan Shah, *Contagious Divides: Epidemics and Race in San Francisco's Chinatown* (Berkeley: University of California Press, 2001), 23–24.

10. "Zaibei Nihonjin wa hatashite anchoku rōdōsha naruka," *Aikoku* 35 (June 24, 1892).

11. See *Shin Sekai*, May 31, June 10, 1906; and Ichioka, *Issei*, 89–90.

12. Michael Weiner, "Discourses of Race, Nation, and Empire in Pre-1945 Japan," *Ethnic and Racial Studies* 18 (July 1995): 450; and Peter Duus, *The Abacus and the Sword: The Japanese Penetration of Korea, 1895–1910* (Berkeley: University of California Press, 1995), 400. The Japanese underclass was often associated with people of outcast origin, who were considered to be of foreign blood lines, such as Ainu, Chinese, and Koreans. On Japan's contemporary program of moral suasion toward and control of the urban poor and prostitutes, see Sheldon Garon, *Molding Japanese Minds: The State in Everyday Life* (Princeton, N.J.: Princeton University Press, 1997), 40–49, 98–106.

13. On this "discourse of nation," see Ann Laura Stoler, *Race and the Education of Desire: Foucault's History of Sexuality and the Colonial Order of Things* (Durham, N.C.: Duke University Press, 1995), 93–136.

14. Speaking of the elite Japanese, Yukiko Koshiro characterizes their "dualistic racial identity" as an "elastic concept, almost like a cultural construct." Yukiko Koshiro, *Trans-Pacific Racisms and the U.S. Occupation of Japan* (New York: Columbia University Press, 1999), 9–10. As powerful modes of classification and exclusion, race and class reinforce each other. Not only does one's racial membership tend to influence one's class positioning in society, but, as David Theo Goldberg points out, "the hierarchical *and* racial connotations [are also] implicit in the concept of the *under*class" (emphasis in original). See David Theo Goldberg, ed., *Anatomy of Racism* (Minneapolis: University of Minnesota Press, 1990), xiv.

15. Shah, *Contagious Divides*, 8. See also Gary Gerstle, *American Crucible: Race and Nation in the Twentieth Century* (Princeton, N.J.: Princeton University Press, 2001), 56–57. For examples of white support for Japanese assimilation, see Ichioka, *Issei*, 189–191; and Rumi Yasutake, "Transnational Women's Activism: The Women's Christian Temperance Union in Japan and Beyond, 1858–1920" (Ph.D. diss., University of California, Los Angeles, 1998), 220–257.

16. Roger Daniels, *The Politics of Prejudice: The Anti-Japanese Movement in California and the Struggle for Japanese Exclusion* (Berkeley: University of California Press, 1962), esp. 49; Spencer C. Olin, Jr., *California's Prodigal Sons: Hiram Johnson and the Progressives, 1911–1917* (Berkeley: University of California Press, 1968); Frank W. Van Nuys, "A Progressive Confronts the Race Question: Chester Rowell, the California Alien Land Law of 1913, and the Twentieth-Century Racial Thought," *California History* 73 (Spring 1994): 2–13; and Kevin Starr, *Inventing the Dream: California through the Progressive Era* (New York: Oxford University Press, 1985), 259–261. Gary Gerstle characterizes the constant interplay of the two positions in twentieth-century American history as that of "civic nationalism and racial nationalism." Gerstle, *American Crucible*, 4–6.

17. George J. Sánchez, "The 'New Nationalism,' Mexican Style: Race and Progressivism in Chicano Political Development during the 1920s," in *California Progressivism Revisited*, ed. William Deverell and Tom Sitton (Berkeley: University of California Press, 1994), 231–232. Sánchez examines a parallel development of collaboration between Mexican diplomats and immigrant leaders in southern California during the 1920s. Forming "honorary committees," the two parties launched Progressive programs based on their shared view of the culturally deprived masses. See ibid., 234–236.

18. Ichioka, *Issei*, 158; and Daniels, *The Politics of Prejudice*, 21. On the impact of this incident on the Chinese community, see Shah, *Contagious Divides*, 120–157.

19. *Shin Sekai*, May 23, 24–26, 1900.

20. *Zaibei Nihonjin Kyōgikai Dai-Ikkai oyobi Dai-Nikai hōkokusho* (1902), 1–2, 8, 10, 46; *Shin Sekai*, July 18, 20, 1900; and Ichioka, *Issei*, 158.

21. Zai Sōkō Nihon Ryōjikan, "Beikoku kaku chihō junkai hōkoku," *SKH* 27 (July 18, 1895): 34–35, 38–40.

22. Mutsu to Komura, August 11, 1898, KHSH, DRO. Tally by the author. See also *Shin Sekai*, March 14, April 21, 1900.

23. *Shin Sekai*, November 13–14, 1908. See also Ichioka, *Issei*, 169–172.

24. *Shin Sekai*, June 6, 19, 1900; and Zai Sōkō Ryōjikan, "Sōkō fukin zairyū honpōjin no jōkyō," *SKH* 66 (February 4, 1899): 21.

25. Daniels, *The Politics of Prejudice*, 31–45.

26. Gaimushō, *NGB* 39.2 (1959): 421–422.

27. Yoichi Tōga, *Nichibei kankei Zaibeikoku Nihonjin hatten shiyō* (Oakland: Beikoku Seisho Kyōkai Nihonjinbu, 1927), 142.

28. Gaimushō, *NGB* 40.3 (1961): 343, also 369–370, 381–386; and Takeuchi, *Beikoku Seihokubu*, 135. There were a few other notable collisions between Issei leaders and diplomats during the 1910s, including a well-known picture bride contro-

versy in 1919. See Ichioka, *Issei*, 173–175, 210–226. In 1905–1906, similar transnational politics took place in the community of their Chinese neighbors within the general context of immigration exclusion. Guanhua Wang, *In Search of Justice: The 1905–1906 Chinese Anti-American Boycott* (Cambridge, Mass.: Harvard University Press, 2001), esp. 108–177.

29. Reports of Ototaka Yamaoka, June 10, 18, 24, July 8, 23, 1907, HGHH, 7, 8, DRO.
30. Gaimushō, *NGB* 40.3 (1961): 375.
31. *Shin Sekai*, May 29, June 7, 28, October 20, 1907.
32. Ibid., June 28, July 21, September 25, 30, October 7, 13, 1907; Zaibei Nihonjinkai, *Zaibei Nihonjinshi* (San Francisco: Zaibei Nihonjinkai, 1940), 778–779; and Saikichi Takezaki, "Zaibei dōhō no seiseki," *Amerika* 11 (March 1908): 10–11.
33. Ichioka, *Issei*, 165–166; and *Shin Sekai*, January 20, 1908, February 4, 1910.
34. *Shin Sekai*, January 23, February 2, 3, 6, 1908; and Ichioka, *Issei*, 160–161.
35. Ichioka, *Issei*, 163–164.
36. *ZNH* 1 (1909): 2–3; ibid. 2 (1910): 4; ibid. 3 (1911): 5; and ibid. 9 (1917): 49–52. Tally by the author.
37. Hara Takashi Monjo Kenkyukai, ed., *Hara Takashi kankei monjo* (Tokyo: Nippon Hōsō Kyōkai Shuppan Kyōkai, 1987), 8:286–287, 348–363; Koike to Yamaza, February 17, 1908, KKST 1, DRO; Koike to Yamaza, c. 1908, KKST 1; Ōhara Satoshi, "Takahashi Sakuei kyōju ate Koike Chōzō, Tatsumi Tetsuo no tegami," *Tokyo Keidai gakkaishi* 29–30 (1960): 395–406; and Ōhara Satoshi, " 'Furesuno Rōdō Dōmeikai' ni tsuite," in *Rōdō mondai kenkyū no gendaiteki kadai*, ed. Fujibayashi Keizō Hakase Kanreki Kinen Ronbun Henshū Iinkai (Tokyo: Daiyamondosha, 1960), 37–38. See also Ichioka, *Issei*, 105–113.
38. Ichioka, *Issei*, 162–163; *Shin Sekai*, January 16, 1910; and Shakai Bunko, *ZSS* (Tokyo: Kashiwa Shobō, 1964), 170–173.
39. *Shin Sekai*, February 16, 19, 24, March 6, 11, 1910; Shakai Bunko, *ZSS*, 173–175, 509, 514–515; and *Yorozu chōhō*, April 5, 1910. A leading Issei in Oakland, working as a consular informant, estimated a total of 160 Japanese socialists and anarchists in California. He also cautioned that upward of 10,000 could turn supportive of the ongoing anti–Japanese association movement out of economic concerns.
40. *Shin Sekai*, March 9–11, 16, 18–19, 30, 1910; and Shakai Bunko, *ZSS*, 176–178.
41. *Shin Sekai*, March 23, April 8, 22, 1910; Ōhara, "Takahashi Sakuei," 407–415; and Shakai Bunko, *ZSS*, 513. See also Yuji Ichioka, "A Buried Past: Early Issei Socialists and the Japanese Community," *Amerasia Journal* 1 (July 1971): 12–15.
42. *ZNH* 3:2–3.
43. Susan Lee Johnson, *Roaring Camp: The Social World of the California Gold Rush* (New York: Norton, 2000), 176–180.
44. Ichioka, *Issei*, 87–88; and Silvia Sun Minnick, *Samfow: The San Joaquin Chinese Legacy* (Fresno, Calif.: Panorama West, 1988), 226.
45. Gaimushō, *NGB* 42.2 (1961): 673–674. The Portland consul estimated that out of 88,600 or so Japanese in the Pacific Coast states, some 78,000 were laborers,

the vast majority of whom might well become good members of the Japanese associations if "guided appropriately." The undesirables, the official confided, would be very difficult to control.

46. *ZNH* 5 (1913): 14–16.

47. *Nichibei Shimbun*, April 22, 1940.

48. Gaimushō, *NGB: Taibei imin mondai keika gaiyō* (1972), 210–211. See also *Ōfu Nippō*, September 15, 1909.

49. KNK 1, October 8, 10, 1915, in box 732, JARP; *Kawashimo Jihō*, October 14, 1915; *Shin Sekai*, October 18, 1915; *Nichibei Shimbun*, January 4, 1916; and *ZNH* 8 (1916): 15–16.

50. *Nichibei Shimbun*, October 18, 19, 22, 28, 1915; and Eiichiro Azuma, "Interethnic Conflict under Racial Subordination: Japanese Immigrants and Their Asian Neighbors in Walnut Grove, California, 1908–1941," *Amerasia Journal* 20 (1994): 33–34.

51. *Ōfu Nippō*, November 25, 1915, January 3, March 2, 4, 1916.

52. KNK 1, June 23, August 4, 1918. See also Ichioka, *Issei*, 177–178.

53. *Ōfu Nippō*, July 13, 1918; and *Shin Sekai*, July 20, 1918.

54. See Ichioka, *Issei*, 185–186.

55. On the Issei's ideas of internal and external assimilation, see Ichioka, *Issei*, 185–187. For a general discussion of Issei assimilationism, see Yūko Matsumoto, " 'Nationalization' and 'the Others': Japanese Immigrants and Americanization in Los Angeles before World War II," *Kiyō Shigakuka* 45 (February 2000): 8–31.

56. *Nichibei Shimbun*, May 29, July 29, August 6, October 1–5, 1915; *Shin Sekai*, July 29, August 19–20, September 17–18, 1915; and *ZNH* 8:2–3.

57. KNK 1, July 3, 1919; *Nichibei Shimbun*, July 8, 1919; and Yamato Ichihashi, "Americanizing the Japanese," in folder 4, box 158, JARP.

58. Ralph F. Burnight, "The Japanese in Rural Los Angeles County," *Studies in Sociology* 4 (June 1920): 13.

59. George J. Sánchez, *Becoming Mexican American: Ethnicity, Culture, and Identity in Chicano Los Angeles, 1900–1945* (New York: Oxford University Press, 1993), 87–125.

60. Beikoku Seihokubu Renraku Nihonjinkai, *Kaimu hōkokusho: March 1–August 31, 1921* (1921): 85–88.

61. Ichioka, *Issei*, 146–147.

62. See, for example, Numano to Makino, November 19, 1913, March 31, 1914, TKUK 1, DRO. Expanding on Numano's program, the foreign office devised multiple channels for official propaganda with the intensification of anti-Japanese agitation and Japan's entry into World War I. In New York, the East & West News Bureau began operation under Toyokichi Iyenaga, a Johns Hopkins graduate.

63. Numano to Makino, July 7, 1913, TKUK 1. See also Makino to Chinda, December 10, 1913, ibid. On Yamato Ichihashi, see Yuji Ichioka, " 'Attorney for the Defense': Yamato Ichihashi and Japanese Immigration," *Pacific Historical Review* 55 (May 1986): 192–225; and Gordon H. Chang, *Morning Glory, Evening Shadow:*

Yamato Ichihashi and His Internment Writings, 1942–1945 (Stanford, Calif.: Stanford University Press, 1997), 35–39.

64. Shibusawa Seien Kinen Zaidan Ryūmonsha, *SED* 25 (1959): 477–478; *ZNH* 1 (1909):5; ibid. 6 (1914): 13–14; ibid. 8 (1916): 7–8, 22–24; and ibid. 9 (1917):15–16; and Zaibei Nihonjinkai, "Zaibei Nihonjinkai ikensho," c. December 1915, TKUK 7.

65. Shibusawa Seien Kinen Zaidan Ryūmonsha, *SED* 33 (1960): 440, also 417–451.

66. J. Soyeda and T. Kamiya, *A Survey of the Japanese Question in California* (San Francisco: Privately printed, 1913), 12–13.

67. Soeda et al., October 20, 1913, TKUK 1.

68. Nihon Imin Kyōkai, *Nihon Imin Kyōkai Yokohama Kōshūjo gairan* (Tokyo: Nihon Imin Kyōkai, 1916); Nihon Imin Kyōkai, *Saikin Ishokumin kenkyū* (Tokyo: Nihon Imin Kyōkai, 1917), 120–121; and Kurachi to Nakamura, January 25, 1917, HIKZ, DRO. After 1917, the institute received financial assistance from the government of Kanagawa Prefecture. In 1920, Japan's Home Ministry nationalized the Yokohama institute while establishing similar emigrant educational facilities in the port cities of Kobe and Nagasaki. From the 1920s on, the state took the initiative in training emigrants for life in Brazil, the Philippines, and other countries.

69. *ZNH* 9:5–6, 9–10; and Zaibei Nihonjinkai, *Shin tobei fujin no shiori* (1919), 2, 23–25. All quotes are from the latter source. On the moral disciplining of picture brides, see also Kei Tanaka, "Japanese Picture Marriage in 1900–1924 California: Construction of Japanese Race and Gender" (Ph.D. diss., Rutgers University, 2002), 179–231.

70. Zaibei Nihonjinkai, *Shin tobei fujin*, 4–8, 12; and *Ōfu Nippō*, May 13, 1919.

71. Yasutake, "Transnational Women's Activism," 234–235.

72. "Kawai Sōkanji no tobei," *JS* 12 (March 1915): 27.

73. Michi Kawai, *My Lantern* (Tokyo: Kyōbunkan, 1939), 137.

74. Kawai Michiko, "Tobei fujin wa seikō shitsutsuariya," *JS* 13 (November 1916): 9–13. Also see Kawai, "Enjerutō no ichinichi," *JS* 12 (September 1915): 51.

75. Sōkō Nihonjin Kirisutokyō Joshi Seinenkai, *Kaiko nijūnen* (San Francisco: Sōkō Nihonjin Kirisutokyō Joshi Seinenkai, 1932), 1–2, in folder 6, box 11, Abiko Family Papers, JARP; Yonako Abiko, "Zaibei Nihonjin Kirisutokyō Joshi Seinenkai sōritsu no shidai," *JS* 9 (October 1912): 101; "Sōkō Joshi Seinenkai," *JS* 11 (December 1914): 41; "Yokohama Joshi Seinenkai," *JS* 13 (September 1916): 61; and Kawai, *My Lantern*, 136. On the role of the Japanese YWCA, see also Tanaka, "Japanese Picture Marriage," 195–220.

76. "Kawai Sōkanji no shōsoku," *JS* 12 (June 1915): 21; "Yokohama Seinenkai no shinjigyō," *JS* 12 (June 1915): 39–40; and "Yokohama Joshi Seinenkai," *JS* 12 (October 1915): 42–43.

77. "Yokohama Seinenkai no shinjigyō," 39–40; and "Yokohama Joshi Seinenkai," *JS* 13 (September 1916): 61.

78. "Report of Helen Topping for May and June 1918," 1–2, JYWCA.

79. There were, however, some white Christian Americanizers who took part in the

reform effort primarily from the standpoint of domestic racial uplift. Yasutake, "Transnational Women's Activism," 242–257. On the parallel work of white women reformers among Chinese immigrant women, see Peggy Pascoe, *Relations of Rescue: The Search for Female Moral Authority in the American West, 1874–1939* (New York: Oxford University Press, 1993), esp. 73–145.

80. "Yu Ai Kai," TKUK: Kyoka undo bu; Martha A. Chickering to Harvey Guy, April 16, 1917, ibid.; *Young Women of Japan* 14 (October 1916): n.p.; "Report to Be Published in 'Christian Movement' 1918," 2, JYWCA. The quotes are from the last two sources. Helen Topping later went to Japan to work for the YWCA in Kobe, where she developed an emigrant assistance program.

81. "Sōkō Nihonjin Joshi Seinenkai," *JS* 12 (November 1915): 45–46; "Kashū sono hoka ni okeru hataraki no ichi-ni," *JS* 13 (June 1916): 28–30; and Hideko Ijūin, "Sōkō dayori," *JS* 14 (February 1917): 29–31.

82. Fūdo Yukie, "Dōhō fujin ni taisuru kibō," n.d., YBP. On the leadership role of her family in Hood Rover, see Eiichiro Azuma, "A History of Oregon's Issei, 1880–1952," *Oregon Historical Quarterly* 94 (Winter 1993–1994): 329–330.

83. Kazuo Itō, *Issei: A History of Japanese Immigrants in North America*, trans. Shinichiro Nakamura and Jean G. Gerard (Seattle, Wash.: Japanese Community Service, 1973), 131; and Lauren Kessler, *Stubborn Twig: Three Generations in the Life of a Japanese American Family* (New York: Random House, 1993), 46–47.

84. Hanihara to Honno, May 24, 1917, and Hanihara to Satō, "Taibei keihatsu undō hōshin oyobi hōhō ni kanshi gushin no ken," both TKUK 9.

85. Ōta, May 8, 1919, TKUK 10.

86. Gaimushō, *NGB* 42.2 (1961):673–674; and *ZNH* 9 (1917):49–52. Tally by the author, excluding non-California data.

87. *Ōfu Nippō*, February 17, 1919; and California State Board of Control, *California and the Oriental: Japanese, Chinese, and Hindus* (Sacramento: California State Printing Office, 1922), 108–109.

88. Ōyama to Uchida, August 15, 1922, HMSC, DRO.

89. Zai Sōkō Sōryōjikan, "Taiheiyō Engan Ryōji Kaigi Honshō shimon jikō ni taisuru iken," 67–68, March 12, 1928, RKKZ 1, DRO.

90. Ibid.; and Zai Sōkō Sōryōjikan, "Dai-Sankai Taiheiyō Engan Ryōji Kaigi gijiroku, gekan," 1928, 229–236, esp. 233, RKKZ: Gijiroku. Reportedly, the gangsters also had the upper hand over the immigrant press to deter the formation of public opinion against them.

91. See Ichioka, *Issei*, 210–243.

92. Zai Sōkō Sōryōjikan, "Taiheiyō Engan Ryōji Kaigi Honshō shimon," 1–13. The San Francisco consul later observed that the cancellation of endorsement rights in 1926 had weakened both the rural Japanese associations and central bodies in terms of their finances and authority. The local entities, however, fared better, since they managed to maintain most of their membership bases by continuing to offer social, legal, and other vital services for Issei residents. Contrarily, on top of the elimination of its key income from certificate fees, the central headquarters lost its main raison d'être.

CHAPTER 3

1. *Nichibei Shimbun*, June 23, 1924.
2. I compiled these statistics from the following sources: *Nichibei nenkan*, vol. 4 (1908), 102–103; vol. 6 (1910), 87–88; vol. 7 (1911), 130–131; vol. 8 (1912), 100–101; vol. 9 (1913), 107–108; vol. 10 (1914), 121–122; vol. 11 (1915), 123–124; Zaibei Nihonjinkai, *Zaibei Nihonjinshi* (San Francisco: Zaibei Nihonjinkai, 1940), 174–175, 187, 192; and Nichibei Shimbunsha, *Zaibei Nihonjin jinmei jiten* (San Francisco: Nichibei Shimbunsha, 1922), 38.
3. Nakaya Shōzō, "Kashū Sakuramento Heiya ni okeru Honpō zairyūmin jijō shisatsu hōkoku," *Imin chōsa hōkoku* (1911; reprint, Tokyo: Gaimushō, 1986), 8:167; U.S. Immigration Commission, *Immigrants in Industries*, pt. 25, *Japanese and Other Immigrant Races in the Pacific Coast and Rocky Mountain States* (Washington, D.C.: GPO, 1911), 358; and Ōfu Nippōsha, *Sakuramento Heigen Nihonjin taisei ichiran* (Sacramento, Calif.: Ōfu Nippō, 1909), 2:65–66.
4. Zaibei Nihonjinkai, *Zaibei Nihonjinshi*, 161; and *Nichibei Shimbun*, April 18, 1940.
5. See Eiichiro Azuma, "Japanese Immigrant Farmers and California Alien Land Laws: A Study of the Walnut Grove Japanese Community," *California History* 73 (Spring 1994): 15–17. On asparagus farming in the delta, see "Asparagus Growing for Canneries," *PRP* 66 (July 19, 1902): 37; and "Asparagus in California," *PRP* 69 (May 6, 1905): 276. On industrialized agriculture and the specialty crops culture in California, see David Vaught, *Cultivating California: Growers, Specialty Crops, and Labor, 1875–1920* (Baltimore, Md.: Johns Hopkins University Press, 1999), 11–157.
6. *Nichibei Shimbun*, April 18, 1940; and KNK 1, August 30, 1909, in box 732, JARP.
7. R. E. Hodges, "Thousands of Acres of Asparagus," *PRP* 96 (October 26, 1918): 452.
8. G. Walter Reed, *History of Sacramento County* (Los Angeles: Historical Record, 1923), 306–309.
9. See Azuma, "Japanese Immigrant Farmers," 17–19.
10. Miscellaneous Book 9, 479–481, SCRO; and Sakae Kaibara, *Kashū Hiroshima kenjin hattenshi* (Sacramento, Calif.: Yorozu Shoten, 1916), 92, 318–319. On the cropping contract, see Azuma, "Japanese Immigrant Farmers," 22.
11. Gaimushō, *Kashū oyobi Kashū Tochihō shiso keika gaiyō* (Tokyo: Gaimushō, 1923), 27.
12. *Ōfu Nippō*, September 27, 1921; and *Shin Sekai*, May 28, 1923.
13. *Nichibei nenkan* 6:112–113; ibid. 12 (1918): 7–10; and Japanese Agricultural Association, *Japanese Farmers in California* (San Francisco: Japanese Agricultural Association, 1918). Computation for the 1909 figure by the author.
14. Noritaka Yagasaki, "Ethnic Cooperativism and Immigrant Agriculture: A Study of Japanese Floriculture and Truck Farming in California" (Ph.D. diss., University of California, Berkeley, 1982).

15. John Modell, *The Economics and Politics of Racial Accommodation: The Japanese of Los Angeles, 1900–1942* (Urbana: University of Illinois Press, 1977), 115–118.

16. Nichibei Shimbunsha, *Zaibei Nihonjin jinmei jiten*, 198; Bangaku Mizutani, *Hokubei Aichi kenjinshi* (Sacramento, Calif.: Hokubei Aichi Kenjinkai, 1919), 10, appendix; and *Shin Sekai*, June 16, 27, 1936.

17. *Nichibei Shimbun*, March 14, 1920. See also *Sacramento Bee*, March 18, 1920. In order to illuminate the economic threat, the *Bee* article was presented as an exhibit at a U.S. congressional hearing on Japanese immigration. See U.S. House, Committee on Immigration and Naturalization, *Japanese Immigration: Hearings before the Committee on Immigration and Naturalization*, pt. 1 (Washington, D.C.: GPO, 1921), 353–354.

18. *Nichibei Shimbun*, December 22, 1923.

19. Ibid., March 14, 1920. By the same token, in other regions, where Issei posed no significant threat, white elites frequently led local political campaigns *against* the land law initiative. In Stockton, a coalition of prominent land owners, business leaders, and Christian ministers circulated leaflets detailing Japanese "contributions" to local agriculture and the expected economic damage that the law, when enacted, would bring to Stockton. Some even flew an airplane on election day to scatter 50,000 copies of the leaflets around the town. In their attempt to influence California voters, several land owners joined a pro-Japanese political lobby, the American Committee of Justice under the leadership of John P. Irish, and a few prominent landlords volunteered to testify before a congressional hearing on behalf of Issei tenant farmers. See Kanzō Ōhashi, *Hokubei Kashū Sutakuton dōhōshi* (Stockton, Calif.: Su-shi Nihonjinkai, 1937), 304–308; and American Committee of Justice, *Arguments against the California Alien Land Law* (Oakland, Calif.: American Committee of Justice, 1920).

20. "Honpōjin nōkōsha no jōkyō ni kansuru chōsa hōkokusho," n.p., December 27, 1926, HKNK, DRO; and "Honpōjin nōkōsha-tō no jōkyō ni kansuru chōsasho shintatsu no ken," n.p., September 16, 1926, HIKZ 3, DRO.

21. "Honpōjin nōkōsha no jōkyō ni kansuru chōsa hōkokusho."

22. "Honpōjin nōkōsha-tō no jōkyō ni kansuru chōsasho shintatsu no ken."

23. Zaibei Nihonjinkai, *Zaibei Nihonjinshi*, 187.

24. Yuji Ichioka, *The Issei: The World of the First Generation Japanese Immigrants, 1885–1924* (New York: Free Press, 1988), 228.

25. See *Rafu Shimpō*, October 7, 13, 1921.

26. KNK 1, September 11, 26, 1921; *Nichibei Shimbun*, September 30, October 4, 1921; and Yada to Uchida, September 15, 1921, BHMZ: Kashū Tochihō, DRO.

27. *Ōfu Nippō*, September 27, 1921.

28. KNK 1, October 2, 6, 1921; *Nichibei Shimbun*, September 30, October 4, 1921; and *Ōfu Nippō*, September 27, October 20, 1921.

29. *Ōfu Nippō*, September 24, 28, 1921; *Nichibei Shimbun*, October 4, 1921; and Kashū Chūō Nōkai, "Kashū Nihonjin nōgyōsha no jitsujō," 7, 14, November 1, 1921, BHMZ: Kashū Tochihō.

30. Kashu Chūō Nōkai, "Kashū Nihonjin nōgyōsha," 11–12, 14, November 1, 1921.

31. Ibid., 5–6; and Ichioka, *Issei*, 229–230.
32. *Rafu Shimpō*, September 28, 1921; Shirō Fujioka, *Beikoku Chūō Nihonjinkaishi* (Los Angeles: Beikoku Chūō Nihonjinkai, 1940), 98–99; and Ichioka, *Issei*, 229–232.
33. *Nichibei Shimbun*, November 21, 1923.
34. *Rafu Shimpō*, November 23, 1923.
35. *Ōfu Nippō*, December 24, 1923.
36. *Taihoku Nippō*, December 4, 1923; and *Shin Sekai*, November 20, 1923.
37. "Honpōjin nōkōsha ni kansuru chōsa hōkokusho."
38. See *Ōfu Nippō*, November 22, 23, 1923; and *Taihoku Nippō*, May 14, 1923.
39. "Honpōjin nōkōsha-tō no jōkyō ni kansuru chōsasho shintatsu no ken"; and "Honpōjin nōkōsha ni kansuru chōsa hōkokusho." See also Tamezō Takimoto, "Warera no jūyō mondai," August 15, 1924, BHMZ.
40. Computation by the author from the following sources: *Nichibei nenkan*, vols. 4, 6, 10, 12; Gaimushō, *Kashū oyobi Kashū Tochihō*, 27; and Zaibei Nihonjinkai, *Zaibei Nihonjinshi*, 187, 192.
41. Numano to Katō, October 14, 1914, BHMZ; and Eiichiro Azuma, "A History of Oregon's Issei," *Oregon Historical Quarterly* 94 (Winter 1993–1994): 328–330.
42. See *Nichibei nenkan*, vol. 4 (1908), 102–103; vol. 6 (1910), 87–88; vol. 7 (1911), 130–131; vol. 8 (1912), 100–101; vol. 9 (1913), 107–108; vol. 10 (1914), 121–122; vol. 11 (1915), 123–124; Zaibei Nihonjinkai, *Zaibei Nihonjinshi*, 174–175; and Nichibei Shimbunsha, *Zaibei Nihonjin jinmei jiten*, 38.
43. Both in Placer and Fresno counties, Japanese landholding farmers belonged to white-run farming guilds. In the towns of Placer and Loomis, Issei farmers ended up borrowing heavily from the local producers' associations, banks, and shipping companies. Membership in such white-run organizations was not necessarily conducive to the interest of Japanese farmers in Fresno, either. There, the Sun Maid Raisin Growers of Delaware held a tight grip on the processing, packing, shipping, and marketing of raisin products. Early in 1925, many farmers, including Japanese, opted to withdraw from the coop, since it had paid them less than half of what nonmembers had received for the same amount of crop on the open market. Sun Maid swiftly mobilized local American Legion members and sent them to punish these "renegades" by arson attacks and random beatings. Many farmers feared the worst and reluctantly returned to Sun Maid despite the obvious economic disadvantages and even deficit operations. See *Nichibei Shimbun*, February 12, 13, 14, 1925; and "Honpōjin nōkōsha-tō no jōkyō ni kansuru chōsasho shintatsu no ken."
44. Ichioka, *Issei*, 148–150; Kesa Noda, *Yamato Colony: 1906–1960* (Livingston, Calif.: Livingston-Merced JACL Chapter, 1981), 1–15, 78; and Valerie J. Matsumoto, *Farming the Home Place: A Japanese American Community in California, 1919–1982* (Ithaca, N.Y.: Cornell University Press, 1993), 25–30.
45. Harvey Guy, "Memorandum on Livingston Situation," 1–2, February 12, 1920, BHMZ: Bessatsu Kashū 1.

46. Ibid., 4; and Harvey Guy, "Memorandum on Situation in Merced County," 2–4, May 17, 1920, BHMZ: Bessatsu Kashū 1.
47. Matsumoto, *Farming the Home Place*, 38–42.
48. *Nichibei Shimbun*, February 3, 1920.
49. Ibid., April 23–26, 1920.
50. Ibid., April 23, May 1, 1920.
51. U.S. Congress, House, *Japanese Immigration*, 847–856, esp. 854.
52. Noda, *Yamato Colony*, 88; and Matsumoto, *Farming the Home Place*, 38–40.
53. *Livingston Chronicle*, December 3, 1920.
54. According to Kesa Noda, some "new settlers" did come to the Yamato Colony in 1920–1921, yet the evidence provided shows that most of them actually came to live with those who had already farmed there. These newcomers tended to be resident employees or relatives rather than additional land owners. Noda, *Yamato Colony*, 89–90, 193–194, 196–198.
55. Modell, *Economics and Politics of Racial Accommodation*, 58. On Issei suburbanization and white segregationist politics in Los Angeles, see Scott Tadao Kurashige, "Transforming Los Angeles: Black and Japanese American Struggles for Racial Equality in the Twentieth Century" (Ph.D. diss., University of California, Los Angeles, 2000), 43–66.
56. Modell, *Economics and Politics of Racial Accommodation*, 62–65, esp. 62; and Kurashige, "Transforming Los Angeles," 52–55.
57. Shibasaki to Uchida, June 1, 1923, BHMZ: Bessatsu Kashū 6.
58. Kikuko Akahori, diary, 6:4, July 1, 1924, in box 1, JARP; and Akira Togawa, diary, July 1, 1924, in folder 3, box 1, TAP, JARP.
59. *Shin Sekai*, April 19, 1924; *Taihoku Nippō*, April 22, 1924; and *Nichibei Shimbun*, July 3, 1924.
60. *Rafu Shimpō*, April 18, 1924.
61. Seizō Abe, *Muteikō shugi seishin dōmei* (Seattle, Wash.: Abe Seizō, 1924), 1.
62. U.S. Department of Labor, Bureau of Immigration, *Annual Report of the Commissioner General of Immigration* (Washington, D.C.: GPO, 1916–1917, 1919, 1922–1927), 128–129, 130–131, 246–247, 135–136, 150–151, 148–149, 178–179, 159–160, 181–182; and Eliot G. Mears, *Resident Orientals on the American Pacific Coast: Their Legal and Economic Status* (Chicago: University of Chicago Press, 1928), 409. According to Masao Suzuki, the massive exodus of Japanese immigrant farmers subsided within several years after 1924. During the 1930s, more laborers than farmers or professionals left for Japan, improving the overall occupational position of Japanese Americans. Masao Suzuki, "Success Story? Japanese Immigrant Economic Achievement and Return Migration, 1920–1930," *Journal of Economic History* 55 (December 1995): 895–896.
63. See "Honpōjin nōkōsha-tō no jōkyō ni kansuru chōsasho shintatsu no ken"; "Honpōjin nōkōsha ni kansuru chōsa hōkokusho"; and Oregon Bureau of Labor, *Census: Japanese Population in Oregon* (Salem: Oregon Bureau of Labor, 1929). Computation of the Oregon figures by the author.
64. *Rafu Shimpō*, April 14, 1922.

65. Tezuka to Shibusawa, July 21, 1924, Zaibei Nihonjin ōfuku, SMA; and Ichioka, *Issei*, 241.

66. For example, see *Rafu Shimpō*, April 10, 22, 1924. In 1925, Fujioka made a one-month trip through Mexico and later published commentaries and a travelogue. Shirō Fujioka, *Minzoku hatten no senkusha* (Tokyo: Dōbunsha, 1926), 167–297.

67. Kitoku Yoshiyama, *Chūmoku subeki Mekishiko* (San Francisco: Nichiboku Kenkyūsha, 1928), 318. See also Tezuka to Shibusawa.

68. Kuga to Tanaka, May 21, 1927, HZKS, DRO. See also Nihonjin Mekishiko Ijūshi Hensan Iinkai, *Nihonjin Mekishiko ijūshi* (Mexico City: Nihonjin Mekishiko Ijūshi Hensan Iinkai, 1971), 184–195.

69. *Shin Sekai*, September 18, 1928.

70. Ibid., May 4, 1926, October 11–15, 1928; and Masasuke Kobayashi, *Yamato minzoku no sekaiteki bōchō* (Tokyo: Keigansha, 1933), 600–602, 605–609. Later, his expansionist friends in San Francisco enshrined Soejima as a racial martyr, celebrating his pioneer spirit and colonialist dedication as a model for all Issei.

71. Nagata Shigeshi, "Zaibei Nihonjin ni atau sho," *Rikkō Sekai* (June 1, 1924): 16–19.

72. Kinenshi Hensan Senmon Iinkai, *Nihon Rikkōkai hyakunen no kōseki* (Tokyo: Nihon Rikkōkai, 1997), 152–154; and Burajiru Rikkōkai, *Burajiru Rikkōkai yonjū-nenshi* (São Paulo, Brazil: Burajiru Rikkōkai, 1966), 97–99.

73. Itō Takuji, *Tenkai no kisoku* (Furukawa, Miyagi: Ōsaki Taimususha, 1987); Hasegawa Yūichi, "Hainichi iminhō to Manshū, Burajiru," in *Nichibei kiki no kigen to Hainichi Iminhō*, ed. Miwa Kimitada (Tokyo: Ronsōsha, 1997), 44–62; and Kimura Kenji, "Senzenki Kaigai yūhi to shisōteki keifu," *Kenkyū nenpō keizai-gaku* 53 (March 1992): 29–40.

74. Toyoji Chiba, *Beikoku Kashū hainichi jijō* (San Francisco: Nichibei Kankei Chōsakai, 1921), 52.

75. Toyoji Chiba, "Chiba Toyoji ikō" (1944), 2:616. Courtesy of Professor Yuji Ichioka.

76. See, for example, Toyoji Chiba, *Manshū no kishō to kansōchi nōgyō* (Dalian, Manchuria: Minami Manshū Tetsudō Kabushiki Gaisha, 1925), 33–35. After Japan set up a virtual colony of Manchukuo in 1932, a significant number of Issei and Nisei moved to Manchuria for better economic opportunities. John J. Stephan, "Hijacked by Utopia: American Nikkei in Manchuria," *Amerasia Journal* 23 (Winter 1997–1998): 1–42.

77. Rogers Brubaker, *Nationalism Reframed: Nationhood and the National Question in the New Europe* (Cambridge: Cambridge University Press, 1996), 4–6.

78. On how the racial "Otherness" of Asian immigrants influenced U.S. national formation, see Najia Aarim-Heriot, *Chinese Immigrants, African Americans, and Racial Anxiety in the United States, 1848–82* (Urbana: University of Illinois Press, 2003); Erika Lee, *At America's Gate: Chinese Immigration during the Exclusion Era, 1882–1943* (Chapel Hill: University of North Carolina Press, 2003), esp. 30–40; and Mae M. Ngai, *Impossible Subjects: Illegal Aliens and the Making of Modern America* (Princeton, N.J.: Princeton University Press, 2004).

79. Shibusawa Seien Kinen Zaidan Ryūmonsha, *SED* 34 (1960): 192. See also Lee A. Makela, "Japanese Attitudes towards the United States Immigration Act of 1924" (Ph.D. diss., Stanford University, 1972).

80. America-Japan Society, *Special Bulletin* 1 (1925): 6; and Nitobe Inazō, *Naikan gaibō* (Tokyo: Jitsugyō no Nihonsha, 1933), 273–274.

81. See, for example, Kanagawa Prefecture, "Shūkai jōkyō hōkoku," July 4, 7, 1924, BHMZ: Naigai hantai undō.

82. See Ukita Kazutami, *Manshū mondai to Nichibei shinzenron* (Tokyo: Hokubun-kan, 1934), 275–276; files and papers concerning Zen Ajia Kyōkai, or the Pan-Asiatic Society, MMKZ 1–2, DRO; and Masayo Umezawa Duus, *The Japanese Conspiracy: The Oahu Sugar Strike of 1920* (Berkeley: University of California Press, 1999), 315–316. Fundamentally, this racism still operated on the Western (modernist) paradigm of a global racial order. See Yukiko Koshiro, *Trans-Pacific Racisms and the U.S. Occupation of Japan* (New York: Columbia University Press, 1999), 11–12. On the ramifications of the 1924 law to long-term U.S.–Japan relations, see Miwa Kimitada, "Tokutomi Sohō no rekishizō to Nichibei Sensō no genriteki kaishi," in *Seiyō no shōgeki to Nihon*, ed. Haga Tōru et al. (Tokyo: Tokyo Daigaku Shuppankai, 1973), 183; and Duus, *Japanese Conspiracy*, 307–317.

83. *Rafu Shimpō*, April 25, 1924.

84. *Shin Sekai*, June 2, 9, 1924.

85. See *Nichibei Shimbun*, June 23, 1924; and Eiichiro Azuma, "Interstitial Lives: Race, Community, and History among Japanese Immigrants Caught between Japan and the United States, 1885–1941" (Ph.D. diss., University of California, Los Angeles, 2000), 178.

CHAPTER 4

1. Shakuma Washizu, "Rekihi inmetsu no tan," 1–97, *Nichibei Shimbun*, April 6–July 14, 1922.

2. Issei historians' publications dealt with various aspects of immigrants' experiences on the U.S. mainland. On general immigrant history, see Mushō Nakagawa, *Zaibei tōshiroku* (Los Angeles: Rafu Shimpōsha, 1932); Nichibei Shimbunsha, *Nichibei taikan* (San Francisco: Nichibei Shimbunsha, 1931); Yoichi Tōga, *Nichibei kankei Zaibeikoku Nihonjin hatten shiyō* (Oakland: Beikoku Seisho Kyōkai Nihonjinbu, 1927); Shakuma Washizu, *Zaibei Nihonjin shikan* (Los Angeles: Rafu Shimpōsha, 1930); and Zaibei Nihonjinkai, *Zaibei Nihonjinshi* (San Francisco: Zaibei Nihonjinkai, 1940). For chronicles of regional development, see Merisubiru Chihō Nihonjinkai, *Hokka yongun Nihonjin hattenshi* (Marysville, Calif.: Merisubiru Chihō Nihonjinkai, 1932); Kanzō Ōhashi, *Hokubei Kashū Sutakuton dōhōshi* (Stockton, Calif.: Su-shi Nihonjinkai, 1937); Hisagorō Saka, *Santa Maria Heigen Nihonjinshi* (Guadalupe, Calif.: Gadarūpu Nihonjinkai, 1936); Takoma Shūhōsha, *Takoma-shi oyobi chihō Nihonjinkai* (Tacoma, Wash.: Takoma Shū-hōsha, 1941); Kōjirō Takeuchi, *Beikoku Seihokubu Nihon iminshi* (Seattle, Wash.:

Taihoku Nippōsha, 1929); Kōsuke Takeuchi, *San Pidoro dōhō hattenroku* (Terminal Island, Calif.: Takeuchi Kōsuke, 1937); and Yakima Nihonjinkai, *Yakima Heigen Nihonjinshi* (Yakima, Wash.: Yakima Nihonjinkai, 1935). For histories organized along the prefectural origins of Issei, see Shirō Endō, *Minami Kashū Okayama kenjin hattenshi* (Los Angeles: Minami Kashū Okayama Kenjin Hattenshi Hensanjo, 1941); Tsunegorō Hirohata, *Zaibei Fukuoka kenjin to jigyō* (Los Angeles: Zaibei Fukuoka Kenjin to Jigyō Hensan Jimusho, 1936); Shurei Hirose, *Zaibei Kōshūjin funtō gojūnenshi* (Los Angeles: Nanka Yamanashi Kaigai Kyōkai, 1934); Katsuma Mukaeda and Masatoshi Nakamura, *Zaibei no Higojin* (Los Angeles: Nanka Kumamoto Kaigai Kyōkai, 1931); Yasuji Satō, *Kashū to Fukushima kenjin: Nanka-hen* (Los Angeles: Kashū Fukushima Kenjin Hattenshi Hensansho, 1929); Jun'ichi Takeda, *Zaibei Hiroshima kenjinshi* (Los Angeles: Zaibei Hiroshima Kenjinshi Hakkōsho, 1929); and Riichirō Yatsu, *Zaibei Miyagi kenjinshi* (Los Angeles: Zaibei Miyagi Kenjinshi Hensan Jimusho, 1933). Other noteworthy works include Shirō Fujioka, *Beikoku Chūō Nihonjinkaishi* (Los Angeles: Beikoku Chūō Nihonjinkai, 1940); Hokka Nihongo Gakuen Kyōkai, *Beikoku Kashū Nihongo gakuen enkakushi* (San Francisco: Hokka Nihongo Gakuen Kyōkai, 1930); Kō Murai, *Zaibei Nihonjin sangyō sōran* (Los Angeles: Beikoku Sangyō Nippōsha 1940); and Hōkō Terakawa, *Hokubei kaikyō enkakushi* (San Francisco: Hongwanji Hokubei Kaikyō Honbu, 1936).

3. Tōga, *Nichibei kankei Zaibeikoku Nihonjin*, "jo." In 1926, for the purpose of commemorating its frustrating struggle with white racism, the Japanese Association of San Francisco organized an "exhibition of historical materials pertaining to the development of the Japanese in America." Its catalog carries a foreword, which is remarkably similar to Tōga's. When composing the quoted "proclamation," he seems to have borrowed key portions from the catalog. The original reads: "No nation without history can be a great one. Any race/nation that is disrespectful of its own past is destined to fall . . . The history of the Japanese in America is already [as long as] 60 years, and there is so much to leave behind in the form of an organized chronicle for the benefit of others. Now the pioneers are advancing in years, and the next generation is rising . . . There is an urgent need to show our historical record of tribulations to the next generation." The organizers of the 1926 exhibition included some individuals who later emerged as prominent Issei historians. See Sōkō Nihonjinkai, *Zaibei Nihonjin hatten shiryō tenrankai kinenshi* (1926), "shogen."

4. *Shin Sekai*, April 18, 24, 1938, January 28, February 14, March 2, 1940; and Zaibei Nihonjinkai, *Zaibei Nihonjinshi*, 4, 1291–1292.

5. Shirō Fujioka, *Minzoku hatten no senkusha* (Tokyo: Dōbunsha, 1927), 3–4, also 167–227.

6. Shirō Fujioka, for example, attended Waseda University in Tokyo before emigrating to the United States in 1899. Before working as a newspaper editor in Seattle and Los Angeles, he studied at Temple and Columbia universities. With no access to white-collar work in mainstream society, most Japanese immigrant historians eked out livelihoods as vernacular newspaper reporters, association sec-

retaries and counselors, religious leaders, and Japanese-language schoolteachers in urban and rural ethnic enclaves.

7. C. S. Miyazaki, "To Our American Sons and Daughters," in *Ōka Nikkei shimin shashin*, ed. Sōsuke Kawai (Tacoma, Wash.: Takoma Shūhōsha, 1938), 54 (English section).

8. Ibid. Issei history resembles the revisionism of new Western historians in its incorporation of an ethnic minority into the frontier narrative and its notion of continuity in "conquest," that is, contestation over land, resources, and the distribution of wealth and power. See Patricia Nelson Limerick, *The Legacy of Conquest: The Unbroken Past of the American West* (New York: Norton, 1987), 18–27.

9. Only a few English-language works have examined *kaigai hattenron*. See Mark R. Peattie, *Nan'yo: The Rise and Fall of the Japanese in Micronesia, 1885–1945* (Honolulu: University of Hawaii Press, 1988), 1–33; and Peter Duus, *The Abacus and the Sword: The Japanese Penetration of Korea, 1895–1910* (Berkeley: University of California Press, 1995), 295–301. On the overseas origins of the prehistoric Japanese, see Stephan Tanaka, *Japan's Orient: Rendering Pasts into History* (Berkeley: University of California Press, 1993), 70–104.

10. *Shin Sekai*, September 30, 1932. On Anglo-American manifest destiny and imperial Japanese racism, see Reginald Horsman, *Race and Manifest Destiny* (Cambridge, Mass.: Harvard University Press, 1981), esp. 272–297; and John W. Dower, *War without Mercy: Race and Power in the Pacific War* (New York: Pantheon, 1986), respectively.

11. Zaibei Nihonjinkai, *Zaibei Nihonjinshi*, 147.

12. Ōhashi, *Hokubei Kashū Sutakuton dōhōshi*, 5–7.

13. See Masasuke Kobayashi, *Nihon minzoku no sekaiteki bōchō* (Tokyo: Keigansha, 1933), 30–33, 42–45. Kobayashi came to the United States in 1902 and graduated from Westminster College in Ogden, Utah. On his ideas and activities in the 1920s, see Brian M. Hayashi, "The Japanese 'Invasion' of California: Major Kobayashi and the Japanese Salvation Army, 1919–1926," *Journal of the West* 23 (1984): 73–82.

14. Seizō Abe, *Muteikō shugi seishin dōmei* (Seattle, Wash.: Abe Seizō, 1924), 2.

15. Nakagawa, *Zaibei tōshiroku*, 2.

16. See Saka, *Santa Maria Heigen Nihonjinshi*, 319–424; Yakima Nihonjinkai, *Yakima Heigen Nihonjinshi*, 314–399; Mukaeda and Nakamura, *Zaibei no Higojin*, 92–940; Takeda, *Zaibei Hiroshima kenjinshi*, 141–616; Hirohata, *Zaibei Fukuoka kenjin to jigyō*, 1–508; Yatsu, *Zaibei Miyagi kenjinshi*, 163–285; and Hirose, *Zaibei Kōshūjin funtō gojūnenshi*, 234–541.

17. Saka, *Santa Maria Heigen Nihonjinshi*.

18. Nakagawa, *Zaibei tōshiroku*, 3, 321–611.

19. On this trajectory, see Yuji Ichioka, *The Issei: The World of the First Generation Japanese Immigrants, 1885–1924* (New York: Free Press, 1988), 150–153.

20. Murai, *Zaibei Nihonjin sangyō sōran*, 1–3, 7; and Zaibei Nihonjinkai, *Zaibei Nihonjinshi*, 130, 146–150. See also Washizu, "Rekishi inmetsu no tan," 97, *Nichibei Shimbun*, July 14, 1922.

21. Unfortunately, the class and gender biases are manifest in the reconstruction of Issei history by professional academicians, too. Due to the control of knowledge production and community politics by Issei male intelligentsia and entrepreneurs, available historical studies tend to represent their views, interests, and positions. The voices of women and laborers are extremely difficult to salvage. To supplement, and often substitute for, the scarce written sources, some scholars have employed oral histories—a methodology that has now become nearly impossible because of the passing of the immigrant generation.

22. Giichi Takamatsu, "Minzoku hatten no senkusha," *Hatarakuhito* 15 (1935): 8, in folder 3, box 3, KGYP, JARP.

23. "Dokusha no koe," *Nichibei Shimbun*, October 30, 1933. See also ibid., November 2, 5, 14, 1933.

24. Saka, *Santa Maria Heigen Nihonjinshi*, 21.

25. Tōga, *Nichibei kankei Zaibeikoku Nihonjin*, "jo."

26. Zaibei Nihonjinkai, *Zaibei Nihonjinshi*, 200–201.

27. Tenyō Yazaki, a Los Angeles Issei journalist who published a youth-oriented monthly, employed the term *Nisei* for the first time when discussing the ramifications of racial discrimination to the ethnic collectivity. The meaning of citizenship relative to the question of racial exclusion was intrinsic to the Japanese immigrant idea of generations. On the origin of the term *Nisei* (and hence *Issei* as its opposite), see Shirō Fujioka, *Ayumi no ato* (Los Angeles: Ayumi no Ato Kankō Kōenkai, 1957), 521.

28. Miyazaki, "To Our American Sons and Daughters," 55. See also Mukaeda and Nakamura, *Zaibei no Higojin*, 34–35. This history of Kumamoto-born Issei contains an English section entitled "Japanese-American Citizens," which reads: "To have the second generation know and understand the trials and sufferings of the first generation is the purpose of this writing. With very meager knowledge of foreign lands and with nothing, save their own bodies, the first generation with a brave and pioneering spirit left their native land and sailed across the wide Pacific Ocean. Confronted by severe racial agitation, kicked and bounced about, excluded there, they withstood misery for forty years. You second generation are the children of these people who with faith fought through these trying situations. May you never forget this."

29. See *Shin Sekai*, November 2, 1940; and Nichibei Shimbunsha, *Nichibei taikan*, 1–2.

30. *Rafu Shimpō*, October 16, 1935.

31. See *Shin Sekai*, January 21, 22, 1938.

32. Kobayashi, *Nihon minzoku no sekaiteki bōchō*, 1–33, 99. The quotation is from 17.

33. Zaibei Nihonjinkai, *Zaibei Nihonjinshi*, 1–4. See also Yatsu, *Zaibei Miyagi kenjinshi*, 1–3.

34. On the concept of genesis amnesia, see Pierre Bourdieu, *Outline of a Theory of Practice* (Cambridge: Cambridge University Press, 1977), 79.

35. Fujioka, *Minzoku hatten no senkusha*, 3. See also Saka, *Santa Maria Heigen Nihonjinshi*, 5; and Mukaeda and Nakamura, *Zaibei no Higojin*, 2.

36. See Yukiko Koshiro, *Trans-Pacific Racisms and the U.S. Occupation of Japan* (New York: Columbia University Press, 1999), 1–13. With the rise of ultranationalistic militarism during the 1930s, the Japanese racial discourse came to assume the superiority of the Yamato race to, rather than compatibility with, the whites, although the shift had begun around 1924. See Dower, *War without Mercy*, 264–281; and Harry Harutoonian and Tetsuo Najita, "Japanese Revolt against the West: Political and Cultural Criticism in the Twentieth Century," in *The Cambridge History of Japan: The Twentieth Century*, ed. Peter Duus (Cambridge: Cambridge University Press, 1988), 711–774.

37. Eileen H. Tamura's definition of Japanese American acculturation, albeit in the Hawaiian context, is most appropriate and informative. She calls it an "adaptation . . . to American middle-class norms," with which ethnic identity persisted. Eileen H. Tamura, *Americanization, Acculturation, and Ethnic Identity: The Nisei Generation in Hawaii* (Urbana: University of Illinois Press, 1994), 52.

38. See David R. Roediger, *The Wages of Whiteness: Race and the Making of the American Working Class* (New York: Verso, 1999); Matthew Frye Jacobson, *Whiteness of a Different Color: European Immigrants and the Alchemy of Race* (Cambridge, Mass.: Harvard University Press, 1998); and Noel Ignatiev, *How the Irish Became White* (New York: Routledge, 1995). While scholars have uncovered the socially constructed nature of whiteness in the United States, their inquiry seems to have been confined to the cases of European immigrants. I would argue that many racial minorities—including Japanese immigrants—engaged in similar practices, albeit not as effectively as people of European ancestry due to the resiliency of biological racism.

39. For examples of this bias against non–Western European immigrants, see Marcus Lee Hansen, *The Atlantic Migration, 1607–1860* (Cambridge, Mass.: Harvard University Press, 1940); and Oscar Handlin, *The Uprooted* (Boston: Little, Brown, 1973). For a critique of historians' focus on permanent settlement in their studies of immigrants, see Virginia Yans-McLaughlin's introduction to *Immigration Reconsidered: History, Sociology, and Politics*, ed. Virginia Yans-McLaughlin (New York: Oxford University Press, 1990), 6–7.

40. On the critique of *dekasegi* practice by advocates of Manchurian colonization, see Louise Young, *Japan's Total Empire: Manchuria and the Culture of Wartime Imperialism* (Berkeley: University of California Press, 1998), 319–320. Due to the stigma associated with the term, Tokyo did away with the conventional term by inventing a brand-new word to refer to those emigrants when Japan sponsored mass emigration into Manchuria from 1935. Under the state program, Manchurian settler-immigrants were no longer *imin*; they were called *takushi*, the "colonial fighters."

41. In addition to the argument for the differences between the current Issei and the earlier laborers, many history books posited a sudden change in social orientation among immigrants from sojourners to permanent settlers, usually prompted by the establishment of families or by the birth of children in America. These mental changes, according to the typical narrative, then ushered in their embrace of

the United States as their "adopted" country, irrespective of citizenship status. See Takeda, *Zaibei Hiroshima kenjinshi*, 20; Hirose, *Zaibei Kōshūjin funtō gojū-nenshi*, 38; and Hirohata, *Zaibei Fukuoka kenjin to jigyō*, 27.

42. Nichibei Shimbunsha, *Nichibei taikan*, 101. Published in 1932, the only English-language history of Japanese immigration by an Issei intellectual, likewise denied any relation between Japanese immigrants and *dekasegi* laborers. Yamato Ichihashi, *Japanese in the United States: A Critical Study of the Problem of the Japanese Immigrants and Their Children* (Stanford, Calif.: Stanford University Press, 1932), 60, 65, 67–68, 81–82, 207–227. On Ichihashi's bias, see Yuji Ichioka, " 'Attorney for the Defense': Yamato Ichihashi and Japanese Immigration," *Pacific Historical Review* 55 (1986): 219–225.

43. Zaibei Nihonjinkai, *Zaibei Nihonjinshi*, 77, and also 32. See Sakata Yasuo, "Wataridori to sono shakai: himerareta kako," in *Zaibei Nihonjin shakai no reimei*, ed. Dōshisha Jinbun Kagaku Kenkyūjo (Tokyo: PMC Shuppan, 1997), 16–20, 59.

44. Miyazaki, "To Our American Sons and Daughters," 59.

45. Zaibei Nihonjinkai, *Zaibei Nihonjinshi*, 19–29; Yūsen Kawamura, *Hainichi sensen o toppa shitsutsu* (Isleton, Calif.: Kawamura Yūsen, 1930), 11–20, 161–182; and Kawamura Yūsen, *Kariforunia kaika hishi* (Tokyo: Kawamura Yūsen, 1934), 50–56. For a general history of Schnell's colony, see John E. Van Sant, *Pacific Pioneers: Japanese Journeys to America and Hawaii, 1850–80* (Urbana: University of Illinois Press, 2000), 117–130.

46. Kawamura, *Hainichi sensen o toppa shitsutsu*, 179.

47. Zaibei Nihonjinkai, *Zaibei Nihonjinshi*, 20–21, 29, 89, 91.

48. On the commemorations as shapers of public memory, see David Lowenthal, "Identity, Heritage, and History," in *Commemorations: The Politics of National Identity*, ed. John R. Gillis (Princeton, N.J.: Princeton University Press, 1997), 41–57; Kirk Savage, "The Politics of Memory: Black Emancipation and the Civil War Monument," in *Commemorations*, 127–149; and John E. Bodnar, *Remaking America: Public Memory, Commemoration, and Patriotism in the Twentieth Century* (Princeton, N.J.: Princeton University Press, 1991), 78–112.

49. *Shin Sekai*, September 12, 1934 (English section). See also ibid., September 6, 1934; and Roy Yoshida, "To Beautify the Tiny Grave of Okei," *Pacific Citizen*, January 1, 1970.

50. *Rafu Shimpō*, March 22, 1935 (English section).

51. Ibid., June 3, 12, November 27, 1937; and Fujioka, *Beikoku Chūō Nihonjinkaishi*, 336.

52. Irie Toraji's expansionist orthodoxy allotted fifteen of its fifty-five chapters to stories of the Issei's tribulations and triumphs, including their "heroic" fight against white racism. The manner in which it treated Japanese experiences in America served as a model for similar works that came out in imperial Japan in the ensuing years. See Irie Toraji, *Hōjin kaigai hattenshi* (Tokyo: Ide Shoten, 1942), 2:326–327.

53. *Kingu* 9 (October 1933): 171.

54. Kaigai Dōhō Chūōkai, *Kigen Nisen Roppyakunen Hōshuku Kaigai Dōhō Tokyo Taikai hōkokusho* (Tokyo: Kaigai Dōhō Chūōkai, 1941), 80–96 (hereafter *Hōkokusho*); and Yuji Ichioka, "Japanese Immigrant Nationalism: The Issei and the Sino-Japanese War, 1937–1941," *California History* 69 (Fall 1990): 269–271. On the activity of the Hawaiian delegation in Tokyo, see John J. Stephan, *Hawaii under the Rising Sun: Japan's Plans for Conquest after Pearl Harbor* (Honolulu: University of Hawaii Press, 1984), 48–53.

55. Kaigai Dōhō Chūōkai, *Hōkokusho*, 2–3, 6.

56. See Eiichiro Azuma, "Interstitial Lives: Race, Community, and History among Japanese Immigrants Caught between Japan and the United States, 1885–1941" (Ph.D. diss., University of California, Los Angeles, 2000), 214–216, 219–220.

57. Ichioka, "Japanese Immigrant Nationalism," 273.

58. *Rafu Shimpō*, November 2, 1940; *Nichibei Shimbun*, November 12, 15, 1940; *Yomiuri Shimbun*, November 3, 1940; *Tokyo Nichi Nichi Shinbun*, November 11, 1940; and Zaibei Nihonjinkai, *Zaibei Nihonjinshi*, 1295. See also Ichioka, "Japanese Immigrant Nationalism," 271, 273. A total of fifty-eight leading Issei men in the U.S. mainland were awarded with a commemorative wooden *sake* cup and a letter of appreciation signed by the foreign minister; four men were separately decorated with prestigious medals for their service and dedication to Japan's overseas development.

59. *Rafu Shimpō*, November 10, 1940.

60. See, for example, Washizu, *Zaibei Nihonjin shikan*, 137–138. On the multilayered racial hierarchy in California and how minorities lived there under white supremacy, see Tomás Almaguer, *Racial Fault Lines: The Historical Origins of White Supremacy in California* (Berkeley: University of California Press, 1994), 1–16; and Michael Omi and Howard Winant, *Racial Formation in the United States: From the 1960s to the 1990s* (New York: Routledge, 1994).

CHAPTER 5

1. A prominent Issei educator in southern California reported to the state's educational officials that it was a long-standing policy to teach Nisei children about their parents' "racial contributions," including "the history of the immigrant Japanese and their pioneer work in America" and "their contribution to the building of America." See "A Resume of the Activities of the Revisory-Editorial Committee of 'the Japanese Reader' Now Being Revised for the Japanese Language School Federation of America" (hereafter "A Resume"), n.d., LANI, JANM.

2. *Shin Sekai*, May 21, 1936.

3. See Zaibei Nihonjinkai, *Zaibei Nihonjinshi* (San Francisco: Zaibei Nihonjinkai, 1940), 1106–1109. Jere Takahashi examines some of the key challenges from the contemporary perspective of Nisei youths. Jere Takahashi, *Nisei/Sansei: Shifting Japanese American Identities and Politics* (Philadelphia, Pa.: Temple University Press, 1997), 35–46.

4. Henry Yu, *Thinking Orientals: Migration, Contact, and Exoticism in Modern America* (New York: Oxford University Press, 2001), 108–123, esp. 109. For a good example of a sociological study dealing with the Nisei problem, see Edward K. Strong, Jr., *The Second-Generation Japanese Problem* (Stanford, Calif.: Stanford University Press, 1934). The Japanese Association of America and Japanese American Citizens League leaders rendered full support to Strong's massive project, which surveyed 10 percent of the Japanese population in California and produced four book-length studies.

5. See, for example, Nichibei Shimbunsha, *Nichibei taikan* (San Francisco: Nichibei Shimbunsha, 1931), 553–573, esp. 553.

6. Zaibei Nihonjinkai, *Zaibei Nihonjinshi*, 130.

7. Ibid., 200; see also U.S. House of Representatives, *Hearings before the Select Committee Investigating National Defense Migration*, pt. 31, *Los Angeles and San Francisco Hearings* (Washington, D.C.: GPO, 1942), 11672–11673.

8. Michael Omi and Howard Winant call this niche an "internal society," which they describe as "an alternative to [the] repressive social system." Michael Omi and Howard Winant, *Racial Formation in the United States: From the 1960s to the 1990s* (New York: Routledge, 1994), 81. On the nature of Japanese immigrant farming, see John Modell, *The Economics and Politics of Racial Accommodation: The Japanese of Los Angeles, 1900–1942* (Urbana: University of Illinois Press, 1977), 96, 106–107.

9. *Kashū Mainichi*, December 4, 1934 (English section), November 15, 1935; and *Rafu Shimpō*, August 27, November 16, 1935. The quote is taken from the first source. See also Edward K. Strong, Jr., *Japanese in California* (Stanford, Calif.: Stanford University Press, 1933), 98–100, 107–108; and Hachirō Shishimoto, *Nikkei Shimin o kataru* (Tokyo: Shōkasha, 1934), 122–127.

10. *Kashū Mainichi*, December 4, 1934 (English section). As the Back-to-the-Farm movement was a statewide program to defend the principal industry of Japanese America, there were also smaller-scale, more localized campaigns to shield other ethnic niches. The origin of Los Angeles's Nisei Week lay in Issei merchants' attempt to bring back Nisei consumers to Little Tokyo businesses from mainstream department stores. The underlying concern was the survival of ethnic retail businesses and Little Tokyo itself, because the enclave depended on Japanese commerce. See Lon Kurashige, "The Problem of Biculturalism: Japanese American Identity and Festival before World War II," *Journal of American History* 86 (March 2000): 1632–1654.

11. *Nichibei Shimbun*, January 1, 1933; and *Rafu Shimpō*, December 1, 1935 (English section). Eileen H. Tamura explains that Issei leaders in Hawaii carried out a similar movement, called the Back-to-the-Plantations campaign, which advocated the return of the second generation to sugar plantation work. What made this campaign unique was that, unlike their mainland counterparts, Hawaii's white elites wholeheartedly supported Japanese labor in agriculture, probably because it had far greater bearing on the local economy. There were not enough replacements for Japanese labor on the sugar plantations should a large number of

them move into other occupations. Hiromi Monobe's recent study unveils a more complex picture of Hawaii Issei's campaign, which began in the mid-1920s with the call for Nisei's involvement in independent farming instead of plantation labor. That position transformed into what Tamura characterizes as accommodationist by the early 1930s, since key Japanese leaders in the islands came to see a diminishing chance for Nisei land ownership and farming in the context of the Depression and legal discrimination. For more detail, see Eileen H. Tamura, *Americanization, Acculturation, and Ethnic Identity: The Nisei Generation in Hawaii* (Urbana: University of Illinois Press, 1994), 129–132; and Hiromi Monobe, "Shaping an Ethnic Leadership: Takie Okumura and the 'Americanization' of the Nisei in Hawaii, 1919–1945" (Ph.D. diss., University of Hawaii, 2004), 107–175.

12. Shakuma Washizu, *Zaibei Nihonjin shikan* (Los Angeles: Rafu Shimposha, 1930), 137–138. See also *Kashū Mainichi*, March 22, 1933; and *Shin Sekai*, September 30, 1932.

13. *Shin Sekai*, June 10, July 22, 1935; and *Nichibei Shimbun*, July 15, 1935, January 1, 1936, January 1, 1938.

14. *Kashū Mainichi*, November 15, 16, 18, 1935. See also *Rafu Shimpō*, December 1, 1935 (English section).

15. *Kashū Mainichi*, December 14, 1935 (English section); and *Rafu Shimpō*, December 14, 1935 (English section).

16. *Rafu Shimpō*, January 10, 1937; and *Shin Sekai*, July 16, 20, 1937.

17. See *Shin Sekai*, June 26, July 20, 1937.

18. *Rafu Shimpō*, June 17, 23, 26, 1939; and *Shin Sekai*, September 4, 1939.

19. *Rafu Shimpō*, April 27, 1940. Also *Kashū Mainichi*, April 26, 29, 1940 (English section); and *Nichibei Shimbun*, May 1, 1940 (English section).

20. Zaibei Nihonjinkai, *Zaibei Nihonjinshi*, 1127.

21. Noson Seinen Taikai (Second Generation Conference on Agricultural Problems) files, in box 8, folder 19, NAJA, UAUW.

22. U.S. House of Representatives, *Hearings*, 11671–11672.

23. On how Issei farmers relied on their own countrymen, see U.S. Immigration Commission, *Immigrants in Industries*, vol. 24, pt. 25, *Japanese and Other Immigrant Races in the Pacific Coast and Rocky Mountain States* (Washington, D.C.: GPO, 1911), 360, 372. Sucheng Chan examines the ways in which Chinese immigrants in the late nineteenth century capitalized on group labor in agriculture— the scheme that the Issei later employed. Sucheng Chan, *This Bittersweet Soil: The Chinese in California Agriculture, 1860–1910* (Berkeley: University of California Press, 1986).

24. The Japanese of the Sacramento–San Joaquin delta tried their hands at a similar program as early as 1930. At first, the Kibei campaign aroused only limited interest in the farming districts where the dwindling of the Japanese labor force after immigration exclusion was acutely felt in the local economy. See *Nichibei Shimbun*, February 4, 1932; and KNK 5, January 10, 1932, January 15, 1933, in box 242, JARP. General descriptions of the Kibei campaign can be found in Yama-

shita Sōen, *Nichibei o tsunagu mono* (Tokyo: Bunseisha, 1938), 186–200; and Shishimoto, *Nikkei Shimin o kataru*, 44–46.

25. KNK 5, July 21, 1935; and *Nichibei Shimbun*, July 24, 1935.

26. *Rafu Shimpō*, September 5, 13, 1935, March 25, 1936; *Shin Sekai*, November 22, 1936; *Kashū Mainichi*, March 30, 1937; *Nichibei Shimbun*, October 25, 1935; and Tomii to Hirota, February 6, 1936, NGKZ, DRO.

27. *Rafu Shimpō*, March 25, 1936. See also Tsunegorō Hirohata, *Zaibei Fukuoka kenjin to jigyō* (Los Angeles: Zaibei Fukuoka kenjin to Jigyō Hensan Jimusho, 1936), 67–72.

28. *Kashū Mainichi*, May 1, 1936; *Rafu Shimpō*, May 19, 1936 (English section); and *Nichibei Shimbun*, May 28, June 3, 1936.

29. *Nichibei Shimbun*, May 19, 1936 (English section).

30. *Miyako Shinbun*, May 1, 1936; and *Yomiuri Shinbun*, May 1, 1936.

31. *Nichibei Shimbun*, February 1, March 14, August 5, 1936; and *Shin Sekai*, December 4, 1936.

32. *Rafu Shimpō*, August 28, 1936; Yamashita, *Nichibei o tsunagu mono*, 195–196; and Fumiko Fukuda, "Mutual Life and Aid among the Japanese in Southern California with Special Reference to Los Angeles" (M.A. thesis, University of Southern California, 1937), 25.

33. *Shin Sekai*, August 27, 1938; and KNK 5, January 12, 1936, January 17, 1937, January 9, 1938.

34. *Shin Sekai*, September 12, 1938. See also Shishimoto, *Nikkei Shimin o kataru*, 133–137; and Yamashita, *Nichibei o tsunagu mono*, 193–195.

35. *Rafu Shimpō*, February 27, 1937; and KNK 5, July 21, 1935. In Walnut Grove, the local Japanese association secretary played the matchmaking role for eighteen Nisei couples between 1938 and 1940.

36. On the reaction of Tokyo and exclusionists in California, see Tomii to Hirota, February 6, 1936, NGKZ; California Joint Immigration Committee, May 27, June 12, 1936, NGKZ; and *Nichibei Shimbun*, June 10, 12, 1936 (English section). On Nisei leaders' views, see Sakamoto to Imazeki, September 21, 1935; Murayama to Sakamoto, c. 1936; and Murata to Sakamoto, March 11, 1937, in boxes 3, 2, 17, respectively, JYSP, UAUW.

37. *Shin Sekai*, October 17, 1936; and *Nichibei Shimbun*, November 30, 1939.

38. Yuji Ichioka, *The Issei: The World of the First Generation Japanese Immigrants, 1885–1924* (New York: Free Press, 1988), 207–210. See also Toyotomi Morimoto, *Japanese Americans and Cultural Continuity: Maintaining Language and Heritage* (New York: Garland, 1997), 35–54. In Seattle, the Japanese of the Pacific Northwest compiled their own textbooks in 1921.

39. Ōhashi Chūichi, "Dōhō Kokugo Gakkō hantairon," *Shin Sekai*, May 24, 1925. His articles ran between May 24 and 28. They also appeared in the *Taihoku Nippō* and the *Hokubei Jiji*, both published in Seattle. Concerned about the negative influence of the immigration question on U.S.–Japan relations, Ōhashi preached to Japanese residents about "permanent residence" and complete "assi-

milationism," which he hoped would relieve him and other diplomats from spending time on "trivial" immigrant matters.

40. *Taihoku Nippō*, June 1–3, 15–27, 1925; *Shin Sekai*, May 29–June 2, 15–21, 1925. See also *Shin Sekai*, June 3–11, 13–14, 1925.

41. *Nichibei Shimbun*, June 1, 1925; and *Rafu Shimpō*, June 5, 1925.

42. See Ōhashi, "Dōhō Kokugo Gakkō hantairon"; Naoki Oka, "Nao imada sakan ni rongichū no Dai-Nisei no kyōiku mondai," *Shin Sekai*, August 13, 1928; and *Taihoku Nippō*, June 23, 1925. On Ōhashi's argument and Issei reactions, see Yuji Ichioka, "The Education of the Second Generation," unpublished article, 1–12. Courtesy of Professor Ichioka.

43. See *Taihoku Nippō*, June 17–18, 20, 1925; and *Shin Sekai*, June 1, 6, 13, 1925.

44. Oka, "Nao imada sakan ni rongichū."

45. *Shin Sekai*, August 21, 1928; and *Nichibei Shimbun*, August 21, 30, 1928.

46. On the impact of the Fukunaga case on Hawaii's Japanese community, see Tamura, *Americanization*, 81–83; Dennis M. Ogawa, *Jan Ken Po: The World of Hawaii's Japanese Americans* (Honolulu: Japanese American Research Center, 1973), 113–149; and Ronald Kotani, *The Japanese in Hawaii: A Century of Struggle* (Honolulu: Hawaii Hochi, 1985), 65–71.

47. *Nichibei Shimbun*, September 30, 1928.

48. *Rafu Shimpō*, September 26, 27, 1928; and *Nichibei Shimbun*, September 25, 1928. See also Ichioka, "The Education of the Second Generation," 23.

49. *Kashū Mainichi*, October 28, 1932.

50. *Nichibei Shimbun*, November 4, 1935 (English section). See also *Shin Sekai*, February 17, 1940; and *Rafu Shimpō*, February 25, 1941. On Nisei crimes, see Strong, *The Second-Generation Japanese Problem*, 177–180; Shishimoto, *Nikkei Shimin o kataru*, 214–222; and Isami Arifuku Waugh, "Hidden Crime and Deviance in the Japanese-American Community, 1920–1946" (Ph.D. diss., University of California, Berkeley, 1978).

51. A. P. Le Grand, "General Japanese Intelligence Survey in the Portland Division," 11–12, January 7, 1941, in box 566, MIDC, RG 165, NACP.

52. *Nichibei Shimbun*, August 27, 1934. On the significance of family education, see Kan'ichi Niisato, *Iminchi aiwa: Dai-Nisei hen* (Tokyo: Shimpōsha, 1934); and Yaemitsu Sugimachi, *Katei shakaigaku* (Los Angeles: Taishūsha, 1935). On the need for moral education, see Yūsen Kawamura, *Hainichi sensen o toppa shitsutsu* (Isleton, Calif.: Privately printed, 1930), 264–265; and *Nichibei Shimbun*, October 6, 26, 1928.

53. Hokka Nihongo Gakuen Kyōkai, *Beikoku Kashū Nihongo Gakuen enkakushi* (San Francisco: Hokka Nihongo Gakuen Kyōkai, 1930), 311.

54. *Rafu Shimpō*, September 28, 1928; Hokka Nihongo Gakuen Kyōkai, *Beikoku Kashū Nihongo*, 345–346; and Beikoku Seihokubu Renraku Nihonjinkai, "Dai-nikai Bei-Ka Nihongo Gakkō kyōiku kondankai," n.p., August 18, 1930, JANA, UAUW.

55. *Nichibei Shimbun*, October 6, 26, 1928; *Shin Sekai*, October 17, 1928; and *Rafu Shimpō*, October 8, 1928.

56. Hokka Nihongo Gakuen Kyōkai, *Beikoku Kashū Nihongo*, 144–147; and Nanka Nihongo Gakuen Kyōkai, *Kyōju to keiei* (Los Angeles: Nanka Nihongo Gakuen Kyōkai, 1932), 6–7.

57. Shimano to Waterman, n.d.; and "A Resume," 3, LANI. Issei educators of California did publish the "revisions" of the state-approved textbooks between 1928 and 1938. However, a careful comparison between the original and the revised versions reveals no substantial changes in content. Likewise, the Washington versions underwent revision in 1928, but the changes were limited to replacing old-style Chinese characters and *kana* letters with newer, more simplified ones. Although a few new chapters were added, the overall contents of the Washington textbooks remained almost identical. On the Washington case, see Sakaguchi Mitsuhiro, "Nihonjin imin to Kokugo kyōiku," *Shisō* 55 (March 1998): 31–34.

58. Hori to Hirota, June 15, 1935, NGCI, DRO; and Sakaguchi, "Nihonjin imin," 37.

59. Tomii to Hirota, June 18, 1935, NGCI.

60. Representatives of the Japanese Language Schools Federation of Southern California, c. January 1942, LANI; and Nanka Nihongo Gakuen Kyōkai, *Kyōju to keiei*, 5–6. The quote is taken from the first source.

61. See Kan'ichi Niisato, *Zaibei no Nihon minzoku gohyakunen no taikei* (Tokyo: Shimpōsha, 1939), 43, 58; *Shin Sekai*, September 30, 1932; *Kashū Mainichi*, April 10, 1932; and *Nichibei Shimbun*, November 21, 1940. To foster racial consciousness among the Nisei, many Issei took advantage of the 1932 Los Angeles Olympics, where Japanese athletes had competed well. Community newspapers were full of nationalistic praise for the athletes, relating their superior performances to their racial heritage. Just as these Japanese had outdone white Americans and other competitors, the Nisei were reminded that they could excel in a multiracial society. See Eiichiro Azuma, "Interstitial Lives: Race, Community, and History among Japanese Immigrants Caught between Japan and the United States, 1885–1941" (Ph.D. diss., University of California, Los Angeles, 2000), 253–256; and Eriko Yamamoto, "Cheers for Japanese Athletes: The 1932 Los Angeles Olympics and the Japanese American Community," *Pacific Historical Review* 69 (August 2000): 399–430.

62. Beikoku Seihokubu Renraku Nihonjinkai, "Dai-nikai Bei-Ka Nihongo Gakkō kyōiku kondankai," n.p. The quote is taken from the statement by Raikaku Nakagawa. See also Takashi Terami, "Dai-Nisei no shimei," *Nichibei Shimbun*, June 22–24, 26–28, 1933.

63. "A Resume," 1–2. This line of thinking also provoked Issei interest in Japanese martial arts as a means of Nisei education. Not only would these traditional "sports," such as *jūdō* and *kendō*, keep youths away from undesirable activities, they would steer the boys and girls toward "exploring the spiritual aspect of Japanese life" in a most practical way. *Kashū Mainichi*, March 25, 1932; Azuma, "Interstitial Lives," 264–268; and Eiichiro Azuma, "Social History of Kendo and Sumo in Japanese America," in *More than a Game: Sport in the Japanese Ameri-*

can Community, ed. Brian Niiya (Los Angeles: Japanese American National Museum, 2000), 78–91.

64. Natori Jun'ichi, "Nikkei Dai-Nisei no shisō to Nippon seishin (2)," *Shin Sekai*, October 24, 1939.

65. On the orthodox Japanese interpretations of *Nippon seishin*, see Kyōiku Shiryō Hensanbu, *Nippon seishin kōwa* (Tokyo: Dai-Ichi Shuppan Kyōkai, 1933), esp. 1–12, 218–221; and Chigaku Tanaka, *What Is Nippon Kokutai? Introduction to Nipponese National Principles* (Tokyo: Shishio Bunko, 1937), esp. 12–23. On the divergence between the Issei and the intellectuals of Japan, see also Eiichiro Azuma, " 'The Pacific Era Has Arrived': Transnational Education among Japanese Americans, 1932–1941," *History of Education Quarterly* 43 (Spring 2003): 66–68.

66. The general absence of statist ideas in the Issei's public discourse does not preclude their ambiguity, multiplicity, and inner contradictions. Some immigrants also appear to have discretely kept their statist inclination to themselves for fear of an exclusionist backlash. See, for example, *Kashū Mainichi*, February 11, 1933; and Shusui Murakami, "Dai-Nisei kyōikuron," *Rafu Shimpō*, April 3–13, 17–20, 1938.

67. R. L. Flanders, "General Japanese Intelligence Survey, Seattle Field Division," 16–17, January 14, 1941, in box 566, MIDC.

68. *Kashū Mainichi*, October 14, 1938. See also ibid., October 28, 1938; *Nichibei Shimbun*, August 31, 1934; *Shin Sekai*, December 2, 1935; *Rafu Shimpō*, March 25, 1938. Fujii and others often used the terms *Nippon seishin*, *Yamato damashii* (Yamato spirit), and *bushidō* (way of warrior) interchangeably.

69. "A Resume," 2.

70. Takeshi Ban, "My Message" (bookmark), RTBF, JANM.

71. Inazo Nitobe, *Bushido: The Soul of Japan* (1905; reprint, Tokyo: Kenkyōsha, 1936), 176. On Nitobe's internationalism, consult Sharlie C. Ushioda, "Man of Two Worlds: An Inquiry into the Value System of Inazo Nitobe (1862–1933)," in *East across the Pacific: Historical and Sociological Studies of Japanese Immigration and Assimilation*, ed. Hilary Conroy and T. Scott Miyakawa (Santa Barbara, Calif.: ABC-Clio, 1972), 187–210.

72. Nitobe, *Bushido*, 88–91.

73. Ibid., 88.

74. See Niisato, *Zaibei no Nihon minzoku gohyakunen no taikei*, 33–35; Hirozumi Ashizawa, *Nippon seishin to jinbutsu yōsei* (Tokyo: Hokubei Butokukai Kōdō Gakuin, 1938), 405–409; *Kashū Mainichi*, October 22, 23, 1935; and *Shin Sekai*, June 24, 1939.

75. Kinya Okajima, "Bushido and Modern Japan," in *Ōka Nikkei Shimin shashin*, ed. Sōsuke Kawai (Tacoma, Wash.: Takoma Shūhōsha, 1938), 28 (English section).

76. On this, see Shurei Hirose, *Zaibei Kōshūjin funtō gojūnenshi* (Los Angeles: Nanka Yamanashi Kaigai Kyōkai, 1934), 136–137; *Kashū Mainichi*, October 23, 1935; *Shin Sekai*, January 1, 1939; and *Nichibei Shimbun*, August 31, 1934.

77. See C. S. Miyazaki, "To Our American Sons and Daughters," in *Ōka Nikkei Shimin shashin*, 62–63 (English section).
78. Sakamoto to Imazeki, January 23, 1933, in box 19, JYSP. On Sakamoto's idea of loyalty, see Yuji Ichioka, "A Study in Dualism: James Yoshinori Sakamoto and the *Japanese American Courier*, 1928–1942," *Amerasia Journal* 13 (1986–1987): 63.
79. *Nichibei Shimbun*, December 5, 1935. See also J.B.W. Waller, "Japanese Language Schools in the United States and the Territory of Hawaii," 1–2, February 4, 1942, in box 3, ODONI, RG 38, NACP.
80. See *Dōhō*, March 20, April 30, 1938, January 15, 1939, March 1, 1941 (English section), October 25, 1941.
81. "Monthly Intelligence Report for June 1940," 2, July 1, 1940, in box 3720, MIDC.
82. *Kashū Mainichi*, May 5, 1934. Nisei compositions sometimes revealed what they were likely taught about the Japanese emperor during the 1930s. A poignant example is the expression of some Nisei's pride in their racial blood, which supposedly originated from the first emperor. Since Issei educators often guided their pupils' hands in writing such pieces, however, it is no exaggeration to say that these essays reflected Issei's views more than Nisei's. For samples of nationalistic Nisei essays, see Rafu Shimpōsha, *Hōshuku kinen taikan* (Los Angeles: Rafu Shimpōsha, 1940), 28–56; and Kōshirō Endō, *Tsuzurikata bunshū: Shina Jihen-gō* (Compton, Calif.: Compton Gakuen, 1938).

CHAPTER 6

1. Goro Murata, "Nisei in Nippon," *Kashū Mainichi*, March 31, 1940 (English section).
2. The extent to which these American-born children might have become assimilated into Japanese society can be conjectured by the fact that the estimated numbers of the Nisei in Japan varied so widely. My estimation of the assimilated American-born in Japan is based on the figures most commonly found (15,000 to 40,000) in the mid-1930s, with the subtraction of 4,000 to 5,000 Nisei *ryūgakusei* and employed individuals. See Yamashita Sōen, *Nichibei o tsunagu mono* (Tokyo: Bunseisha, 1938), 144, 204; and Yuji Ichioka, "Beyond National Boundaries: The Complexity of Japanese-American History," *Amerasia Journal* 23 (Winter 1997–1998): viii.
3. Tally made by the author from 1933 reports on the population of the American-born Japanese, NGKZ, DRO.
4. Reportedly, in 1935, no more than 600 Nisei were employed in Japan with about half residing in Tokyo. See Yamashita Sōen, *Nikkei Shimin no Nihon ryūgaku jijō* (Tokyo: Bunseidō, 1935), 303–346; Hachirō Shishimoto, *Nikkei Shimin o kataru* (Tokyo: Shōkasha, 1934), 176–177, 184–188; *Nichibei Shimbun*, August 18, 23, 1939 (English section); and John J. Stephan, "Hijacked by Utopia: American Nikkei in Manchuria," *Amerasia Journal* 23 (Winter 1997–1998): 1–42.

5. Shibata to Sakamoto, October 4, 1932, in box 18, JYSP, UAUW. On the impact of occupational racism, see John Modell, *The Economics and Politics of Racial Accommodation: The Japanese of Los Angeles, 1900–1942* (Urbana: University of Illinois Press, 1977), 127–153; and Jere Takahashi, *Nisei/Sansei: Shifting Japanese American Identities and Politics* (Philadelphia, Pa.: Temple University Press, 1997), 37–42. Chinese Americans similarly crossed the Pacific for better occupational opportunities in their ancestral land. Unlike their Nisei counterparts, this group did not seem to have included a significant number of students. See Gloria H. Chun, "Go West . . . to China: Chinese American Identity in the 1930s," in *Claiming America: Constructing Chinese American Identities during the Exclusion Era*, ed. K. Scott Wong and Sucheng Chan (Philadelphia, Pa.: Temple University Press, 1998), 170–180.

6. Wallace S. Wharton, "Japanese Activities," October 6, 1933, in box 227, SCAC, RG 38, NACP.

7. A reliable source estimated approximately 3,700 Nisei students in Japanese secondary education and above in 1936. Some 1,700 of them were *ryūgakusei*, who had come to Japan alone in pursuit of education, and the rest lived with their extended families or relatives in Japan. Tokyo was the temporary home for about 700 students, whereas other parts of Japan accommodated 3,000. See Yamashita, *Nichibei o tsunagu mono*, 177–178, 319–332. For a list of such schools, see ibid., 321–328; and Nisei Survey Committee, *The Nisei: A Survey of Their Educational, Vocational, and Social Problems* (Tokyo: Keisen Girls' School, 1939), 53–55.

8. Yamashita, *Nikkei Shimin no Nihon ryūgaku jijō*, 4–8. Computation by the author.

9. See ibid., 8–18; Tsunemitsu Kōnen, *Nihon ryūgaku no jissai* (Tokyo: Runbini Shuppansha, 1936), 21–22; and Toyotomi Morimoto, *Japanese Americans and Cultural Continuity: Maintaining Language and Heritage* (New York: Garland, 1997), 88–92.

10. Akira Iriye, *Cultural Internationalism and World Order* (Baltimore, Md.: Johns Hopkins University Press, 1997), 91, also 119–125. Iriye argues that cultural internationalism was increasingly overpowered by "exclusionary nationalism, racism, aggression, and mass murder [militarism]" during the 1930s. Here, and throughout this chapter, I use the term *internationalism* according to the common usage in diplomatic history. The term is to be distinguished from the notion of *transnationalism*. Internationalism focuses on the relations between two nation-states, while transnationalism illuminates the agency, imagination, and practice of immigrants relative to them.

11. Shishimoto, *Nikkei Shimin o kataru*, 253–266, 275–282; Shin'ichirō Hasegawa, *Zaibei Nihonjin no mita Beikoku to Beikokujin* (Tokyo: Jitsugyō no Nihonsha, 1937), 4–14, 39–48; and Morimoto, *Japanese Americans and Cultural Continuity*, 59, 67–72.

12. Yuji Ichioka, "Kengakudan: The Origin of Nisei Study Tours of Japan," *California History* 73 (Spring 1994): 34–39.

13. Roy Hidemichi Akagi, *The Second Generation Problem: Some Suggestions toward Its Solution* (New York: Japanese Student Christian Association, 1926), 37. On the JSCA, see David K. Yoo, *Growing Up Nisei: Race, Generation, and Culture among Japanese Americans of California, 1924–1949* (Urbana: University of Illinois Press, 2000), 59–63.

14. Yuji Ichioka, "A Study in Dualism: James Yoshinori Sakamoto and the *Japanese American Courier*, 1928–1942," *Amerasia Journal* 13 (1986–1987): 49–81; and also Takahashi, *Nisei/Sansei*, 49–53.

15. See Yamashita, *Nikkei Shimin no Nihon ryūgaku jijō*, 2–4.

16. Tsunemitsu, *Nihon ryūgaku no jissai*, 147–149; Nihon Beifu Kyōkai, *Dai-Nisei to kokuseki mondai* (Tokyo: Nihon Beifu Kyōkai, 1938), 46–51, in box 362, JARP; and Hōkō Terakawa, *Hokubei kaikyō enkakushi* (San Francisco: Hongwanji Hokubei Kaikyō Honbu, 1936), 556.

17. Richard F. Boyce, "Second-Generation Japanese Program," 23–24, September 20, 1935, RUSD, RG 59, NACP.

18. Tsunemitsu Kōnen, "Amerika o megurite," 1–5, *Rafu Shimpō*, February 22–25, 1937. His attempt to stay tuned translated into frequent visits to the United States—a rare practice among Japanese "experts" in Nisei education. In 1933, 1935, and 1937, Tsunemitsu spent three to six months each year in the immigrant society, meeting with Issei educators and parents to gather their views of his school's operation.

19. Nihon Beifu Kyōkai, *Nihon ryūgaku no atarashii hōhō* (Tokyo: Nihon Beifu Kyōkai, 1938), 9–44, in box 362, JARP; and *Nichibei Shimbun*, February 26, 1937.

20. Nihon Beifu Kyōkai, *Nihon ryūgaku no atarashiki hōhō*, 15–16, 21–23, 37–38; and *Shin Sekai*, September 25, 1939, July 28–29, 1940.

21. Nihon Beifu Kyōkai, *Nihon ryūgaku no atarashiki hōhō*, 17.

22. Michi Kawai, *My Lantern* (Tokyo: Kyōbunkan, 1939), 91, 199. See also Kawai, "Kami to tomoni hataraku warera," *Keisen* 46 (January 1937): 1, KWCA.

23. Kawai, *My Lantern*, 200, 206.

24. Kikuchi to Wilson, January 13, 1968, 4, in folder 13, box 160, JARP.

25. Nisei Survey Committee, *Nisei*, 3, 45.

26. Tsuyuko Kimura, "Ninenkan o kaerimite," *Keisen* 74 (July 1939): 4, KWCA.

27. "Dai-Nisei no tokubetsu kōza," *Keisen* 31 (October 1935): 1, KWCA; and Nakajima Naoto, "Dai-Nisei ryūgakusei no nayami," *Kaizō* 18 (August 1936): 18.

28. *Shin Sekai*, January 27, 1932, September 11, 1934; *Nichibei Shimbun*, August 6, 1934; and *Rafu Shimpō*, February 26, 1935. See also Brian M. Hayashi, *"For the Sake of Our Japanese Brethren": Assimilation, Nationalism, and Protestantism among the Japanese of Los Angeles, 1895–1942* (Stanford, Calif.: Stanford University Press, 1995), 119.

29. Graduating Class, *Japanese Cooking and Etiquette* (Tokyo: Keisen Girls' School, 1941).

30. Sadako Nagasaki, "A Nisei Philosophy," *Keisen News* 14 (July 1938): 3, KWCA.

31. Horace M. Kallen coined the term *cultural pluralism* in 1924. On "the battles between the assimilationist and the pluralist perspectives" around World War I, see Werner Sollors, "Foreword: Theories of Ethnicity," in *Theories of Ethnicity: A Classical Reader*, ed. Werner Sollors (New York: New York University Press, 1996), xxvi–xxvii. Milton Gordon defines cultural pluralism as a variation of assimilationist theories, for it tends not to challenge the centrality of Anglo sociopolitical institutions in American life. Milton Gordon, *Assimilation in American Life* (Oxford: Oxford University Press, 1964), 60–83.

32. Nisei Survey Committee, *Nisei*, 43–44.

33. Kimura, "Ninenkan o kaerimite," 4.

34. Keisen Jo Gakuen, *Gojūnen no ayumi* (Tokyo: Keisen Jo Gakuen, 1979), 159.

35. See, for example, Inazo Nitobe, "The Japanese Nation: Its Land, Its People, and Its Life," *Nitobe Inazō zenshū* (Tokyo: Kyōbunkan, 1969), 13:26–27, 32; *Kashū Mainichi*, January 1, 1933; *Japanese American Courier*, January 21, 1933; and Ryūkichi Kihara, *Hawai Nihonjinshi* (Tokyo: Bunseisha, 1935), 826–827.

36. Ichioka, "A Study in Dualism," 58–59, and "Kengakudan," 42.

37. Division of Far Eastern Affairs, Memorandom, March 25, 1940, RUSDS, RG 59, NACP. During the 1930s, Japanese diplomats on the West Coast employed several Nisei for the purposes mentioned by the American diplomat. In Seattle, the local consulate kept one full-time Nisei press attaché throughout the decade. A veteran journalist, Bill Hosokawa worked in that capacity for a few years in the mid-1930s before being recruited for work in Singapore as the chief editor of an English-language propaganda paper subsidized by the Japanese foreign office. See ZKSC, DRO; Okamoto to Arita, 6–8, 10–11, August 14, 1936, RKKZ 2, DRO; and Hosokawa to Sakamoto, c. 1939, in box 17, JYSP.

38. See Ōtsuka Kō, *Ishokumin to kyōiku mondai* (Tokyo: Tōkō Shoin, 1933); and Kojima Masaru, *Zaigai shitei kyōikuron no keifu* (Kyoto: Ryūkoku Gakkai, 1993). The involvement of the state in the education of foreign-born Japanese was extensive in the regions outside North America and Europe, since Japanese officials felt less concerned about the diplomatic ramifications of such actions, which could register as violating the rights of other sovereign states. Yet, insofar as the American Nisei stayed within the reach of its state power and institutions, Tokyo was not as inhibited. Indeed, the *ryūgakusei* were easy prey to Japan's educational manipulations, which were not possible if they were in the United States.

39. Sano Yasutarō, "Kaigai ni okeru kokugo kyōiku," *Iwanami kōza: Kokugo kyōiku* (Tokyo: Iwanami Shoten, 1936), 17–18, 20; Kojima Ken, "Zaigai Hōjin Dai-Nisei mondai no tenbō," in *Zaigai Hōjin Dai-Nisei mondai*, ed. Aoyagi Ikutarō (Tokyo: Imin Mondai Kenkyūkai, 1940), 2–5, 14, 18–19; and Satō Masashi, ed., *Kaigai Nisei kyōiku no taiken o kataru* (Tokyo: Kaigai Kyōiku Kyōkai, 1933), 1–2. It appears that leaders of Nazi Germany and fascist Italy had similarly contemplated the political use of German and Italian Americans through heritage learning. According to a study on the German-American Bund, the Nazi government annually sponsored selected members of the Bund's youth auxiliaries to receive six-week-long courses on National Socialism and anti-Semitism along with a host of

other politicocultural activities. Italy, too, hosted summer camps for Italian-American youngsters during the 1930s. See Susan Canedy, *America's Nazis, a Democratic Dilemma: A History of the German American Bund* (Menlo Park, Calif.: Markgraf, 1990), 99; and Dino Cinel, *From Italy to San Francisco: The Immigrant Experience* (Stanford, Calif.: Stanford University Press, 1982), 252–253.

40. Kojima, "Zaigai Hōjin Dai-Nisei mondai no tenbō," 4–5, 13, 18–20.

41. *Japanese American Courier*, January 1, 1939. See also *Nichibei Shimbun*, October 25, 1931; *Shin Sekai*, November 27, 1932, April 15, 1933; *Rafu Shimpō*, January 1, 1932 (English section); and *Kashū Mainichi*, June 4, 1933 (English section).

42. For a typical "blood will tell" argument, see Tsutsumi Fujio, "Sonchō subeki Hokubei Dai-Nisei no tokken," in *Bimyō naru kagi no shoyūsha* (Tokyo: Kō-A Kokusai Kyōkai, 1939), 32–35.

43. "Gaikokujin jidō no shōgakkō nyūgaku toriatsukaikata," 130, July 18, 1935; "Nikkei Beijin chūgakkō, kōtō jogakkō-tō nyūgaku toriatsukaikata," 463, February 19, 1935; and "Migi fūtsū gakumukyoku kaitō," 6, February 26, 1935, all in GSS, NAJ.

44. Eiichiro Azuma, "Interstitial Lives: Race, Community, and History among Japanese Immigrants Caught between Japan and the United States, 1885–1941" (Ph.D. diss., University of California, Los Angeles, 2000), 287–288.

45. Statistics from "The Institute's World," *International Youth* 1:1 (December 1938): 82; and Jun'ichi Natori, "Waseda International Institute and Its Educational Ideal," *International Youth* 1:3 (February 1941): 21, WUHA.

46. Natori, "Waseda International Institute and Its Educational Ideal," 21.

47. *Shin Sekai*, May 16, 1935; "Waseda Kokusai Gakuin ni tsuite," *Rikkō Sekai* 375 (March 1936): 28–32; and "Waseda Kokusai Gakuin narabi ni Keiei Kōgakubu setsuritsu keikaku," *Waseda Daigaku-shi kiyō* 14 (July 1981): 161–162, 166–167.

48. Natori, "Waseda International Institute and Its Educational Ideal," 22.

49. Richard F. Boyce, "American Citizens of Japanese Race Residing in Japan," 11, January 29, 1940, RUSDS.

50. Kay Tateishi, "A Typical Nisei," *Amerasia Journal* 23 (Winter 1997–1998): 203; *Heishikan News* 1 (August 10, 1940): 1, in Heishikan collection, JOMM, Yokohama; and Tamotsu Murayama, "Rajio Puresu (RP) no tanjō to sono ayunda michi," c. 1960s, 5–6, in Tamotsu Murayama file, *Pacific Citizen*, Los Angeles. Courtesy of Professor Yuji Ichioka.

51. *Dōhō*, August 15, 1939 (English section).

52. Morino Masayoshi, "Boku Bei kansō hōkoku," November 25, 1941 (Chōsabu Dai-Rokka), DRO.

53. *Dōhō*, August 15, 1939 (English section); Nemichi to Arita, August 22, 1939, HSYK, DRO; and Tateishi, "A Typical Nisei," 202–204.

54. Tateishi, "A Typical Nisei," 203; *Heishikan News* 1 (August 10, 1940): 1; and ibid. 5 (June 15, 1942): 19, in Heishikan collection, JOMM. Though they lost U.S. citizenship and remained in Japan after the war, the former Heishikan members have protested the label of having been Japan's "spies" or apologists, usually citing the bridge concept, which Kawai calculatedly defined as the intended pur-

pose of the academy. That it still allows them to entertain a sanitized understanding of the Heishikan project succinctly shows the political utility of the bridge concept—one that is now often invoked in both U.S. and Japanese public discourses to the effect of neutralizing the meaning of global capital expansion and domination. On the wartime and postwar experiences of the Heishikan members, see Kumei Teruko, "Shinkō no rensa," in *Zaigai shitei kyōiku no kenkyū*, ed. Kojima Masaru (Tokyo: Tamagawa Daigaku Shuppanbu, 2003): 128–156.

55. "What about Japan for the Nisei," *Rafu Shimpō*, December 29, 1940 (English section).

56. "Not Fair to Think Nisei Want to Leave U.S. for Nippon, Says Writer," *Nichibei Shimbun*, May 11, 1940 (English section). Another Nisei journalist mentioned the presence of "the [Japanese] militarist who may envision . . . tasks for the nisei in the event of world hostilities." *Nichibei Shimbun*, December 22, 1935 (English section); also Sam Hataye, "Misunderstood Nisei," *Nichibei Shimbun*, December 21, 1936 (English section); and *Rafu Shimpō*, May 26, 1938. On Uno, see Yuji Ichioka, "The Meaning of Loyalty: The Case of Kazumaro Buddy Uno," *Amerasia Journal* 23 (Winter 1997–1998): 45–72.

57. Beifu Kyōkai, *Dai-Nisei to Bukkyō* (Kyoto: Shinran Kenkyū Hakkōsho, 1935), 42–43, in box 295, JARP.

58. *Shin Sekai*, January 1, 1938 (English section).

59. Boyce, "American Citizens of Japanese Race Residing in Japan," 13.

60. *Shin Sekai*, September 2, 1935 (English section).

61. Nisei Survey Committee, *Nisei*, 29. See also Boyce, "Second-Generation Japanese in Japan," 15–18.

62. *Nichibei Shimbun*, December 10, 1936; *Shin Sekai*, May 28, 1935, September 5, 1938 (English section); Ken Katō, "Nisei wa doko ni," *Kaigai ijū* 11 (October 1938): 52; *Rafu Shimpō*, December 22, 1939 (English section), December 29, 1940 (English section); "Kaigai Hōjin Dai-Nisei no kyōiku taiken o kataru zadankai," *Kaigai ijū* 12 (July 1939): 10; Yamashita, *Nichibei o tsunagu mono*, 297–301; and Tsunemitsu, *Nihon ryūgaku no jissai*, 47–53. On anti-Americanism in Japan, see Miriam Silverberg, "Constructing the Japanese Ethnography of Modernity," *Journal of Asian Studies* 51 (February 1992): 49–50.

63. Yamashita, *Nichibei o tsunagu mono*, 382–385, 419–421; and *Miyako Shinbun*, October 30, 1933.

64. Yamashita, *Nichibei o tsunagu mono*, 414–418; *Rafu Shimpō*, October 27, November 11–17, 1933; *Shin Sekai*, October 29, 1933; *Tokyo Asahi Shinbun*, October 9–10, 1933; and *Yomiuri Shinbun*, October 9–10, 1933. See also a police report in Fujinuma to Yamamoto et al., October 9, 1933, NGKZ.

65. *Shin Sekai*, November 22, 1933; *Rafu Shimpō*, December 15, 1933; and Yamashita, *Nichibei o tsunagu mono*, 420–421.

66. Fujinuma to Yamamoto et al., December 15, 1933, NGKZ.

67. *Rafu Shimpō*, November 23, 1934 (English section). See also *Nichibei Shimbun*, January 18, 1937; and *Shin Sekai*, September 12, 1937. According to another Nisei

leader, about 80 percent of the Nisei in Tokyo were considered undesirable, and the vast majority of them were also placed on the police blacklist.

68. Baba Yoshitsugu, "Saikin ni okeru Wagakuni ni taisuru gaichō katsudō ni tsuite," *Shisō jitsumuka kaidō kōenshu* (January 1940), in *Shakai mondai shiryō sōsho*, ed. Shakai Mondai Shiryō Kenkyūkai (Tokyo: Tōyō Bunkasha, 1976), 1:129–148, esp. 132–133, 137–139.

69. Boyce, "American Citizens of Japanese Race Residing in Japan," 9–10.

70. *Shin Sekai*, May 16, July 10, 1936, August 3, 1941; and *Rafu Shimpō*, May 26, 1938.

71. *Nichibei Shimbun*, February 11, 1937. See also Iwakiri Noboru, "Dai-Nisei mondai no jūyōsei," *Kaigai no Nippon* 14 (April 1940): 6.

72. *Nichibei Shimbun*, February 9–12, 1937. The coverage by the Japanese press was so negative that the Nisei was constantly referred to as a "traitor." See *Tokyo Asahi Shinbun*, March 22, April 10, 1936. Combined with the wife's illness, living in Japan proved to be a disappointment, and only a few months later, the couple decided to go back to the United States.

73. *Shin Sekai*, September 4–6, 1940; and Murayama to Sakamoto, June 13, September 16, 1938, in box 2, JYSP. While in Japan, Murayama frequently contributed to the *Shin Sekai* and *Pacific Citizen*. He reported on Nisei life in Japan, the Sino-Japanese War as a war correspondent, and the current news of Japanese society. He also played an instrumental role in producing Radio Tokyo short-wave programs for North America. During the war, Murayama continued to act as a "defender" of the Nisei in Japan, a role that caused him to be detained by the police on numerous occasions. Working as an auxiliary to a prisoner-of-war camp in Tokyo, Murayama was reportedly one of the few that behaved "sympathetically" toward Allied prisoners of war—a dogged adherence to internationalism that later saved him from war crimes prosecution during the American occupation. Unable to restore his U.S. citizenship, Murayama remained in Japan after the war, serving as the publisher of the *Japan Times* and the president of the Japan Boy Scout Association until his death in December 1968.

74. Murayama to Sakamoto, June 13, 1938.

75. *Shin Sekai*, September 4–6, 1940.

76. Since the early 1930s, Nisei students had organized themselves into school-based fraternities, as well as regional and alumni associations. In addition, there was a more broadly organized Pacific Young People's Society (PYPS), which included approximately 100 leading Nisei and some prominent Japanese. The PYPS offered the second generation a welcome place of "relaxation and relief," where, as the American consul aptly put it, the members could " 'be themselves' in exactly the same way as other foreigners in Japan do in their 'foreign colony' activities." That "foreign colony" character of the PYPS, however, led law enforcement to hold the organization in extremely low regard. The authorities labeled the society "secretive" and conspiratorial, a view reinforced by the frequent attendance of a U.S. military attaché at its meetings. Eventually, because of police meddling, the PYPS ceased to function in the mid-1930s. Other Nisei associations served only

the specific social interests of a small segment of their American-born members, thereby disqualifying them as lobbyists for the overall Nisei population in Japan. None of the existing groups could speak as the Nisei voice, as Murayama envisaged. See Boyce, "Second-Generation Japanese in Japan," 12; Yamashita, *Nikkei Shimin no Nihon ryūgaku jijō*, 267–273; and Fujinuma to Yamamoto et al., December 15, 1933.

77. *Shin Sekai*, June 30, 1937.

78. Izumi Hirobe, *Japanese Pride, American Prejudice: Modifying the Exclusion Clause of the 1924 Immigration Act* (Stanford, Calif.: Stanford University Press, 2001), esp. 10–14.

79. *Pan-Pacific Youth* 1 (Autumn 1939): 4, enclosure 4, in Boyce, "American Citizens of Japanese Race Residing in Japan." See also Nisei Survey Committee, *Nisei*, 50, iii (supplement).

80. Tamotsu Murayama, "Nisei Information Bureau Proposed," June 20, 1939, in box 20, JYSP; and Murayama to Sakamoto, November 1, 1939, in box 2, JYSP.

81. Murayama to Sakamoto, November 1, 1939. See also "Nisei Information Service," December 1939, in box 2, GCWC, RG 338, NACP.

82. *Shin Sekai*, February 11–12, 1941.

83. Ibid., May 27, 1941. See also ibid., November 18, 1939 (English section), July 26, 1940; and *Rafu Shimpō*, December 29, 1940.

84. Naimushō Keihokyoku, "Shōwa 16-nenchū ni okeru Gaiji keisatsu gaikyō" (1941), reprinted in *Gaiji Keisatsu gaikyō* (Tokyo: Ryūkei Shosha, 1980), 6:164; and GTZK: Hokubei no bu 1–5, DRO. Tally by the author from the records of visas issued to the Nisei between July 1 and December 13, 1940. The last steamship for the United States left Yokohama in July 1941.

85. Naimushō Keihokyoku, "Shōwa 17-nen chū ni okeru Gaiji Keisatsu gaikyō" (1942), reprinted in *Gaiji Keisatsu gaikyō* (Tokyo: Ryūkei Shosha, 1980), 8:77; and Tamotsu Murayama, *Shūsen no koro* (Tokyo: Jiji Tsūshin, 1968), 23–24, 156. See also the autobiographies of such Nisei in *Amerasia Journal* 23 (1997): 145–216; Masayo Duus, *Tokyo Rose: Orphan of the Pacific* (New York: Kodansha International, 1979); Russell Warren Howe, *The Hunt for "Tokyo Rose"* (Lanham, Md.: Madison, 1990); and Mary Kimoto Tomita, *Dear Miye: Letters from Japan, 1939–1946*, ed. Robert G. Lee (Stanford, Calif.: Stanford University Press, 1996).

86. Willard Price, *Children of the Rising Sun* (New York: Reynal & Hitchcock, 1938), 280. Led by V. S. McClatchy, a long-time leader of the anti-Japanese movement, the California Joint Immigration Committee criticized the return of Japan-reared Nisei to the United States as a new wave of Japanese immigration in disguise. Primarily targeting the Issei-initiated Return-to-America campaign, McClatchy alleged that the youth posed a greater menace to the United States than ordinary immigrants, for they were legally American citizens, albeit with unflinching "loyalty to Japan." Many Americans similarly perceived the Nisei returnees as embodying an enhanced danger to U.S. national security and interest. See *Nichibei Shimbun*, June 10, 1936 (English section).

87. An Intelligence Officer [Kenneth D. Ringle], "Japanese in America: The Problem and the Solution," *Harper's Magazine* 185 (1942): 492.

CHAPTER 7

1. Yuji Ichioka, "Japanese Immigrant Nationalism: The Issei and the Sino-Japanese War, 1937–1941," *California History* 69 (Fall 1990): 260–275, 310–311; and Brian M. Hayashi, *"For the Sake of Our Japanese Brethren": Assimilation, Nationalism, and Protestantism among the Japanese of Los Angeles, 1895–1942* (Stanford, Calif.: Stanford University Press, 1995). On Japanese immigrant nationalism in Hawaii, see John J. Stephan, *Hawaii under the Rising Sun: Japan's Plans for Conquest after Pearl Harbor* (Honolulu: University of Hawaii Press, 1984), 23–40.
2. Matthew Frye Jacobson, *Special Sorrows: The Diasporic Imagination of Irish, Polish, and Jewish Immigrants in the United States* (Berkeley: University of California Press, 2002); Renqui Yu, *To Save China, to Save Ourselves: The Chinese Hand Laundry Alliance of New York* (Philadelphia, Pa.: Temple University Press, 1992), esp. 77–99; Wayne Patterson, *The Ilse: First Generation Korean Immigrants in Hawaii, 1903–1973* (Honolulu: University of Hawaii Press, 2000), 100–116; Joan Jensen, *Passage from India: Asian Indian Immigrants in North America* (New Haven, Conn.: Yale University Press, 1988), 179–180.
3. There are a few notable studies on German and Italian immigrant nationalism: Susan Canedy, *America's Nazis, a Democratic Dilemma: A History of the German American Bund* (Menlo Park, Calif.: Markgraf, 1990); Leland V. Bell, *In Hitler's Shadow: The Anatomy of American Nazism* (Port Washington, N.Y.: Kennikat, 1973); and Dino Cinel, *From Italy to San Francisco: The Immigrant Experience* (Stanford, Calif.: Stanford University Press, 1982), 228–255. On the consequences of their prewar nationalisms, see Jörg Nagler, "Internment of German Enemy Aliens in the United States during the First and Second World Wars," in *Alien Justice: Wartime Internment in Australia and North America*, ed. Kay Saunders and Roger Daniels (Queensland, Australia: University of Queensland Press, 2002), 66–79; and George E. Pozzetta, "Alien Enemies or Loyal Americans? The Internment of Italian-Americans," in *Alien Justice*, 80–92.
4. *Nichibei Shimbun*, September 21, 1931; and *Shin Sekai*, October 21, 1931.
5. *Rafu Shimpō*, November 28–30, 1931.
6. Ibid., November 28–30, December 2, 5, 1931.
7. *Nichibei Shimbun*, November 27, 1931.
8. KNK 5, December 5, 8, 1931, in box 242, JARP.
9. "Gunshikin kennōkin meisaihyō," NSSG 1, DRO.
10. *Nichibei Shimbun*, November 27, 1931; and *Rafu Shimpō*, November 30, 1931.
11. *Nichibei Shimbun*, July 17, 18, 23, 27, 1937; *Shin Sekai*, July 26, 1937; and *Kashū Mainichi*, July 30, 1937.
12. *Rafu Shimpō*, July 20, August 5, 1937, February 1, 1938; *Kashū Mainichi*, July 20,

1937, February 22, 1938; *Nichibei Shimbun*, July 22, 1937; Shirō Fujioka, *Beikoku Chūō Nihonjinkaishi* (Los Angeles: Beikoku Chūō Nihonjinkai, 1940), 330–333; and Hanboku Yusa, *Hanboku zenshū* (Santa Maria, Calif.: Yusa Hanboku, 1940), 26–29.

13. "Kaimu hōkoku," 4, April 2, May 3, 27, August 18, September 29, 1938, JANA, UAUW.

14. IJAR, September 28, 1937, in box 734, JARP; and Zaibei Nihonjinkai, *Zaibei Nihonjinshi* (San Francisco: Zaibei Nihonjinkai, 1940), 924–925.

15. In Japanese immigrant society, a man who could read, write, and speak English well had a far better chance to gain the job of the Japanese association secretary, one of the most prestigious and influential positions. Education, be it Japanese or American, also enabled one to become a Japanese-language teacher or newspaper reporter/correspondent, who shaped public opinion and the dominant current of thought among Issei. Material wealth and, often, "right" prefectural origins—for example, Hiroshima and Wakayama if in southern California—could translate into social prestige, that is, the presidency or board membership in the Japanese associations and other community organizations. These individual advantages formed the original social capitals in Issei society.

16. I built my argument for Japanese immigrant patriotism as a new social field and nationalist contributions as a new capital on the theory of Pierre Bourdieu. My idea of position taking in patriotic competition also derives from his study of the cultural field within the social structures of power. See Pierre Bourdieu, *The Field of Cultural Production* (New York: Columbia University Press, 1993), and *In Other Words: Essays toward a Reflective Sociology* (Stanford, Calif.: Stanford University Press, 1990), 140–149. Those who did not subscribe to the legitimacy of the new field, and the meaning of the capital associated with it, did not opt to take part in the competition; rather, they stayed out and often attacked it from outside at the cost of severe criticism and ridicule from the general population. The most notable such dissidents were leftists and communists.

17. Ōta to Ugaki, July 10, 1938, ZHHT: Beikoku no bu, DRO; and Shiozaki to Ugaki, July 15, 1938, ibid.

18. A. P. Le Grand, "General Japanese Intelligence Survey in the Portland Division," 8, January 7, 1941, in box 566, MIDC, RG 165, NACP. See also *Rafu Shimpō*, November 29, 1931; and *Nichibei Shimbun*, August 19, 1937.

19. On the consequences of noncompliance, see Ōta to Ugaki; *Dōhō*, October 15, 1937, July 15, 1939, March 15, 1940, November 5, 1941 (English section); *Nichibei Shimbun*, September 6, 1937; and *Shin Sekai*, December 15, 1940.

20. *Rafu Shimpō*, October 6, 1938; *Kashū Mainichi*, August 13, 1938, January 1, 1939; *Nichibei Shimbun*, July 6, 1940; Mikami Hiroyuki, "Jihenka ni okeru Zaibei dōhō," *Rajio kōen kōza* 35 (May 5, 1938): 57, 61–62; and Tanaka Gunkichi, "Kikika no Zaibei Hōjin kinjō," *Genchi hōkoku* 4 (April 1941): 134–143. I converted the original yen figures into dollar amounts at an exchange rate of four to one. The gift of the aircraft to the Japanese military can be also seen as part of such transnational competition. As did the southern California residents, the Japanese

in Argentina, Mexico, Peru, Dutch East Indies, Davao (the Philippines), and Hilo (Hawaii) raised enough funds for donations of their own "patriotic airplanes" in 1937–1938.

21. Western Defense Command Headquarters, "Heimusha Kai," June 1944, 1–9, esp. 5, in box 1, GCWC, RG 338, NACP.
22. "Kanefugi Utsunomiya," 3, April 9, 1942, in box 89, EACF, RG 85, NAPS.
23. Western Defense Command Headquarters, "Heimusha Kai," 16–17.
24. IJAR, December 17, 1937, January 20, 1938; and *Utah Nippō*, January 10, 1938.
25. Ōta to Ugaki; Ichioka, "Japanese Immigrant Nationalism," 263–264; *Shin Sekai*, August 25, 1939; and Western Defense Command Headquarters, "Heimusha Kai," 7.
26. Western Defense Command Headquarters, "Heimusha Kai," 6–7.
27. Robert Howard Ross, "Social Distance as It Exists between the First and Second Generation Japanese in the City of Los Angeles and Vicinity" (M.A. thesis, University of Southern California, 1939), 138; and Sinclair Gannon, "Purchase of Airplane for Japanese Army," January 11, 1938, in box 226, SCAC, RG 38, NACP.
28. *Nichibei Shimbun*, December 6, 1937; and *Utah Nippō*, December 17, 1937, January 10, 12, 1938.
29. *Nichibei Shimbun*, August 15, 1938; and *Rafu Shimpō*, June 2, 1940.
30. "Zenbei yakuin kaigi ketsugibun," 1938, in folder 1, box 2, KGYP, JARP. See also "Speaker's Outline," June 1938, in folder 1, box 2, ibid. On forced donations, see *Dōhō*, October 15, 1937, July 15, 1939, March 15, 1940. A *Dōhō* writer commented that Issei women had become particularly critical about war-related donations because they were more "concerned about" the impact of forced contributions on the household finances for which they were responsible.
31. Masao Dodō, *Taiheiyō jidai to Beikoku* (Los Angeles: Rafu Shimpōsha, 1933), 2–12; Wakasugi to Shidehara, and Satō to Shidehara, November 12, 13, 1931, respectively, MJYS 1, DRO; and *Shin Sekai*, February 28, 29, 1932. On the Chinese-American boycott and nationalism, see Yu, *To Save China, to Save Ourselves*, 77–137; and Mei Zheng, "Chinese Americans in San Francisco and New York City during the Anti-Japanese War: 1937–1945" (M.A. thesis, University of California, Los Angeles, 1990). According to Yu, Chinese immigrants, too, employed the people's diplomacy idea in search of white American sympathies.
32. *Rafu Shimpō*, October 21, 1931; *Nichibei Shimbun*, October 26, 1931; and *Shin Sekai*, February 29, March 10, 1932. See also *Rafu Shimpō*, February 8, 1933; and "Taibei senden kōsaku to Zaibei Nihonjin no tachiba," *Nippon to Amerika* 7 (January 1938): 22.
33. They included 28,000 copies of *The Present Situation in Shanghai*, 5,000 copies of *Japan's Right to Defend Herself*, and 4,000 reprints of *The Sino-Japanese Question from a Different Angle* from the prestigious *Far Eastern Review*. See Wakasugi to Yoshizawa, April 30, 1932, MJYS 5.
34. *Shin Sekai*, March 7, 1932 (English section).
35. *Nichibei Shimbun*, March 29, 1932 (English section).
36. *Nichibei Shimbun*, October 9, 1931; and Peter C. Y. Leung, *One Day, One Dollar:*

Locke, California, and the Chinese Farming Experience in the Sacramento Delta (El Cerrito, Calif.: Chinese/Chinese American History Project, 1984), 31.

37. KNK, March 20, 31, 1932.
38. Ibid.
39. Wakasugi to Yoshizawa, April 23, 1932, MJYS 5.
40. Uchiyama to Yoshizawa, March 29, 1932, MJYS 4.
41. Ibid.
42. Zai Sōkō Sōryōjikan, "Taiheiyō Engan Ryōji Kaigi Honshō shimon jikō ni taisuru iken," 1–13, March 12, 1928, RKKZ 1, DRO.
43. Wakasugi to Shidehara, July 28, 1931, ZNKZ 2, DRO.
44. Satō to Hirota, December 27, 1933, ibid.
45. See *Shin Sekai*, February 29, 1932; and Wakasugi to Yoshizawa, April 23, 1932.
46. *Nichibei Shimbun*, February 16, 1932. See also ibid., March 8, 1934; and *Rafu Shimpō*, February 28, 1933.
47. *Rafu Shimpō*, March 8, 1932; and Dodō, *Taiheiyō jidai to Beikoku*, 39–40.
48. Wakasugi to Yoshizawa, April 23, 1932.
49. *Nichibei Shimbun*, June 25, 1933, October 18, 1937.
50. See, for instance, Hori to Hirota, December 28, 1934, 36–37, NGKZ, DRO.
51. Kōshirō Endō, *Tsuzurikata bunshū: Shina Jihen-gō* (Compton, Calif.: Compton Gakuen, 1938), 10.
52. Taiheiyō Bunka Kyōikukai, "Shuisho oyobi seiki," 2–3, RTBF, JANM. Another notable program of Ban's academy was the annual English-language lecture series for Los Angeles Nisei under the theme of the "Japanese racial culture." Taught by the reverend and a number of other Issei educators and leaders, the 1937–1938 program featured eighteen lectures, including the "truth" about the Sino-Japanese War and its relevance to the second generation. See Pacific Society of Religious Education, "The Fourth Lecture of the Japanese Racial Culture," July 1937–June 1938, RTBF; *Shin Sekai*, July 11, 1933; and *Nichibei Shimbun*, May 15, 1934.
53. Daily activity journals, vols. 3–4, RTBF.
54. Ibid., 3:54, 70, 85–87, 93–95; 4:31–32, 35, 41, 57; and *Nichibei Shimbun*, May 15, 1934. Tally by the author.
55. "Dr. Takeshi Ban," 3–4, 9, January 21, 1942, in box 36, EACF; Taiheiyō Bunka Kyōikukai, "Bunkyō jigyō no kukakuteki yakushin," n.p., and "Bunkyō Eiga tsumitate shikin kiyakusho," n.p., both in RTBF; and Wallace Nobuo Ban, *Taiheiyō ni hashi o kakeyo* (Osaka: Gendai Kyoiku Shuppan Kenkyūjo, 1982), 72.
56. "Dr. Takeshi Ban," 2–3, 7, 9.
57. Ban, *Taiheiyō ni hashi o kakeyo*, 72, 79–80.
58. Wakasugi to Saitō, June 9, 1932, MJYS 6.
59. Uchiyama to Saitō, May 26, 1932, MJYS 5; and W. Perkins, "Japanese Activities in Seattle, Wash., and Portland, Ore.," 4–7, October 20, 1932, in box 227, SCAC. On Sakamoto's activities, see Yuji Ichioka, "A Study in Dualism: James Yoshinori Sakamoto and the *Japanese American Courier*, 1928–1942," *Amerasia Journal* 13 (1986–1987): 63–64, 79.

60. *Rafu Shimpō*, March 2, 1935; *Kashū Mainichi*, June 19, 1936; Fujioka, *Beikoku Chūō Nihonjinkaishi*, 283–284, 301, 331–332; and Nihon Bunka Kyōkai, *Nihon Bunka Kyōkai setsuritsu keika* (Los Angeles: Nihon Bunka Kyōkai, 1939).
61. Nihon Bunka Kyōkai, *Nihon Bunka Kyōkai setsuritsu keika*, 2.
62. In 1934, Tokyo adopted cultural propaganda as an integral part of its overall diplomacy. Modeled after the examples of Italy, Germany, and France, the Foreign Ministry formed the Kokusai Bunka Shinkōkai (Society for International Cultural Relations) with an eye to manipulating public opinion overseas in favor of Japan through the dissemination of selected philosophies, traditional arts, and enchanting images. In the context of its estrangement from the international community after 1933, imperial Japan expected such cross-cultural communications and international exchanges to help it win the sympathies of white Americans and Europeans. A small number of Nisei in Japan were recruited to work as "cultural ambassadors," who frequently traveled to the United States for sponsored lectures. On the KBS, see Akira Iriye, *Cultural Internationalism and World Order* (Baltimore, Md.: Johns Hopkins University Press, 1997), 119–125; Eriko Yamamoto, "Miya Sannomiya Kikuchi: A Pioneer Nisei Woman's Life and Identity," *Amerasia Journal* 23 (Winter 1997–1998): 87–89; and Eiichiro Azuma, "Interstitial Lives: Race, Community, and History among Japanese Immigrants Caught between Japan and the United States, 1885–1941" (Ph.D. diss., University of California, Los Angeles, 2000), 286–287, 338.
63. On the crossroads of race and gender in the white American appreciation of East Asian cultures, see Mari Yoshihara, *Embracing the East: White Women and American Orientalism* (New York: Oxford University Press, 2003), esp. 15–73.
64. Nihon Bunka Kyōkai, *Nihon Bunka Kyōkai setsuritsu keika*, 2.
65. Gaimushō Jōhōbu, "Shina Jihen ni okeru jōhō senden kōsaku gaiyō," pt. 2 (1938), 31, DRO.
66. Fujioka, *Beikoku Chūō Nihonjinkaishi*, 334–335; and *Beikoku Sangyō Nippō*, October 14, December 10, 1937.
67. Tamaki, "Hokushi jiken to gādenā," *Nanka Gādenā Renmei geppō*, 4, August 10, 1937, in folder 2, box 5, KGYP.
68. "Nisshi Jihen no himatsu," *Nanka Gādenā Renmei geppō*, 6, October 10, 1937, ibid.
69. Tahara Haruji, "Kaigai dōhō wa Jihen o dou ninshiki shitaka," *Tairiku* 1 (November 1938): 108.
70. Ōta to Ugaki; and Ichioka, "Japanese Immigrant Nationalism," 263.
71. *Kashū Mainichi*, August 9, 1938; *Nichibei Shimbun*, August 11, 1938; *Shin Sekai*, August 13, 1938; and Ichioka, "Japanese Immigrant Nationalism," 264.
72. Larry S. Tajiri, "$140 in Prizes in Nichi-Bei Essay Contest to Justify Japan Case in Far East: Propaganda against Nippon Menaces Nisei in U.S.," *Nichibei Shimbun*, December 10, 1937.
73. *Rafu Shimpō*, October 8, 14, 1937 (English section); *Nichibei Shimbun*, October 10, 1937 (English section); and Satow to Sakamoto, October 22, 1937, in box 11, JYSP, UAUW.

74. Sugahara to Sakamoto, October 5, 1937, in box 11, JYSP.

75. Ōta, 1938, RKKZ: Gijiroku 3, DRO.

76. Kay Sugahara, "Boycott—Boon or Boomerang?" *Nichibei Shimbun*, November 14, 1937.

77. Bob Kumamoto, "The Search for Spies: American Counterintelligence and the Japanese American Community, 1931–1942," *Amerasia Journal* 6 (Fall 1979): 45–75.

78. *Kashū Mainichi*, July 10, August 3, 1939; *Dōhō*, May 15, 1940; and *Nichibei Shimbun*, October 25, 1940.

79. *Nichibei Shimbun*, February 8, 1941.

80. On their part, Japanese diplomats "relaxed the former policy of 'cultural propaganda and enlightenment,' " abandoning the use of the Japanese associations as the front for it. Instead, they devoted their energies to consolidating the clandestine intelligence network, involving mainly "citizens of foreign extraction, aliens, communists, negroes, labor union members, and anti-semites [*sic*]." No longer were Japanese Americans—Issei and Nisei alike—central in this new scheme. See "Japanese Intelligence and Propaganda in the United States during 1941," 1–2, December 4, 1941, in box 222, SCAC.

81. Shin'ichi Katō, *Minami Kashū Nihonjin nanajūnenshi* (Los Angeles: Nanka Nikkeijin Shōgyō Kaigisho, 1960), 390–391; *Rafu Shimpō*, April 16, 1941; and *Kashū Mainichi*, February 23, 1941. See also *Rafu Shimpō*, January 1, 28, 1941; and *Nichibei Shimbun*, February 21, 1941.

82. *Rafu Shimpō*, May 28, 1941; Katō, *Minami Kashū Nihonjin nanajūnenshi*, 391; and "Full Loyalty to America Pledged in World Crisis by Japanese Association," *Japanese American Review*, June 28, 1941. The English statement quoted is from the last source.

83. Gary Gerstle, *Working-Class Americanism: The Politics of Labor in a Textile City, 1914–1960* (Princeton, N.J.: Princeton University Press, 2002), 8–13.

84. Tsuyoshi Matsumoto, "The Japanese in California: An Account of Their Contributions to the Growth and Development of the State and of Their Part in the Community Life," 1941, 2–3, in folder 15, box 160, JARP.

85. Ibid., 45–46.

86. Katō, *Minami Kashū Nihonjin nanajūnenshi*, 392–394; and *Rafu Shimpō*, November 14, 1941. On how the attorney general compromised to override the constitutional rights of Nisei citizens, see Peter Irons, *Justice at War: The Story of the Japanese American Internment Cases* (New York: Oxford University Press, 1983), 3–74.

CHAPTER 8

1. *Nichibei Shimbun*, February 10, 14, 1930. On the same incident from a Filipino perspective, see Arleen de Vera, "The Tapia-Saiki Incident: Interethnic Conflict and Filipino Responses to the Anti-Filipino Exclusion Movement," in *Over the*

Edge: Remapping the American West, ed. Valerie Matsumoto and Blake Allmen-dinger (Berkeley: University of California Press, 1999), 201–214.

2. *Shin Sekai*, February 11, 12, 21, March 26, 27, 1930; and *Three Stars*, February 15, 1930. The quote is from the latter source.

3. *Nichibei Shimbun*, February 15, 16, 18, 1930.

4. *Shin Sekai*, March 17, 1930.

5. *Nichibei Shimbun*, March 15, 16, 24, 1930; and *Shin Sekai*, March 15, 19, 1930.

6. In translating the term *minzoku*, Japanese often used the sociologically distinct concepts of "race," "ethnicity," and "nation" interchangeably. Because the delta's Issei tended to stress the physiological difference between themselves and Filipi-nos as the precondition for their cultural differences, I have employed the term *race* (or *racialized ethnicity*) for *minzoku* in this chapter. In different contexts, however, other terms may be employed for *minzoku*.

7. These two dimensions of nationalism were not unique to Japanese immigrants. Kevin M. Doak has discussed the notions of "state nationalism" and "ethnic na-tionalism" in imperial Japan. According to him, many people in Japan envisaged a natural ethnic body as a national community, which differed from the state-centered political community. Japanese often found their national community as-saulted by the modern state, which undermined the foundation of preexisting ties, unity, and order. Doak contends that ethnic nationalism enabled these Japa-nese to oppose the state by providing an alternative community—at least con-ceptually. See Kevin M. Doak, "Ethnic Nationalism and Romanticism in Early Twentieth-Century Japan," *Journal of Japanese Studies* 22 (1996): 78–79; and Kevin M. Doak, "What Is a Nation and Who Belongs? National Narratives and the Ethnic Imagination in Twentieth-Century Japan," *American Historical Review* 102 (April 1997): 283–286. The case of Issei nationalism shows more complex re-lations between the state and ethnic dimensions than what Doak argues. Japa-nese immigrant nationalism resembles what Matthew Frye Jacobson calls "the diasporic imagination" of European immigrant groups more than that of the people of Japan, insofar as his study subjects similarly overlapped visions of a homeland and aspirations to claim a place in America. Of course, there was a significant difference between them. While Jacobson's subjects could obtain white status through acculturation, Issei could not due to their racial origin. Matthew Frye Jacobson, *Special Sorrows: The Diasporic Imagination of Irish, Po-lish, and Jewish Immigrants in the United States* (Berkeley: University of Califor-nia Press, 2002).

8. On the Chinese in the delta, see George Chu, "Chinatown in the Delta: The Chinese in the Sacramento–San Joaquin Delta, 1870–1960," *California Historical Quarterly* 49 (March 1970): 21–37; and Sucheng Chan, *This Bittersweet Soil: The Chinese in California Agriculture, 1860–1910* (Berkeley: University of California Press, 1986), 158–224.

9. See Kanzo Ōhashi, *Hokubei Kashū Sutokuton dōhōshi* (Stockton, Calif.: Su-Shi Nihonjinkai, 1937), 7–12, 20–24, 64; and California State Department of Indus-trial Relations, *Facts about Filipino Immigration into California* (San Francisco:

Department of Industrial Relations, 1930), 46–47, 57, 60, 66–72. Although no population statistics are available for the delta proper, census figures indicate that the number of Filipinos in California dramatically increased during the 1920s from 2,674 to 30,470.

10. *Nichibei Shimbun*, February 18, March 4, 1930; and *Shin Sekai*, March 15, 19, 1930.

11. Zaibei Nihonjinkai, *Zaibei Nihonjinshi* (San Francisco: Zaibei Nihonjinkai, 1940), 588–590; Ōhashi, *Hokubei Kashū Sutokuton dōhōshi*, 80; and *Nichibei Shimbun*, January 1, 1933. According to state statistics, over 93 percent of approximately 29,000 Filipinos admitted into California were male immigrants, mostly young bachelors.

12. *Shin Sekai*, March 20, 1930. See also Ōhashi, *Hokubei Kashū Sutokuton dōhōshi*, 74–75. In Stockton, there were a few other cases of interethnic love affairs. Prior to the 1930 marriage, the wife of a Japanese laundryman ran away with a Filipino laborer, leaving behind her child and husband. This woman was caught and sent back to Japan after her husband divorced her. In the 1930s, there was another documented case of Nisei-Filipino marriage, and there were probably others as well.

13. John W. Dower, *War without Mercy: Race and Power in the Pacific War* (New York: Pantheon, 1986), 274–278.

14. See Suzuki Yūko, *Jūgun ianfu, naisen kekkon* (Tokyo: Miraisha, 1992); Yoon Keun-Cha, *Nihon kokuminron* (Tokyo: Chikuma Shobō, 1997), 108–109, 259; and Eiji Oguma, *A Genealogy of "Japanese" Self Image* (Melbourne, Australia: Trans Pacific, 2002).

15. *Nichibei Shimbun*, May 5, 1937.

16. See Ann Laura Stoler, *Race and the Education of Desire: Foucault's History of Sexuality and the Colonial Order of Things* (Durham, N.C.: Duke University Press, 1995), esp. 143; Peggy Pascoe, "Race, Gender, and the Privileges of Prosperity: On the Significance of Miscegenation Law in the U.S. West," in *Over the Edge*, 215–230; Peggy Pascoe, "Miscegenation Law, Court Cases, and Ideologies of 'Race' in Twentieth-Century America," *Journal of American History* 83 (June 1996): 44–69; Megumi Dick Osumi, "Asians and California's Anti-Miscegenation Laws," in *Asian and Pacific American Experience: Women's Perspectives*, ed. Nobuya Tsuchida (Minneapolis: Asian/Pacific American Learning Resource Center, University of Minnesota, 1982), 1–27; and Cynthia Nakashima, "An Invisible Monster: The Creation and Denial of Mixed-Race People in America," in *Racially Mixed People in America*, ed. Maria P. P. Root (Newbury Park, Calif.: Sage, 1992), 162–178.

17. "Yamato minzoku no tadashii chisuji," *Nichibei Shimbun*, April 28, 1933.

18. *Shin Sekai*, January 10, 1941.

19. Ibid., August 12, 1940 (English section).

20. *Nichibei Shimbun*, January 1, 1933.

21. Michael Omi and Howard Winant, *Racial Formations in the United States: From the 1960s to the 1990s* (New York: Routledge, 1994), 80–81, also 66–67.

22. No substantial study is yet available on the subject of Filipino farm labor in the delta. The following studies deal with their activities in other regions of California in the 1930s. Federal Writers' Project, *Unionization of Filipinos in California Agriculture* (Oakland: Federal Writers' Project, 1939), 11–13; Howard DeWitt, *Violence in the Fields: California Filipino Farm Labor Unionization during the Great Depression* (Saratoga, Calif.: Century Twenty One, 1980), 74–110; and Howard DeWitt, "The Filipino Labor Union: The Salinas Lettuce Strike of 1934," *Amerasia Journal* 5 (1978): 1–22. General studies of California's farm labor history have given scant, if any, attention to the role of Filipinos (and other racial minorities). For instance, the most influential works depict minority farmworkers as if they were helpless masses, who always needed guidance from white labor organizers. This kind of bias (or patronizing view) seems to stem from the authors' inability to use immigrant-language materials, the indispensable sources that in fact most likely express a high level of awareness and reveal various types of activism. See Cletus E. Daniel, *Bitter Harvest: A History of California Farmworkers, 1870–1941* (Berkeley: University of California Press, 1982); and Carey McWilliams, *Factories in the Fields: The Story of Migratory Farm Labor in California* (Boston: Little, Brown, 1939), esp. 211–282. For a succinct review of the literature, see Chris Friday, "Asian American Labor and Historical Interpretation," *Labor History* 35 (Fall 1994): 524–525.

23. *Nichibei Shimbun*, November 20, 25, December 4, 1936; *Shin Sekai*, November 30, December 3, 4, 1936; undated leaflet, in box 1, KGYP, JARP; and U.S. Senate, Committee on Education and Labor, *Violations of Free Speech and Rights of Labor: Hearings before a Subcommittee of the Committee on Education and Labor*, pt. 72 (Washington, D.C.: GPO, 1940), 26685–26686.

24. On white shippers and land owners in the delta's celery industry, see Kō Murai, *Zaibei Nihonjin sangyō sōran* (Los Angeles: Beikoku Sangyō Nippō, 1940), 199–202. On multilayered race relations in the American West, see Tomás Almaguer, *Racial Fault Lines: The Historical Origins of White Supremacy in California* (Berkeley: University of California Press, 1994), esp. 1–17. Almaguer contends that whites reserved the top position for themselves, while Mexicans, African Americans, Asians, and Native Americans followed in rank order. The author, however, does not concern himself with the emergence of stratification among Asian immigrant groups in their changing relationships with the white ruling class.

25. Chris Friday has analyzed a similar system of ethnic labor recruitment, as well as the emergence of ethnically based "cannery communities." Chris Friday, *Organizing Asian American Labor: The Pacific Coast Canned-Salmon Industry, 1870–1942* (Philadelphia, Pa.: Temple University Press, 1994), 109–112.

26. Matsumoto Yūko sheds light on the coexistence of working-class and farming-class "ethnic solidarity" in the Los Angeles Japanese community, whereas John Modell examines the clash between two versions of ethnic loyalties espoused by a Nisei labor union and a large Issei-owned business in Los Angeles. Their studies suggest that Japanese American nationalism—and the ethnic solidarity result-

ing from it—was not a monolithic constant but rather an arena in which conflicting interests collided and engaged for legitimacy. Friday also traces the emergence of working-class nationalism in the workplace, which led to ethnic factionalism in the cannery industry of the Pacific Northwest. See Matsumoto Yūko, "1936-nen Rosuanjerusu serori sutoraiki to Nikkei nōgyō komyuniti," *Shirin* 75 (July 1992): 44–73; John Modell, *The Economics and Politics of Racial Accommodation: The Japanese of Los Angeles, 1900–1942* (Urbana: University of Illinois Press, 1977), 127–153; and Friday, *Organizing Asian American Labor*, 112–114, 149–192.

27. On this effect of ideology, see Louis Althusser, *Lenin and Philosophy and Other Essays*, trans. Ben Brewster (New York: Monthly Review Press, 1971), 162–165, 182. In southern California, different social dynamics rendered contrasting racial meanings to Filipinos. In 1933 and 1936, Mexican workers struck against Japanese farmers in the districts of El Monte and Venice, respectively. My reading of local Japanese newspapers reveals that, in those instances, Filipinos often became a "good" race—that is, friends of the Issei farming class who served as scabs—while Mexicans were considered the chief menace that almost paralyzed their farm operations. On Filipinos in the El Monte strike, see *Rafu Shimpō*, June 12, 13, 15, 28, 1933; and *Kashū Mainichi*, June 28, 1933. Though it does not explore the different patterns of racialization in the labor-ethnic disputes, the following study details the Japanese-Mexican estrangement: Charles Wollenberg, "Race and Class in Rural California: The El Monte Berry Strike of 1933," *California Historical Quarterly* 51 (Summer 1972): 155–164.

28. In addition to Omi and Winant's conception of a "war of maneuver," I have relied on Pierre Bourdieu's formulations of "struggle" and "position" in the analysis of interethnic conflict in the delta. Speaking primarily of what he calls the artistic field and the religious field, Bourdieu has argued that the position that an agent occupies in society structures his disposition, or "habitus," which then leads him to a conscious or unconscious struggle for the defense of his position. Insofar as such an action has the effect of protecting the status quo, Bourdieu has called it the "doxic acceptance" of the established order. Based on that habitus, a quest for "distinction" is a logical product of the struggle to keep one's position. In the case of delta Issei, their distinction would be their firm allegiance to the rule of the landed local whites. See Pierre Bourdieu, *The Logic of Practice* (Stanford, Calif.: Stanford University Press, 1990), 136–141; and Bourdieu, *The Field of Cultural Production* (New York: Columbia University Press, 1993), 61–67.

29. *Nichibei Shimbun*, November 28, 1936.
30. *Shin Sekai*, December 10, 1936.
31. *Philippine Journal*, November 11, 1939.
32. Louis Yamamoto, "Celery Strike Won!" *Dōhō*, December 15, 1939 (English section).
33. *Nichibei Shimbun*, December 1, 1939.
34. *Shin Sekai*, November 29, 30, 1939 (English section).

35. *Nichibei Shimbun*, December 2, 1939.

36. Ibid., December 2, 1939, January 13, 1940; *Shin Sekai*, December 2, 6, 1939; and *Philippine Journal*, December 22, 1939. In his semiautobiographical account, Carlos Bulosan vividly depicts the scene of the Filipino boycott and the rise of anti-Japanese sentiments among Filipino union laborers. Carlos Bulosan, *America Is in the Heart* (Seattle: University of Washington Press, 1973), 275–277.

37. *Nichibei Shimbun*, December 28, 1939; *Shin Sekai*, December 29, 1939; and *Philippine Journal*, January 4, 1940.

38. *Dōhō*, February 1, 1940; and *Nichibei Shimbun*, January 4, 1940.

39. *Shin Sekai*, January 15, 18, 1940. Also see *Nichibei Shimbun*, January 13, 15, 24, 1940. The quote is taken from *Shin Sekai*, January 15, 1940. The computation of new employment for Japanese was made by the author from newspaper advertisements.

40. David Thompson, "The Filipino Federation of America, Incorporated: A Study in the Natural History of a Social Institution," *Social Process in Hawaii* 7 (November 1941): 24–34; and Steffi San Buenaventura, "Filipino Folk Spirituality and Immigration: From Mutual Aid to Religion," *Amerasia Journal* 22 (Spring 1996): 3–9, 17–22.

41. Thompson, "The Filipino Federation of America, Incorporated," 33–34; and *Philippine Journal*, February 15, 1940. Moncado had his men oppose the Filipino Labor Union in the 1934 Salinas strike, making his group an ally of white and Japanese growers there as well. See DeWitt, "The Filipino Labor Union," 9.

42. Interestingly, the FALA, too, saw a federation member as something less than a real Filipino—a selfish traitor to the race. In the union publication, the FALA president proclaimed the racial authenticity of his union: "[T]he Filipino now is a new man. He is already awakened; he knows the value of himself in particular and to his own people as a whole. He knows that these groups who want him to fight his own people are doing that for their own selfish interests. He knows that whatever reward he gets by being a traitor to his people are [*sic*] only immediate and temporary, and that in the final analysis, he is a Filipino first, last, and always!" See Macario D. Bautista, "You Cannot Destroy This Unity!" *Philippine Journal*, January 23, 1940.

43. The "unofficial" nature of Morimoto's activities is clear in that her doings rarely entered into the pages of Japanese newspapers. When they did, reports usually suggested that she was acting on her own, responding to private requests from Issei merchants. By contrast, the union publication depicted her activities as the core of anti-Filipino sabotage by Japanese. Later, in November 1940, her employment office became the scene of an assassination attempt, where a disgruntled FALA member fired ten shots. Though no one was hurt, this incident resulted in the sudden end of Morimoto's anti-union activities and the subsequent divorce of the couple. Kay Morimoto later moved to Los Angeles. See *Stockton Record*, November 29, 30, 1940; and *Nichibei Shimbun*, December 1, 2, 1940.

44. "Poor Mrs. Morimoto: She Must Think Filipinos Dumb," *Philippine Journal*, January 23, 1940; and *Shin Sekai*, January 19, 1940.

45. "Japanese Meddlers Not Wanted," *Philippine Journal*, August 17, 1940.
46. "An Open Letter to Growers," *Philippine Journal*, February 15, 1940.
47. "FALA Will Fight Traitors and Movements against It," *Philippine Journal*, July 31, 1940; "Filipino Labor, Not Japanese Should Be Given Preference," *Philippine Journal*, October 28, 1940. The quote is from the latter.
48. "Filipino Leader Predicts Aid of Japan," *Stockton Record*, July 1, 1940; "Filipino Chief Says People Loyal," *Stockton Record*, July 12, 1940; and "Dr. Bautista Condemns Moncado's Statements," *Philippine Journal*, June 29, 1940.
49. *Nichibei Shimbun*, July 14, 1940.
50. "Peace Plea in Field Labor Ranks Made," *Stockton Record*, August 12, 1940; and *Shin Sekai*, August 14, 1940.
51. *Philippine Journal*, August 17, 31, 1940; *Nichibei Shimbun*, December 1, 1940; and *Stockton Record*, August 12, 1940.
52. *Nichibei Shimbun*, November 13, 23, 1940; *Shin Sekai*, November 15, 1940; and *Stockton Record*, November 20, 1940.
53. *Shin Sekai*, October 20, 1940. There was a pro-union Filipino Business Association of Stockton, which consisted of twenty-nine member stores. Many of the businesses competed directly with Japanese merchants. See FALA, *FALA Yearbook: 2nd Annual Convention* (Stockton, Calif.: FALA, 1940), in box 15, Carey McWilliams Papers, Young Research Library, UCLA. In addition, the union attempted to free its members from Japanese "exploitation" by forming a grocery store of its own. Established in January 1940, the Filipino Mercantile Corporation offered union members provisions at reasonable prices, and it reportedly earned $40,000 during the 1940 asparagus season. See *Philippine Journal*, February 15, March 30, April 22, 1940. A contemporary observer commented that this program designed to help union members was "[e]ntirely unique in farm labor history." See Harry Schwarts, "Recent Development among Farm Labor Unions," *Journal of Farm Economics* 23 (November 1941): 838–839.
54. *Philippine Journal*, August 17, 31, 1940; and *Nichibei Shimbun*, December 1, 1940.
55. "Picketing Is Started on Unfair List," *Philippine Journal*, October 28, 1940.
56. *Stockton Record*, October 18, 29, 1940; and *Philippine Journal*, October 28, 1940.
57. *Nichibei Shimbun*, November 10, 1940; and *Stockton Record*, November 20, 1940. The latter source also reports the presence of 513 white workers and 82 Mexicans, blacks, and Asian Indians.
58. *Shin Sekai*, November 27, 1940.
59. *Nichibei Shimbun*, June 9, 1939 (English section).
60. Robert M. Jiobu points out that ethnic hegemony in a certain economic sector could enable a subordinate group to achieve "upward mobility" by allowing its members access to jobs and means of negotiation. In the case of the delta Japanese, it seems that ethnic hegemony in agriculture was not the real situation but an ideal one that they constantly pursued in vain. Interethnic competition was so fierce in the delta that no groups could elevate themselves relative to the dominant one. As I detailed in chapter 3, it is my interpretation that the Japanese of California were generally in a similar state of racial subordination despite

their apparent dominance in the production of certain labor-intensive crops. See Robert M. Jiobu, "Ethnic Hegemony and the Japanese of California," *American Sociological Review* 53 (June 1988): 353–367.

61. *Nichibei Shimbun*, December 5, 8, 9, 1940, February 2, 1941; and *Shin Sekai*, November 27, December 2, 8, 9, 1940.

62. *Shin Sekai*, January 6, 7, 1941.

63. I compiled these data by comparing the names of the union officials with a Japanese immigrant directory of 1941: Shin Sekai Asahi, *1941 Shin Sekai Asahi nenkan*, 282–305.

64. *Shin Sekai*, December 9, 1940.

65. Ibid., February 2, 3, 1941; and *Nichibei Shimbun*, February 2, 14, April 10, May 17, 1941 (English section).

66. *Shin Sekai*, April 12, 1941 (English section); and *Nichibei Shimbun*, April 13, 1941.

67. *Shin Sekai*, January 7, 1941.

68. On class unconsciousness, see Russell Jacoby, *Dialectic of Defeat: Contours of Western Marxism* (Cambridge: Cambridge University Press, 1981), 117–126; and Pierre Bourdieu, *Language and Symbolic Power* (Cambridge, Mass.: Harvard University Press, 1991), 235–238.

69. For cases of interethnic solidarity, see Ronald Takaki, *Pau Hana: Plantation Life and Labor in Hawaii* (Honolulu: University of Hawaii Press, 1985), 153–176; Edward D. Beechert, *Working in Hawaii: A Labor History* (Honolulu: University of Hawaii Press, 1985), 196–247; and Friday, *Organizing Asian American Labor*, 149–171. Takaki constructs an idealized "progressive" history from ethnic division to interethnic labor solidarity in the Hawaiian strike of 1920 among plantation workers, while Beechert illuminates the exceptional nature of the 1920 case by stressing the difficulty of maintaining working-class unity. Friday also considers the conflicting forces toward ethnic division and unionization, underlining the volatile nature of labor unity among Asian cannery workers in the Pacific Northwest.

70. *Nichibei Shimbun*, February 21, April 2, 17, 1942.

EPILOGUE

1. Otto Brower, dir., *Little Tokyo USA* (Twentieth Century–Fox, 1942).

2. Etienne Balibar, "Paradoxes of Universality," in *Anatomy of Racism*, ed. David Theo Goldberg (Minneapolis: University of Minnesota Press, 1990), 283–285.

3. U.S. Department of War, *Final Report: Japanese Evacuation from the West Coast, 1942* (Washington, D.C.: GPO, 1943), 34.

4. On Asian Otherness, see Lisa Lowe, *Immigrant Acts: On Asian American Cultural Politics* (Durham, N.C.: Duke University Press, 1996), 4–6.

5. This does *not* mean that Issei's way of thinking also turned binary. However unfavorable the circumstances were, Japanese immigrants, along with their sons and daughters, still acted on their own beliefs rather than being acted upon by the

forces of others' making. The point here is that whatever they did was interpreted according to the polarized notions of loyal and disloyal, pro-America and pro-Japan, and good and evil. Overall, there were three ways in which Issei negotiated the difficult situations in the camps. The first type of Issei saw no alternative but to align themselves with the hyper-Americanism that the War Relocation Authority (WRA) and the JACL had been promoting. On the other hand, having provided "disloyal" answers to the WRA-sponsored loyalty registration, other immigrants consciously gave up on America out of an ungovernable rage at white racism, uncontrollable stupefaction following the total destruction of their development, or the despair that saw no possibility of a future in the hostile land. Between these contrasts stood the vast majority of Issei men and women, who continued to swing between Japan and the United States. Even the WRA was aware of the complexities of Issei positions. U.S. War Relocation Authority, *WRA: A Story of Human Conservation* (Washington, D.C.: GPO, 1946), 50. For insightful analyses of the "disloyal" behavior, see Mae M. Ngai, *Impossible Subjects: Illegal Aliens and the Making of Modern America* (Princeton, N.J.: Princeton University Press, 2004), 177–201; and Brian Masaru Hayashi, *Democratizing the Enemy: The Japanese American Internment* (Princeton, N.J.: Princeton University Press, 2004).

6. John W. Dower, *War without Mercy: Race and Power in the Pacific War* (New York: Pantheon, 1986), 32.

7. During the war, nothing revealed Issei sentiments better than Japanese poetry, which provided ordinary immigrants with one of the few ways of expressing (remnants of) their dualism and eclecticism. Poetry, as a forum of intellectual exchange, was not new to Japanese immigrants, but the elevation of its discursive importance resulted from the wartime intrusion of state power into other venues of public discourse. As Issei were deprived of political and social roles, many of them found a venue of self-assertion, if not realization, in uncensored, recreational cultural activities. Informal literary groups sprang up in all of the internment camps, often compiling mimeographed poetry collections and journals for their own consumption. Although rough in style and aesthetically unsophisticated, Japanese poems offered many Issei a refuge from wartime nationalism.

8. Banka, in *Poston bungei* 5 (June 1943): 48, in box 12, TAP, JARP.

9. Ryūji, ibid.

10. Shisei Tsuneishi, *Hātosan Ginsha kushū* (1945), 58.

11. See Paul Spickard, *Japanese Americans: The Formation and Transformation of an Ethnic Group* (Boston: Twayne, 1996), 133–143; Jere Takahashi, *Nisei/Sansei: Shifting Japanese American Identities and Politics* (Philadelphia, Pa.: Temple University Press, 1997), 113–131; and Lon Kurashige, *Japanese American Celebration and Conflict: A History of Ethnic Identity and Festival, 1934–1990* (Berkeley: University of California Press, 2002), 119–150. Kurashige makes an important distinction between assimilation and integration in the postwar social strategy of many Nisei— an analysis that stands alone in existing historiography. The JACL policy of integration, according to him, did not necessarily mean "total *immersion* in white

America, the severing of ties to Japan and Japanese culture, or . . . interracial marriage with whites" (121). This integrationist politics still incorporated "the practice of ethnic pluralism" to a degree, while the main goal of "*inclusion* into society's main institutions" always carried pivotal weight.

12. David K. Yoo, *Growing Up Nisei: Race, Generation, and Culture among Japanese Americans of California, 1924–1949* (Urbana: University of Illinois Press, 2000), 174.

13. In the mainstream discourse, the myth of Japanese Americans as a model minority became popularized by white academicians and observers at the height of the civil rights movement. See William Peterson, "Success Story, Japanese-American Style," *New York Times Magazine*, January 9, 1966; William Peterson, *Japanese Americans: Oppression and Success* (New York: Random House, 1971); and "Success Story: Outwhiting the Whites," *Newsweek*, June 21, 1971. Peterson's 1971 synthesis set the basic tone of conservative academic discussions on the "triumph" of Japanese Americans, or more precisely, the Nisei—a myth that has come under critical reevaluation by Asian American scholars in recent years. See Deborah Woo, *Glass Ceilings and Asian Americans: The New Face of Workplace Barriers* (Walnut Creek, Calif.: AltaMira, 2000), 3–41; and Robert G. Lee, *Orientals: Asian Americans in Popular Culture* (Philadelphia, Pa.: Temple University Press 1999), 145–203.

14. See Bill Hosokawa, *Nisei, the Quiet Americans: The Story of a People* (New York: Morrow, 1969), esp. 494; and Mike Masaoka, *They Call Me Moses Masaoka* (New York: Morrow, 1987), 176.

15. On the construction of a new identity in postwar Japanese America, see T. Fujitani, "Go for Broke, the Movie: Japanese American Soldiers in U.S. National, Military, and Racial Discourses," in *Perilous Memories: The Asia-Pacific War(s)*, ed. T. Fujitani, Geoffrey M. White, and Lisa Yoneyama (Durham, N.C.: Duke University Press, 2001), 239–266; and Caroline Chung Simpson, *An Absent Presence: Japanese Americans in Postwar American Culture, 1945–1960* (Durham, N.C.: Duke University Press, 2001), esp. 43–57. For postwar master narratives, see Hosokawa, *Nisei*; Peterson, *Japanese Americans*; Robert A. Wilson and Bill Hosokawa, *East to America: A History of the Japanese in the United States* (New York: Morrow, 1980); and Bill Hosokawa, *JACL: In Quest of Justice* (New York: Morrow, 1982). The production and mass distribution of Hosokawa's works were commissioned by the JACL and hence considered to be official histories among many Japanese Americans.

16. After the Pacific War, many Issei and Nisei leaders avoided talking about their support of Japan during the 1930s. In addition to this self-censorship, there were even blatant attempts of total fabrication. An Issei minister of a Konkōkyō church in San Francisco was a case in point. While being detained in a Justice Department internment camp, this individual advocated the remigration of Japanese immigrants to South Pacific islands after the war on grounds that triumphant Japan would dramatically expand the boundaries of the empire. Later, in 1957, this Issei wrote an autobiography in which he unabashedly depicted himself

as having always believed in American democracy and opposed Japanese militarism. This may present an extreme case of self-invention, but the tendency to keep quiet about their prewar activities was not uncommon among many Issei and older Nisei.

17. Bill Hosokawa, "Maybe Nisei Have Flopped as 'Bridges' across the Pacific," *Pacific Citizen*, December 20, 1957, 4.

18. See Rogers Brubaker, *Nationalism Reframed: Nationhood and the National Question in the New Europe* (Cambridge: Cambridge University Press, 1996), 4–6. Brubaker characterizes the nationalism of a national minority as "a political stance, not an ethnodemographic fact," which such a group exhibits when it deals with either its "external homeland" to which it owes "ethnonational affinity," or the "nationalizing state" in which it presently lives. In the case of Japanese immigrants, they demanded recognition of their membership in the nation of Japan, as well as that of their rightful presence in the United States despite their lack of citizenship ties.

19. Donna R. Gabaccia, "Liberty, Coercion, and the Making of Immigrant Historians," *Journal of American History* 84 (September 1997): 570–575, esp. 575. For a useful critique of the immigrant paradigm, see Donna R. Gabaccia, "Is Everywhere Nowhere? Nomads, Nations, and the Immigrant Paradigm of United States History," *Journal of American History* 86 (December 1999): 1115–1134.

20. See David Theo Goldberg's introduction to *Anatomy of Racism*, xii.

21. See Gary Y. Okihiro, *Margins and Mainstreams: Asians in American History and Culture* (Seattle: University of Washington Press, 1994), 31–63. My proposal for the treatment of Japanese immigrants as a racial category should not be seen as a dismissal of the existing "Asian racial-formation" approach. In fact, there are a number of studies that have examined the racial dynamics of American society admirably by using Asians as a single analytical category. Because the dominant society has been prone to lump different Asian groups into the "Oriental" Other, it is still valid to analyze their varied experiences in an integrated manner. See Tomás Almaguer, *Racial Fault Lines: The Historical Origins of White Supremacy in California* (Berkeley: University of California Press, 1994); and Chris Friday, "Competing Communities at Work: Asian Americans, European Americans, and Native Alaskans in the Pacific Northwest, 1938–1947," in *Over the Edge: Remapping the American West*, ed. Valerie J. Matsumoto and Blake Allmendinger (Berkeley: University of California Press, 1999), 307–328.

22. For studies of inter-Asian relations, see Eiichiro Azuma, "Interethnic Conflict under Racial Subordination: Japanese Immigrants and Their Asian Neighbors in Walnut Grove, California, 1908–1941," *Amerasia Journal* 20 (1994): 27–56; Edwin Grant Burrow, *Chinese and Japanese in Hawaii during the Sino-Japanese Conflict* (Honolulu: Hawaii Groups, American Council, Institute of Pacific Relations, 1939); Arleen de Vera, "The Tapia-Saiki Incident: Interethnic Conflict and Filipino Responses to the Anti-Filipino Exclusion Movement," in *Over the Edge*, 201–214; and Chris Friday, *Organizing Asian American Labor: The Pacific Coast*

Canned-Salmon Industry, 1870–1942 (Philadelphia, Pa.: Temple University Press, 1994).

23. Gary Gerstle, *American Crucible: Race and Nation in the Twentieth Century* (Princeton, N.J.: Princeton University Press, 2001), 4–6, esp. 4.

24. Balibar, "Paradoxes of Universality," 283–285.

25. Gerstle, *American Crucible*, 115–116.

26. Yuji Ichioka, "The Meaning of Loyalty: The Case of Kazumaro Buddy Uno," *Amerasia Journal* 23 (Winter 1997–1998): 62–63.

27. For example, Ronald Takaki's history of multicultural America still privileges "loyalty" and "contribution" to illustrate the diverse but unified American experience, and the author singles out the doings of Issei in California agriculture and those of Nisei internees and servicemen during the war. See Ronald Takaki, *A Different Mirror: A History of Multicultural America* (New York: Little, Brown, 1993), 246–277, 376–385, 401–402.

Bibliography

MANUSCRIPT MATERIALS

Diplomatic Records Office, Tokyo *(DRO)*

Meiji-Taishō Series
Beikoku ni okeru Hainichi Mondai zakken (BHMZ).
Hokubei Gasshūkoku ni oite Honpōjin tokō seigen oyobi haiseki ikken (HGHH).
Honpō Imin kankei zakken (HIKZ).
Honpōjin Mibun oyobi Seikō chōsa: Zaigai Honpōjin (HMSC).
Honshō shokuin yōsei kankei zakken (HSYK).
Kaigai ni okeru honpō Shūgyōfu no insū oyobi sono jyōkyō to nen nikai Hōkōku
  kata kuntatsu ikken (KHSH).
Kagekiha sonota Kiken Shugisha torishimari kankei zakken (KKST).
Minzoku mondai kankei zakken (MMKZ).
Nihon Jinmin Hawaikoku e dekasegi ikken: Dekaseginin kaiyaku kikoku no bu
  (NJHD).
Nichiro sen'eki ni saishi gunshikin kennō zakken (NSSG).
Ryōji Kaigi kankei zakken (RKKZ).
Taibei keihatsu undō ni kansuru ken (TKUK).
Zaibei Honpōjin no jōkyō narabi tobeisha torishimari kankei zassan (ZHJT).

Shōwa Series
Gaikokujin ni taisuru Zaigai Kōkan hakkyū sashō hōkoku ikken (GTZK).
Honpōjin no Kaigai nōgyō kankei zakken (HKNK).

Honshō narabi Zaigai Kōkan'in shucchō kankei zakken: Zaibei kakkan (HZKS).
Manshū Jihen yoron narabi Shinbun ronchō yoron keihatsu kankei (MJYS).
Nihongo Gakkō chōsa ikken (NGCI).
Nikkei Gaijin kankei zakken (NGKZ).
Zaigai Honpōjin hogo narabi torishimari kankei zakken (ZHHT).
Zaigai Kōkan shiyōnin chōsa narabi hōkoku (ZKSC).
Zaigai Nihonjinkai kankei zakken (ZNKZ).

Japan Young Women's Christian Association National Headquarters Archives, Tokyo (JYWCA)

Japanese American National Museum, Los Angeles (JANM)

Los Angeles Nippon Institute (Rafu Daini Gakuen) Collection (LANI).
Reverend Takeshi Ban Family Collection (RTBF).

Japanese American Research Project, University of California, Los Angeles (JARP)

Abiko Family Papers.
Akahori Masaru Papers.
Central Japanese Association of Southern California Records.
Intermountain Japanese Association Records (IJAR).
Japanese Association of Los Angeles (Rafu Nihonjinkai) Records.
Karl G. Yoneda Papers (KGYP).
Kawashimo Nihonjinkjai kiroku (Japanese Association of Walnut Grove Records) (KNK).
T. Scott Miyakawa Papers.
Togawa Akira Papers (TAP).

Japanese Overseas Migration Museum, Yokohama (JOMM)

Heishikan Collection.

Keisen Women's College Archives, Tokyo (KWCA)

National Archives of Japan, Tokyo (NAJ)

Education Ministry (Monbushō) Papers, Gakusei seito sōki (GSS).
Home Ministry (Naimushō) Papers.
2,600th Anniversary Collection.

Nihon Rikkōkai Archives, Tokyo

Emigration Collection.

Oregon Historical Society, Portland

Yasui Brothers Family Papers (YBP).

Sacramento County Recorder's Office, California *(SCRO)*

Shibusawa Memorial Archives, Tokyo *(SMA)*

U.S. National Archives, College Park, Maryland *(NACP)*

Record Group 38 (RG 38): Records of the Office of the Chief of Naval Operations
Office of Naval Intelligence, Security Classified Administrative Correspondence, 1942–
    1946 (SCAC).
Oriental Desk, Office of Naval Intelligence (ODONI).

Record Group 59 (RG 59): State Department Central Decimal File
Records of the U.S. Department of State relating to the Internal Affairs of Japan,
    1930–1939 (RUSD).
Records of the U.S. Department of State relating to the Internal Affairs of Japan,
    1940–1944 (RUSDS).

*Record Group 165 (RG 165): Records of the War Department General and Special
    Staffs*
Military Intelligence Division Correspondence, 1917–1941 (MIDC).

Record Group 338 (RG 338): Western Defense Command and Fourth Army
Wartime Civil Control Administration and Civil Affairs Division, General Correspon-
    dence 1942–1946 (GCWC).

U.S. National Archives, Pacific Southwest Region, Laguna Niguel, California
(NAPS)

Record Group 85 (RG 85): Records of Immigration and Naturalization Service
Enemy Alien Case Files (EACF).

University Archives, University of Washington, Seattle *(UAUW)*

James Y. Sakamoto Papers (JYSP).
Japanese Association of North America Records (JANA).
North American Japanese Association Records (NAJA).

Waseda University History Archives, Tokyo *(WUHA)*

NEWSPAPERS AND PERIODICALS

United States

Aikoku. 1892 (San Francisco).
Beikoku Sangyō Nippō (*Sangyō Nippō*). 1937–1938 (Los Angeles).
Dai-Jūkyūseiki. 1888–1889 (San Francisco).
Dōhō (*Doho*). 1937–1941 (Los Angeles).
Japanese American Courier. 1931–1940 (Seattle).
Japanese American Weekly. 1941 (New York).
Japanese El Rodeo. 1912 (Los Angeles).
Kashū Chūō Nōkai Geppō. 1916–1918 (San Francisco).
Kashū Mainichi (*Japan California Daily News*). 1931–1942 (Los Angeles).
Nanka Gādenā Renmei Geppō. 1937–1938 (Los Angeles).
Nichibei Shimbun (*Japanese American News*). 1912–1942 (San Francisco).
Ōfu Nippō (*Sacramento Daily News*). 1908–1925 (Sacramento).
Pacific Rural Press (*PRP*). 1902–1920 (San Francisco).
Philippine Journal. 1939–1941 (Stockton).
Rafu Shimpō (L.A. *Japanese Daily News*). 1920–1942 (Los Angeles).
Sacramento Bee. 1921–1923.
San Francisco Chronicle. 1918–1919.
Shin Sekai (*New World Daily and New World-Sun*). 1899–1900, 1906–1942 (San Francisco).
Stockton Record. 1939–1940.
Taihoku Nippō (*Great Northern Daily News*). 1923–1925 (Seattle).
Utah Nippō. 1937–1940 (Salt Lake City).

Japan

Amerika (*America*). 1907–1909 (Tokyo).
Gaiko Jihō (*Revue Diplomatique*). 1924–1941 (Tokyo).
International Youth. 1938–1941 (Tokyo).
Joshi Seinenkai (*JS*). 1915–1919 (Tokyo).
Kaigai no Nippon. 1937–1941 (Tokyo).

Keisen (*Keisen News*). 1932–1941 (Tokyo).
Miyako Shinbun. 1933, 1940 (Tokyo).
Nihonjin. 1893–1894, 1896–1897 (Tokyo).
Nippon to Amerika (*Japan and America*). 1938–1941 (Tokyo).
Pan-Pacific Youth. 1939 (Tokyo).
Rikkō Sekai. 1923–1940 (Tokyo).
Shokumin Kyōkai hōkoku (*SKH*). 1893–1902 (Tokyo).
Tokyo Asahi Shinbun. 1933, 1936, 1940 (Tokyo).
Yomiuri Shinbun. 1933, 1940 (Tokyo).
Young Women of Japan. 1916–1918 (Tokyo).

PUBLISHED GOVERNMENT SOURCES

United States

California State Board of Control. *California and the Oriental: Japanese, Chinese, and Hindus.* Sacramento: California State Printing Office, 1922.
California State Department of Industrial Relations. *Facts about Filipino Immigration into California.* San Francisco: Department of Industrial Relations, 1930.
Oregon Bureau of Labor. *Census: Japanese Population in Oregon.* Salem: Oregon Bureau of Labor, 1929.
U.S. Congress. House of Representatives. Committee on Immigration and Naturalization. *Japanese Immigration: Hearings before the Committee on Immigration and Naturalization.* Washington, D.C.: GPO, 1921.
———. House of Representatives. Select Committee Investigating National Defense Migration. *Hearings before the Select Committee Investigating National Defense Migration.* Part 31: *Los Angeles and San Francisco Hearings.* Washington, D.C.: GPO, 1942.
———. Senate. Committee on Education and Labor. *Violations of Free Speech and Rights of Labor: Hearings before a Subcommittee of the Committee on Education and Labor.* Washington, D.C.: GPO, 1940.
———. Senate. Subcommittee of the Committee on Education and Labor. *Report: Violations of Free Speech and Rights of Labor.* Part 72. Washington, D.C.: GPO, 1942.
U.S. Department of Labor. Bureau of Immigration. *Annual Report of the Commissioner General of Immigration.* Washington, D.C.: GPO, 1916–1917, 1919, 1922–1927.
U.S. Department of War. *Final Report: Japanese Evacuation from the West Coast, 1942.* Washington, D.C.: GPO, 1943.
U.S. Immigration Commission. *Immigrants in Industries.* Part 25: *Japanese and Other Immigrant Races in the Pacific Coast and Rocky Mountain States.* Washington, D.C.: GPO, 1911.
U.S. War Relocation Authority. *WRA: A Story of Human Conservation.* Washington, D.C.: GPO, 1946.

Japan

Gaimushō. Amerika-kyoku. "Jikyokuka ni okeru Zaibei-Ka Hōjin no genjō narabi sono taisaku" (May 1941). DRO.

———. Jōhōbu. "Shina Jihen ni okeru Jōhō senden kōsaku gaiyō" (September 1938). Pt. 2. DRO.

———. Tsūshōkyoku Iminka. "Kashū oyobi Kashū Tochihō shiso keika gaiyō" (1923). DRO.

———. *Nihon Gaikō bunsho* (*NGB*). Vols. 24–26, 39–42 (1891–1893, 1906–1909). Tokyo: Nihon Kokusai Rengō Kyōkai, 1952–1961.

———. *Nihon Gaikō bunsho*. Taishō 2:3 (1913). Tokyo: Gaimushō, 1965.

———. *Nihon Gaikō bunsho: Taibei imin mondai keika gaiyō*. Tokyo: Gaimushō, 1972.

Naikaku Jōhōbu. *Kigen Nisen Roppyakunen Shukuten kiroku*. Vols. 1–13. Tokyo: Naikaku Jōhōbu, 1942.

Naimushō Keihokyoku. *Shōwa 16-nenchū ni okeru Gaiji Keisatsu gaikyō*. 1941. Reprinted in *Gaiji Keisatsu gaiyō* 7. Tokyo: Ryūkei Shosha, 1980.

———. *Shōwa 17-nenchū ni okeru Gaiji Keisatsu jōkyō*. 1943. Reprinted in *Gaiji Keisatsu gaiyō* 8. Tokyo: Ryūkei Shosha, 1980.

Rafu Nihon Ryōjikan. "Ohanashi taikai oyobi sakubun kyōgi taikai." Los Angeles: Rafu Nihon Ryōjikan, 1933.

Shūgiin. *Teikoku Gikai Shūgiin Iinkaigiroku: Shōwa-hen*. Vol. 85 (1937–1938). Reprint. Tokyo: Tokyo Daigaku Shuppan, 1995.

SELECTED PRIMARY SOURCES

Abe, Seizō. *Muteikō shugi seishin dōmei*. Seattle, Wash.: Abe Seizō, 1924.

Akagi, Roy Hidemichi. *The Second Generation Problem: Some Suggestions toward Its Solution*. New York: Japanese Student Christian Association, 1926.

Akamine, Seichirō. *Beikoku ima fushigi*. Tokyo: Jitsugakusha Eigakkō, 1886.

America-Japan Society. *Special Bulletin* 1. Tokyo: America-Japan Society, 1925.

Aoyagi, Ikutarō, ed. *Zaigai Hōjin Dai-Nisei mondai*. Tokyo: Imin Mondai Kenkyūkai, 1940.

Ban, Shinzaburō. "Ban Shinzaburō kun no hokubei dan." *Shokumin Kyōkai hōkoku* 12 (April 1894): 47–67.

———. "Yo wa Beikoku nite yonsen no dōhō to tomoni sūko no tetsudō o shisetsu shitari." *Jitsugyō no Nihon* 12 (August 1909): 23–34.

Chiba, Toyoji. *Beikoku Kashū hainichi jijō*. San Francisco: Nichibei Kankei Chōsakai, 1921.

———. "Chiba Toyoji ikō," Vol 2. Unpublished manuscript, 1944.

Dodō, Masao. *Taiheiyō jidai to Beikoku*. Los Angeles: Rafu Shimpōsha, 1933.

Ebihara, Hachirō. *Kaigai Hōji shinbun zasshi-shi*. Tokyo: Gakuji Shobō, 1936.

Endō, Kōshirō. *Kanputon ryō gakuen enpō.* Compton, Calif.: Privately printed, 1936, 1940.

Endō, Kōshirō, ed. *Tsuzurikata bunshū: Shina Jihen-gō.* Compton, Calif.: Compton Gakuen, 1938.

Endō, Shirō. *Minami Kashū Okayama kenjin hattenshi.* Los Angeles: Minami Kashū Okayama Kenjin Hattenshi Hensanjo, 1941.

Fujioka, Shirō. *Ayumi no ato.* Los Angeles: Ayumi no Ato Kankō Kōenkai, 1957.

———. *Beikoku Chūō Nihonjinkaishi.* Los Angeles: Beikoku Chūō Nihonjinkai, 1940.

———. *Minzoku hatten no senkusha.* Tokyo: Dōbunsha, 1927.

Fukuzawa, Yukichi. *Fukuzawa Yukichi zenshū (FYZ).* Vols. 9–11. Tokyo: Iwanami Shoten, 1932.

Hasegawa, Shin'ichirō. *Zaibei Hōjin no mitaru Beikoku to Beikokujin.* Tokyo: Jitsugyō no Nihonsha, 1937.

Hirohata, Tsunegorō. *Zaibei Fukuoka kenjinshi.* Los Angeles: Zaibei Fukuoka Kenjinshi Hensan Jimusho, 1931.

———. *Zaibei Fukuoka kenjin to jigyō.* Los Angeles: Zaibei Fukuoka Kenjin to Jigyō Hensan Jimusho, 1936.

Hirose, Shurei. *Zaibei Kōshūjin funtō gojūnenshi.* Los Angeles: Nanka Yamanashi Kaigai Kyōkai, 1934.

Hokka Nihongo Gakuen Kyōkai. *Beikoku Kashū Nihongo Gakuen enkakushi.* San Francisco: Hokka Nihongo Gakuen Kyōkai, 1930.

Ichihashi, Yamato. *Japanese in the United States.* Stanford, Calif.: Stanford University Press, 1932.

Irie, Toraji. *Hōjin kaigai hattenshi.* Vols. 1–2. Tokyo: Ide Shoten, 1942.

Ishikawa, Kanmei. *Fukuzawa Yukichi den.* Vol. 2. Tokyo: Iwanami Shoten, 1932.

Japanese Agricultural Association. *Japanese Farmers in California.* San Francisco: Japanese Agricultural Association, 1918.

Kaibara, Sakae. *Kashū Hiroshima kenjin hattenshi.* Sacramento: Yorozu Shoten, 1916.

Kaigai Dōhō Chūōkai. *Kigen Nisen Roppyakunen Hōshuku Kaigai Dōhō Tokyo Taikai hōkokusho.* Tokyo: Kaigai Dōhō Chūōkai, 1941.

Kanai, Shigeo, and Banshō Ito. *Hokubei no Nihonjin.* San Francisco: Japan Insatsu Kaisha, 1909.

Katayama, Sen. *Shin tobei.* Tokyo: Rōdō Shimbunsha, 1904.

———. *Tobei annai.* Tokyo: Rōdō Shimbunsha, 1901.

Katō, Shi'nichi. *Minami Kashū Nihonjin nanajūnenshi.* Los Angeles: Nanka Nikkeijin Shōgyō Kaigisho, 1960.

Kawai, Michi. *My Lantern.* Tokyo: Kyōbunkan, 1939.

Kawai, Sōsuke, ed. *Ōka Nikkei Shimin shashin.* Tacoma, Wash.: Takoma Shūhōsha, 1938.

Kawamura, Yūsen. *Hainichi sensen o toppa shitsutsu.* Isleton, Calif.: Kawamura Yūsen, 1930.

Kawashima, Isami. *Nichibei gaikōshi.* San Francisco: Hatae Minoru, 1932.

Kihara, Ryūkichi. *Hawai Nihonjinshi*. Tokyo: Bunseisha, 1935.

Kobayashi, Masasuke. *Nihon minzoku no sekaiteki bōchō*. Tokyo: Keigansha, 1933.

Mears, Eliot Grinnell. *Resident Orientals on the American Pacific Coast: Their Legal and Economic Status*. Chicago: University of Chicago Press, 1928.

Mizutani, Bangaku. *Hokubei Aichi kenjinshi*. Sacramento, Calif.: Aichi Kenjinkai, 1920.

Mizutani, Shōzō. *Nyūyōku Nihonjin hattenshi*. New York: Nyūyōku Nihonjinkai, 1921.

Mukaeda, Katsuma, and Masatoshi Nakamura. *Zaibei no Higojin*. Los Angeles: Nanka Kumamoto Kaigai Kyōkai, 1931.

Murai, Kō. *Zaibei Nihonjin sangyō sōran*. Los Angeles: Beikoku Sangyō Nippōsha, 1940.

Murayama, Tamotsu. *Shūsen no koro*. Tokyo: Jiji Tsūshin, 1968.

Nakagawa, Mushō. *Zaibei tōshiroku*. Los Angeles: Rafu Shimpōsha, 1932.

Nanka Nihongo Gakuen Kyōkai. *Kyōju to keiei*. Los Angeles: Nanka Nihongo Gakuen Kyōkai, 1932.

———. *Kyōyō to shokugyō*. Los Angeles: Nanka Nihongo Gakuen Kyōkai, 1928.

Nanka Nihonjin Kirisuto Kyōkai Renmei. *Zaibei Nihonjin Kirisutokyō gojūnenshi*. Los Angeles: Nanka Nihonjin Kirisutokyō Kyōkai Renmei, 1932.

Nichibei Shimbunsha. *Nichibei nenkan*. Vols. 4, 6–12. San Francisco: Nichibei Shimbunsha, 1908, 1910–1918.

———. *Nichibei taikan*. San Francisco: Nichibei Shimbunsha, 1931.

———. *Zaibei Nihonjin jinmei jiten*. San Francisco: Nichibei Shimbunsha, 1922.

Nihon Beifu Kyōkai. *Dai-Nisei sōsho*. Tokyo: Nihon Beifu Kyokai, 1938.

Nihon Bunka Kyōkai. *Nihon Bunka Kyōkai setsuritsu keika*. Los Angeles: Nihon Bunka Kyōkai, 1939.

Niisato, Kan'ichi. *Iminchi aiwa*. Tokyo: Shimpōsha, 1934, 1935.

———. *Zaibei no Nihon minzoku gohyakunen no taikei*. Tokyo: Shimpōsha, 1939.

Nisei Survey Committee. *The Nisei: A Survey of Their Educational, Vocational, and Social Problems*. Tokyo: Keisen Girls' School, 1939.

Nitobe, Inazō. *Bushido: The Soul of Japan*. Tokyo: Kenkyōsha, 1936.

———. *Nitobe Inazō zenshū*. Vols. 6, 12, 13. Tokyo: Kyōbunkan, 1969.

Ōfu Nippōsha. *Sakuramento Heigen Nihonjin taisei ichiran*. Vol. 2. Sacramento, Calif.: Ōfu Nippō, 1909.

Ōhashi, Kanzō. *Hokubei Kashū Sutokuton dōhōshi*. Stockton, Calif.: Su-shi Nihonjinkai, 1937.

Ōtsuka, Kō. *Ishokumin to kyōiku mondai*. Tokyo: Tōkō Shoin, 1933.

Ōtsuka, Zentarō. *Nichibei gaikōron*. Tokyo: Sagamiya Shoten, 1910.

Price, Willard. *Children of the Rising Sun*. New York: Reynal & Hitchcock, 1938.

Rafu Shimpōsha. *Hōshuku kinen taikan*. Los Angeles: Rafu Shimpōsha, 1940.

———. *Rafu nenkan, 1937–1938*. Los Angeles: Rafu Shimpōsha, 1937.

Ringle, Kenneth D. "Japanese in America: The Problem and the Solution." *Harper's Magazine* 185 (1942): 489–497.

Saka, Hisagorō. *Santa Maria Heigen Nihonjinshi*. Guadalupe, Calif.: Gadarūpu Nihonjinkai, 1936.

Satō, Masashi. *Kaigai Nisei kyōiku no taiken o kataru*. Tokyo: Kaigai Kyōiku Kyōkai, 1933.

Shakai Bunko, ed. *Zaibei Shakai shugisha Museifu shugisha enkaku (ZSS)*. Tokyo: Kashiwa Shobō, 1964.

Shibayama, Taketoku. *Zaigai dōhō o mukaete*. Tokyo: Nihon Takushoku Kyōkai, 1941.

Shibusawa Seien Kinen Zaidan Ryūmonsha, ed. *Shibusawa Eiichi denki shiryō (SED)*. Vols. 25, 33, 34, 37. Tokyo: Shibusawa Eiichi Denki Shiryō Kankōkai, 1959–1961.

Shimanuki, Hyōdayū. *Tobei annai taizen*. Tokyo: Chūyōdō, 1901.

Shishimoto, Hachirō. *Nikkei Shimin o kataru*. Tokyo: Shōkasha, 1934.

Shūyū, Sanjin (pseud.), and Kumajirō Ishida. *Kitare Nihonjin*. Tokyo: Kaishindō, 1887.

Sōkō Nihonjin Kirisutokyō Joshi Seinenkai. *Kaiko nijūnen*. San Francisco: Sōkō Nihonjin Kirisutokyō Joshi Seinenkai, 1932.

Soyeda, J., and T. Kamiya. *A Survey of the Japanese Question in California*. San Francisco: Privately printed, 1913.

Takeda, Jun'ichi. *Zaibei Hiroshima kenjinshi*. Los Angeles: Zaibei Hiroshima Kenjinshi Hakkōsho, 1929.

Takeuchi, Kojirō. *Beikoku Seihokubu Nihon iminshi*. Seattle, Wash.: Taihoku Nippōsha, 1929.

Takeuchi, Kōsuke. *San Pidoro dōhō hattenroku*. Terminal Island, Calif.: Takeuchi Kōsuke, 1937.

Takoma Shūhōsha. *Takoma-shi oyobi chihō Nihonjinkai*. Tacoma, Wash.: Takoma Shūhōsha, 1941.

Terakawa, Hōkō. *Hokubei kaikyō enkakushi*. San Francisco: Hongwanji Hokubei Kaikyō Honbu, 1936.

Tōga, Yoichi. *Nichibei kankei Zaibeikoku Nihonjin hatten shiyō*. Oakland: Beikoku Seisho Kyōkai Nihonjinbu, 1927.

Tsunemitsu, Kōnen. *Nihon ryūgaku no jissai*. Tokyo: Runbini Shuppansha, 1936.

Washizu, Shakuma (Bunzō). *Zaibei Nihonjin shikan*. Los Angeles: Rafu Shimpōsha, 1930.

Yakima Nihonjinkai. *Yakima Heigen Nihonjinshi*. Yakima, Wash.: Yakima Nihonjinkai, 1935.

Yamada, Tatsumi. *Kaigai Dai-Nisei mondai*. Tokyo: Kibundō, 1936.

Yamane, Goichi. *Saikin tobei annai*. Tokyo: Tobei Zasshisha, 1906.

Yamashita, Sōen. *Nichibei o tsunagu mono*. Tokyo: Bunseisha, 1938.

———. *Nikkei shimin no Nihon ryūgaku jijō*. Tokyo: Bunseido, 1935.

Yatsu, Riichirō. *Zaibei Miyagi kenjinshi*. Los Angeles: Zaibei Miyagi Kenjinshi Hensan Jimusho, 1933.

Yusa, Hanboku (Keizō). *Hanboku zenshū*. Santa Maria, Calif.: Yusa Hanboku, 1940.

Zaibei Nihonjinkai. *Shin tobei fujin no shiori*. San Francisco: Zaibei Nihonjinkai, 1919.

———. *Zaibei Nihonjinkai hōkōkusho (ZNH)*. Vols. 1–10. San Francisco: Zaibei Nihonjinkai, 1909–1918.

———. *Zaibei Nihonjinshi*. San Francisco: Zaibei Nihonjinkai, 1940.

SELECTED SECONDARY SOURCES

Adelman, Jeremy, and Stephen Aaron. "From Borderlands to Borders: Empires, Nation-States, and the Peoples in Between in North American History." *American Historical Review* 104 (June 1999): 814–841.

Almaguer, Tomás. *Racial Fault Lines: The Historical Origins of White Supremacy in California.* Berkeley: University of California Press, 1994.

Azuma, Eiichiro. "Historical Overview of Japanese Emigration, 1868–2000." In *Encyclopedia of Japanese Descendants in the Americas: An Illustrated History of the Nikkei*, ed. Akemi Kikumura-Yano, 32–48. Walnut Creek, Calif.: AltaMira, 2002.

———. "A History of Oregon's Issei, 1880–1952." *Oregon Historical Quarterly* 94 (Winter 1993–1994): 315–367.

———. "Interethnic Conflict under Racial Subordination: Japanese Immigrants and Their Asian Neighbors in Walnut Grove, California, 1908–1941." *Amerasia Journal* 20 (1994): 27–56.

———. "Interstitial Lives: Race, Community, and History among Japanese Immigrants Caught between Japan and the United States, 1885–1941." Ph.D. diss., University of California, Los Angeles, 2000.

———. "Japanese Immigrant Farmers and California Alien Land Laws: A Study of the Walnut Grove Japanese Community." *California History* 73 (Spring 1994): 14–29.

Blacker, Carmen. *The Japanese Enlightenment: A Study of the Writings of Fukuzawa Yukichi.* Cambridge: Cambridge University Press, 1964.

Bodnar, John E. *Remaking America: Public Memory, Commemoration, and Patriotism in the Twentieth Century.* Princeton, N.J.: Princeton University Press, 1991.

Bonacich, Edna. "Asian Labor in the Development of California and Hawaii." In *Labor Immigration under Capitalism: Asian Workers in the United States before World War II*, ed. Edna Bonacich and Lucie Cheng, 130–185. Berkeley: University of California Press, 1984.

Bourdieu, Pierre. *The Field of Cultural Production.* New York: Columbia University Press, 1993.

———. *In Other Words: Essays towards a Reflective Sociology.* Stanford, Calif.: Stanford University Press, 1990.

———. *The Logic of Practice.* Stanford, Calif.: Stanford University Press, 1990.

Bowen, Roger. *Rebellion and Democracy in Meiji Japan.* Berkeley: University of California Press, 1980.

Brubaker, Rogers. *Nationalism Reframed: Nationhood and the National Question in the New Europe.* Cambridge: Cambridge University Press, 1996.

Chan, Sucheng. *This Bittersweet Soil: The Chinese in California Agriculture, 1860–1910.* Berkeley: University of California Press, 1986.

Chang, Gordon H. "History and Postmodernism." *Amerasia Journal* 21 (1995): 89–93.

———. *Morning Glory, Evening Shadow: Yamato Ichihashi and His Internment Writings, 1942–1945.* Stanford, Calif.: Stanford University Press, 1997.

Chen, Yong. *Chinese San Francisco, 1850–1943: A Trans-Pacific Community.* Stanford, Calif.: Stanford University Press, 2000.

Chun, Gloria H. "Go West . . . to China: Chinese American Identity in the 1930s." In *Claiming America: Constructing Chinese American Identities during the Exclusion Era*, ed. K. Scott Wong and Sucheng Chan, 170–180. Philadelphia, Pa.: Temple University Press, 1998.

Cinel, Dino. *From Italy to San Francisco: The Immigrant Experience*. Stanford, Calif.: Stanford University Press, 1982.

Clifford, James. "Diaspora." *Cultural Anthropology* 9 (1994): 302–338.

Craig, Albert. "Fukuzawa Yukichi: The Political Foundations of Meiji Nationalism." In *Political Development in Modern Japan*, ed. Robert E. Ward, 99–148. Princeton, N.J.: Princeton University Press, 1973.

Daniel, Cletus E. *Bitter Harvest: A History of California Farmworkers, 1870–1941*. Berkeley: University of California Press, 1982.

Daniels, Roger. "American Historians and East Asian Immigrants." *Pacific Historical Review* 43 (November 1974): 449–472.

———. *The Politics of Prejudice: The Anti-Japanese Movement in California and the Struggle for Japanese Exclusion*. Berkeley: University of California Press, 1962.

———. "Westerners from the East: Oriental Immigrants Reappraised." *Pacific Historical Review* 35 (November 1966): 373–384.

De Vera, Arleen. "Constituting Community: A Study of Nationalism, Colonialism, Gender, and Identity among Filipinos in California, 1919–1946." Ph.D. diss., University of California, Los Angeles, 2002.

———. "The Tapia-Saiki Incident: Interethnic Conflict and Filipino Responses to the Anti-Filipino Exclusion Movement." In *Over the Edge: Remapping the American West*, ed. Valerie Matsumoto and Blake Allmendinger, 201–214. Berkeley: University of California Press, 1999.

DeWitt, Howard. *Violence in the Fields: California Filipino Farm Labor Unionization during the Great Depression*. Saratoga, Calif.: Century Twenty One, 1980.

Dirlik, Arif. "Asians on the Rim: Transnational Capital and Local Community in the Making of Contemporary Asian America." *Amerasia Journal* 22 (1996): 1–24.

Doak, Kevin M. "Ethnic Nationalism and Romanticism in Early Twentieth-Century Japan." *Journal of Japanese Studies* 22 (1996): 77–103.

———. "What Is a Nation and Who Belongs? National Narratives and the Ethnic Imagination in Twentieth-Century Japan." *American Historical Review* 102 (April 1997): 283–309.

Doi, Yatarō. *Yamaguchi-ken Ōshima-gun Hawai iminshi*. Tokuyama: Matsuno Shoten, 1980.

Dower, John. *War without Mercy: Race and Power in the Pacific War*. New York: Pantheon, 1986.

Duus, Masayo Umezawa. *The Japanese Conspiracy: The Oahu Sugar Strike of 1920*. Berkeley: University of California Press, 1999.

———. *Tokyo Rose: Orphan of the Pacific*. New York: Kodansha International, 1979.

Duus, Peter. *The Abacus and the Sword: The Japanese Penetration of Korea, 1895–1910*. Berkeley: University of California Press, 1995.

Espiritu, Augusto Fauni. "Expatriate Affirmations: The Performance of Nationalism and Patronage in Filipino American Intellectual Life." Ph.D. diss., University of California, Los Angeles, 2000.

Friday, Chris. "Asian American Labor and Historical Interpretation." *Labor History* 35 (Fall 1994): 524–546.

——. "Competing Communities at Work: Asian Americans, European Americans, and Native Alaskans in the Pacific Northwest, 1938–1947." In *Over the Edge: Remapping the American West*, ed. Valerie Matsumoto and Blake Allmendinger, 307–328. Berkeley: University of California Press, 1999.

——. *Organizing Asian American Labor: The Pacific Coast Canned-Salmon Industry, 1870–1942*. Philadelphia, Pa.: Temple University Press, 1994.

Fujitani, T. "Go for Broke, the Movie: Japanese American Soldiers in U.S. National, Military, and Racial Discourses." In *Perilous Memories: The Asia-Pacific War(s)*, ed. T. Fujitani et al., 239–266. Durham, N.C.: Duke University Press, 2001.

Fujitani, Takashi. *Splendid Monarchy: Power and Pageantry in Modern Japan*. Berkeley: University of California Press, 1996.

Gabaccia, Donna R. "Is Everywhere Nowhere? Nomads, Nations, and the Immigrant Paradigm of United States History." *Journal of American History* 86 (December 1999): 1115–1134.

——. "Liberty, Coercion, and the Making of Immigrant Historians." *Journal of American History* 84 (September 1997): 570–575.

Garon, Sheldon. *Molding Japanese Minds: The State in Everyday Life*. Princeton, N.J.: Princeton University Press, 1997.

Gerstle, Gary. *American Crucible: Race and Nation in the Twentieth Century*. Princeton, N.J.: Princeton University Press, 2001.

——. *Working-Class Americanism: The Politics of Labor in a Textile City, 1914–1960*. Princeton, N.J.: Princeton University Press, 2002.

Gillis, John R., ed. *Commemorations: The Politics of National Identity*. Princeton, N.J.: Princeton University Press, 1997.

Gilroy, Paul. *The Black Atlantic: Modernity and Double Consciousness*. Cambridge, Mass.: Harvard University Press, 1993.

Glenn, Evelyn Nakano. *Unequal Freedom: How Race and Gender Shaped American Citizenship and Labor*. Cambridge, Mass.: Harvard University Press, 2002.

Gluck, Carol. *Japan's Modern Myths: Ideology in the Late Meiji Period*. Princeton, N.J.: Princeton University Press, 1985.

Goldberg, David Theo, ed. *Anatomy of Racism*. Minneapolis: University of Minnesota Press, 1990.

Guarnizo, Luis Eduardo, and Michael Peter Smith. "The Locations of Transnationalism." In *Transnationalism from Below*, ed. Michael Smith and Luis Eduardo Guarnizo, 3–34. New Brunswick, N.J.: Transaction, 1998.

Hall, Stuart. "Cultural Identity and Diaspora." In *Identity: Community, Culture, Difference*, ed. J. Rutherford, 222–237. London: Lawrence, 1990.

Hannerz, Ulf. *Transnational Connections*. New York: Routledge, 1996.

Harutoonian, Harry, and Tetsuo Najita. "Japanese Revolt against the West: Political and Cultural Criticism in the Twentieth Century." In *The Cambridge History of*

Japan. Vol. 6: *The Twentieth Century*, ed. Peter Duus, 711–774. Cambridge: Cambridge University Press, 1988.

Hayashi, Brian M. *Democratizing the Enemy: The Japanese American Internment.* Princeton, N.J.: Princeton University Press, 2004.

————. *"For the Sake of Our Japanese Brethren": Assimilation, Nationalism, and Protestantism among the Japanese of Los Angeles, 1895–1942.* Stanford, Calif.: Stanford University Press, 1995.

————. "The Japanese 'Invasion' of California: Major Kobayashi and the Japanese Salvation Army, 1919–1926." *Journal of the West* 23 (April 1984): 73–82.

Hirobe, Izumi. *Japanese Pride, American Prejudice: Modifying the Exclusion Clause of the 1924 Immigration Act.* Stanford, Calif.: Stanford University Press, 2001.

Horsman, Reginald. *Race and Manifest Destiny.* Cambridge, Mass.: Harvard University Press, 1981.

Hosokawa, Bill. *JACL: In Quest of Justice.* New York: Morrow, 1982.

————. *Nisei, the Quiet Americans: The Story of a People.* New York: Morrow, 1969.

Hoston, Germaine A. "The State, Modernity, and the Fate of Liberalism in Prewar Japan." *Journal of Asian Studies* 51 (May 1992): 287–316.

Howes, John F., ed. *Nitobe Inazo: Japan's Bridge across the Pacific.* Boulder, Colo.: Westview, 1995.

Hsu, Madeline Y. *Dreaming of Gold, Dreaming of Home: Transnationalism and Migration between the United States and South China, 1882–1943.* Stanford, Calif.: Stanford University Press, 2000.

Hu-DeHart, Evelyn, ed. *Across the Pacific: Asian Americans and Globalization.* Philadelphia, Pa.: Temple University Press, 2000.

Hune, Shirley. "Asian American Studies and Asian Studies: Boundaries and Borderlands of Ethnic Studies and Area Studies." In *Color-Line to Borderlands: The Matrix of American Ethnic Studies*, ed. Johnnella E. Butler, 227–239. Seattle: University of Washington Press, 2001.

Ichioka, Yuji. " 'Attorney for the Defense': Yamato Ichihashi and Japanese Immigration." *Pacific Historical Review* 55 (1986): 192–225.

————. *Before Internment: Essays in Prewar Japanese-American History,* ed. Arif Dirlik, Eiichiro Azuma, and Gordon H. Chang. Stanford, Calif.: Stanford University Press, forthcoming.

————. "Beyond National Boundaries: The Complexity of Japanese-American History." *Amerasia Journal* 23 (Winter 1997–1998): vii–xi.

————. "A Historian by Happenstance." *Amerasia Journal* 26 (2000): 32–53.

————. *The Issei: The World of the First Generation Japanese Immigrants, 1885–1924.* New York: Free Press, 1988.

————. "Japanese Immigrant Nationalism: The Issei and the Sino-Japanese War, 1937–1941." *California History* 69 (Fall 1990): 260–275.

————. "Kengakudan: The Origin of Nisei Study Tours of Japan." *California History* 73 (Spring 1994): 31–42.

————. "The Meaning of Loyalty: The Case of Kazumaro Buddy Uno." *Amerasia Journal* 23 (Winter 1997–1998): 45–71.

———. "A Study in Dualism: James Yoshinori Sakamoto and the *Japanese American Courier*, 1928–1942." *Amerasia Journal* 13 (1986–1987): 49–81.

Ignatiev, Noel. *How The Irish Became White*. New York: Routledge, 1995.

Iriye, Akira. *Cultural Internationalism and World Order*. Baltimore, Md.: Johns Hopkins University Press, 1997.

———. *Pacific Estrangement: Japanese and American Expansion, 1897–1911*. Cambridge, Mass.: Harvard University Press, 1972.

Itō, Kazuo. *Issei: A History of Japanese Immigrants in North America*. Seattle, Wash.: Japanese Community Service, 1973.

Jacobson, Matthew Frye. *Barbarian Virtues: The United States Encounters Foreign Peoples at Home and Abroad, 1876–1917*. New York: Hill and Wang, 2000.

———. *Special Sorrows: The Diasporic Imagination of Irish, Polish, and Jewish Immigrants in the United States*. Berkeley: University of California Press, 2002.

———. *Whiteness of a Different Color: European Immigrants and the Alchemy of Race*. Cambridge, Mass.: Harvard University Press, 1998.

Jacoby, Russell. *Dialectic of Defeat: Contours of Western Marxism*. Cambridge: Cambridge University Press, 1981.

Jiobu, Robert M. "Ethnic Hegemony and the Japanese of California." *American Sociological Review* 53 (June 1988): 353–367.

Johnson, Susan Lee. *Roaring Camp: The Social World of the California Gold Rush*. New York: Norton, 2000.

Kelly, Robin D. G. "But a Local Phase of a World Problem: Black History's Global Vision, 1883–1950." *Journal of American History* 86 (December 1999): 1045–1077.

Kinmonth, Earl H. *The Self-Made Man in Meiji Japanese Thought: From Samurai to Salary Man*. Berkeley: University of California Press, 1981.

Kodama, Masaaki. *Nihon iminshi kenkyū josetsu*. Hiroshima: Keisuisha, 1992.

Kojima, Masaru. *Zaigai shitei kyōikuron no keifu*. Kyoto: Ryūkoku Gakkai, 1993.

Koshiro, Yukiko. *Trans-Pacific Racisms and the U.S. Occupation of Japan*. New York: Columbia University Press, 1999.

Kotani, Ronald. *The Japanese in Hawaii: A Century of Struggle*. Honolulu: Hawaii Hochi, 1985.

Kublin, Hyman. *Asian Revolutionary: The Life of Sen Katayama*. Princeton, N.J.: Princeton University Press, 1964.

Kumamoto, Bob. "The Search for Spies: American Counterintelligence and the Japanese American Community, 1931–1942." *Amerasia Journal* 6 (Fall 1979): 45–75.

Kumei, Teruko. *Gaikokujin o meguru shakaishi*. Tokyo: Yūsankaku, 1995.

Kurashige, Lon. *Japanese American Celebration and Conflict: A History of Ethnic Identity and Festival, 1934–1990*. Berkeley: University of California Press, 2002.

———. "The Problem of Biculturalism: Japanese American Identity and Festival before World War II." *Journal of American History* 86 (March 2000): 1632–1654.

Kurashige, Scott Tadao. "Transforming Los Angeles: Black and Japanese American Struggles for Racial Equality in the Twentieth Century." Ph.D. diss., University of California, Los Angeles, 2000.

Lasker, Bruno, and Agnes Roman. *Propaganda from China and Japan: A Case Study in Propaganda Analysis.* New York: Institute of Pacific Relations, 1938.

Lee, Erika. *At America's Gate: Chinese Immigration during the Exclusion Era, 1882–1943.* Chapel Hill: University of North Carolina Press, 2003.

Lee, Robert G. *Orientals: Asian Americans in Popular Culture.* Philadelphia, Pa.: Temple University Press, 1999.

Limerick, Patricia Nelson. *The Legacy of Conquest: The Unbroken Past of the American West.* New York: Norton, 1987.

Lowe, Lisa. *Immigrant Acts: On Asian American Cultural Politics.* Durham, N.C.: Duke University Press, 1996.

Makela, Lee A. "Japanese Attitudes towards the United States Immigration Act of 1924." Ph.D. diss., Stanford University, 1972.

Masaoka, Mike. *They Call Me Moses Masaoka.* New York: Morrow, 1987.

Matsumoto, Valerie J. "Desperately Seeking 'Deirdre': Gender Roles, Multicultural Relations, and Nisei Women Writers of the 1930s." *Frontier* 12 (1991): 19–32.

———. *Farming the Home Place: A Japanese American Community in California, 1919–1982.* Ithaca, N.Y.: Cornell University Press, 1993.

———. "Redefining Expectations: Nisei Women in the 1930s." *California History* 73 (Spring 1994): 44–53.

Matsumoto, Yūko. " 'Nationalization' and 'the Others': Japanese Immigrants and Americanization in Los Angeles before World War II." *Kiyō, Shigakuka* 45 (February 2000): 1–62.

———. "1936-nen Rosuanjerusu serori sutoraiki to Nikkei nōgyō komyuniti." *Shirin* 75 (July 1992): 44–73.

Miwa, Kimitada, ed. *Nichibei kiki no kigen to hainichi iminhō.* Tokyo: Ronsōsha, 1997.

Modell, John. *The Economics and Politics of Racial Accommodation: The Japanese of Los Angeles, 1900–1942.* Urbana: University of Illinois Press, 1977.

Monobe, Hiromi. "Shaping an Ethnic Leadership: Takie Okumura and the 'Americanization' of the Nisei in Hawaii, 1919–1945." Ph.D. diss., University of Hawaii, Manoa, 2004.

Morimoto, Toyotomi. *Japanese Americans and Cultural Continuity: Maintaining Language and Heritage.* New York: Garland, 1997.

Moriyama, Alan Takeo. *Imingaisha: Japanese Emigration Companies and Hawaii, 1894–1908.* Honolulu: University of Hawaii Press, 1985.

Myers, Ramon H., and Mark R. Peattie, eds. *The Japanese Colonial Empire, 1895–1945.* Princeton, N.J.: Princeton University Press, 1984.

Ngai, Mae M. *Impossible Subjects: Illegal Aliens and the Making of Modern America.* Princeton, N.J.: Princeton University Press, 2004.

Noda, Kesa. *Yamato Colony: 1906–1960.* Livingston, Calif.: Livingston-Merced JACL Chapter, 1981.

Notehelfer, F. G. *Kotoku Shusui: Portrait of a Japanese Radical.* Cambridge: Cambridge University Press, 1971.

Odo, Franklin. *No Sword to Bury: Japanese Americans in Hawaii during World War II.* Philadelphia, Pa.: Temple University Press, 2004.

Ogawa, Dennis M. *Jan Ken Po: The World of Hawaii's Japanese Americans.* Honolulu, Hawaii: Japanese American Research Center, 1973.

Oguma, Eiji. *A Genealogy of 'Japanese' Self Image.* Melbourne, Australia: Trans Pacific, 2002.

Okamoto, Shumpei. "Meiji Imperialism: Pacific Emigration or Continental Expansionism?" In *Japan Examined: Perspectives on Modern Japanese History*, ed. Harry Wray and Hilary Conroy, 141–148. Honolulu: University of Hawaii Press, 1983.

Okihiro, Gary Y. *Cane Fires: The Anti-Japanese Movement in Hawaii, 1865–1945.* Philadelphia, Pa.: Temple University Press, 1991.

———. *Margins and Mainstreams: Asians in American History and Culture.* Seattle: University of Washington, 1994.

Olin, Spencer C., Jr. *California's Prodigal Sons: Hiram Johnson and the Progressives, 1911–1917.* Berkeley: University of California Press, 1968.

Omi, Michael, and Howard Winant. *Racial Formation in the United States: From the 1960s to the 1990s.* New York: Routledge, 1994.

Palumbo-Liu, David. *Asian/American: Historical Crossings of a Racial Frontier.* Stanford, Calif.: Stanford University Press, 1999.

Pascoe, Peggy. "Miscegenation Law, Court Cases, and Ideologies of 'Race' in Twentieth-Century America." *Journal of American History* 83 (June 1996): 44–69.

———. *Relations of Rescue: The Search for Female Moral Authority in the American West, 1874–1939.* New York: Oxford University Press, 1993.

Peattie, Mark R. *Nan'yo: The Rise and Fall of the Japanese in Micronesia, 1885–1945.* Honolulu: University of Hawaii Press, 1988.

Peterson, William. *Japanese Americans: Oppression and Success.* New York: Random House, 1971.

Pyle, Kenneth B. *The New Generation in Meiji Japan: Problems in Cultural Identity, 1885–1895.* Stanford, Calif.: Stanford University Press, 1969.

Roediger, David R. *The Wages of Whiteness: Race and the Making of the American Working Class.* New York: Verso, 1999.

Safran, William. "Diasporas in Modern Societies: Myths of Homeland and Return." *Diaspora* 1 (1991): 83–99.

Sakaguchi, Mitsuhiko. "Nihonjin imin to kokugo kyōiku." *Shisō* 55 (March 1998): 19–42.

Sakata, Yasuo. "Datsua no shishi to tozasareta Hakusekijin no rakuen." In *Beikoku shoki no Nihongo shinbun*, ed. Tamura Norio et al., 47–194. Tokyo: Keisō Shobō, 1986.

———. " 'Wataridori (birds-of-passage)' to sono shakai." In *Zaibei Nihonjin shakai no reimei*, ed. Dōshisha Jinbun Kagaku Kenkyūjo, 3–78. Tokyo: Gendai Shiryō Shuppan, 1997.

San Buenaventura, Steffi. "Filipino Folk Spirituality and Immigration: From Mutual Aid to Religion." *Amerasia Journal* 22 (Spring 1996): 1–30.

Sánchez, George J. *Becoming Mexican American: Ethnicity, Culture, and Identity in Chicano Los Angeles, 1900–1945.* New York: Oxford University Press, 1993.

———. "The 'New Nationalism,' Mexican Style: Race and Progressivism in Chicano Political Development during the 1920s." In *California Progressivism Revisited*, ed. William Deverell and Tom Sitton, 229–244. Berkeley: University of California Press, 1994.

Sawada, Mitziko. *Tokyo Life, New York Dreams: Urban Japanese Visions of America, 1890–1924.* Berkeley: University of California Press, 1996.

Schiller, Nina Glick, Linda Basch, and Cristina Blanc-Szanton. "Transnationalism: A New Analytical Framework for Understanding Migration." In *Towards a Transnational Perspective on Migration: Race, Class, Ethnicity, and Nationalism Reconsidered*, ed. Nina Glick Schiller et al., 1–24. New York: New York Academy of Sciences, 1992.

Shah, Nayan. *Contagious Divides: Epidemics and Race in San Francisco's Chinatown.* Berkeley: University of California Press, 2001.

Silverberg, Miriam. "Constructing the Japanese Ethnography of Modernity." *Journal of Asian Studies* 51 (February 1992): 30–54.

Simpson, Caroline Chung. *An Absent Presence: Japanese Americans in Postwar American Culture, 1945–1960.* Durham, N.C.: Duke University Press, 2001.

Spickard, Paul. *Japanese Americans: The Formation and Transformation of an Ethnic Group.* Boston: Twayne, 1996.

Stephan, John J. *Hawaii under the Rising Sun: Japan's Plans for Conquest after Pearl Harbor.* Honolulu: University of Hawaii Press, 1984.

———. "Hijacked by Utopia: American Nikkei in Manchuria." *Amerasia Journal* 23 (Winter 1997–1998): 1–42.

Stephens, Michelle A. "Black Transnationalism and the Politics of National Identity: West Indian Intellectuals in Harlem in the Age of War and Revolution." *American Quarterly* 50 (September 1998): 592–608.

Stoler, Ann Laura. *Race and the Education of Desire: Foucault's History of Sexuality and the Colonial Order of Things.* Durham, N.C.: Duke University Press, 1995.

Strong, Edward K., Jr. *Japanese in California.* Stanford, Calif.: Stanford University Press, 1933.

———. *The Second-Generation Japanese Problem.* Stanford, Calif.: Stanford University Press, 1934.

Suzuki, Masao. "Success Story? Japanese Immigrant Economic Achievement and Return Migration, 1920–1930." *Journal of Economic History* 55 (December 1995): 889–901.

Takahashi, Jere. *Nisei/Sansei: Shifting Japanese American Identities and Politics.* Philadelphia, Pa.: Temple University Press, 1997.

Takaki, Ronald. *A Different Mirror: A History of Multicultural America.* New York: Little, Brown, 1993.

———. *Strangers from a Different Shore: A History of Asian Americans.* Boston: Back Bay, 1998.

Tamura, Eileen H. *Americanization, Acculturation, and Ethnic Identity: The Nisei Generation in Hawaii.* Urbana: University of Illinois Press, 1994.

Tanaka, Kei. "Japanese Picture Marriage in 1900–1924 California: Construction of Japanese Race and Gender." Ph.D. diss., Rutgers University, 2002.

Tanaka, Stephan. *Japan's Orient: Rendering Pasts into History.* Berkeley: University of California Press, 1993.

Tateishi, Kay. "A Typical Nisei." *Amerasia Journal* 23 (Winter 1997–1998): 199–216.

Thompson, David. "The Filipino Federation of America, Incorporated: A Study in the Natural History of a Social Institution." *Social Process in Hawaii* 7 (November 1941): 24–34.

Tomita, Mary Kimoto. *Dear Miye: Letters Home from Japan, 1939–1946.* Edited by Robert G. Lee. Stanford, Calif.: Stanford University Press, 1996.

Ushioda, Sharlie C. "Man of Two Worlds: An Inquiry into the Value System of Inazo Nitobe." In *East across the Pacific: Historical and Sociological Studies of Japanese Immigration and Assimilation,* ed. Hilary Conroy and T. Scott Miyakawa, 187–210. Santa Barbara, Calif.: ABC-Clio, 1972.

Van Nuys, Frank W. "A Progressive Confronts the Race Question: Chester Rowell, the California Alien Land Law of 1913, and the Twentieth-Century Racial Thought." *California History* 73 (Spring 1994): 2–13.

Vertovec, Steven. "Three Meanings of 'Diaspora,' Exemplified among South Asian Religions." *Diaspora* 6 (1997): 277–299.

Waugh, Isami Arifuku. "Hidden Crime and Deviance in the Japanese-American Community, 1920–1946." Ph.D. diss., University of California, Berkeley, 1978.

Weiner, Michael. "Discourses of Race, Nation, Empire in Pre-1945 Japan." *Ethnic and Racial Studies* 18 (July 1995): 433–456.

Wilson, Robert A., and Bill Hosokawa. *East to America: A History of the Japanese in the United States.* New York: Morrow, 1980.

Wollenberg, Charles. "Race and Class in Rural California: The El Monte Berry Strike of 1933." *California Historical Quarterly* 51 (Summer 1972): 155–164.

Wong, Sau-Ling C. "Denationalization Reconsidered: Asian American Cultural Criticism at a Theoretical Crossroads." *Amerasia Journal* 21 (1995): 1–27.

Yagasaki, Noritaka. "Ethnic Cooperativism and Immigrant Agriculture: A Study of Japanese Floriculture and Truck Farming in California." Ph.D. diss., University of California, Berkeley, 1982.

Yamamoto, Eriko. "Cheers for Japanese Athletes: The 1932 Los Angeles Olympics and the Japanese American Community." *Pacific Historical Review* 69 (August 2000): 399–430.

———. "Miya Sannomiya Kikuchi: A Pioneer Nisei Woman's Life and Identity." *Amerasia Journal* 23 (Winter 1997–1998): 73–101.

Yans-McLaughlin, Virginia, ed. *Immigration Reconsidered.* New York: Oxford University Press, 1990.

Yasutake, Rumi. "Transnational Women's Activism: The Women's Christian Temperance Union in Japan and Beyond, 1858–1920." Ph.D. diss., University of California, Los Angeles, 1998.

Yoo, David K. *Growing Up Nisei: Race, Generation, and Culture among Japanese Americans of California, 1924–1949*. Urbana: University of Illinois Press, 2000.

Young, Louise. *Japan's Total Empire: Manchuria and the Culture of Wartime Imperialism*. Berkeley: University of California Press, 1998.

Yu, Henry. *Thinking Orientals: Migration, Contact, and Exoticism in Modern America*. New York: Oxford University Press, 2001.

Yu, Renqui. *To Save China, to Save Ourselves: The Chinese Hand Laundry Alliance of New York*. Philadelphia, Pa.: Temple University Press, 1992.

Zheng, Mei. "Chinese Americans in San Francisco and New York City during the Anti-Japanese War: 1937–1945." M.A. thesis, University of California, Los Angeles, 1990.

Index

CPSIA information can be obtained at www.ICGtesting.com
Printed in the USA
BVOW040717231111

276677BV00002B/1/P